The Perfect

AMAZON BASICS

BREAD MACHINE COOKBOOK

UNLOCK THE FULL POTENTIAL OF YOUR BREAD MACHINE WITH 1500-DAY EASY-TO-FOLLOW RECIPES FOR BEGINNERS TO ALWAYS HAVE FRESH, DELICIOUS HOMEMADE BREAD

KATHERINE VOLPE

CONTENTS

HERB AND SPICE BREAD RECIPES 56

VEGETABLE BREAD RECIPES 72

CAKE RECIPES/QUICK BREAD/SWEET ROLLS 88

HOLIDAY BREAD RECIPES 104

SOURDOUGH BREAD RECIPES 122

GLUTEN-FREE RECIPES 132

INTERNATIONAL BREAD RECIPES..**205**

RECIPE INDEX..**215**

INTRODUCTION

How Does the Amazon Basics Bread Maker Work?

The best thing about using an automated bread maker is that the machine does the above procedures. A bread maker is described as a compact electric oven. It can hold a single bread tin, and the tins come in a variety of sizes. These tins come with attractive designs, such as having an axle at the bottom. Many bread makers in the market will come with glass lids, which helps the user see the bread being created. You also get to see steam coming out from the vent indication fresh bread is ready.

Top Reasons to Invest in the Amazon Basics Bread Maker

Having a bread machine in your kitchen comes with many benefits. Most importantly, it gives the chance to enjoy fresh and tasty bread whenever you want. It gives you control over the ingredients you have on your bread and an assurance that what you are having is good for your health. You can get a decent unit by asking for recommendations from friends that have used them before. On the other hand, you might consider reading reviews about the same. That said, here are some reasons why these appliances are a must have in any kitchen.

1.   It is a quick and easy mixing bread maker.

One of the main reasons why bread machines are recommended for bread making is how they simplify the entire bread making operation. With a bread maker, mixing the dough is simplified by automatic functions of the machine. Moreover, you can always set aside some of the dough for later in your refrigerator for later use. With a bread machine, you do not have to worry about the complexity of the recipe as everything is done as you watch.

2.   It could save your time and money.

Bread machines are fairly priced. Are you aware that you can get a bread machine for as little as $50? Therefore, you have every reason to have this appliance in your kitchen considering that store-bought loaves of bread are relatively expensive. Baking your own is cheaper. It also gives you the liberty to enjoy pizza and rolls cheaply.

Most people do not even think about making their bread due to time constraints. Interestingly, preparing your bread takes less than 20 minutes of your time. Considering that most bread makers are fully automated, you do not need to spend your time monitoring the progress. You only need to key in some commands and let the machine do what it does best. Some models also notify you when the bread is ready.

3.   You could enjoy the aroma of fresh baking bread.

Brad making machines let you enjoy the aroma of well-cooked and tasty bred right from your home. Having a nice and cool aroma comes with a feeling of satisfaction. Considering that most bread makers come with a couple of recipes, you also get to tryout different combinations and see what they have to offer. Imagine the aroma of fresh bread baking just before you get to eat, it is certainly appetizing.

4.   You will be taking pride in quality baking.

Bread Baking is not everyone's job. However, bread making machines make baking easy and comfortable for everyone. With a bread-making machine, you enjoy the bragging rights as much as the appliance does everything for you. With the right recipes, you family or guests will applaud you not knowing where the secrete lies.

If you are yet to have a bread machine, these four reasons are enough to make you buy one. Bread machines not only save time, they also give you the chance to enjoy fresh and healthy bread.

Using Tips for Your Amazon Basics Bread Maker

Here you're provided with a short list of bread machine tips to go!

1)   The order of your ingredient matter a lot. Most of the times what we do we just collect all the ingredients that we need and then put it as our wish. You may think to add the liquid at the first or at the last both are same, but it's actually not. So please maintain the order of the ingredients. Put the liquid, yeast first and other at the last!

2)   Attach the wand before you pour the ingredients into it. Somehow, if you forget to check out whether the mixing wand is doing appropriately or not, can mess the whole thing. So check this before starting.

3)   Make sure that you are pulling out the basket out when you are pouring the ingredients in. This is a must thing, that you have to follow. Once you have poured all the ingredients then put your basket in the machine.

4)   If you want to give a twist to your bread and want to add some extra ingredients like nuts, cheese, oats or any spice, you have to be a little careful. Add these extra ingredients you have to wait until the ball is just foaming. Don't add these before that. After the foaming is done add or sprinkles the extra ingredients.

5)   If you are willing making carrot bread, ensure the dough ball is formed and then include the shredded carrots in it. Always glow slowly when you are mixing the ingredients. Remember, mixing these extra ingredients at first can ruin your bread.

6)   We know that it is a bread machine and it is supposed to make a good bread. However, that does not mean you don't have anything to do. You have to check your creation time to time. We all have one fixed bread recipe that we follow for our everyday bread. Maybe the recipe is all okay and same but still, it doesn't go well occasionally. So, make sure you check all the ingredients and the mixture properly.

7)   You should not keep the loaf for a long time. Sometimes we think that as it is ready it is cool to keep it for a long time. This is the reason you will see that the bottom of the loaf is not good. Try to get the loaf as soon as it cools.

8)   If you see that the loaf is dense and short then you have to look into the consistency. After 5 minutes of kneading, check the consistency of the dough. Even, you see that it is still too dry then include 1 tablespoon of liquid at a time. The reason for drying dough can also be what kind of flour you are using. Try to use the high protein bread flour.

Cleaning Tips for the Amazon Basics Bread Machine Users:

1. To keep your kitchen cleaner, spoon and measure the flour over your sink or a large baking tray so the mess is corralled.

2. To keep your bread machine tidier, fill the bread pan away from the machine. Then snap the pan in place in the machine.

3. To remove bits of ingredients or browned flour from the bottom of your bread machine, remove the bread pan, unplug the machine and wait for it to cool. Then use the wand attachment of a vacuum cleaner to gently suction out the debris without disturbing the heating element or clamps.

4. To wash the bread pan and kneading paddle(s), follow your manual's directions. Most instruct you to use a mild detergent and a soft cloth. If the kneading paddle is stuck in the bottom of the pan, place the pan in the sink and fill it with warm water. Let it soak for 30 minutes, then gently twist the paddle to remove it. Washing the bread pan in the dishwasher can result in discoloration, pitting and/or rust.

5. To clean the window of the bread machine, inside and out, use a damp cloth.

6. To store your bread machine while it's not in use, place the clean bread pan and paddle inside the machine and store it in a cool, dry, covered area, such as a kitchen cabinet.

BREAKFAST BREAD RECIPES

Hot Jalapeño Bread With Longhorn Cheese

Ingredients:
- 8 slices (1 pound)
- 2/3 cup water
- 2 cups bread flour
- 5/8 cup shredded longhorn cheddar cheese (2 1/2 ounces)
- 2 tablespoons nonfat dry milk
- 2 canned jalapeño chiles, seeded and diced
- 3/4 tablespoon sugar
- 3/4 teaspoon salt
- 1 1/4 teaspoons SAF yeast or 1/2 tablespoon bread machine yeast
- 12 slices (1 ½ pounds)
- 1 cup water
- 3 cups bread flour
- 1 cup shredded longhorn cheddar cheese (4 ounces)
- 3 tablespoons nonfat dry milk
- 3 canned jalapeño chiles, seeded and diced
- 1 tablespoon sugar
- 1 teaspoon salt
- 2 teaspoons SAF yeast or 21/2 teaspoons bread machine yeast
- 16 slices (2 pounds)
- 11/3 cups water
- 4 cups bread flour
- 11/4 cups shredded longhorn cheddar cheese (5 ounces)
- 4 tablespoons nonfat dry milk
- 4 canned jalapeño chiles, seeded and diced
- 1 1/2 tablespoons sugar
- 1 1/2 teaspoons salt
- 2 1/2 teaspoons SAF yeast or 1 tablespoon bread machine yeast

Directions:
1. Choose the size of loaf you would like to make and measure your ingredients.
2. Add the ingredients to the bread pan in the order listed above.
3. Place the pan in the bread machine and close the lid.
4. Turn on the bread maker. Select the Basic setting, then the loaf size, and finally the crust color. Start the cycle. (This recipe is not suitable for use with the Delay Timer.)
5. When the cycle is finished and the bread is baked, carefully remove the pan from the machine. Use a potholder as the handle will be very hot. Let rest for a few minutes.
6. Remove the bread from the pan and allow to cool on a wire rack for at least 10 minutes before slicing.

Crescia Al Formaggio

Ingredients:
- 8 slices (1 pound)
- 1/3 cup plus 2/3 tablespoon water
- 2 large eggs
- 2 tablespoons olive oil
- 2 1/6 cups bread flour
- 1/2 cup grated Asiago or Locatelli cheese
- 1 tablespoon nonfat dry milk
- 2/3 tablespoon sugar
- 1 1/3 teaspoons gluten
- 3/4 teaspoon salt
- 1 1/3 teaspoons SAF yeast or 1 2/3 teaspoons bread machine yeast
- 12 slices (1 ½ pounds)
- 1/2 cup plus 1 tablespoon water
- 3 large eggs
- 3 tablespoons olive oil
- 31/4 cups bread flour
- 3/4 cup grated Asiago or Locatelli cheese
- 11/2 tablespoons nonfat dry milk
- 1 tablespoon sugar
- 2 teaspoons gluten
- 1/2 teaspoon salt
- 2 teaspoons SAF yeast or 21/2 teaspoons bread machine yeast
- 16 slices (2 pounds)
- 2/3 cup plus 1 1/3 tablespoons water
- 4 large eggs

- 4 tablespoons olive oil
- 4 1/3 cups bread flour
- 1 cup grated Asiago or Locatelli cheese
- 2 tablespoons nonfat dry milk
- 1 1/3 tablespoons sugar
- 2 2/3 teaspoons gluten
- 1 1/2 teaspoons salt
- 2 2/3 teaspoons SAF yeast or 3 1/3 teaspoons bread machine yeast

Directions:

1. Choose the size of loaf you would like to make and measure your ingredients.
2. Add the ingredients to the bread pan in the order listed above.
3. Place the pan in the bread machine and close the lid.
4. Turn on the bread maker. Select the Basic setting, then the loaf size, and finally the crust color. Start the cycle.
5. When the cycle is finished and the bread is baked, carefully remove the pan from the machine. Use a potholder as the handle will be very hot. Let rest for a few minutes.
6. Remove the bread from the pan and allow to cool on a wire rack for at least 10 minutes before slicing.

Orange-cinnamon Bread

Ingredients:

- 8 slices (1 pound)
- For the dough:
- 1/3 cup orange juice
- 1/4 cup milk
- 1/2 large egg
- 2 tablespoons unsalted butter, cut into pieces
- 2 cups bread flour
- 1/6 cup sugar
- Grated zest of 1/2 orange
- 1/2 tablespoon plus 1/2 teaspoon gluten
- 1 1/4 teaspoons ground cinnamon
- 3/4 teaspoons salt
- 1 1/8 teaspoons SAF yeast or 1 3/8 teaspoons bread machine yeast
- For the vanilla-orange glaze:
- 3/8 cup sifted confectioners' sugar
- 3/4 to 1 tablespoons orange juice
- 1/2 teaspoon vanilla extract
- 12 slices (1 ½ pounds)
- For the dough:
- 1/2 cup orange juice
- 1/3 cup milk
- 1 large egg
- 3 tablespoons unsalted butter, cut into pieces
- 3 cups bread flour
- 1/4 cup sugar
- Grated zest of 1 orange
- 1 tablespoon gluten
- 2 teaspoons ground cinnamon
- 11/4 teaspoons salt
- 2 teaspoons SAF yeast or 21/2 teaspoons bread machine yeast
- For the vanilla-orange glaze:
- 3/4 cup sifted confectioners' sugar
- 11/2 to 2 tablespoons orange juice
- 1 teaspoon vanilla extract
- 16 slices (2 pounds)
- For the dough:
- 2/3 cup orange juice
- 1/2 cup milk
- 1 large egg
- 4 tablespoons unsalted butter, cut into pieces
- 4 cups bread flour
- 1/3 cup sugar
- Grated zest of 1 orange
- 1 tablespoon plus 1 teaspoon gluten
- 21/2 teaspoons ground cinnamon
- 11/2 teaspoons salt
- 21/4 teaspoons SAF yeast or 23/4 teaspoons bread machine yeast
- For the vanilla-orange glaze:
- 3/4 cup sifted confectioners' sugar
- 11/2 to 2 tablespoons orange juice
- 1 teaspoon vanilla extract

Directions:

1. Choose the size of loaf you would like to make and measure your ingredients.
2. To make the dough, add all the dough ingredients to the bread pan in the order listed above.

3. Place the pan in the bread machine and close the lid.

4. Turn on the bread maker. Select the Basic setting, then the loaf size, and finally the crust color. Start the cycle. (This recipe is not suitable for use with the Delay Timer.)

5. When the cycle is finished and the bread is baked, carefully remove the pan from the machine. Use a potholder as the handle will be very hot. Let rest for a few minutes.

6. To prepare the glaze, combine the confectioners' sugar, orange juice, and vanilla in a small bowl; beat with a small whisk until smooth. With a large spoon, drizzle the bread with the glaze, letting it drip down the sides. Cool to room temperature to set the glaze.

7. Remove the bread from the pan and allow to cool on a wire rack for at least 10 minutes before slicing.

Egg Bread

Ingredients:
- 8 slices (1 pound)
- 2/3 cup water
- 1/2 large egg
- 2 cups bread flour
- 3/4 tablespoon sugar
- 1/2 tablespoon plus 1/2 teaspoon gluten
- 3/4 teaspoon salt
- 1 1/4 teaspoons SAF yeast or 1/2 tablespoon bread machine yeast
- 12 slices (1 ½ pounds)
- 1 cup water
- 1 large egg
- 3 cups bread flour
- 1 tablespoon sugar
- 1 tablespoon gluten
- 11/4 teaspoons salt
- 2 teaspoons SAF yeast or 21/2 teaspoons bread machine yeast
- 16 slices (2 pounds)
- 11/3 cups water
- 1 large egg
- 4 cups bread flour
- 11/2 tablespoons sugar
- 1 tablespoon plus 1 teaspoon gluten

- 11/2 teaspoons salt
- 21/2 teaspoons SAF yeast or 1 tablespoon bread machine yeast

Directions:
1. Choose the size of loaf you would like to make and measure your ingredients.

2. Pour the boiling water over the cracked rye in a bowl. Add the brown sugar, butter, and salt. Let stand 1 hour on the counter to soften.

3. Add the ingredients to the bread pan in the order listed above. Adding the grain and its soaking liquid as the liquid ingredients.

4. Place the pan in the bread machine and close the lid.

5. Turn on the bread maker. Select the Basic/French setting, then the loaf size, and finally the crust color. Start the cycle.

6. When the cycle is finished and the bread is baked, carefully remove the pan from the machine. Use a potholder as the handle will be very hot. Let rest for a few minutes.

7. Remove the bread from the pan and allow to cool on a wire rack for at least 10 minutes before slicing.

Granola Bread

Ingredients:
- 8 slices (1 pound)
- 3/4 cup buttermilk
- 1 1/2 tablespoons vegetable oil
- 1 1/2 tablespoons honey
- 1 3/8 cups bread flour
- 1/2 cup whole wheat flour
- 2/3 cup granola
- 1/2 tablespoon plus 1/2 teaspoon gluten
- 1 teaspoon salt
- 3/4 teaspoon ground cinnamon
- 1 1/4 teaspoons SAF yeast or 1/2 tablespoon bread machine yeast
- 12 slices (1 ½ pounds)
- 11/8 cups buttermilk
- 2 tablespoons vegetable oil
- 2 tablespoons honey
- 21/8 cups bread flour
- 3/4 cup whole wheat flour

- 11/4 cups granola
- 1 tablespoon gluten
- 11/2 teaspoons salt
- 1 teaspoon ground cinnamon
- 2 teaspoons SAF yeast or 21/2 teaspoons bread machine yeast
- 16 slices (2 pounds)
- 11/2 cups buttermilk
- 3 tablespoons vegetable oil
- 3 tablespoons honey
- 23/4 cups bread flour
- 1 cup whole wheat flour
- 11/3 cups granola
- 1 tablespoon plus 1 teaspoon gluten
- 2 teaspoons salt
- 11/2 teaspoons ground cinnamon
- 21/2 teaspoons SAF yeast or 1 tablespoon bread machine yeast

Directions:

1. Choose the size of loaf you would like to make and measure your ingredients.
2. Add the ingredients to the bread pan in the order listed above.
3. Place the pan in the bread machine and close the lid.
4. Turn on the bread maker. Select the White/Basic setting, then the loaf size, and finally the crust color. Start the cycle.
5. When the cycle is finished and the bread is baked, carefully remove the pan from the machine. Use a potholder as the handle will be very hot. Let rest for a few minutes.
6. Remove the bread from the pan and allow to cool on a wire rack for at least 10 minutes before slicing.

Parmesan Cheddar Bread

Ingredients:
- 8 slices (1 pound)
- 5/6 cup lukewarm milk
- 2 teaspoons unsalted butter, melted
- 1 1/3 tablespoons sugar
- 2/3 teaspoon table salt
- 1/3 teaspoon freshly ground black pepper
- Pinch cayenne pepper
- 1 cup shredded aged sharp Cheddar cheese
- 1/3 cup shredded Parmesan cheese
- 2 cups white bread flour
- 5/6 teaspoon bread machine yeast
- 12 slices (1 ½ pounds)
- 1¼ cups lukewarm milk
- 1 tablespoon unsalted butter, melted
- 2 tablespoons sugar
- 1 teaspoon table salt
- ½ teaspoon freshly ground black pepper
- Pinch cayenne pepper
- 1½ cups shredded aged sharp Cheddar cheese
- ½ cup shredded or grated Parmesan cheese
- 3 cups white bread flour
- 1¼ teaspoons bread machine yeast
- 16 slices (2 pounds)
- 1⅔ cups lukewarm milk
- 4 teaspoons unsalted butter, melted
- 2⅔ tablespoons sugar
- 1⅓ teaspoons table salt
- ⅔ teaspoon freshly ground black pepper
- Pinch cayenne pepper
- 2 cups shredded aged sharp Cheddar cheese
- ⅔ cup shredded Parmesan cheese
- 4 cups white bread flour
- 1⅔ teaspoons bread machine yeast

Directions:

1. Choose the size of loaf you would like to make and measure your ingredients.
2. Add the ingredients to the bread pan in the order listed above.
3. Place the pan in the bread machine and close the lid.
4. Turn on the bread maker. Select the White/Basic setting, then the loaf size, and finally the crust color. Start the cycle.
5. When the cycle is finished and the bread is baked, carefully remove the pan from the machine. Use a potholder as the handle will be very hot. Let rest for a few minutes.
6. Remove the bread from the pan and allow to cool on a wire rack for at least 10 minutes before slicing.

Italian Lemon-ricotta Bread

Ingredients:

- 8 slices (1 pound)
- 1/4 cup milk
- 3/8 cup ricotta cheese
- 1 1/2 large egg yolks
- 1 teaspoons anise extract
- 1/4 cup (1/2 stick) plus 1/2 tablespoon unsalted butter, cut into pieces
- 2 cups bread flour
- 1/4 cup walnuts
- 1/4 cup golden raisins
- 1 3/4 tablespoons sugar
- Grated zest of 1 lemons
- 1/2 tablespoon plus 1/2 teaspoon gluten
- 1 teaspoons salt
- 1 1/4 teaspoons SAF yeast or 1/2 tablespoon bread machine yeast
- 12 slices (1 ½ pounds)
- 1/3 cup milk
- 2/3 cup ricotta cheese
- 2 large egg yolks
- 11/2 teaspoons anise extract
- 7 tablespoons unsalted butter, cut into pieces
- 3 cups bread flour
- 1/3 cup walnuts
- 1/3 cup golden raisins
- 3 tablespoons sugar
- Grated zest of 1 lemon
- 1 tablespoon gluten
- 11/2 teaspoons salt
- 21/4 teaspoons SAF yeast or 23/4 teaspoons bread machine yeast
- 16 slices (2 pounds)
- 1/2 cup milk
- 3/4 cup ricotta cheese
- 3 large egg yolks
- 2 teaspoons anise extract
- 1/2 cup (1 stick) plus 1 tablespoon unsalted butter, cut into pieces
- 4 cups bread flour
- 1/2 cup walnuts
- 1/2 cup golden raisins
- 31/2 tablespoons sugar
- Grated zest of 2 lemons
- 1 tablespoon plus 1 teaspoon gluten
- 2 teaspoons salt
- 21/2 teaspoons SAF yeast or 1 tablespoon bread machine yeast

Directions:

1. Choose the size of loaf you would like to make and measure your ingredients.

2. Add the ingredients to the bread pan in the order listed above.

3. Place the pan in the bread machine and close the lid.

4. Turn on the bread maker. Select the Basic setting, then the loaf size, and finally the crust color. Start the cycle. (This recipe is not suitable for use with the Delay Timer.)

5. When the cycle is finished and the bread is baked, carefully remove the pan from the machine. Use a potholder as the handle will be very hot. Let rest for a few minutes.

6. Remove the bread from the pan and allow to cool on a wire rack for at least 10 minutes before slicing.

Buttermilk Cheese Bread

Ingredients:

- 8 slices (1 pound)
- 5/8 cup buttermilk
- 1/3 cup water
- 2 1/4 cups bread flour
- 5/8 cup shredded Swiss cheese (2 1/2 ounces)
- 1 tablespoon sugar
- 3/4 teaspoon baking powder
- 1 teaspoon salt
- 1 1/4 teaspoons SAF yeast or 1/2 tablespoon bread machine yeast
- 12 slices (1 ½ pounds)
- 1 cup buttermilk
- 1/2 cup water
- 31/2 cups bread flour
- 1 cup shredded Swiss cheese (4 ounces)
- 11/2 tablespoons sugar
- 11/4 teaspoons baking powder
- 11/2 teaspoons salt

- 2 teaspoons SAF yeast or 21/2 teaspoons bread machine yeast
- 16 slices (2 pounds)
- 1 1/4 cups buttermilk
- 2/3 cup water
- 4 1/2 cups bread flour
- 1 1/4 cups shredded Swiss cheese (5 ounces)
- 2 tablespoons sugar
- 1 1/2 teaspoons baking powder
- 2 teaspoons salt
- 2 1/2 teaspoons SAF yeast or 1 tablespoon bread machine yeast

Directions:

1. Choose the size of loaf you would like to make and measure your ingredients.
2. Add the ingredients to the bread pan in the order listed above.
3. Place the pan in the bread machine and close the lid.
4. Turn on the bread maker. Select the Basic setting, then the loaf size, and finally the crust color. Start the cycle.
5. When the cycle is finished and the bread is baked, carefully remove the pan from the machine. Use a potholder as the handle will be very hot. Let rest for a few minutes.
6. Remove the bread from the pan and allow to cool on a wire rack for at least 10 minutes before slicing.

Dutch Sugar Loaf

Ingredients:

- 8 slices (1 pound)
- 3/8 cup sugar cubes
- 1 teaspoon ground cinnamon
- Small pinch of ground cloves
- 2/3 cup fat-free milk
- 1 tablespoon unsalted butter or margarine, cut into pieces
- 2 cups bread flour
- 1/2 tablespoon plus 1/2 teaspoon gluten
- 7/8 teaspoon salt
- 1 1/4 teaspoons SAF yeast or 1/2 tablespoon bread machine yeast
- 12 slices (1 ½ pounds)

- 2/3 cup sugar cubes
- 11/2 teaspoons ground cinnamon
- Small pinch of ground cloves
- 11/8 cups fat-free milk
- 1 tablespoon unsalted butter or margarine, cut into pieces
- 3 cups bread flour
- 1 tablespoon gluten
- 11/4 teaspoons salt
- 2 teaspoons SAF yeast or 21/2 teaspoons bread machine yeast
- 16 slices (2 pounds)
- 3/4 cup sugar cubes
- 2 teaspoons ground cinnamon
- Small pinch of ground cloves
- 11/3 cups fat-free milk
- 2 tablespoons unsalted butter or margarine, cut into pieces
- 4 cups bread flour
- 1 tablespoon plus 1 teaspoon gluten
- 13/4 teaspoons salt
- 21/2 teaspoons SAF yeast or 1 tablespoon bread machine yeast

Directions:

1. Choose the size of loaf you would like to make and measure your ingredients.
2. Add the ingredients to the bread pan in the order listed above(except the spice-coated sugar cubes).
3. Place the pan in the bread machine and close the lid.
4. Turn on the bread maker. Select the Sweet Bread setting, then the loaf size, and finally the crust color. Start the cycle. Five minutes into the kneading segment, press Pause and sprinkle in half of the sugar cube mixture. Press Start to resume the cycle. Three minutes later, press Pause and add the rest of the sugar cube mixture. Press Start to resume the cycle.
5. When the cycle is finished and the bread is baked, carefully remove the pan from the machine. Use a potholder as the handle will be very hot. Let rest for a few minutes.
6. Remove the bread from the pan and allow to cool on a wire rack for at least 10 minutes before slicing.

Chocolate Challah

Ingredients:

- 8 slices (1 pound)
- 5/8 cup water
- 1 large egg
- 1 1/2 tablespoons vegetable oil
- 1/2 tablespoon vanilla extract
- 2 cups bread flour
- 1/3 cup sugar
- 1/6 cup unsweetened Dutch-process cocoa powder
- 2/3 tablespoon gluten
- 1 teaspoon salt
- 1 teaspoon SAF yeast or 1 1/4 teaspoons bread machine yeast
- 1/3 cup semisweet chocolate chips
- 12 slices (1½ pounds)
- 1 cup water
- 1 large egg plus 1 egg yolk
- 2 tablespoons vegetable oil
- 2 teaspoons vanilla extract
- 3 cups bread flour
- 1/2 cup sugar
- 1/4 cup unsweetened Dutch-process cocoa powder
- 1 tablespoon gluten
- 11/2 teaspoons salt
- 13/4 teaspoons SAF yeast or 21/4 teaspoons bread machine yeast
- 1/2 cup semisweet chocolate chips
- 16 slices (2 pounds)
- 11/4 cups water
- 2 large eggs
- 3 tablespoons vegetable oil
- 1 tablespoon vanilla extract
- 4 cups bread flour
- 2/3 cup sugar
- 1/3 cup unsweetened Dutch-process cocoa powder
- 1 tablespoon plus 1 teaspoon gluten
- 2 teaspoons salt
- 2 teaspoons SAF yeast or 21/2 teaspoons bread machine yeast
- 2/3 cup semisweet chocolate chips

Directions:

1. Choose the size of loaf you would like to make and measure your ingredients.
2. Add the ingredients to the bread pan in the order listed above (except the chocolate chips).
3. Place the pan in the bread machine and close the lid.
4. Turn on the bread maker. Select the Basic/Sweet Bread setting, then the loaf size, and finally the crust color. Start the cycle.
5. At the beep, add the chocolate chips.
6. When the cycle is finished and the bread is baked, carefully remove the pan from the machine. Use a potholder as the handle will be very hot. Let rest for a few minutes.
7. Remove the bread from the pan and allow to cool on a wire rack for at least 10 minutes before slicing.

Cheddar Bacon Bread

Ingredients:

- 8 slices (1 pound)
- 1/3 cup lukewarm milk
- 1 teaspoon unsalted butter, melted
- 1 tablespoon honey
- 1 teaspoon table salt
- 1/3 cup green chilies, chopped
- 1/3 cup grated Cheddar cheese
- 1/3 cup cooked bacon, chopped
- 2 cups white bread flour
- 1 1/4 teaspoons bread machine yeast
- 12 slices (1 ½ pounds)
- ½ cup lukewarm milk
- 1½ teaspoons unsalted butter, melted
- 1½ tablespoons honey
- 1½ teaspoons table salt
- ½ cup green chilies, chopped
- ½ cup grated Cheddar cheese
- ½ cup cooked bacon, chopped
- 3 cups white bread flour
- 2 teaspoons bread machine yeast
- 16 slices (2 pounds)
- ⅔ cup lukewarm milk
- 2 teaspoons unsalted butter, melted
- 2 tablespoons honey
- 2 teaspoons table salt

- ⅔ cup green chilies, chopped
- ⅔ cup grated Cheddar cheese
- ⅔ cup cooked bacon, chopped
- 4 cups white bread flour
- 2½ teaspoons bread machine yeast

Directions:

1. Choose the size of loaf you would like to make and measure your ingredients.

2. Add the ingredients to the bread pan in the order listed above.

3. Place the pan in the bread machine and close the lid.

4. Turn on the bread maker. Select the White/Basic setting, then the loaf size, and finally the crust color. Start the cycle.

5. When the cycle is finished and the bread is baked, carefully remove the pan from the machine. Use a potholder as the handle will be very hot. Let rest for a few minutes.

6. Remove the bread from the pan and allow to cool on a wire rack for at least 10 minutes before slicing.

Blue Cheese Onion Bread

Ingredients:

- 8 slices (1 pound)
- ¾ cup + 1 tablespoon water at 80 degrees F
- 1 whole egg
- 2 teaspoons melted butter, cooled
- 3 tablespoons powdered skim milk
- 2 teaspoons sugar
- ½ teaspoon salt
- 1/3 cup crumbled blue cheese
- 2 teaspoons dried onion flakes
- 2 cups white bread flour
- 3 tablespoons instantly mashed potato flakes
- ¾ teaspoons bread machine/ active dry yeast
- 12 slices (1 ½ pounds)
- 1 1/8 cups + 1 tablespoon water at 80 degrees F
- 1 1/2 whole eggs
- 3 teaspoons melted butter, cooled
- 4 1/2 tablespoons powdered skim milk
- 3 teaspoons sugar
- 3/4 teaspoon salt
- 1/2 cup crumbled blue cheese

- 3 teaspoons dried onion flakes
- 3 cups white bread flour
- 4 1/2 tablespoons instantly mashed potato flakes
- 1 1/8 teaspoons bread machine/ active dry yeast
- 16 slices (2 pounds)
- 1 1/2 cups + 2 tablespoons water at 80 degrees F
- 2 whole eggs
- 4 teaspoons melted butter, cooled
- 6 tablespoons powdered skim milk
- 4 teaspoons sugar
- 1 teaspoon salt
- 2/3 cup crumbled blue cheese
- 4 teaspoons dried onion flakes
- 4 cups white bread flour
- 6 tablespoons instantly mashed potato flakes
- 1 1/2 teaspoons bread machine/ active dry yeast

Directions:

1. Choose the size of loaf you would like to make and measure your ingredients.

2. Add the ingredients to the bread pan in the order listed above.

3. Place the pan in the bread machine and close the lid.

4. Turn on the bread maker. Select the White/Basic setting, then the loaf size, and finally the crust color. Start the cycle.

5. When the cycle is finished and the bread is baked, carefully remove the pan from the machine. Use a potholder as the handle will be very hot. Let rest for a few minutes.

6. Remove the bread from the pan and allow to cool on a wire rack for at least 10 minutes before slicing.

Mozza Salami Bread

Ingredients:

- 8 slices (1 pound)
- ¾ cup water, at 80 degrees F
- 1/3 cup shredded mozzarella cheese
- 4 teaspoons sugar
- 2/3 teaspoon salt
- 2/3 teaspoon dried basil
- Pinch of garlic powder
- 2 cups + 2 tablespoons white bread flour
- 1 teaspoon bread machine/ instant yeast

- ½ cup finely diced hot salami
- 12 slices (1 ½ pounds)
- 1 1/8 cups water, at 80 degrees F
- 1/2 cup shredded mozzarella cheese
- 6 teaspoons sugar
- 1 teaspoon salt
- 1 teaspoon dried basil
- Pinch of garlic powder
- 3 cups + 3 tablespoons white bread flour
- 1 1/2 teaspoons bread machine/ instant yeast
- 3/4 cup finely diced hot salami
- 16 slices (2 pounds)
- 1 1/2 cups water, at 80 degrees F
- 2/3 cup shredded mozzarella cheese
- 8 teaspoons sugar
- 1 1/3 teaspoons salt
- 1 1/3 teaspoons dried basil
- Pinch of garlic powder
- 4 cups + 4 tablespoons white bread flour
- 2 teaspoons bread machine/ instant yeast
- 1 cup finely diced hot salami

Directions:

1. Choose the size of loaf you would like to make and measure your ingredients.
2. Add the ingredients to the bread pan in the order listed above (except salami).
3. Place the pan in the bread machine and close the lid.
4. Turn on the bread maker. Select the White/Basic setting, then the loaf size, and finally the crust color. Start the cycle.
5. Add salami once the machine signals.
6. When the cycle is finished and the bread is baked, carefully remove the pan from the machine. Use a potholder as the handle will be very hot. Let rest for a few minutes.
7. Remove the bread from the pan and allow to cool on a wire rack for at least 10 minutes before slicing.

Pan D'angiol (bread Of The Angels)

Ingredients:
- 8 slices (1 pound)
- 5/6 cups milk
- 3/8 teaspoon almond extract
- 3/4 tablespoons butter, cut into pieces
- 2 tablespoons almond paste, cut into pieces
- 2 cups bread flour
- 1/8 cup sugar
- 1/2 tablespoon plus 1/2 teaspoon gluten
- 1 teaspoons salt
- 1 1/4 teaspoons SAF yeast or 1/2 tablespoon bread machine yeast
- 1/3 cup chopped dried sour cherries
- 1/6 cup slivered blanched almonds
- 12 slices (1 ½ pounds)
- 11/4 cups milk
- 1/2 teaspoon almond extract
- 1 tablespoon butter, cut into pieces
- 3 tablespoons almond paste, cut into pieces
- 3 cups bread flour
- 3 tablespoons sugar
- 1 tablespoon gluten
- 11/2 teaspoons salt
- 2 teaspoons SAF yeast or 21/2 teaspoons bread machine yeast
- 1/2 cup chopped dried sour cherries
- 1/2 cup slivered blanched almonds
- 16 slices (2 pounds)
- 12/3 cups milk
- 3/4 teaspoon almond extract
- 11/2 tablespoons butter, cut into pieces
- 4 tablespoons almond paste, cut into pieces
- 4 cups bread flour
- 1/4 cup sugar
- 1 tablespoon plus 1 teaspoon gluten
- 2 teaspoons salt
- 21/2 teaspoons SAF yeast or 1 tablespoon bread machine yeast
- 2/3 cup chopped dried sour cherries
- 1/3 cup slivered blanched almonds

Directions:

1. Choose the size of loaf you would like to make and measure your ingredients.
2. Add the ingredients to the bread pan in the order listed above (except the cherries and almonds)
3. Place the pan in the bread machine and close the lid.

4. Turn on the bread maker. Select the Basic/Fruit and Nut setting, then the loaf size, and finally the crust color. Start the cycle. (This recipe is not suitable for use with the Delay Timer.)

5. When the machine beeps, or between Knead 1 and Knead 2, add the cherries and almonds.

6. When the cycle is finished and the bread is baked, carefully remove the pan from the machine. Use a potholder as the handle will be very hot. Let rest for a few minutes.

7. Remove the bread from the pan and allow to cool on a wire rack for at least 10 minutes before slicing.

Jalapeno Cheddar Bread

Ingredients:
- 8 slices (1 pound)
- 2/3 cup lukewarm buttermilk
- 1/6 cup unsalted butter, melted
- 1 egg, at room temperature
- 1/3 teaspoon table salt
- 1/2 jalapeno pepper, chopped
- 1/3 cup Cheddar cheese, shredded
- 1/6 cup sugar
- 1 cup all-purpose flour
- 2/3 cup cornmeal
- 3/4 tablespoon baking powder
- 12 slices (1 ½ pounds)
- 1 cup lukewarm buttermilk
- ¼ cup unsalted butter, melted
- 2 eggs, at room temperature
- ½ teaspoon table salt
- 1 jalapeno pepper, chopped
- ½ cup Cheddar cheese, shredded
- ¼ cup sugar
- 1⅓ cups all-purpose flour
- 1 cup cornmeal
- 1 tablespoon baking powder
- 16 slices (2 pounds)
- 1⅓ cups lukewarm buttermilk
- ⅓ cup unsalted butter, melted
- 2 eggs, at room temperature
- ⅔ teaspoon table salt
- 1 jalapeno pepper, chopped
- ⅔ cup Cheddar cheese, shredded
- ⅓ cup sugar
- 2 cups all-purpose flour
- 1⅓ cups cornmeal
- 1½ tablespoons baking powder

Directions:
1. Choose the size of loaf you would like to make and measure your ingredients.

2. Add the ingredients to the bread pan in the order listed above.

3. Place the pan in the bread machine and close the lid.

4. Turn on the bread maker. Select the Rapid/Quick setting, then the loaf size, and finally the crust color. Start the cycle.

5. When the cycle is finished and the bread is baked, carefully remove the pan from the machine. Use a potholder as the handle will be very hot. Let rest for a few minutes.

6. Remove the bread from the pan and allow to cool on a wire rack for at least 10 minutes before slicing.

Dried Apricot Whole Wheat Bread

Ingredients:
- 8 slices (1 pound)
- 1/2 cup apple or pear juice
- 3 1/2 tablespoons water
- 1 1/4 tablespoons honey
- 1 1/4 tablespoons nut or vegetable oil
- 1 1/6 cups bread flour
- 1/2 cup whole wheat flour
- 1/3 cup rolled oats
- 1/2 tablespoon plus 1/2 teaspoon gluten
- 3/4 teaspoons salt
- 1 1/4 teaspoons SAF yeast or 1/2 tablespoon bread machine yeast
- 1/3 cup finely chopped dried apricots
- 12 slices (1 ½ pounds)
- 3/4 cup apple or pear juice
- 6 tablespoons water
- 2 tablespoons honey
- 2 tablespoons nut or vegetable oil
- 11/2 cups bread flour
- 1 cup whole wheat flour

- 1/2 cup rolled oats
- 1 tablespoon gluten
- 11/4 teaspoons salt
- 2 teaspoons SAF yeast or 21/2 teaspoons bread machine yeast
- 1/2 cup finely chopped dried apricots
- 16 slices (2 pounds)
- 1 cup apple or pear juice
- 7 tablespoons water
- 21/2 tablespoons honey
- 21/2 tablespoons nut or vegetable oil
- 21/3 cups bread flour
- 1 cup whole wheat flour
- 2/3 cup rolled oats
- 1 tablespoon plus 1 teaspoon gluten
- 11/2 teaspoons salt
- 21/2 teaspoons SAF yeast or 1 tablespoon bread machine yeast
- 2/3 cup finely chopped dried apricots

Directions:

1. Choose the size of loaf you would like to make and measure your ingredients.

2. Add the ingredients to the bread pan in the order listed above (except the apricots).

3. Place the pan in the bread machine and close the lid.

4. Turn on the bread maker. Select the Whole Wheat/Fruit and Nut setting, then the loaf size, and finally the crust color. Start the cycle. (This recipe is not suitable for use with the Delay Timer)

5. When the machine beeps, or between Knead 1 and Knead 2, add the apricots.

6. When the cycle is finished and the bread is baked, carefully remove the pan from the machine. Use a potholder as the handle will be very hot. Let rest for a few minutes.

7. Remove the bread from the pan and allow to cool on a wire rack for at least 10 minutes before slicing.

American Cheese Beer Bread

Ingredients:

- 8 slices (1 pound)
- 5/6 cup warm beer
- 3/4 tablespoon sugar
- 1 teaspoon table salt
- 3/4 tablespoon unsalted butter, melted
- 3/8 cup American cheese, shredded
- 3/8 cup Monterrey Jack cheese, shredded
- 2 cups white bread flour
- 1 teaspoon bread machine yeast
- 12 slices (1 ½ pounds)
- 1¼ cups warm beer
- 1 tablespoon sugar
- 1½ teaspoons table salt
- 1 tablespoon unsalted butter, melted
- ½ cup American cheese, shredded
- ½ cup Monterrey Jack cheese, shredded
- 3 cups white bread flour
- 1½ teaspoons bread machine yeast
- 16 slices (2 pounds)
- 1⅔ cups warm beer
- 1½ tablespoons sugar
- 2 teaspoons table salt
- 1½ tablespoons unsalted butter, melted
- ¾ cup American cheese, shredded
- ¾ cup Monterrey Jack cheese, shredded
- 4 cups white bread flour
- 2 teaspoons bread machine yeast

Directions:

1. Choose the size of loaf you would like to make and measure your ingredients.

2. Add the ingredients to the bread pan in the order listed above.

3. Place the pan in the bread machine and close the lid.

4. Turn on the bread maker. Select the White/Basic setting, then the loaf size, and finally the crust color. Start the cycle.

5. When the cycle is finished and the bread is baked, carefully remove the pan from the machine. Use a potholder as the handle will be very hot. Let rest for a few minutes.

6. Remove the bread from the pan and allow to cool on a wire rack for at least 10 minutes before slicing.

Parmesan Nut Bread

Ingredients:

- 8 slices (1 pound)
- 2/3 cup water
- 1 tablespoon olive oil
- 2 cups bread flour
- 3/8 cup grated Parmesan cheese
- 2/3 tablespoon gluten
- Pinch of sugar
- 3/8 teaspoon salt
- 1 1/4 teaspoons SAF yeast or 1/2 tablespoon bread machine yeast
- 1/4 cup pine nuts, coarsely chopped
- 1/3 cup walnuts, coarsely chopped
- 12 slices (1 ½ pounds)
- 1 cup water
- 11/2 tablespoons olive oil
- 3 cups bread flour
- 2/3 cup grated Parmesan cheese
- 1 tablespoon gluten
- Pinch of sugar
- 1/2 teaspoon salt
- 2 teaspoons SAF yeast or 21/2 teaspoon bread machine yeast
- 1/3 cup pine nuts, coarsely chopped
- 1/2 cup walnuts, coarsely chopped
- 16 slices (2 pounds)
- 11/3 cups water
- 2 tablespoons olive oil
- 4 cups bread flour
- 3/4 cup grated Parmesan cheese
- 1 tablespoon plus 1 teaspoon gluten
- Pinch of sugar
- 3/4 teaspoon salt
- 21/2 teaspoons SAF yeast or 1 tablespoon bread machine yeast
- 1/2 cup pine nuts, coarsely chopped
- 2/3 cup walnuts, coarsely chopped

Directions:

1. Choose the size of loaf you would like to make and measure your ingredients.
2. Add the ingredients to the bread pan in the order listed above (except the nuts).
3. Place the pan in the bread machine and close the lid.
4. Turn on the bread maker. Select the Basic setting, then the loaf size, and finally the crust color. Start the cycle. (This recipe is not suitable for use with the Delay Timer.)
5. When the machine beeps, or between Knead 1 and Knead 2, add the nuts.
6. When the cycle is finished and the bread is baked, carefully remove the pan from the machine. Use a potholder as the handle will be very hot. Let rest for a few minutes.
7. Remove the bread from the pan and allow to cool on a wire rack for at least 10 minutes before slicing.

Brioche Bread

Ingredients:

- 8 slices (1 pound)
- 1/4 cup plus 1 tablespoon milk
- 1 large egg
- 1 egg yolk
- 1 3/8 cups bread flour
- 1 1/4 tablespoons sugar
- 1/2 tablespoon gluten
- 1/2 teaspoon salt
- 7/8 teaspoon SAF yeast or 1 1/8 teaspoon bread machine yeast
- 1/4 cup plus 1 tablespoons (5/8 stick) unsalted butter, cut into pieces
- 12 slices (1 ½ pounds)
- 1/3 cup milk
- 2 large eggs
- 1 egg yolk
- 2 cups bread flour
- 2 tablespoons sugar
- 2 teaspoons gluten
- 3/4 teaspoon salt
- 11/4 teaspoons SAF yeast or 13/4 teaspoons bread machine yeast
- 7 tablespoons unsalted butter, cut into pieces
- 16 slices (2 pounds)
- 1/2 cup plus 1 tablespoon milk
- 2 large eggs
- 2 egg yolks

- 23/4 cups bread flour
- 21/2 tablespoons sugar
- 1 tablespoon gluten
- 1 teaspoon salt
- 13/4 teaspoons SAF yeast or 21/4 teaspoons bread machine yeast
- 1/2 cup plus 2 tablespoons (11/4 sticks) unsalted butter, cut into pieces

Directions:

1. Choose the size of loaf you would like to make and measure your ingredients.
2. Add the ingredients to the bread pan in the order listed above (except the butter).
3. Place the pan in the bread machine and close the lid.
4. Turn on the bread maker. Select the Basic setting, then the loaf size, and finally the crust color. Start the cycle.
5. About 10 minutes into Knead 2, open the lid while the machine is running. Add a piece or two of the butter, allowing it to be incorporated before adding more pieces. It will take a full minute or two to add all the butter. Close the lid.
6. When the cycle is finished and the bread is baked, open the lid and let the bread sit in the pan for 15 minutes, later remove the pan from the machine carefully. Use a potholder as the handle will be very hot. Let rest for a few minutes.
7. Remove the bread from the pan and allow to cool on a wire rack for at least 10 minutes before slicing.

FRUIT BREAD RECIPES

Applesauce Bread

Ingredients:

- 8 slices (1 pound)
- 1/4 cup apple juice
- 3/8 cup unsweetened applesauce
- 1/2 large egg
- 1 1/2 tablespoons unsalted butter, cut into pieces
- 2 cups bread flour
- 1/8 cup light brown sugar, optional
- 1/2 tablespoon plus 1/2 teaspoon gluten
- 1 teaspoon salt
- 5/8 teaspoon ground cinnamon or apple pie spice
- 1/4 teaspoon baking soda
- 1 1/8 teaspoons SAF yeast or 1 3/8 teaspoons bread machine yeast
- 12 slices (1 ½ pounds)
- 1/4 cup apple juice
- 1/2 cup unsweetened applesauce
- 1 large egg
- 2 tablespoons unsalted butter, cut into pieces
- 3 cups bread flour
- 3 tablespoons light brown sugar, optional
- 1 tablespoon gluten
- 11/2 teaspoons salt
- 1 teaspoon ground cinnamon or apple pie spice
- 1/3 teaspoon baking soda
- 2 teaspoons SAF yeast or 21/2 teaspoons bread machine yeast
- 16 slices (2 pounds)
- 1/2 cup apple juice
- 3/4 cup unsweetened applesauce
- 1 large egg
- 3 tablespoons unsalted butter, cut into pieces
- 4 cups bread flour
- 1/4 cup light brown sugar, optional
- 1 tablespoon plus 1 teaspoon gluten
- 2 teaspoons salt
- 11/4 teaspoons ground cinnamon or apple pie spice
- 1/2 teaspoon baking soda
- 21/4 teaspoons SAF yeast or 23/4 teaspoons bread machine yeast

Directions:

1. Choose the size of loaf you would like to make and measure your ingredients.
2. Add the ingredients to the bread pan in the order listed above.
3. Place the pan in the bread machine and close the lid.
4. Turn on the bread maker. Select the Basic/Sweet Bread setting, then the loaf size, and finally the crust color. Start the cycle.
5. When the cycle is finished and the bread is baked, carefully remove the pan from the machine. Use a potholder as the handle will be very hot. Let rest for a few minutes.
6. Remove the bread from the pan and allow to cool on a wire rack for at least 10 minutes before slicing.

Cranberry Orange Pecan Bread

Servings: 16
Cooking Time: 2 Hours 50 Minutes

Ingredients:

- 1 cup water
- 1/4 cup orange juice
- 2 teaspoons salt
- 1/3 cup sugar
- 2 1/2 tablespoons nonfat dry milk
- 2 1/2 tablespoons butter, cubed
- 4 cups bread flour
- 2 1/2 teaspoons orange zest
- 2 1/2 teaspoons bread machine yeast
- 1/2 cup dried cranberries
- 1/2 cup pecans, chopped

Directions:

1. Set aside cranberries and pecans, then place all other ingredients in the bread maker pan in order listed.
2. Choose Sweet cycle, light crust and press Start.
3. Add cranberries and pecans at the end of the kneading cycle.
4. Transfer to a plate and let cool 10 minutes before slicing with a bread knife.

Nutrition:

- al Info Calories: 247 Sodium: 311 Dietary Fiber: 2.6 g, Fat: 11.5 g, Carbs: 31.5 g, Protein: 5.4 g.

Cappuccino Orange Bread

Ingredients:
- 8 slices (1 pound)
- 1 cup water
- 1 tablespoon instant coffee granules
- 2 tablespoons butter, soften
- 1 teaspoon orange peel, grated
- 3 cups bread flour
- 2 tablespoons dry milk
- ¼ cup sugar
- 1¼ teaspoons salt
- 2¼ teaspoons bread machine yeast
- 12 slices (1 ½ pounds)
- 1 1/2 cups water
- 1 1/2 tablespoons instant coffee granules
- 3 tablespoons butter, soften
- 1 1/2 teaspoons orange peel, grated
- 4 1/2 cups bread flour
- 3 tablespoons dry milk
- 3/8 cup sugar
- 1 7/8 teaspoons salt
- 3 3/8 teaspoons bread machine yeast
- 16 slices (2 pounds)
- 2 cups water
- 2 tablespoons instant coffee granules
- 4 tablespoons butter, soften
- 2 teaspoons orange peel, grated
- 6 cups bread flour
- 4 tablespoons dry milk
- 1/2 cup sugar
- 2 1/2 teaspoons salt
- 4 1/2 teaspoons bread machine yeast

Directions:

1. Choose the size of loaf you would like to make and measure your ingredients.

2. Add the ingredients to the bread pan in the order listed above.

3. Place the pan in the bread machine and close the lid.

4. Turn on the bread maker. Select the White/Basic setting, then the loaf size, and finally the crust color. Start the cycle.

5. When the cycle is finished and the bread is baked, carefully remove the pan from the machine. Use a potholder as the handle will be very hot. Let rest for a few minutes.

6. Remove the bread from the pan and allow to cool on a wire rack for at least 10 minutes before slicing.

Cinnamon Figs Bread

Ingredients:
- 8 slices (1 pound)
- 3/4 cup lukewarm water
- 1 1/2 tablespoons unsalted butter, melted
- 1/8 cup sugar
- 1/2 teaspoon table salt
- 1/4 teaspoon cinnamon, ground
- 1/2 teaspoon orange zest
- Pinch ground nutmeg
- 1 1/4 cups whole-wheat flour
- 3/4 cup white bread flour
- 1 teaspoon bread machine yeast
- 5/8 cup chopped fresh plums or sliced figs
- 12 slices (1 ½ pounds)
- 1⅛ cups lukewarm water
- 2¼ tablespoons unsalted butter, melted
- 3 tablespoons sugar
- ¾ teaspoon table salt
- ⅓ teaspoon cinnamon, ground
- ¾ teaspoon orange zest
- Pinch ground nutmeg
- 1⅞ cups whole-wheat flour
- 1⅛ cups white bread flour
- 1½ teaspoons bread machine yeast
- 1 cup chopped plums or sliced figs
- 16 slices (2 pounds)
- 1½ cups lukewarm water
- 3 tablespoons unsalted butter, melted
- ¼ cup sugar
- 1 teaspoon table salt
- ½ teaspoon cinnamon, ground
- 1 teaspoon orange zest
- Pinch ground nutmeg
- 2½ cups whole-wheat flour
- 1½ cups white bread flour
- 2 teaspoons bread machine yeast
- 1¼ cups chopped fresh plums or sliced figs

Directions:

1.   Choose the size of loaf you would like to make and measure your ingredients.

2.   Add all of the ingredients except for the plums to the bread pan in the order listed above.

3.   Place the pan in the bread machine and close the lid.

4.   Turn on the bread maker. Select the White/Basic or Fruit/Nut (if your machine has this setting) setting, then the loaf size, and finally the crust color. Start the cycle.

5.   When the machine signals to add ingredients, add the plums. (Some machines have a fruit/nut hopper where you can add the plums when you start the machine. The machine will automatically add them to the dough during the baking process.)

6.   When the cycle is finished and the bread is baked, carefully remove the pan from the machine. Use a potholder as the handle will be very hot. Let rest for a few minutes.

7.   Remove the bread from the pan and allow to cool on a wire rack for at least 10 minutes before slicing.

Cocoa Date Bread

Ingredients:
- 8 slices (1 pound)
- 1/2 cup lukewarm water
- 1/4 cup lukewarm milk
- 1 tablespoon unsalted butter, melted
- 1 1/2 tablespoons honey
- 1 1/2 tablespoons molasses
- 1/2 tablespoon sugar
- 1 1/2 tablespoons skim milk powder
- 1/2 teaspoon table salt
- 1 cup white bread flour
- 1 1/4 cups whole-wheat flour
- 1/2 tablespoon cocoa powder, unsweetened
- 3/4 teaspoon bread machine yeast
- 1/2 cup dates, chopped
- 12 slices (1 ½ pounds)
- ¾ cup lukewarm water
- ½ cup lukewarm milk
- 2 tablespoons unsalted butter, melted
- ¼ cup honey
- 3 tablespoons molasses

- 1 tablespoon sugar
- 2 tablespoons skim milk powder
- 1 teaspoon table salt
- 1¼ cups white bread flour
- 2¼ cups whole-wheat flour
- 1 tablespoon cocoa powder, unsweetened
- 1½ teaspoons bread machine yeast
- ¾ cup dates, chopped
- 16 slices (2 pounds)
- 1 cup lukewarm water
- ½ cup lukewarm milk
- 2 tablespoons unsalted butter, melted
- 5 tablespoons honey
- 3 tablespoons molasses
- 1 tablespoon sugar
- 3 tablespoons skim milk powder
- 1 teaspoon table salt
- 2 cups white bread flour
- 2½ cups whole-wheat flour
- 1 tablespoon cocoa powder, unsweetened
- 1½ teaspoons bread machine yeast
- 1 cup dates, chopped

Directions:

1.   Choose the size of loaf you would like to make and measure your ingredients.

2.   Add all of the ingredients except for the dates to the bread pan in the order listed above.

3.   Place the pan in the bread machine and close the lid.

4.   Turn on the bread maker. Select the White/Basic or Fruit/Nut (if your machine has this setting) setting, then the loaf size, and finally the crust color. Start the cycle.

5.   When the machine signals to add ingredients, add the dates. (Some machines have a fruit/nut hopper where you can add the dates when you start the machine. The machine will automatically add them to the dough during the baking process.)

6.   When the cycle is finished and the bread is baked, carefully remove the pan from the machine. Use a potholder as the handle will be very hot. Let rest for a few minutes.

7.   Remove the bread from the pan and allow to cool on a wire rack for at least 10 minutes before slicing.

Spice Peach Bread

Ingredients:

- 8 slices (1 pound)
- 1/4 cup lukewarm heavy whipping cream
- 1/2 egg, beaten
- 3/4 tablespoon unsalted butter, melted
- 1 1/2 tablespoons sugar
- 3/4 teaspoon table salt
- 1/8 teaspoon nutmeg, ground
- 1/4 teaspoon cinnamon, ground
- 1 3/4 cups white bread flour
- 1/4 cup whole-wheat flour
- 3/4 teaspoon bread machine yeast
- 1/2 cup canned peaches, drained and chopped
- 12 slices (1 ½ pounds)
- ⅓ cup lukewarm heavy whipping cream
- 1 egg, beaten
- 1 tablespoon unsalted butter, melted
- 2¼ tablespoons sugar
- 1⅛ teaspoons table salt
- ⅛ teaspoon nutmeg, ground
- ⅓ teaspoon cinnamon, ground
- 2⅔ cups white bread flour
- ⅓ cup whole-wheat flour
- 1⅛ teaspoons bread machine yeast
- ¾ cup canned peaches, drained and chopped
- 16 slices (2 pounds)
- ½ cup lukewarm heavy whipping cream
- 1 egg, beaten
- 1½ tablespoons unsalted butter, melted
- 3 tablespoons sugar
- 1½ teaspoons table salt
- ¼ teaspoon nutmeg, ground
- ½ teaspoon cinnamon, ground
- 3½ cups white bread flour
- ½ cup whole-wheat flour
- 1½ teaspoons bread machine yeast
- 1 cup canned peaches, drained and chopped

Directions:

1. Choose the size of loaf you would like to make and measure your ingredients.

2. Add all of the ingredients except for the peach to the bread pan in the order listed above.

3. Place the pan in the bread machine and close the lid.

4. Turn on the bread maker. Select the White/Basic or Fruit/Nut (if your machine has this setting) setting, then the loaf size, and finally the crust color. Start the machine.

5. When the machine signals to add ingredients, add the peaches. (Some machines have a fruit/nut hopper where you can add the peaches when you start the machine. The machine will automatically add them to the dough during the baking process.)

6. When the cycle is finished and the bread is baked, carefully remove the pan from the machine. Use a potholder as the handle will be very hot. Let rest for a few minutes.

7. Remove the bread from the pan and allow to cool on a wire rack for at least 10 minutes before slicing.

Pineapple Carrot Bread

Servings: 12

Cooking Time: 3 Hours

Ingredients:

- 1 (8-ounce) can crushed pineapple, with juice
- 1/2 cup carrots, shredded
- 2 eggs
- 2 tablespoons butter
- 4 cups bread flour
- 3 tablespoons sugar
- 1 teaspoon salt
- 3/4 teaspoon ground ginger
- 1 1/4 teaspoons active dry yeast

Directions:

1. Add all of the ingredients (except yeast) to the bread maker pan in the order listed above.

2. Make a well in the center of the dry ingredients and add the yeast.

3. Select the Basic bread cycle and press Start.

4. Transfer baked loaf to a cooling rack for 15 minutes before slicing to serve.

Nutrition:

- al Info Calories: 203, Sodium: 222 mg, Dietary Fiber: 1.6 g, Fat: 3.1 g, Carbs: 38 g, Protein: 5.6 g.

Tomato Bread

Ingredients:

- 8 slices (1 pound)
- 3/4 cup water
- 1/8 cup tomato paste
- 1/4 cup chopped oil-packed sun-dried tomatoes, with their oil
- 1 5/6 cups bread flour
- 1/3 cup whole wheat flour
- 1 tablespoon gluten
- 1 teaspoon salt
- 1 1/8 teaspoons SAF yeast or 1 3/8 teaspoons bread machine yeast
- 12 slices (1 ½ pounds)
- 11/4 cups water
- 3 tablespoons tomato paste
- 1/3 cup chopped oil-packed sun-dried tomatoes, with their oil
- 23/4 cups bread flour
- 1/2 cup whole wheat flour
- 11/2 tablespoons gluten
- 11/2 teaspoons salt
- 2 teaspoons SAF yeast or 21/2 teaspoons bread machine yeast
- 16 slices (2 pounds)
- 11/2 cups water
- 1/4 cup tomato paste
- 1/2 cup chopped oil-packed sun-dried tomatoes, with their oil
- 32/3 cups bread flour
- 2/3 cup whole wheat flour
- 2 tablespoons gluten
- 2 teaspoons salt
- 21/4 teaspoons SAF yeast or 23/4 teaspoons bread machine yeast

Directions:

1. Choose the size of loaf you would like to make and measure your ingredients.
2. Add the ingredients to the bread pan in the order listed above.
3. Place the pan in the bread machine and close the lid.
4. Turn on the bread maker. Select the Basic setting, then the loaf size, and finally the crust color. Start the cycle.
5. When the cycle is finished and the bread is baked, carefully remove the pan from the machine. Use a potholder as the handle will be very hot. Let rest for a few minutes.
6. Remove the bread from the pan and allow to cool on a wire rack for at least 10 minutes before slicing.

Blueberry Honey Bread

Ingredients:

- 8 slices (1 pound)
- 1/2 cup plain yogurt
- 1/3 cup lukewarm water
- 1/8 cup honey
- 2 teaspoons unsalted butter, melted
- 1 teaspoon table salt
- 3/4 teaspoon lime zest
- 1/3 teaspoon lemon extract
- 2 cups white bread flour
- 1 1/8 teaspoons bread machine yeast
- 2/3 cup dried blueberries
- 12 slices (1 ½ pounds)
- ¾ cup plain yogurt
- ½ cup lukewarm water
- 3 tablespoons honey
- 1 tablespoon unsalted butter, melted
- 1½ teaspoons table salt
- 1 teaspoon lime zest
- ½ teaspoon lemon extract
- 3 cups white bread flour
- 2¼ teaspoons bread machine yeast
- 1 cup dried blueberries
- 16 slices (2 pounds)
- 1 cup plain yogurt
- ⅔ cup lukewarm water
- ¼ cup honey
- 4 teaspoons unsalted butter, melted
- 2 teaspoons table salt
- 1½ teaspoons lime zest
- ⅔ teaspoon lemon extract
- 4 cups white bread flour

- 2¼ teaspoons bread machine yeast
- 1⅓ cups dried blueberries

Directions:

1. Choose the size of loaf you would like to make and measure your ingredients.

2. Add all of the ingredients except for the blueberries to the bread pan in the order listed above.

3. Place the pan in the bread machine and close the lid.

4. Turn on the bread maker. Select the White/Basic or Fruit/Nut (if your machine has this setting) setting, then the loaf size, and finally the crust color. Start the cycle.

5. When the machine signals to add ingredients, add the blueberries. (Some machines have a fruit/nut hopper where you can add the blueberries when you start the machine. The machine will automatically add them to the dough during the baking process.)

6. When the cycle is finished and the bread is baked, carefully remove the pan from the machine. Use a potholder as the handle will be very hot. Let rest for a few minutes.

7. Remove the bread from the pan and allow to cool on a wire rack for at least 10 minutes before slicing.

Wild Rice Cranberry Delight

Ingredients:

- 8 slices (1 pound)
- 1¼ cups water
- ¼ cup skim milk powder
- 1¼ teaspoon salt
- 2 tablespoons liquid honey
- 1 tablespoon extra-virgin olive oil
- 3 cups all-purpose flour
- ¾ cup cooked wild rice
- ¼ cup pine nuts
- ¾ teaspoon celery seeds
- 1 teaspoon bread machine yeast
- 2/3 cup dried cranberries
- 1/8 teaspoon black pepper, ground
- 12 slices (1 ½ pounds)
- 1 7/8 cups water
- 3/8 cup skim milk powder
- 1 7/8 teaspoons salt
- 3 tablespoons liquid honey

- 1 1/2 tablespoons extra-virgin olive oil
- 4 1/2 cups all-purpose flour
- 1 1/8 cups cooked wild rice
- 3/8 cup pine nuts
- 1 1/8 teaspoons celery seeds
- 1 1/2 teaspoons bread machine yeast
- 1 cup dried cranberries
- 3/16 teaspoon black pepper, ground
- 16 slices (2 pounds)
- 2 1/2 cups water
- 1/2 cup skim milk powder
- 2 1/2 teaspoons salt
- 4 tablespoons liquid honey
- 2 tablespoon extra-virgin olive oil
- 6 cups all-purpose flour
- 1 1/2 cups cooked wild rice
- 1/2 cup pine nuts
- 1 1/2 teaspoons celery seeds
- 2 teaspoons bread machine yeast
- 1 1/3 cups dried cranberries
- 1/4 teaspoon black pepper, ground

Directions:

1. Choose the size of loaf you would like to make and measure your ingredients.

2. Add the ingredients to the bread pan in the order listed above (except cranberries).

3. Place the pan in the bread machine and close the lid.

4. Turn on the bread maker. Select the White/Basic setting, then the loaf size, and finally the crust color. Start the cycle.

5. Once the machine beeps, add cranberries.

6. When the cycle is finished and the bread is baked, carefully remove the pan from the machine. Use a potholder as the handle will be very hot. Let rest for a few minutes.

7. Remove the bread from the pan and allow to cool on a wire rack for at least 10 minutes before slicing.

Garlic Olive Bread

Ingredients:

- 8 slices (1 pound)
- 2/3 cup lukewarm milk
- 1 tablespoon unsalted butter, melted

- 2/3 teaspoon garlic, minced
- 1 tablespoon sugar
- 2/3 teaspoon table salt
- 2 cups white bread flour
- 3/4 teaspoon bread machine yeast
- 1/4 cup black olives, chopped
- 12 slices (1 ½ pounds)
- 1 cup lukewarm milk
- 1½ tablespoons unsalted butter, melted
- 1 teaspoon garlic, minced
- 1½ tablespoons sugar
- 1 teaspoon table salt
- 3 cups white bread flour
- 1 teaspoon bread machine yeast
- ⅓ cup black olives, chopped
- 16 slices (2 pounds)
- 1⅓ cups lukewarm milk
- 2 tablespoons unsalted butter, melted
- 1⅓ teaspoons garlic, minced
- 2 tablespoons sugar
- 1⅓ teaspoons table salt
- 4 cups white bread flour
- 1½ teaspoons bread machine yeast
- ½ cup black olives, chopped

Directions:

1. Choose the size of loaf you would like to make and measure your ingredients.

2. Add all of the ingredients except for the olives to the bread pan in the order listed above.

3. Place the pan in the bread machine and close the lid.

4. Turn on the bread maker. Select the White/Basic or Fruit/Nut (if your machine has this setting) setting, then the loaf size, and finally the crust color. Start the machine.

5. When the machine signals to add ingredients, add the olives. (Some machines have a fruit/nut hopper where you can add the olives when you start the machine. The machine will automatically add them to the dough during the baking process.)

6. When the cycle is finished and the bread is baked, carefully remove the pan from the machine. Use a potholder as the handle will be very hot. Let rest for a few minutes.

7. Remove the bread from the pan and allow to cool on a wire rack for at least 10 minutes before slicing.

Toasted Coconut Bread

Ingredients:
- 8 slices (1 pound)
- 11/4 cups (about 21/2 ounces) shredded unsweetened coconut
- 11/8 cups half-and-half (regular or fat-free)
- 2 large eggs
- 1/4 cup canola oil
- 2 teaspoons coconut extract
- 1 teaspoon vanilla extract
- 3/4 cup sugar
- 2 cups unbleached all-purpose flour
- 1 tablespoon baking powder
- 1/2 teaspoon salt
- 12 slices (1 ½ pounds)
- 1 7/8 cups (about 21/2 ounces) shredded unsweetened coconut
- 1 11/16 cups half-and-half (regular or fat-free)
- 3 large eggs
- 3/8 cup canola oil
- 3 teaspoons coconut extract
- 1 1/2 teaspoons vanilla extract
- 1 1/8 cups sugar
- 3 cups unbleached all-purpose flour
- 1 1/2 tablespoons baking powder
- 3/4 teaspoon salt
- 16 slices (2 pounds)
- 2 1/2 cups (about 21/2 ounces) shredded unsweetened coconut
- 2 1/4 cups half-and-half (regular or fat-free)
- 4 large eggs
- 1/2 cup canola oil
- 4 teaspoons coconut extract
- 2 teaspoons vanilla extract
- 1 1/2 cups sugar
- 4 cups unbleached all-purpose flour
- 2 tablespoons baking powder
- 1 teaspoon salt

Directions:

1.   Choose the size of loaf you would like to make and measure your ingredients.

2.   Preheat the oven to 350°F.

3.   Sprinkle the coconut on an ungreased baking sheet and toast in the oven until lightly browned, about 3 minutes. Transfer immediately to a small bowl and let cool to room temperature.

4.   Add the ingredients to the bread pan in the order listed above. Adding the coconut with the dry ingredients.

5.   Place the pan in the bread machine and close the lid.

6.   Turn on the bread maker. Select the Quick Bread/Cake setting, then the loaf size, and finally the crust color. Start the cycle.

7.   When the cycle is finished and the bread is baked, carefully remove the pan from the machine. Use a potholder as the handle will be very hot. Let rest for a few minutes.

8.   Remove the bread from the pan and allow to cool on a wire rack for at least 10 minutes before slicing.

Cranberry Honey Bread

Ingredients:
- 8 slices (1 pound)
- 5/8 cup + 1/2 tablespoon lukewarm water
- 1/8 cup unsalted butter, melted
- 1 1/2 tablespoons honey or molasses
- 2 cups white bread flour
- 1/4 cup cornmeal
- 1 teaspoon table salt
- 1 1/4 teaspoons bread machine yeast
- 3/8 cup cranberries, dried
- 12 slices (1 ½ pounds)
- 1 cup + 1 tablespoon lukewarm water
- 2 tablespoons unsalted butter, melted
- 3 tablespoons honey or molasses
- 3 cups white bread flour
- ⅓ cup cornmeal
- 1½ teaspoons table salt
- 2 teaspoons bread machine yeast
- ½ cup cranberries, dried
- 16 slices (2 pounds)
- 1¼ cups + 1 tablespoon lukewarm water

- ¼ cup unsalted butter, melted
- 3 tablespoons honey or molasses
- 4 cups white bread flour
- ½ cup cornmeal
- 2 teaspoons table salt
- 2½ teaspoons bread machine yeast
- ¾ cup cranberries, dried

Directions:

1.   Choose the size of loaf you would like to make and measure your ingredients.

2.   Add all of the ingredients except for the dried cranberries to the bread pan in the order listed above.

3.   Place the pan in the bread machine and close the lid.

4.   Turn on the bread maker. Select the White/Basic or Fruit/Nut (if your machine has this setting) setting, then the loaf size, and finally the crust color. Start the cycle.

5.   When the machine signals to add ingredients, add the dried cranberries. (Some machines have a fruit/nut hopper where you can add the dried cranberries when you start the machine. The machine will automatically add them to the dough during the baking process.)

6.   When the cycle is finished and the bread is baked, carefully remove the pan from the machine. Use a potholder as the handle will be very hot. Let rest for a few minutes.

7.   Remove the bread from the pan and allow to cool on a wire rack for at least 10 minutes before slicing.

Cinnamon Apple Bread

Ingredients:
- 8 slices (1 pound)
- 2/3 cup lukewarm milk
- 1 2/3 tablespoons butter, melted
- 1 1/3 tablespoons sugar
- 1 teaspoon table salt
- 2/3 teaspoon cinnamon, ground
- A pinch ground cloves
- 2 cups white bread flour
- 1 1/8 teaspoons bread machine yeast
- 2/3 cup peeled apple, finely diced
- 12 slices (1 ½ pounds)
- 1 cup lukewarm milk
- 2½ tablespoons butter, melted

- 2 tablespoons sugar
- 1½ teaspoons table salt
- 1 teaspoon cinnamon, ground
- A pinch ground cloves
- 3 cups white bread flour
- 2¼ teaspoons bread machine yeast
- 1 cup peeled apple, finely diced
- 16 slices (2 pounds)
- 1⅓ cups lukewarm milk
- 3⅓ tablespoons butter, melted
- 2⅔ tablespoons sugar
- 2 teaspoons table salt
- 1⅓ teaspoons cinnamon, ground
- A pinch ground cloves
- 4 cups white bread flour
- 2¼ teaspoons bread machine yeast
- 1⅓ cups peeled apple, finely diced

Directions:

1. Choose the size of loaf you would like to make and measure your ingredients.

2. Add the ingredients to the bread pan in the order listed above (except for the apples).

3. Place the pan in the bread machine and close the lid.

4. Turn on the bread maker. Select the Basic/Fruit and Nut setting, then the loaf size, and finally the crust color. Start the cycle.

5. When the machine signals to add ingredients, add the apples.

6. When the cycle is finished and the bread is baked, carefully remove the pan from the machine. Use a potholder as the handle will be very hot. Let rest for a few minutes.

7. Remove the bread from the pan and allow to cool on a wire rack for at least 10 minutes before slicing.

Hawaiian Banana Bread

Ingredients:

- 8 slices (1 pound)
- ½ cup mashed banana
- ½ cup crushed pineapple and juice
- 1 whole egg
- ¼ cup milk
- ¼ cup margarine, soft
- ½ teaspoon salt
- 1/3 cup white sugar
- ½ cup instant potato flakes
- 3 cups bread flour
- 1½ teaspoons active dry yeast
- 12 slices (1 ½ pounds)
- 3/4 cup mashed banana
- 3/4 cup crushed pineapple and juice
- 2/3 whole egg
- 3/8 cup milk
- 3/8 cup margarine, soft
- 3/4 teaspoon salt
- 1/2 cup white sugar
- 3/4 cup instant potato flakes
- 4 1/2 cups bread flour
- 2 1/4 teaspoons active dry yeast
- 16 slices (2 pounds)
- 1 cup mashed banana
- 1 cup crushed pineapple and juice
- 2 whole eggs
- 1/2 cup milk
- 1/2 cup margarine, soft
- 1 teaspoon salt
- 2/3 cup white sugar
- 1 cup instant potato flakes
- 6 cups bread flour
- 3 teaspoons active dry yeast

Directions:

1. Choose the size of loaf you would like to make and measure your ingredients.

2. Add the ingredients to the bread pan in the order listed above.

3. Place the pan in the bread machine and close the lid.

4. Turn on the bread maker. Select the White/Basic setting, then the loaf size, and finally the crust color. Start the cycle.

5. Once the bread maker signals, add fruits.

6. When the cycle is finished and the bread is baked, carefully remove the pan from the machine. Use a potholder as the handle will be very hot. Let rest for a few minutes.

7. Remove the bread from the pan and allow to cool on a wire rack for at least 10 minutes before slicing.

Succulent Cranberry Cinnamon Bread

Ingredients:
- 8 slices (1 pound)
- 1¼ cup water
- 2 tablespoons soft butter
- 2½ tablespoons sugar
- 3½ cups bread flour
- 2¼ teaspoons dry yeast
- 1 cup dried cranberries
- 1½ teaspoons cinnamon
- 12 slices (1 ½ pounds)
- 1 7/8 cups water
- 3 tablespoons soft butter
- 3 3/4 tablespoons sugar
- 5 1/4 cups bread flour
- 3 3/8 teaspoons dry yeast
- 1 1/2 cups dried cranberries
- 2 1/4 teaspoons cinnamon
- 16 slices (2 pounds)
- 2 1/2 cups water
- 4 tablespoons soft butter
- 5 tablespoons sugar
- 7 cups bread flour
- 4 1/2 teaspoons dry yeast
- 2 cups dried cranberries
- 3 teaspoons cinnamon

Directions:

1. Choose the size of loaf you would like to make and measure your ingredients.

2. Add the ingredients to the bread pan in the order listed above (except cranberries).

3. Place the pan in the bread machine and close the lid.

4. Turn on the bread maker. Select the White/Basic setting, then the loaf size, and finally the crust color. Start the cycle.

5. When the cycle is finished and the bread is baked, carefully remove the pan from the machine. Use a potholder as the handle will be very hot. Let rest for a few minutes.

6. Remove the bread from the pan and allow to cool on a wire rack for at least 10 minutes before slicing.

Super Spice Bread

Ingredients:
- 8 slices (1 pound)
- 2/3 cup lukewarm milk
- 1 egg, at room temperature
- 1 tablespoon unsalted butter, melted
- 1 1/3 tablespoons honey
- 2/3 teaspoon table salt
- 2 cups white bread flour
- 2/3 teaspoon ground cinnamon
- 1/3 teaspoon ground cardamom
- 1/3 teaspoon ground nutmeg
- 1 1/8 teaspoons bread machine yeast
- 12 slices (1 ½ pounds)
- 1 cup lukewarm milk
- 2 eggs, at room temperature
- 1½ tablespoons unsalted butter, melted
- 2 tablespoons honey
- 1 teaspoon table salt
- 3 cups white bread flour
- 1 teaspoon ground cinnamon
- ½ teaspoon ground cardamom
- ½ teaspoon ground nutmeg
- 2 teaspoons bread machine yeast
- 16 slices (2 pounds)
- 1⅓ cups lukewarm milk
- 2 eggs, at room temperature
- 2 tablespoons unsalted butter, melted
- 2⅔ tablespoons honey
- 1⅓ teaspoons table salt
- 4 cups white bread flour
- 1⅓ teaspoons ground cinnamon
- ⅔ teaspoon ground cardamom
- ⅔ teaspoon ground nutmeg
- 2¼ teaspoons bread machine yeast

Directions:

1. Choose the size of loaf you would like to make and measure your ingredients.

2. Add the ingredients to the bread pan in the order listed above.

3. Place the pan in the bread machine and close the lid.

4. Turn on the bread maker. Select the White/Basic setting, then the loaf size, and finally the crust color. Start the cycle.

5. When the cycle is finished and the bread is baked, carefully remove the pan from the machine. Use a potholder as the handle will be very hot. Let rest for a few minutes.

6. Remove the bread from the pan and allow to cool on a wire rack for at least 10 minutes before slicing.

Orange Bread

Ingredients:

- 8 slices (1 pound)
- 5/8 cup lukewarm milk
- 1/8 cup orange juice
- 1/8 cup sugar
- 3/4 tablespoon unsalted butter, melted
- 5/8 teaspoon table salt
- 2 cups white bread flour
- Zest of 1/2 orange
- 7/8 teaspoon bread machine yeast
- 12 slices (1 ½ pounds)
- 1 cup lukewarm milk
- 3 tablespoons orange juice
- 3 tablespoons sugar
- 1 tablespoon unsalted butter, melted
- 1 teaspoon table salt
- 3 cups white bread flour
- Zest of 1 orange
- 1¼ teaspoons bread machine yeast
- 16 slices (2 pounds)
- 1¼ cups lukewarm milk
- ¼ cup orange juice
- ¼ cup sugar
- 1½ tablespoons unsalted butter, melted
- 1¼ teaspoons table salt
- 4 cups white bread flour
- Zest of 1 orange
- 1¾ teaspoons bread machine yeast

Directions:

1. Choose the size of loaf you would like to make and measure your ingredients.

2. Add the ingredients to the bread pan in the order listed above.

3. Place the pan in the bread machine and close the lid.

4. Turn on the bread maker. Select the White/Basic setting, then the loaf size, and finally the crust color. Start the cycle.

5. When the cycle is finished and the bread is baked, carefully remove the pan from the machine. Use a potholder as the handle will be very hot. Let rest for a few minutes.

6. Remove the bread from the pan and allow to cool on a wire rack for at least 10 minutes before slicing.

Dried Cranberry Tea Bread

Ingredients:

- 8 slices (1 pound)
- 11/2 cups dried cranberries
- Boiling water
- 2 large eggs
- 2 teaspoons almond extract
- 1 teaspoon vanilla extract
- 1/4 cup canola or vegetable oil
- 3/4 cup frozen unsweetened apple juice concentrate, thawed
- 1 cup sugar
- 11/4 cups unbleached all-purpose flour
- 1 cup whole wheat pastry flour
- 1 tablespoon baking powder
- 1/2 teaspoon baking soda
- 1 teaspoon ground cinnamon
- 1/2 teaspoon fresh-ground nutmeg
- 1/2 teaspoon salt
- 12 slices (1 ½ pounds)
- 2 1/4 cups dried cranberries
- Boiling water
- 3 large eggs
- 3 teaspoons almond extract
- 1 1/2 teaspoons vanilla extract
- 3/8 cup canola or vegetable oil
- 1 1/8 cups frozen unsweetened apple juice concentrate, thawed
- 1 1/2 cups sugar
- 1 7/8 cups unbleached all-purpose flour

* 1 1/2 cups whole wheat pastry flour
* 1 1/2 tablespoons baking powder
* 3/4 teaspoon baking soda
* 1 1/2 teaspoons ground cinnamon
* 3/4 teaspoon fresh-ground nutmeg
* 3/4 teaspoon salt
* 16 slices (2 pounds)
* 3 cups dried cranberries
* Boiling water
* 4 large eggs
* 4 teaspoons almond extract
* 2 teaspoons vanilla extract
* 1/2 cup canola or vegetable oil
* 1 1/2 cups frozen unsweetened apple juice concentrate, thawed
* 2 cups sugar
* 2 1/2 cups unbleached all-purpose flour
* 2 cups whole wheat pastry flour
* 2 tablespoons baking powder
* 1 teaspoon baking soda
* 2 teaspoons ground cinnamon
* 1 teaspoon fresh-ground nutmeg
* 1 teaspoon salt

Directions:

1. Choose the size of loaf you would like to make and measure your ingredients.

2. Cover the cranberries with boiling water in a small bowl, and let stand for 20 minutes to soften. Drain and pat dry with paper towels. Set aside.

3. Add the ingredients to the bread pan in the order listed above. Adding the cranberries with the dry ingredients.

4. Place the pan in the bread machine and close the lid.

5. Turn on the bread maker. Select the Quick Bread/Cake setting, then the loaf size, and finally the crust color. Start the cycle.

6. When the cycle is finished and the bread is baked, carefully remove the pan from the machine. Use a potholder as the handle will be very hot. Let rest for a few minutes.

7. Remove the bread from the pan and allow to cool on a wire rack for at least 10 minutes before slicing.

Raisin Candied Fruit Bread

Ingredients:

* 8 slices (1 pound)
* 1/2 egg, beaten
* 3/4 cup + 1/2 tablespoon lukewarm water
* 1/3 teaspoon ground cardamom
* 5/8 teaspoon table salt
* 1 tablespoon sugar
* 1/6 cup butter, melted
* 2 cups bread flour
* 5/8 teaspoon bread machine yeast
* 1/4 cup raisins
* 1/4 cup mixed candied fruit
* 12 slices (1 ½ pounds)
* 1 egg, beaten
* 1⅛ cup lukewarm water
* ½ teaspoon ground cardamom
* 1 teaspoon table salt
* 1½ tablespoons sugar
* ¼ cup butter, melted
* 3 cups bread flour
* 1 teaspoon bread machine yeast
* ⅓ cup raisins
* ⅓ cup mixed candied fruit
* 16 slices (2 pounds)
* 1 egg, beaten
* 1½ cups + 1 tablespoon lukewarm water
* ⅔ teaspoon ground cardamom
* 1¼ teaspoons table salt
* 2 tablespoons sugar
* ⅓ cup butter, melted
* 4 cups bread flour
* 1¼ teaspoons bread machine yeast
* ½ cup raisins
* ½ cup mixed candied fruit

Directions:

1. Choose the size of loaf you would like to make and measure your ingredients.

2. Add all of the ingredients except for the candied fruits and raisins to the bread pan in the order listed above.

3. Place the pan in the bread machine and close the lid.

4.   Turn on the bread maker. Select the White/Basic or Fruit/Nut (if your machine has this setting) setting, then the loaf size, and finally the crust color. Start the cycle.

5.   When the machine signals to add ingredients, add the candied fruits and raisins. (Some machines have a fruit/nut hopper where you can add the fruits and raisins when you start the machine. The machine will automatically add them to the dough during the baking process.)

6.   When the cycle is finished and the bread is baked, carefully remove the pan from the machine. Use a potholder as the handle will be very hot. Let rest for a few minutes.

7.   Remove the bread from the pan and allow to cool on a wire rack for at least 10 minutes before slicing.

Raisin Bread

Servings: 12
Cooking Time: 3 Hours

Ingredients:
- 1 cup warm water
- 3 tablespoons vegetable oil
- 3 cups flour
- 1 teaspoon cinnamon
- 1/8 teaspoon nutmeg
- 1/3 cup sugar
- 1 1/2 teaspoons salt
- 1 packet instant dry yeast
- 3/4 cup raisins

Directions:
1.   Add the water and oil to the bread maker.
2.   Add flour and sprinkle with cinnamon and nutmeg.
3.   On top of the flour, add sugar to one corner of the bread maker, salt in the other corner and yeast in another corner, so the yeast is not touching sugar and salt.
4.   Set to Basic bread cycle, medium crust color, and press Start.
5.   Add the raisins when the dough cycle is finished.
6.   When the baking cycle is finished, transfer to a cooling rack for 15 minutes before slicing.

Nutrition:
- al Info Calories: 193, Sodium: 1068 mg, Dietary Fiber: 1.3 g, Fat: 3.8 g, Carbs: 36.8 g, Protein: 3.5 g.

Cherry–wheat Berry Bread

Ingredients:
- 8 slices (1 pound)
- 1/4 cup wheat berries
- 1/2 cup water
- 5/8 cup water
- 1/2 large egg white
- 1 1/2 tablespoons canola oil
- 1/6 cup honey
- 2 cups bread flour
- 1/2 tablespoon gluten
- 1 teaspoon salt
- 1/2 tablespoon SAF yeast or 1/2 tablespoon plus 1/4 teaspoon bread machine yeast
- 1/3 cup tart dried cherries tossed with 1/2 tablespoon flour
- 12 slices (1 ½ pounds)
- 1/3 cup wheat berries
- 1 cup water
- 1 cup water
- 1 large egg white
- 2 tablespoons canola oil
- 1/4 cup honey
- 3 cups bread flour
- 2 teaspoons gluten
- 11/2 teaspoons salt
- 21/2 teaspoons SAF yeast or 1 tablespoon bread machine yeast
- 1/2 cup tart dried cherries tossed with 1 tablespoon flour
- 16 slices (2 pounds)
- 1/2 cup wheat berries
- 1 cup water
- 11/4 cups water
- 1 large egg white
- 3 tablespoons canola oil
- 1/3 cup honey
- 4 cups bread flour
- 1 tablespoon gluten
- 2 teaspoons salt
- 1 tablespoon SAF yeast or 1 tablespoon plus 1/2 teaspoon bread machine yeast

- 2/3 cup tart dried cherries tossed with 1 tablespoon flour

Directions:

1. Choose the size of loaf you would like to make and measure your ingredients.

2. Combine the wheat berries and the 1 cup of water in a saucepan. Bring to a boil. Reduce the heat, partially cover, and simmer for about 45 minutes, until chewy and tender. Drain off the excess water.

3. Add the ingredients to the bread pan in the order listed above (except the wheat berries and the cherries).

4. Place the pan in the bread machine and close the lid.

5. Turn on the bread maker. Select the Basic setting, then the loaf size, and finally the crust color. Start the cycle. (This recipe is not suitable for use with the Delay Timer.)

6. When the machine beeps, or at the pause between Knead 1 and 2, add the wheat berries and the cherries.

7. When the cycle is finished and the bread is baked, carefully remove the pan from the machine. Use a potholder as the handle will be very hot. Let rest for a few minutes.

8. Remove the bread from the pan and allow to cool on a wire rack for at least 10 minutes before slicing.

Strawberry Oat Bread

Ingredients:

- 8 slices (1 pound)
- 3/4 cup lukewarm milk
- 1/8 cup unsalted butter, melted
- 1/8 cup sugar
- 1 teaspoon table salt
- 3/4 cup quick oats
- 1 1/2 cups white bread flour
- 1 teaspoon bread machine yeast
- 1/2 cup strawberries, sliced
- 12 slices (1 ½ pounds)
- 1⅛ cups lukewarm milk
- 3 tablespoons unsalted butter, melted
- 3 tablespoons sugar
- 1½ teaspoons table salt
- 1 cup quick oats
- 2¼ cups white bread flour

- 1½ teaspoons bread machine yeast
- ¾ cup strawberries, sliced
- 16 slices (2 pounds)
- 1½ cups lukewarm milk
- ¼ cup unsalted butter, melted
- ¼ cup sugar
- 2 teaspoons table salt
- 1½ cups quick oats
- 3 cups white bread flour
- 2 teaspoons bread machine yeast
- 1 cup strawberries, sliced

Directions:

1. Choose the size of loaf you would like to make and measure your ingredients.

2. Add all of the ingredients except for the strawberries to the bread pan in the order listed above.

3. Place the pan in the bread machine and close the lid.

4. Turn on the bread maker. Select the White/Basic or Fruit/Nut (if your machine has this setting) setting, then the loaf size, and finally the crust color. Start the cycle.

5. When the machine signals to add ingredients, add the strawberries. (Some machines have a fruit/nut hopper where you can add the strawberries when you start the machine. The machine will automatically add them to the dough during the baking process.)

6. When the cycle is finished and the bread is baked, carefully remove the pan from the machine. Use a potholder as the handle will be very hot. Let rest for a few minutes.

7. Remove the bread from the pan and allow to cool on a wire rack for at least 10 minutes before slicing.

Fruity French Bread

Ingredients:

- 8 slices (1 pound)
- ¾ cup canned pears, mashed
- ¼ cup water
- 1 tablespoon honey
- 1 egg, slightly beaten
- 3 cups bread flour
- 1/8 teaspoon pepper
- 1 teaspoon dry yeast
- 12 slices (1 ½ pounds)

- 1 1/8 cups canned pears, mashed
- 3/8 cup water
- 1 1/2 tablespoons honey
- 1 1/2 eggs, slightly beaten
- 4 1/2 cups bread flour
- 3/16 teaspoon pepper
- 1 1/2 teaspoons dry yeast
- 16 slices (2 pounds)
- 1 1/2 cups canned pears, mashed
- 1/2 cup water
- 2 tablespoons honey
- 2 eggs, slightly beaten
- 6 cups bread flour
- 1/4 teaspoon pepper
- 2 teaspoons dry yeast

Directions:

1. Choose the size of loaf you would like to make and measure your ingredients.

2. Add the ingredients to the bread pan in the order listed above.

3. Place the pan in the bread machine and close the lid.

4. Turn on the bread maker. Select the White/Basic setting, then the loaf size, and finally the crust color. Start the cycle.

5. When the cycle is finished and the bread is baked, carefully remove the pan from the machine. Use a potholder as the handle will be very hot. Let rest for a few minutes.

6. Remove the bread from the pan and allow to cool on a wire rack for at least 10 minutes before slicing.

Cranberry Walnut Wheat Bread

Ingredients:
- 8 slices (1 pound)
- 1 cup warm water
- 1 tablespoon molasses
- 2 tablespoons butter
- 1 teaspoon salt
- 2 cups 100% whole wheat flour
- 1 cup unbleached flour
- 2 tablespoons dry milk
- 1 cup cranberries
- 1 cup walnuts, chopped
- 2 teaspoons active dry yeast
- 12 slices (1 ½ pounds)
- 1 1/2 cups warm water
- 1 1/2 tablespoons molasses
- 3 tablespoons butter
- 1 1/2 teaspoons salt
- 3 cups 100% whole wheat flour
- 1 1/2 cups unbleached flour
- 3 tablespoons dry milk
- 1 1/2 cup cranberries
- 1 1/2 cups walnuts, chopped
- 3 teaspoons active dry yeast
- 16 slices (2 pounds)
- 2 cups warm water
- 2 tablespoons molasses
- 4 tablespoons butter
- 2 teaspoons salt
- 4 cups 100% whole wheat flour
- 2 cups unbleached flour
- 4 tablespoons dry milk
- 2 cups cranberries
- 2 cups walnuts, chopped
- 4 teaspoons active dry yeast

Directions:

1. Choose the size of loaf you would like to make and measure your ingredients.

2. Add the ingredients to the bread pan in the order listed above (except the yeast, walnuts and cranberries).

3. Place the pan in the bread machine and close the lid.

4. Turn on the bread maker. Select the Wheat Bread setting, then the loaf size, and finally the crust color. Start the cycle.

5. Add cranberries and walnuts after first kneading cycle is finished.

6. When the cycle is finished and the bread is baked, carefully remove the pan from the machine. Use a potholder as the handle will be very hot. Let rest for a few minutes.

7. Remove the bread from the pan and allow to cool on a wire rack for at least 10 minutes before slicing.

NUT AND SEED BREAD RECIPES

Zuni Indian Bread

Ingredients:

- 8 slices (1 pound)
- 2/3 cup buttermilk
- 1/2 large egg
- 1 1/2 tablespoons sunflower seed oil
- 1 1/4 cups bread flour
- 1/2 cup whole wheat flour
- 1/4 cup cornmeal
- 1/3 cup raw sunflower seeds
- 1 1/2 tablespoons dark brown sugar
- 1 tablespoon gluten
- 1 teaspoon salt
- 1 1/4 teaspoons SAF yeast or 1/2 tablespoon bread machine yeast
- 12 slices (1 ½ pounds)
- 1 cup buttermilk
- 1 large egg
- 2 tablespoons sunflower seed oil
- 2 cups bread flour
- 2/3 cup whole wheat flour
- 1/3 cup cornmeal
- 1/2 cup raw sunflower seeds
- 2 tablespoons dark brown sugar
- 11/2 tablespoons gluten
- 11/2 teaspoons salt
- 21/4 teaspoons SAF yeast or 23/4 teaspoons bread machine yeast
- 16 slices (2 pounds)
- 11/3 cups buttermilk
- 1 large egg
- 3 tablespoons sunflower seed oil
- 21/2 cups bread flour
- 1 cup whole wheat flour
- 1/2 cup cornmeal
- 2/3 cup raw sunflower seeds
- 3 tablespoons dark brown sugar
- 2 tablespoons gluten
- 2 teaspoons salt

- 21/2 teaspoons SAF yeast or 1 tablespoon bread machine yeast

Directions:

1. Choose the size of loaf you would like to make and measure your ingredients.
2. Add the ingredients to the bread pan in the order listed above.
3. Place the pan in the bread machine and close the lid.
4. Turn on the bread maker. Select the Whole Wheat setting, then the loaf size, and finally the crust color. Start the cycle.
5. When the cycle is finished and the bread is baked, carefully remove the pan from the machine. Use a potholder as the handle will be very hot. Let rest for a few minutes.
6. Remove the bread from the pan and allow to cool on a wire rack for at least 10 minutes before slicing.

Pistachio Horseradish Apple Bread

Ingredients:

- 8 slices (1 pound)
- 1 1/2 cups wheat flour
- 1 whole egg, beaten
- 1 1/2 tablespoons horseradish, grated
- 1/4 cup apple puree
- 1/2 tablespoon sugar
- 2 tablespoons olive oil
- 1/4 cup pistachios, peeled and chopped
- 1/2 teaspoon instant yeast
- 1/2 cup + 1/2 tablespoon water
- 1/2 teaspoon salt
- 12 slices (1 ½ pounds)
- 2 1/4 cups wheat flour
- 1 1/2 whole eggs, beaten
- 2 1/4 tablespoons horseradish, grated
- 3/8 cup apple puree
- 3/4 tablespoon sugar
- 3 tablespoons olive oil
- 3/8 cup pistachios, peeled and chopped
- 3/4 teaspoon instant yeast
- 3/4 cup + 3/4 tablespoon water

- 3/4 teaspoon salt
- 16 slices (2 pounds)
- 3 cups wheat flour
- 2 whole eggs, beaten
- 3 tablespoons horseradish, grated
- ½ cup apple puree
- 1 tablespoon sugar
- 4 tablespoons olive oil
- ½ cup pistachios, peeled and chopped
- 1 teaspoon instant yeast
- 1 cup + 1 tablespoon water
- 1 teaspoon salt

Directions:

1. Choose the size of loaf you would like to make and measure your ingredients.
2. Add the ingredients to the bread pan in the order listed above.
3. Place the pan in the bread machine and close the lid.
4. Turn on the bread maker. Select the White/Basic setting, then the loaf size, and finally the crust color. Start the cycle.
5. When the cycle is finished and the bread is baked, carefully remove the pan from the machine. Use a potholder as the handle will be very hot. Let rest for a few minutes.
6. Remove the bread from the pan and allow to cool on a wire rack for at least 10 minutes before slicing.

Delicious Flax Honey Bread

Ingredients:

- 8 slices (1 pound)
- ¾ cup milk, at room temperature
- 1 tablespoon melted butter
- 1 tablespoon honey
- ¾ teaspoon salt
- 2 tablespoons flaxseeds
- 2 cups white bread flour
- ¾ teaspoon bread machine yeast
- 12 slices (1 ½ pounds)
- 1 1/8cups milk, at room temperature
- 1 1/2 tablespoons melted butter
- 1 1/2 tablespoons honey
- 1 1/8 teaspoons salt

- 3 tablespoons flaxseeds
- 3 cups white bread flour
- 1 1/8 teaspoons bread machine yeast
- 16 slices (2 pounds)
- 1 1/2 cups milk, at room temperature
- 2 tablespoons melted butter
- 2 tablespoons honey
- 1 1/2 teaspoons salt
- 4 tablespoons flaxseeds
- 4 cups white bread flour
- 1 1/2 teaspoons bread machine yeast

Directions:

1. Choose the size of loaf you would like to make and measure your ingredients.
2. Add the ingredients to the bread pan in the order listed above.
3. Place the pan in the bread machine and close the lid.
4. Turn on the bread maker. Select the White/Basic setting, then the loaf size, and finally the crust color. Start the cycle.
5. When the cycle is finished and the bread is baked, carefully remove the pan from the machine. Use a potholder as the handle will be very hot. Let rest for a few minutes.
6. Remove the bread from the pan and allow to cool on a wire rack for at least 10 minutes before slicing.

Bourbon Nut Bread

Ingredients:

- 8 slices (1 pound)
- 1/4 cup nut oil or vegetable oil
- 2 large eggs
- 11/2 teaspoons almond extract
- 11/2 cups sour cream
- 1/2 cup bourbon
- 1 cup light brown sugar
- 21/4 cups unbleached all-purpose flour
- 21/2 teaspoons baking powder
- 1/2 teaspoon baking soda
- 1/2 teaspoon salt
- 11/2 teaspoons ground nutmeg
- 1 teaspoon instant espresso powder

- 11/4 cups (6 ounces) coarsely chopped pecans or walnuts
- 12 slices (1 ½ pounds)
- 3/8 cup nut oil or vegetable oil
- 3 large eggs
- 2 1/4 teaspoons almond extract
- 2 1/4 cups sour cream
- 3/4 cup bourbon
- 1 1/2 cups light brown sugar
- 3 3/8 cups unbleached all-purpose flour
- 3 3/4 teaspoons baking powder
- 3/4 teaspoon baking soda
- 3/4 teaspoon salt
- 2 1/4 teaspoons ground nutmeg
- 1 1/2 teaspoons instant espresso powder
- 1 7/8 cups (9 ounces) coarsely chopped pecans or walnuts
- 16 slices (2 pounds)
- 1/2 cup nut oil or vegetable oil
- 4 large eggs
- 3 teaspoons almond extract
- 3 cups sour cream
- 1 cup bourbon
- 2 cups light brown sugar
- 4 1/2 cups unbleached all-purpose flour
- 5 teaspoons baking powder
- 1 teaspoon baking soda
- 1 teaspoon salt
- 3 teaspoons ground nutmeg
- 2 teaspoons instant espresso powder
- 2 1/2 cups (3 ounces) coarsely chopped pecans or walnuts

Directions:

1. Choose the size of loaf you would like to make and measure your ingredients.

2. Add the ingredients to the bread pan in the order listed above.

3. Place the pan in the bread machine and close the lid.

4. Turn on the bread maker. Select the Quick Bread/Cake setting, then the loaf size, and finally the crust color. Start the cycle.

5. When the cycle is finished and the bread is baked, carefully remove the pan from the machine. Use a potholder as the handle will be very hot. Let rest for a few minutes.

6. Remove the bread from the pan and allow to cool on a wire rack for at least 10 minutes before slicing.

Toasted Walnut Bread

Ingredients:

- 8 slices (1 pound)
- 1/2 cup (2 to 2 1/2 ounces) walnut pieces
- 2/3 cup water
- 1 large egg white, lightly beaten
- 1 tablespoon butter, cut into pieces
- 2 cups bread flour
- 1 1/2 tablespoons sugar
- 1 1/2 tablespoons nonfat dry milk
- 2/3 tablespoon gluten
- 1/2 teaspoon salt
- 1 teaspoon SAF yeast or 1 1/4 teaspoons bread machine yeast
- 12 slices (1 ½ pounds)
- 3/4 cup (3 to 4 ounces) walnut pieces
- 1 cup water
- 2 large egg whites, lightly beaten
- 11/2 tablespoons butter, cut into pieces
- 3 cups bread flour
- 2 tablespoons sugar
- 2 tablespoons nonfat dry milk
- 1 tablespoon gluten
- 3/4 teaspoon salt
- 11/2 teaspoons SAF yeast or 2 teaspoons bread machine yeast
- 16 slices (2 pounds)
- 1 cup (4 to 5 ounces) walnut pieces
- 11/3 cups water
- 2 large egg whites, lightly beaten
- 2 tablespoons butter, cut into pieces
- 4 cups bread flour
- 3 tablespoons sugar
- 3 tablespoons nonfat dry milk
- 1 tablespoon plus 1 teaspoon gluten
- 1 teaspoon salt
- 2 teaspoons SAF yeast or 21/2 teaspoons bread machine yeast

Directions:

1. Choose the size of loaf you would like to make and measure your ingredients.
2. Preheat the oven to 350°F.
3. Spread the walnuts on a baking sheet and place in the center of the oven for 4 minutes to toast lightly. Set aside to cool.
4. Add the ingredients to the bread pan in the order listed above (except the walnuts).
5. Place the pan in the bread machine and close the lid.
6. Turn on the bread maker. Select the Basic/Fruit and Nut cycle setting, then the loaf size, and finally the crust color. Start the cycle. (This recipe is not suitable for use with the Delay Timer.)
7. When the cycle is finished and the bread is baked, carefully remove the pan from the machine. Use a potholder as the handle will be very hot. Let rest for a few minutes.
8. When the machine beeps, or between Knead 1 and Knead 2, add the walnuts.
9. Remove the bread from the pan and allow to cool on a wire rack for at least 10 minutes before slicing.

Mix Seed Raisin Bread

Ingredients:
- 8 slices (1 pound)
- 3/4 cup lukewarm milk
- 1 tablespoon unsalted butter, melted
- 1 tablespoon honey
- 1/2 teaspoon table salt
- 11/4 cups white bread flour
- 1/8 cup flaxseed
- 1/8 cup sesame seeds
- 3/4 cup whole-wheat flour
- 11/8 teaspoons bread machine yeast
- 1/4 cup raisins
- 12 slices (1 ½ pounds)
- 1⅛ cups lukewarm milk
- 1½ tablespoons unsalted butter, melted
- 1½ tablespoons honey
- ¾ teaspoon table salt
- 1¾ cups white bread flour
- 3 tablespoons flaxseed

- 3 tablespoons sesame seeds
- 1¼ cups whole-wheat flour
- 1¾ teaspoons bread machine yeast
- ⅓ cup raisins
- 16 slices (2 pounds)
- 1½ cups lukewarm milk
- 2 tablespoons unsalted butter, melted
- 2 tablespoons honey
- 1 teaspoon table salt
- 2½ cups white bread flour
- ¼ cup flaxseed
- ¼ cup sesame seeds
- 1½ cups whole-wheat flour
- 2¼ teaspoons bread machine yeast
- ½ cup raisins

Directions:

1. Choose the size of loaf you would like to make and measure your ingredients.
2. Add the ingredients to the bread pan in the order listed above.
3. Place the pan in the bread machine and close the lid.
4. Turn on the bread maker. Select the White/Basic setting, then the loaf size, and finally the crust color. Start the cycle.
5. When the cycle is finished and the bread is baked, carefully remove the pan from the machine. Use a potholder as the handle will be very hot. Let rest for a few minutes.
6. Remove the bread from the pan and allow to cool on a wire rack for at least 10 minutes before slicing.

Polish Poppy Seed Bread

Ingredients:
- 8 slices (1 pound)
- 12 slices (1 ½ pounds)
- 16 slices (2 pounds)
- 11/2-POUND LOAF
- 1 cup (for 14-ounce mix) or 1 cup plus 2 tablespoons (for 1-pound mix) fat-free milk
- 1 egg yolk
- 1 teaspoon almond extract
- One 14-ounce or 1-pound box white bread machine mix

- 1/2 cup chopped slivered blanched almonds
- 1/3 cup currants
- 1 tablespoon poppy seeds
- 1 tablespoon light brown sugar
- 2 teaspoons gluten
- 1 yeast packet (included in mix)

Directions:

1. Place all the ingredients in the pan according to the order in the manufacturer's instructions. Set the crust for medium and program for the Basic cycle; press Start.

2. When the baking cycle ends, immediately remove the bread from the pan and place it on a rack. Let cool to room temperature before slicing.

Brazilian Nuts & Nutmeg Loaf

Ingredients:

- 8 slices (1 pound)
- 1¼ cups water
- 2 tablespoons olive oil
- 1 tablespoon honey
- 3 cups wholemeal bread flour
- 1½ teaspoons salt
- 1 teaspoon fresh grated nutmeg
- 1½ teaspoons active dried yeast
- ¾ cup brazil nuts, coarsely chopped
- 12 slices (1 ½ pounds)
- 1 7/8 cups water
- 3 tablespoons olive oil
- 1 1/2 tablespoons honey
- 4 1/2 cups wholemeal bread flour
- 2 1/4 teaspoons salt
- 1 1/2 teaspoons fresh grated nutmeg
- 2 1/4 teaspoons active dried yeast
- 1 1/8 cups brazil nuts, coarsely chopped
- 16 slices (2 pounds)
- 2 1/2 cups water
- 4 tablespoons olive oil
- 2 tablespoons honey
- 6 cups wholemeal bread flour
- 3 teaspoons salt
- 2 teaspoons fresh grated nutmeg
- 3 teaspoons active dried yeast
- 1 1/2 cups brazil nuts, coarsely chopped

Directions:

1. Choose the size of loaf you would like to make and measure your ingredients.

2. Add the ingredients to the bread pan in the order listed above (except nuts).

3. Place the pan in the bread machine and close the lid.

4. Turn on the bread maker. Select the White/Basic setting, then the loaf size, and finally the crust color. Start the cycle.

5. Add nuts once the machine beeps.

6. When the cycle is finished and the bread is baked, carefully remove the pan from the machine. Use a potholder as the handle will be very hot. Let rest for a few minutes.

7. Remove the bread from the pan and allow to cool on a wire rack for at least 10 minutes before slicing.

California Nut Bread

Ingredients:

- 8 slices (1 pound)
- 1/2 cup (2 to 2 1/2 ounces) nutmeat pieces
- 5/6 cup buttermilk
- 1/4 cup nut oil
- 2 cups bread flour
- 3/4 tablespoon dark brown sugar
- 2/3 tablespoon gluten
- 1 teaspoon salt
- 1/2 tablespoon SAF yeast or 1/2 tablespoon plus 1/4 teaspoon bread machine yeast
- 12 slices (1 ½ pounds)
- 3/4 cup (3 to 4 ounces) nutmeat pieces
- 11/4 cups buttermilk
- 1/3 cup nut oil
- 3 cups bread flour
- 1 tablespoon dark brown sugar
- 1 tablespoon gluten
- 11/2 teaspoons salt
- 21/2 teaspoons SAF yeast or 1 tablespoon bread machine yeast
- 16 slices (2 pounds)
- 1 cup (4 to 5 ounces) nutmeat pieces
- 12/3 cups buttermilk
- 1/2 cup nut oil

- 4 cups bread flour
- 11/2 tablespoons dark brown sugar
- 1 tablespoon plus 1 teaspoon gluten
- 2 teaspoons salt
- 1 tablespoon SAF yeast or 1 tablespoon plus 1/2 teaspoon bread machine yeast

Directions:

1. Choose the size of loaf you would like to make and measure your ingredients.
2. Preheat the oven to 350°F.
3. Spread the nuts evenly on a baking sheet. Bake until lightly toasted, about 5 to 7 minutes. Remove from the oven and let cool.
4. Add the ingredients to the bread pan in the order listed above (except the nuts).
5. Place the pan in the bread machine and close the lid.
6. Turn on the bread maker. Select the Basic setting, then the loaf size, and finally the crust color. Start the cycle.
7. When the machine beeps or between Knead 1 and Knead 2, add the nuts.
8. When the cycle is finished and the bread is baked, carefully remove the pan from the machine. Use a potholder as the handle will be very hot. Let rest for a few minutes.
9. Remove the bread from the pan and allow to cool on a wire rack for at least 10 minutes before slicing.

Pecan Raisin Bread

Ingredients:

- 8 slices (1 pound)
- 5/8 cup (about 3 ounces) pecan halves
- 3/4 cup water
- 3/4 tablespoon butter, cut into pieces
- 1 2/3 cups bread flour
- 1/3 cup dark rye flour
- 3/4 tablespoon dark brown sugar
- 1/2 tablespoon plus 1 teaspoons gluten
- 1 teaspoon salt
- 1 1/4 teaspoons SAF yeast or 1/2 tablespoon bread machine yeast
- 1/4 cup dark raisins
- 12 slices (1 ½ pounds)
- 1 cup (about 4 ounces) pecan halves

- 1 cup plus 2 tablespoons water
- 1 tablespoon butter, cut into pieces
- 21/2 cups bread flour
- 1/2 cup dark rye flour
- 1 tablespoon dark brown sugar
- 1 tablespoon plus 1 teaspoon gluten
- 11/2 teaspoons salt
- 21/4 teaspoons SAF yeast or 23/4 teaspoons bread machine yeast
- 1/3 cup dark raisins
- 16 slices (2 pounds)
- 11/4 cups (about 6 ounces) pecan halves
- 11/2 cups water
- 11/2 tablespoons butter, cut into pieces
- 31/3 cups bread flour
- 2/3 cup dark rye flour
- 11/2 tablespoons dark brown sugar
- 1 tablespoon plus 2 teaspoons gluten
- 2 teaspoons salt
- 21/2 teaspoons SAF yeast or 1 tablespoon bread machine yeast
- 1/2 cup dark raisins

Directions:

1. Choose the size of loaf you would like to make and measure your ingredients.
2. Preheat the oven to 350°F.
3. Spread the nuts on a baking sheet. Bake for 10 minutes, stirring twice. Cool on the baking sheet. Chop the nuts into large pieces and set aside.
4. Add the ingredients to the bread pan in the order listed above (except the nuts and the raisins).
5. Place the pan in the bread machine and close the lid.
6. Turn on the bread maker. Select the Basic/Fruit and Nut setting, then the loaf size, and finally the crust color. Start the cycle. (This recipe is not suitable for use with the Delay Timer.)
7. When the machine beeps, or between Knead 1 and Knead 2, add the nuts and the raisins.
8. When the cycle is finished and the bread is baked, carefully remove the pan from the machine. Use a potholder as the handle will be very hot. Let rest for a few minutes.
9. Remove the bread from the pan and allow to cool on a wire rack for at least 10 minutes before slicing.

Corn, Poppy Seeds & Sour Cream Bread

Ingredients:

* 8 slices (1 pound)
* 1 3/4 cups wheat flour
* 7/8 cup cornflour
* 2 1/2 ounces sour cream
* 1 tablespoon corn oil
* 1 teaspoon active dried yeast
* 1 teaspoon salt
* 8 1/8 ounces water
* poppy seeds for sprinkling
* 12 slices (1 ½ pounds)
* 2 5/8 cups wheat flour
* 1 5/16 cups cornflour
* 3 3/4 ounces sour cream
* 1 1/2tablespoons corn oil
* 1 1/2 teaspoons active dried yeast
* 1 1/2teaspoons salt
* 12 3/16 ounces water
* poppy seeds for sprinkling
* 16 slices (2 pounds)
* 3½ cups wheat flour
* 1¾ cups cornflour
* 5 ounces sour cream
* 2 tablespoons corn oil
* 2 teaspoons active dried yeast
* 2 teaspoons salt
* 16 ¼ ounces water
* poppy seeds for sprinkling

Directions:

1. Choose the size of loaf you would like to make and measure your ingredients.
2. Add the ingredients to the bread pan in the order listed above (except the poppy seeds).
3. Place the pan in the bread machine and close the lid.
4. Turn on the bread maker. Select the White/Basic setting, then the loaf size, and finally the crust color. Start the cycle.
5. When the cycle is finished and the bread is baked, carefully remove the pan from the machine. Use a potholder as the handle will be very hot. Let rest for a few minutes.
6. Moisten the surface with water and sprinkle with poppy seeds.
7. Remove the bread from the pan and allow to cool on a wire rack for at least 10 minutes before slicing.

Orange Walnut Candied Loaf

Ingredients:

* 8 slices (1 pound)
* 1/3 cup warm whey
* 2/3 tablespoon bread machine yeast
* 2 2/3 tablespoons sugar
* 1 1/3 orange juice
* 2 2/3 cups flour
* 2/3 teaspoon salt
* 1 tablespoons salt
* 2 teaspoons orange zest
* 4/9 teaspoon vanilla
* 2 tablespoons (walnut + almonds)
* 1/3 cup candied fruit
* 12 slices (1 ½ pounds)
* ½ cup warm whey
* 1 tablespoon bread machine yeast
* 4 tablespoons sugar
* 2 orange juice
* 4 cups flour
* 1 teaspoon salt
* 1½ tablespoons salt
* 3 teaspoons orange zest
* ⅓ teaspoon vanilla
* 3 tablespoons (walnut + almonds)
* ½ cup candied fruit
* 16 slices (2 pounds)
* 2/3 cup warm whey
* 1 1/3 tablespoons bread machine yeast
* 5 1/3 tablespoons sugar
* 2 2/3 orange juice
* 5 1/3 cups flour
* 1 1/3 teaspoons salt
* 2 tablespoons salt
* 4 teaspoons orange zest
* 8/9 teaspoon vanilla
* 4 tablespoons (walnut + almonds)
* 2/3 cup candied fruit

Directions:

1. Choose the size of loaf you would like to make and measure your ingredients.

2. Add the ingredients to the bread pan in the order listed above.

3. Place the pan in the bread machine and close the lid.

4. Turn on the bread maker. Select the White/Basic/Sweet Bread setting, then the loaf size, and finally the crust color. Start the cycle.

5. When the cycle is finished and the bread is baked, carefully remove the pan from the machine. Use a potholder as the handle will be very hot. Let rest for a few minutes.

6. Remove the bread from the pan and allow to cool on a wire rack for at least 10 minutes before slicing.

Caramel Apple Pecan Loaf

Ingredients:

- 8 slices (1 pound)
- 1 cup water
- 2 tablespoons butter
- 3 cups bread flour
- ¼ cup packed brown sugar
- ¾ teaspoon ground cinnamon
- 1 teaspoon salt
- 2 teaspoons quick yeast
- ½ cup apple, chopped
- ⅓ cup coarsely chopped pecans, toasted
- 12 slices (1 ½ pounds)
- 1 1/2 cups water
- 3 tablespoons butter
- 4 1/2 cups bread flour
- 3/8 cup packed brown sugar
- 1 1/8 teaspoons ground cinnamon
- 1 1/2 teaspoons salt
- 3 teaspoons quick yeast
- 3/4 cup apple, chopped
- 1/2 cup coarsely chopped pecans, toasted
- 16 slices (2 pounds)
- 2 cups water
- 4 tablespoons butter
- 6 cups bread flour
- 1/2 cup packed brown sugar

- 1 1/2 teaspoons ground cinnamon
- 2 teaspoons salt
- 4 teaspoons quick yeast
- 1 cup apple, chopped
- 2/3 cup coarsely chopped pecans, toasted

Directions:

1. Choose the size of loaf you would like to make and measure your ingredients.

2. Add the ingredients to the bread pan in the order listed above (except apples and pecans).

3. Place the pan in the bread machine and close the lid.

4. Turn on the bread maker. Select the White/Basic setting, then the loaf size, and finally the crust color. Start the cycle.

5. Once the bread maker beeps, add pecans and apples.

6. When the cycle is finished and the bread is baked, carefully remove the pan from the machine. Use a potholder as the handle will be very hot. Let rest for a few minutes.

7. Remove the bread from the pan and allow to cool on a wire rack for at least 10 minutes before slicing.

Sunflower Oatmeal Bread

Ingredients:

- 8 slices (1 pound)
- 1/3 cup water
- 1/2 cup buttermilk
- 1/2 large egg
- 1 tablespoon butter, cut into pieces
- 1 1/2 tablespoons honey
- 3/4 tablespoon molasses
- 1 2/3 cups bread flour
- 1/3 cup rolled oats
- 1/3 cup whole wheat flour
- 1/3 cup raw sunflower seeds
- 2/3 tablespoon gluten
- 1 teaspoon salt
- 1 1/8 teaspoons SAF yeast or 1 3/8 teaspoons bread machine yeast
- 12 slices (1 ½ pounds)
- 1/2 cup water
- 5/8 cup buttermilk
- 1 large egg

- 11/2 tablespoons butter, cut into pieces
- 2 tablespoons honey
- 1 tablespoon molasses
- 21/2 cups bread flour
- 1/2 cup rolled oats
- 1/2 cup whole wheat flour
- 1/2 cup raw sunflower seeds
- 1 tablespoon gluten
- 11/2 teaspoons salt
- 2 teaspoons SAF yeast or 21/2 teaspoons bread machine yeast
- 16 slices (2 pounds)
- 2/3 cup water
- 7/8 cup buttermilk
- 1 large egg
- 2 tablespoons butter, cut into pieces
- 3 tablespoons honey
- 11/2 tablespoons molasses
- 31/3 cups bread flour
- 2/3 cup rolled oats
- 2/3 cup whole wheat flour
- 2/3 cup raw sunflower seeds
- 1 tablespoon plus 1 teaspoon gluten
- 2 teaspoons salt
- 21/4 teaspoons SAF yeast or 23/4 teaspoons bread machine yeast

Directions:

1. Choose the size of loaf you would like to make and measure your ingredients.

2. Add the ingredients to the bread pan in the order listed above.

3. Place the pan in the bread machine and close the lid.

4. Turn on the bread maker. Select the Basic setting, then the loaf size, and finally the crust color. Start the cycle.

5. When the cycle is finished and the bread is baked, carefully remove the pan from the machine. Use a potholder as the handle will be very hot. Let rest for a few minutes.

6. Remove the bread from the pan and allow to cool on a wire rack for at least 10 minutes before slicing.

Sunflower Seeds & Oatmeal Bread

Ingredients:

- 8 slices (1 pound)
- 1 cup water
- ¼ cup honey
- 2 tablespoons butter
- 3 cups bread flour
- ½ cup quick-cooking oats
- 2 tablespoons dry milk
- 1¼ teaspoons salt
- 2¼ teaspoons bread machine yeast
- ½ cup sunflower seeds
- 12 slices (1 ½ pounds)
- 1 1/2 cups water
- 3/8 cup honey
- 3 tablespoons butter
- 4 1/2 cups bread flour
- 3/4 cup quick-cooking oats
- 3 tablespoons dry milk
- 1 7/8 teaspoons salt
- 3 3/8 teaspoons bread machine yeast
- 3/4 cup sunflower seeds
- 16 slices (2 pounds)
- 2 cups water
- 1/2 cup honey
- 4 tablespoons butter
- 6 cups bread flour
- 1 cup quick-cooking oats
- 4 tablespoons dry milk
- 2 1/2 teaspoons salt
- 4 1/2 teaspoons bread machine yeast
- 1 cup sunflower seeds

Directions:

1. Choose the size of loaf you would like to make and measure your ingredients.

2. Add the ingredients to the bread pan in the order listed above (except seeds).

3. Place the pan in the bread machine and close the lid.

4. Turn on the bread maker. Select the White/Basic setting, then the loaf size, and finally the crust color. Start the cycle.

5. Once the machine beeps, add seeds.

6.   When the cycle is finished and the bread is baked, carefully remove the pan from the machine. Use a potholder as the handle will be very hot. Let rest for a few minutes.

7.   Remove the bread from the pan and allow to cool on a wire rack for at least 10 minutes before slicing.

Olive Oil–pine Nut Bread

Ingredients:
- 8 slices (1 pound)
- 1/3 cup water
- 1/3 cup dry white wine
- 1/6 cup olive oil
- 1 1/3 cups bread flour
- 1/2 cup whole wheat flour
- 1/6 cup rye flour
- 2/3 tablespoon gluten
- 1/2 tablespoon plus 1 teaspoon sugar
- 1 teaspoon salt
- 1 1/4 teaspoons SAF yeast or 1/2 tablespoon bread machine yeast
- 1/4 cup pine nuts, coarsely chopped
- 12 slices (1 ½ pounds)
- 1/2 cup water
- 1/2 cup dry white wine
- 1/4 cup olive oil
- 2 cups bread flour
- 3/4 cup whole wheat flour
- 1/4 cup rye flour
- 1 tablespoon gluten
- 1 tablespoon sugar
- 11/2 teaspoons salt
- 2 teaspoons SAF yeast or 21/2 teaspoons bread machine yeast
- 1/3 cup pine nuts, coarsely chopped
- 16 slices (2 pounds)
- 2/3 cup water
- 2/3 cup dry white wine
- 1/3 cup olive oil
- 22/3 cups bread flour
- 1 cup whole wheat flour
- 1/3 cup rye flour
- 1 tablespoon plus 1 teaspoon gluten

- 1 tablespoon plus 2 teaspoons sugar
- 2 teaspoons salt
- 21/2 teaspoons SAF yeast or 1 tablespoon bread machine yeast
- 1/2 cup pine nuts, coarsely chopped

Directions:
1.   Choose the size of loaf you would like to make and measure your ingredients.
2.   Add the ingredients to the bread pan in the order listed above (except the pine nuts).
3.   Place the pan in the bread machine and close the lid.
4.   Turn on the bread maker. Select the Basic or French Bread setting, then the loaf size, and finally the crust color. Start the cycle. (This recipe is not suitable for use with the Delay Timer.)
5.   Five minutes into Knead 2, sprinkle in the pine nuts.
6.   When the cycle is finished and the bread is baked, carefully remove the pan from the machine. Use a potholder as the handle will be very hot. Let rest for a few minutes.
7.   Remove the bread from the pan and allow to cool on a wire rack for at least 10 minutes before slicing.

Brown Sugar Date Nut Swirl Bread

Ingredients:
- 8 slices (1 pound)
- 1 cup milk
- 1 large egg
- 4 tablespoons butter
- 4 tablespoons sugar
- 1 teaspoon salt
- 4 cups flour
- 1 2/3 teaspoons yeast
- For the filling:
- 1/2 cup packed brown sugar
- 1 cup walnuts, chopped
- 1 cup medjool dates, pitted and chopped
- 2 teaspoons cinnamon
- 2 teaspoons clove spice
- 1 1/3 tablespoons butter
- Powdered sugar, sifted
- 12 slices (1 ½ pounds)
- 1 1/2 cups milk

- 1 1/2 large eggs
- 6 tablespoons butter
- 6 tablespoons sugar
- 1 1/2 teaspoons salt
- 6 cups flour
- 2 1/2 teaspoons yeast
- For the filling:
- 1/2 cup packed brown sugar
- 1 cup walnuts, chopped
- 1 cup medjool dates, pitted and chopped
- 2 teaspoons cinnamon
- 2 teaspoons clove spice
- 1 1/3 tablespoons butter
- Powdered sugar, sifted
- 16 slices (2 pounds)
- 2 cups milk
- 2 large eggs
- 8 tablespoons butter
- 8 tablespoons sugar
- 2 teaspoons salt
- 8 cups flour
- 3 1/3 teaspoons yeast
- For the filling:
- 1 cup packed brown sugar
- 2 cups walnuts, chopped
- 2 cups medjool dates, pitted and chopped
- 4 teaspoons cinnamon
- 4 teaspoons clove spice
- 2 2/3 tablespoons butter
- Powdered sugar, sifted

Directions:

1. Choose the size of loaf you would like to make and measure your ingredients.

2. Add the ingredients to the bread pan in the order listed above (except yeast).

3. Make a well in the center of the dry ingredients and add the yeast.

4. Place the pan in the bread machine and close the lid.

5. Turn on the bread maker. Select the Dough setting, then the loaf size, and finally the crust color. Start the cycle.

6. When the cycle is finished and the bread is baked, carefully remove the pan from the machine. Use a potholder as the handle will be very hot. Let rest for a few minutes.

7. Mix the brown sugar with walnuts, dates and spices; set aside.

8. Roll the dough into a rectangle, on a lightly floured surface.

9. Baste with a tablespoon of butter, add the filling.

10. Start from the short side and roll the dough to form a jelly roll shape.

11. Place the roll into a greased loaf pan and cover.

12. Let it rise in a warm place, until nearly doubled in size; about 30 minutes.

13. Bake at 350°F for approximately 30 minutes.

14. Cover with foil during the last 10 minutes of cooking.

15. Transfer to a cooling rack for 15 minutes; sprinkle with the powdered sugar and serve.

Fig And Walnut Bread

Ingredients:

- 8 slices (1 pound)
- 12 slices (1 ½ pounds)
- 16 slices (2 pounds)
- 11/2-POUND LOAF
- 1 cup water (for 14-ounce mix) or 1 cup plus 2 tablespoons water (for 1-pound mix)
- One 14-ounce or 1-pound box white bread machine mix
- 2 teaspoons gluten
- 1 yeast packet (included in mix)
- 3/4 cup chopped dried figs
- 1/4 cup chopped walnuts

Directions:

1. Place the ingredients, except the figs and walnuts, in the pan according to the order in the manufacturer's instructions. Set the crust for dark and program for the Basic or Fruit and Nut cycle; press Start. When the machine beeps, or between Knead 1 and Knead 2, add the figs and walnuts.

2. When the baking cycle ends, immediately remove the bread from the pan and place it on a rack. Let cool to room temperature before slicing.

Potato Bread With Caraway Seeds

Ingredients:

- 8 slices (1 pound)
- 5/6 cup warm water
- 1 1/2 tablespoons instant potato flakes
- 1 tablespoon butter or lard
- 1 3/4 cups bread flour
- 1/4 cup potato starch flour
- 1 tablespoon sugar
- 1/2 tablespoon gluten
- 1/2 tablespoon caraway seeds
- 1 teaspoon salt
- 1 teaspoon SAF yeast or 1 1/4 teaspoons bread machine yeast
- 12 slices (1 ½ pounds)
- 11/3 cups warm water
- 2 tablespoons instant potato flakes
- 11/2 tablespoons butter or lard
- 22/3 cups bread flour
- 1/3 cup potato starch flour
- 11/2 tablespoons sugar
- 2 teaspoons gluten
- 2 teaspoons caraway seeds
- 11/2 teaspoons salt
- 13/4 teaspoons SAF yeast or 21/4 teaspoons bread machine yeast
- 16 slices (2 pounds)
- 12/3 cups warm water
- 3 tablespoons instant potato flakes
- 2 tablespoons butter or lard
- 31/2 cups bread flour
- 1/2 cup potato starch flour
- 2 tablespoons sugar
- 1 tablespoon gluten
- 1 tablespoon caraway seeds
- 2 teaspoons salt
- 2 teaspoons SAF yeast or 21/2 teaspoons bread machine yeast

Directions:

1. Choose the size of loaf you would like to make and measure your ingredients.

2. Place the instant potato flakes in the water in a bowl. Let stand for 5 minutes. The flakes will expand and soften, and the water become cloudy.

3. Add the ingredients to the bread pan in the order listed above. Adding the potato water with the butter or lard as the liquid ingredients.

4. Place the pan in the bread machine and close the lid.

5. Turn on the bread maker. Select the Quick Yeast Bread/Rapid setting, then the loaf size, and finally the crust color. Start the cycle.

6. If the dough rises more than two-thirds of the way up the pan, gently deflate the dough a bit. This will keep the dough from hitting the window during baking.

7. When the cycle is finished and the bread is baked, carefully remove the pan from the machine. Use a potholder as the handle will be very hot. Let rest for a few minutes.

8. Remove the bread from the pan and allow to cool on a wire rack for at least 10 minutes before slicing.

Herb Light Rye Bread

Ingredients:

- 8 slices (1 pound)
- 3/8 teaspoon dill seed
- 3/8 teaspoon poppy seeds
- 1/6 teaspoon celery seeds
- 9/16 cup plus 1/2 tablespoon water
- 1/2 large egg
- 1 tablespoon minced shallot
- 3/4 tablespoon molasses
- 1 1/2 cups bread flour
- 1/2 cup medium or dark rye flour
- 1/2 tablespoon plus 1 teaspoon gluten
- 2/3 teaspoon caraway seed
- 1 1/8 teaspoons salt
- 1 1/4 teaspoons SAF yeast or 1/2 tablespoon bread machine yeast
- 12 slices (1 ½ pounds)
- 1/2 teaspoon dill seed
- 1/2 teaspoon poppy seeds
- 1/4 teaspoon celery seeds
- 7/8 cup water
- 1 large egg

* 11/2 tablespoons minced shallot
* 1 tablespoon molasses
* 21/4 cups bread flour
* 3/4 cup medium or dark rye flour
* 1 tablespoon gluten
* 11/2 teaspoons caraway seed
* 13/4 teaspoons salt
* 2 teaspoons SAF yeast or 21/2 teaspoons bread machine yeast
* 16 slices (2 pounds)
* 3/4 teaspoon dill seed
* 3/4 teaspoon poppy seeds
* 1/3 teaspoon celery seeds
* 11/8 cups plus 1 tablespoon water
* 1 large egg
* 2 tablespoons minced shallot
* 11/2 tablespoons molasses
* 3 cups bread flour
* 1 cup medium or dark rye flour
* 1 tablespoon plus 1 teaspoon gluten
* 11/3 teaspoons caraway seed
* 21/4 teaspoons salt
* 21/2 teaspoons SAF yeast or 1 tablespoon bread machine yeast

Directions:

1. Choose the size of loaf you would like to make and measure your ingredients.
2. Using a mortar and pestle, combine the dill seeds, poppy seeds, and celery seeds and crush them together coarsely. Or place the seeds between 2 sheets of waxed paper and crush them with a rolling pin.
3. Add the ingredients to the bread pan in the order listed above. Adding the crushed seeds with the dry ingredients.
4. Place the pan in the bread machine and close the lid.
5. Turn on the bread maker. Select the Basic setting, then the loaf size, and finally the crust color. Start the cycle.
6. When the cycle is finished and the bread is baked, carefully remove the pan from the machine. Use a potholder as the handle will be very hot. Let rest for a few minutes.

7. Remove the bread from the pan and allow to cool on a wire rack for at least 10 minutes before slicing.

Basic Pecan Bread

Ingredients:
* 8 slices (1 pound)
* 2/3 cups lukewarm milk
* 11/3 tablespoons unsalted butter, melted
* 1/2 egg, at room temperature
* 1 1/3 tablespoons sugar
* 2/3 teaspoons table salt
* 2 cups white bread flour
* 1 teaspoons bread machine yeast
* 2/3 cups chopped pecans, toasted
* 12 slices (1 ½ pounds)
* 1 cup lukewarm milk
* 2 tablespoons unsalted butter, melted
* 1 egg, at room temperature
* 2 tablespoons sugar
* 1 teaspoon table salt
* 3 cups white bread flour
* 1½ teaspoons bread machine yeast
* 1 cup chopped pecans, toasted
* 16 slices (2 pounds)
* 1⅓ cups lukewarm milk
* 2⅔ tablespoons unsalted butter, melted
* 1 egg, at room temperature
* 2⅔ tablespoons sugar
* 1⅓ teaspoons table salt
* 4 cups white bread flour
* 2 teaspoons bread machine yeast
* 1⅓ cups chopped pecans, toasted

Directions:

1. Choose the size of loaf you would like to make and measure your ingredients.
2. Add all of the ingredients except for the toasted pecans to the bread pan in the order listed above.
3. Place the pan in the bread machine and close the lid.
4. Turn on the bread maker. Select the White/Basic or Fruit/Nut (if your machine has this setting) setting, then the loaf size, and finally the crust color. Start the cycle.
5. When the machine signals to add ingredients, add the toasted pecans. (Some machines have a fruit/nut

hopper where you can add the toasted pecans when you start the machine. The machine will automatically add them to the dough during the baking process.)

6. When the cycle is finished and the bread is baked, carefully remove the pan from the machine. Use a potholder as the handle will be very hot. Let rest for a few minutes.

7. Remove the bread from the pan and allow to cool on a wire rack for at least 10 minutes before slicing.

Mesmerizing Walnut Bread

Ingredients:

- 8 slices (1 pound)
- 2 cups wheat flour
- 1/4 cup water
- 1/4 cup milk
- 1 whole egg, beaten
- 1/4 cup walnut
- 1/2 tablespoon vegetable oil
- 1/2 tablespoon sugar
- 1/2 teaspoon salt
- 1/2 teaspoon bread machine yeast
- 12 slices (1 ½ pounds)
- 3 cups wheat flour
- 3/8 cup water
- 3/8 cup milk
- 1 1/2 whole eggs, beaten
- 3/8 cup walnut
- 3/4 tablespoon vegetable oil
- 3/4 tablespoon sugar
- 3/4 teaspoon salt
- 3/4 teaspoon bread machine yeast
- 16 slices (2 pounds)
- 4 cups wheat flour
- ½ cup water
- ½ cup milk
- 2 whole eggs, beaten
- ½ cup walnut
- 1 tablespoon vegetable oil
- 1 tablespoon sugar
- 1 teaspoon salt
- 1 teaspoon bread machine yeast

Directions:

1. Choose the size of loaf you would like to make and measure your ingredients.

2. Add the ingredients to the bread pan in the order listed above (except the walnuts) .

3. Place the pan in the bread machine and close the lid.

4. Turn on the bread maker. Select the French Bread setting, then the loaf size, and finally the crust color. Start the cycle.

5. Slightly fry the walnuts in a dry frying pan until crispy; then let them cool.

6. Once the bread maker gives the signal, add the walnuts to the bread maker and mix with a spatula.

7. Let the remaining cycle complete.

8. When the cycle is finished and the bread is baked, carefully remove the pan from the machine. Use a potholder as the handle will be very hot. Let rest for a few minutes.

9. Remove the bread from the pan and allow to cool on a wire rack for at least 10 minutes before slicing.

Orange-cumin Bread

Ingredients:

- 8 slices (1 pound)
- 1/3 cup orange juice
- 1/2 cup fat-free milk
- 2 tablespoons butter, cut into pieces
- 1 3/4 cups bread flour
- 1/4 cup whole wheat flour
- 1/6 cup light brown sugar
- 2/3 tablespoon gluten
- 1 teaspoon cumin seed, crushed in a mortar and pestle
- 1 teaspoon salt
- 1 1/8 teaspoons SAF yeast or 1 3/8 teaspoons bread machine yeast
- 12 slices (1 ½ pounds)
- 1/2 cup orange juice
- 2/3 cup fat-free milk
- 3 tablespoons butter, cut into pieces
- 22/3 cups bread flour
- 1/3 cup whole wheat flour
- 1/4 cup light brown sugar
- 1 tablespoon gluten

- 11/2 teaspoons cumin seed, crushed in a mortar and pestle
- 11/2 teaspoons salt
- 2 teaspoons SAF yeast or 21/2 teaspoons bread machine yeast
- 16 slices (2 pounds)
- 2/3 cup orange juice
- 7/8 cup fat-free milk
- 4 tablespoons butter, cut into pieces
- 31/2 cups bread flour
- 1/2 cup whole wheat flour
- 1/3 cup light brown sugar
- 1 tablespoon plus 1 teaspoon gluten
- 2 teaspoons cumin seed, crushed in a mortar and pestle
- 2 teaspoons salt
- 21/4 teaspoons SAF yeast or 23/4 teaspoons bread machine yeast

Directions:

1. Choose the size of loaf you would like to make and measure your ingredients.
2. Add the ingredients to the bread pan in the order listed above.
3. Place the pan in the bread machine and close the lid.
4. Turn on the bread maker. Select the Basic setting, then the loaf size, and finally the crust color. Start the cycle.
5. When the cycle is finished and the bread is baked, carefully remove the pan from the machine. Use a potholder as the handle will be very hot. Let rest for a few minutes.
6. Remove the bread from the pan and allow to cool on a wire rack for at least 10 minutes before slicing.

Sesame Seeds & Onion Bread

Ingredients:
- 8 slices (1 pound)
- 3/10 cup water
- 1 7/15 cups flour
- 3/10 cup cottage cheese
- 4/5 tablespoon soft butter
- 4/5 tablespoon sugar
- 3/5 teaspoon salt
- 3/5 tablespoon sesame seeds
- 4/5 tablespoon dried onion
- 1/2 teaspoon dry yeast
- 12 slices (1 ½ pounds)
- 9/20 cup water
- 2 1/5 cups flour
- 9/20 cup cottage cheese
- 1 1/5 tablespoons soft butter
- 1 1/5 tablespoons sugar
- 9/10 teaspoon salt
- 9/10 tablespoon sesame seeds
- 1 1/5 tablespoons dried onion
- 3/4 teaspoon dry yeast
- 16 slices (2 pounds)
- 3/5 cup water
- 2 14/15 cups flour
- 3/5 cup cottage cheese
- 1 3/5 tablespoons soft butter
- 1 3/5 tablespoons sugar
- 1 1/5 teaspoons salt
- 1 1/5 tablespoons sesame seeds
- 1 3/5 tablespoons dried onion
- 1 teaspoon dry yeast

Directions:

1. Choose the size of loaf you would like to make and measure your ingredients.
2. Add the ingredients to the bread pan in the order listed above.
3. Place the pan in the bread machine and close the lid.
4. Turn on the bread maker. Select the White/Basic setting, then the loaf size, and finally the crust color. Start the cycle.
5. When the cycle is finished and the bread is baked, carefully remove the pan from the machine. Use a potholder as the handle will be very hot. Let rest for a few minutes.
6. Remove the bread from the pan and allow to cool on a wire rack for at least 10 minutes before slicing.

Pistachio Cherry Bread

Ingredients:

- 8 slices (1 pound)
- 3/16 cup lukewarm water
- 1/2 egg, at room temperature
- 1/8 cup butter, softened
- 1/8 cup packed dark brown sugar
- 3/4 teaspoon table salt
- 1 7/8 cups white bread flour
- 1/4 teaspoon ground nutmeg
- Dash allspice
- 1 teaspoon bread machine yeast
- 1/2 cup dried cherries
- 1/4 cup unsalted pistachios, chopped
- 12 slices (1 ½ pounds)
- ¾ cup lukewarm water
- 1 egg, at room temperature
- 3 tablespoons butter, softened
- 3 tablespoons packed dark brown sugar
- 1⅛ teaspoons table salt
- 2¾ cups white bread flour
- ½ teaspoon ground nutmeg
- Dash allspice
- 1½ teaspoons bread machine yeast
- ¾ cup dried cherries
- ⅓ cup unsalted pistachios, chopped
- 16 slices (2 pounds)
- 1⅛ cups lukewarm water
- 1 egg, at room temperature
- ¼ cup butter, softened
- ¼ cup packed dark brown sugar
- 1½ teaspoons table salt
- 3¾ cups white bread flour
- ½ teaspoon ground nutmeg
- Dash allspice
- 2 teaspoons bread machine yeast
- 1 cup dried cherries
- ½ cup unsalted pistachios, chopped

Directions:

1. Choose the size of loaf you would like to make and measure your ingredients.

2. Add all of the ingredients except for the pistachios and cherries to the bread pan in the order listed above.

3. Place the pan in the bread machine and close the lid.

4. Turn on the bread maker. Select the White/Basic or Fruit/Nut (if your machine has this setting) setting, then the loaf size, and finally the crust color. Start the cycle.

5. When the machine signals to add ingredients, add the pistachios and cherries. (Some machines have a fruit/nut hopper where you can add the pistachios and cherries when you start the machine. The machine will automatically add them to the dough during the baking process.)

6. When the cycle is finished and the bread is baked, carefully remove the pan from the machine. Use a potholder as the handle will be very hot. Let rest for a few minutes.

7. Remove the bread from the pan and allow to cool on a wire rack for at least 10 minutes before slicing.

HERB AND SPICE BREAD RECIPES

Basil Cheese Bread

Ingredients:
- 8 slices (1 pound)
- 2/3 cup lukewarm milk
- 2 teaspoons unsalted butter, melted
- 2 teaspoons sugar
- 5/8 teaspoon dried basil
- 1/2 teaspoon table salt
- 1/2 cup sharp Cheddar cheese, shredded
- 2 cups white bread flour
- 1 teaspoon bread machine yeast
- 12 slices (1 ½ pounds)
- 1 cup lukewarm milk
- 1 tablespoon unsalted butter, melted
- 1 tablespoon sugar
- 1 teaspoon dried basil
- ¾ teaspoon table salt
- ¾ cup sharp Cheddar cheese, shredded
- 3 cups white bread flour
- 1½ teaspoons bread machine yeast
- 16 slices (2 pounds)
- 1⅓ cups lukewarm milk
- 4 teaspoons unsalted butter, melted
- 4 teaspoons sugar
- 1¼ teaspoons dried basil
- 1 teaspoon table salt
- 1 cup sharp Cheddar cheese, shredded
- 4 cups white bread flour
- 2 teaspoons bread machine yeast

Directions:
1. Choose the size of loaf you would like to make and measure your ingredients.
2. Add the ingredients to the bread pan in the order listed above.
3. Place the pan in the bread machine and close the lid.
4. Turn on the bread maker. Select the White/Basic setting, then the loaf size, and finally the crust color. Start the cycle.
5. When the cycle is finished and the bread is baked, carefully remove the pan from the machine. Use a potholder as the handle will be very hot. Let rest for a few minutes.
6. Remove the bread from the pan and allow to cool on a wire rack for at least 10 minutes before slicing.

Potato Rosemary Loaf

Ingredients:
- 8 slices (1 pound)
- 1 3/5 cups wheat flour
- 2/5 tablespoon sugar
- 2/5 tablespoon sunflower oil
- 3/5 teaspoon salt
- 3/5 cup water
- 2/5 teaspoon dry yeast
- 2/5 cup mashed potatoes, ground through a sieve
- crushed rosemary to taste
- 12 slices (1 ½ pounds)
- 1 7/5 cups wheat flour
- 3/5 tablespoon sugar
- 3/5 tablespoon sunflower oil
- 9/10 teaspoon salt
- 9/10 cup water
- 3/5 teaspoon dry yeast
- 3/5 cup mashed potatoes, ground through a sieve
- crushed rosemary to taste
- 16 slices (2 pounds)
- 3 1/5 cups wheat flour
- 4/5 tablespoon sugar
- 4/5 tablespoon sunflower oil
- 1 1/5 teaspoons salt
- 1 1/5 cups water
- 4/5 teaspoon dry yeast
- 4/5 cup mashed potatoes, ground through a sieve
- crushed rosemary to taste

Directions:
1. Choose the size of loaf you would like to make and measure your ingredients.
2. Add the ingredients to the bread pan in the order listed above (except mashed potatoes, and chopped rosemary).
3. Place the pan in the bread machine and close the lid.

4. Turn on the bread maker. Select the Bread with Filling setting, then the loaf size, and finally the crust color. Start the cycle.

5. Once the bread maker beeps and signals to add more ingredients, open lid, add mashed potatoes, and chopped rosemary.

6. When the cycle is finished and the bread is baked, carefully remove the pan from the machine. Use a potholder as the handle will be very hot. Let rest for a few minutes.

7. Remove the bread from the pan and allow to cool on a wire rack for at least 10 minutes before slicing.

Whole Wheat Basil Bread

Ingredients:

- 8 slices (1 pound)
- 1/2 cup buttermilk
- 1/4 cup water
- 1 1/2 tablespoons butter, cut into pieces
- 1 1/2 tablespoons honey
- 2 cups white whole wheat flour
- 1/6 cup chopped fresh basil
- 1/6 cup pine nuts, chopped
- 2/3 tablespoon gluten
- 1 teaspoon salt
- 1 1/4 teaspoons SAF yeast or 1/2 tablespoon bread machine yeast
- 12 slices (1½ pounds)
- 3/4 cup buttermilk
- 1/3 cup water
- 2 tablespoons butter, cut into pieces
- 2 tablespoons honey
- 3 cups white whole wheat flour
- 1/4 cup chopped fresh basil
- 1/4 cup pine nuts, chopped
- 1 tablespoon gluten
- 11/2 teaspoons salt
- 2 teaspoons SAF yeast or 21/2 teaspoons bread machine yeast
- 16 slices (2 pounds)
- 1 cup buttermilk
- 1/2 cup water
- 3 tablespoons butter, cut into pieces

- 3 tablespoons honey
- 4 cups white whole wheat flour
- 1/3 cup chopped fresh basil
- 1/3 cup pine nuts, chopped
- 1 tablespoon plus 1 teaspoon gluten
- 2 teaspoons salt
- 21/2 teaspoons SAF yeast or 1 tablespoon bread machine yeast

Directions:

1. Choose the size of loaf you would like to make and measure your ingredients.

2. Add the ingredients to the bread pan in the order listed above.

3. Place the pan in the bread machine and close the lid.

4. Turn on the bread maker. Select the Basic setting, then the loaf size, and finally the crust color. Start the cycle.

5. When the cycle is finished and the bread is baked, carefully remove the pan from the machine. Use a potholder as the handle will be very hot. Let rest for a few minutes.

6. Remove the bread from the pan and allow to cool on a wire rack for at least 10 minutes before slicing.

Awesome Rosemary Bread

Ingredients:

- 8 slices (1 pound)
- ¾ cup + 1 tablespoon water at 80 degrees F
- 1⅔ tablespoons melted butter, cooled
- 2 teaspoons sugar
- 1 teaspoon salt
- 1 tablespoon fresh rosemary, chopped
- 2 cups white bread flour
- 1⅓ teaspoons instant yeast
- 12 slices (1 ½ pounds)
- 1 1/8 cups + 1 1/2 tablespoons water at 80 degrees F
- 4 1/6 tablespoons melted butter, cooled
- 3 teaspoons sugar
- 1 1/2 teaspoons salt
- 1 1/2 tablespoons fresh rosemary, chopped
- 3 cups white bread flour
- 2 teaspoons instant yeast
- 16 slices (2 pounds)

- 1 1/2 cups + 2 tablespoons water at 80 degrees F
- 3 1/3 tablespoons melted butter, cooled
- 4 teaspoons sugar
- 2 teaspoons salt
- 2 tablespoons fresh rosemary, chopped
- 4 cups white bread flour
- 2 2/3 teaspoons instant yeast

Directions:

1. Choose the size of loaf you would like to make and measure your ingredients.
2. Add the ingredients to the bread pan in the order listed above.
3. Place the pan in the bread machine and close the lid.
4. Turn on the bread maker. Select the White/Basic setting, then the loaf size, and finally the crust color. Start the cycle.
5. When the cycle is finished and the bread is baked, carefully remove the pan from the machine. Use a potholder as the handle will be very hot. Let rest for a few minutes.
6. Remove the bread from the pan and allow to cool on a wire rack for at least 10 minutes before slicing.

- 1½ teaspoons salt
- 1½ tablespoons sugar
- 1 tablespoon dry yeast
- 1¾ cups water
- 2 tablespoons cumin
- 3 tablespoons sunflower oil

Directions:

1. Choose the size of loaf you would like to make and measure your ingredients.
2. Add the ingredients to the bread pan in the order listed above.
3. Place the pan in the bread machine and close the lid.
4. Turn on the bread maker. Select the French Bread setting, then the loaf size, and finally the crust color. Start the cycle.
5. Once the maker beeps, add cumin.
6. When the cycle is finished and the bread is baked, carefully remove the pan from the machine. Use a potholder as the handle will be very hot. Let rest for a few minutes.
7. Remove the bread from the pan and allow to cool on a wire rack for at least 10 minutes before slicing.

Cumin Tossed Fancy Bread

Ingredients:
- 8 slices (1 pound)
- 2 2/3 cups wheat flour
- 3/4 teaspoon salt
- 3/4 tablespoon sugar
- 1/2 tablespoon dry yeast
- 7/8 cup water
- 1 tablespoon cumin
- 1 1/2 tablespoons sunflower oil
- 12 slices (1 ½ pounds)
- 4 cups wheat flour
- 1 1/8 teaspoons salt
- 1 1/8 tablespoons sugar
- 3/4 tablespoon dry yeast
- 1 5/16 cups water
- 1 1/2 tablespoons cumin
- 2 1/4 tablespoons sunflower oil
- 16 slices (2 pounds)
- 5⅓ cups wheat flour

Ricotta & Chive Loaf

Ingredients:
- 8 slices (1 pound)
- 1 cup lukewarm water
- 1/3 cup whole ricotta cheese
- 1½ teaspoons salt
- 1 tablespoon granulated sugar
- 3 cups bread flour
- ½ cup chopped chives
- 2½ teaspoons instant yeast
- 12 slices (1 ½ pounds)
- 1 1/2 cups lukewarm water
- 1/2 cup whole ricotta cheese
- 2 1/4 teaspoons salt
- 1 1/2 tablespoons granulated sugar
- 4 1/2 cups bread flour
- 3/4 cup chopped chives
- 3 3/4 teaspoons instant yeast
- 16 slices (2 pounds)
- 2 cups lukewarm water

- 2/3 cup whole ricotta cheese
- 3 teaspoons salt
- 2 tablespoons granulated sugar
- 6 cups bread flour
- 1 cup chopped chives
- 5 teaspoons instant yeast

Directions:

1. Choose the size of loaf you would like to make and measure your ingredients.
2. Add the ingredients to the bread pan in the order listed above (except dried fruits).
3. Place the pan in the bread machine and close the lid.
4. Turn on the bread maker. Select the White/Basic setting, then the loaf size, and finally the crust color. Start the cycle.
5. Once the machine beeps, add fruits.
6. When the cycle is finished and the bread is baked, carefully remove the pan from the machine. Use a potholder as the handle will be very hot. Let rest for a few minutes.
7. Remove the bread from the pan and allow to cool on a wire rack for at least 10 minutes before slicing.

Buttermilk Bread With Lavender

Ingredients:

- 8 slices (1 pound)
- 1/4 cup water
- 7/16 cup buttermilk
- 1/8 cup olive oil
- 2 cups bread flour
- 1 1/2 tablespoons finely chopped fresh lavender leaves
- 5/8 teaspoon finely chopped fresh lavender flowers
- Grated zest of 1/2 small lemon
- 2/3 tablespoon gluten
- 1 teaspoon salt
- 1 1/8 teaspoons SAF yeast or 1 3/8 teaspoons bread machine yeast
- 12 slices (1½ pounds)
- 1/3 cup water
- 3/4 cup buttermilk
- 3 tablespoons olive oil
- 3 cups bread flour

- 2 tablespoons finely chopped fresh lavender leaves
- 1 teaspoon finely chopped fresh lavender flowers
- Grated zest of 1 small lemon
- 1 tablespoon gluten
- 11/2 teaspoons salt
- 2 teaspoons SAF yeast or 21/2 teaspoons bread machine yeast
- 16 slices (2 pounds)
- 1/2 cups water
- 7/8 cup buttermilk
- 1/4 cup olive oil
- 4 cups bread flour
- 3 tablespoons finely chopped fresh lavender leaves
- 11/4 teaspoons finely chopped fresh lavender flowers
- Grated zest of 1 small lemon
- 1 tablespoon plus 1 teaspoon gluten
- 2 teaspoons salt
- 21/4 teaspoons SAF yeast or 23/4 teaspoons bread machine yeast

Directions:

1. Choose the size of loaf you would like to make and measure your ingredients.
2. Add the ingredients to the bread pan in the order listed above.
3. Place the pan in the bread machine and close the lid.
4. Turn on the bread maker. Select the Basic setting, then the loaf size, and finally the crust color. Start the cycle.
5. When the cycle is finished and the bread is baked, carefully remove the pan from the machine. Use a potholder as the handle will be very hot. Let rest for a few minutes.
6. Remove the bread from the pan and allow to cool on a wire rack for at least 10 minutes before slicing.

Cinnamon-flavored Raisin Bread

Ingredients:

- 8 slices (1 pound)
- ¾ cup milk at 80 degrees F
- 1 tablespoon melted butter, cooled
- 1 tablespoon sugar
- ¾ teaspoon salt
- ½ teaspoon ground cinnamon

- 2 cups white bread flour
- 1 teaspoon instant yeast
- ½ cup golden raisins
- 12 slices (1 ½ pounds)
- 1 1/8 cups milk at 80 degrees F
- 1 1/2 tablespoons melted butter, cooled
- 1 1/2 tablespoons sugar
- 1 1/8 teaspoons salt
- 3/4 teaspoon ground cinnamon
- 3 cups white bread flour
- 1 1/2 teaspoons instant yeast
- 3/4 cup golden raisins
- 16 slices (2 pounds)
- 1 1/2 cups milk at 80 degrees F
- 2 tablespoons melted butter, cooled
- 2 tablespoons sugar
- 1 1/2 teaspoons salt
- 1 teaspoon ground cinnamon
- 4 cups white bread flour
- 2 teaspoons instant yeast
- 1 cup golden raisins

Directions:

1. Choose the size of loaf you would like to make and measure your ingredients.

2. Add the ingredients to the bread pan in the order listed above (except raisins).

3. Place the pan in the bread machine and close the lid.

4. Turn on the bread maker. Select the Sweet Bread setting, then the loaf size, and finally the crust color. Start the cycle.

5. Add raisins at the raisin/nut signal (should be after 1 - 1½ hours).

6. When the cycle is finished and the bread is baked, carefully remove the pan from the machine. Use a potholder as the handle will be very hot. Let rest for a few minutes.

7. Remove the bread from the pan and allow to cool on a wire rack for at least 10 minutes before slicing.

Turmeric Raisin Saffron Loaf

Ingredients:
- 8 slices (1 pound)
- 3/5 cup milk at 80 degrees F
- 4/5 tablespoon sugar
- 3/5 teaspoon salt
- 1/10 teaspoon powdered saffron + turmeric
- 4/5 tablespoon butter
- 2/5 tablespoon vanilla sugar
- 11 1/4 cups flour
- 2/5 teaspoon bread machine yeast
- 2/5 cup raisins
- 12 slices (1 ½ pounds)
- 9/10 cup milk at 80 degrees F
- 1 1/5 tablespoons sugar
- 9/10 teaspoon salt
- 3/20 teaspoon powdered saffron + turmeric
- 1 1/5 tablespoons butter
- 3/5 tablespoon vanilla sugar
- 16 7/8 cups flour
- 3/5 teaspoon bread machine yeast
- 3/5 cup raisins
- 16 slices (2 pounds)
- 1 1/5 cups milk at 80 degrees F
- 1 3/5 tablespoons sugar
- 1 1/5 teaspoons salt
- 1/5 teaspoon powdered saffron + turmeric
- 1 3/5 tablespoons butter
- 4/5 tablespoon vanilla sugar
- 22 1/2 cups flour
- 4/5 teaspoon bread machine yeast
- 4/5 cup raisins

Directions:

1. Choose the size of loaf you would like to make and measure your ingredients.

2. Add the ingredients to the bread pan in the order listed above (except raisins).

3. Place the pan in the bread machine and close the lid.

4. Turn on the bread maker. Select the White/Basic setting, then the loaf size, and finally the crust color. Start the cycle.

5. Once the bread maker gives the signal for adding more ingredients, add raisins.

6. When the cycle is finished and the bread is baked, carefully remove the pan from the machine. Use a potholder as the handle will be very hot. Let rest for a few minutes.

7. Remove the bread from the pan and allow to cool on a wire rack for at least 10 minutes before slicing.

Brooklyn Botanic Garden Herb Bread

Ingredients:

- 8 slices (1 pound)
- 1/2 cup milk
- 1/2 large egg
- 1 1/2 tablespoons unsalted butter, cut into pieces
- 2 cups bread flour
- 2/3 tablespoon gluten
- 2/3 tablespoon caraway seed, crushed
- 5/8 teaspoon dried sage
- 5/8 teaspoon fresh grated nutmeg
- 1 teaspoon salt
- 1 1/4 teaspoons SAF yeast or 1/2 tablespoon bread machine yeast
- 12 slices (1 ½ pounds)
- 3/4 cup milk
- 1 large egg
- 2 tablespoons unsalted butter, cut into pieces
- 3 cups bread flour
- 1 tablespoon gluten
- 1 tablespoon caraway seed, crushed
- 1 teaspoon dried sage
- 1 teaspoon fresh grated nutmeg
- 11/4 teaspoons salt
- 2 teaspoons SAF yeast or 21/2 teaspoons bread machine yeast
- 16 slices (2 pounds)
- 1 cup milk
- 1 large egg
- 3 tablespoons unsalted butter, cut into pieces
- 4 cups bread flour
- 1 tablespoon plus 1 teaspoon gluten
- 1 tablespoon plus 1 teaspoon caraway seed, crushed
- 11/4 teaspoons dried sage
- 11/4 teaspoons fresh grated nutmeg
- 2 teaspoons salt
- 21/2 teaspoons SAF yeast or 1 tablespoon bread machine yeast

Directions:

1. Choose the size of loaf you would like to make and measure your ingredients.
2. Add the ingredients to the bread pan in the order listed above.
3. Place the pan in the bread machine and close the lid.
4. Turn on the bread maker. Select the Basic setting, then the loaf size, and finally the crust color. Start the cycle.
5. When the cycle is finished and the bread is baked, carefully remove the pan from the machine. Use a potholder as the handle will be very hot. Let rest for a few minutes.
6. Remove the bread from the pan and allow to cool on a wire rack for at least 10 minutes before slicing.

Oregano Mozza-cheese Bread

Ingredients:

- 8 slices (1 pound)
- 1/2 cup (milk + egg) mixture
- 1/4 cup mozzarella cheese
- 1 1/8 cup flour
- 3/8 cup whole grain flour
- 1 tablespoon sugar
- 1/2 teaspoon salt
- 1 teaspoon oregano
- 3/4 teaspoon dry yeast
- 12 slices (1 ½ pounds)
- 3/4 cup (milk + egg) mixture
- 3/8 cup mozzarella cheese
- 1 11/16 cups flour
- 9/16 cup whole grain flour
- 1 1/2 tablespoons sugar
- 3/4 teaspoon salt
- 1 1/2 teaspoon oregano
- 1 1/8 teaspoon dry yeast
- 16 slices (2 pounds)
- 1 cup (milk + egg) mixture
- ½ cup mozzarella cheese
- 2¼ cups flour
- ¾ cup whole grain flour
- 2 tablespoons sugar
- 1 teaspoon salt
- 2 teaspoons oregano
- 1½ teaspoons dry yeast

Directions:

1. Choose the size of loaf you would like to make and measure your ingredients.

2. Add the ingredients to the bread pan in the order listed above.

3. Place the pan in the bread machine and close the lid.

4. Turn on the bread maker. Select the White/Basic setting, then the loaf size, and finally the crust color. Start the cycle.

5. When the cycle is finished and the bread is baked, carefully remove the pan from the machine. Use a potholder as the handle will be very hot. Let rest for a few minutes.

6. Remove the bread from the pan and allow to cool on a wire rack for at least 10 minutes before slicing.

Cinnamon Milk Bread

Ingredients:
- 8 slices (1 pound)
- 5/6 cup lukewarm milk
- 1/2 egg, at room temperature
- 1/6 cup unsalted butter, melted
- 1/3 cup sugar
- 1/3 teaspoon table salt
- 2 cups white bread flour
- 1 teaspoon ground cinnamon
- 1 1/8 teaspoons bread machine yeast
- 12 slices (1 ½ pounds)
- 1 cup lukewarm milk
- 1 egg, at room temperature
- ¼ cup unsalted butter, melted
- ½ cup sugar
- ½ teaspoon table salt
- 3 cups white bread flour
- 1½ teaspoons ground cinnamon
- 2 teaspoons bread machine yeast
- 16 slices (2 pounds)
- 1⅔ cups lukewarm milk
- 1 egg, at room temperature
- ⅓ cup unsalted butter, melted
- ⅔ cup sugar
- ⅔ teaspoon table salt
- 4 cups white bread flour
- 2 teaspoons ground cinnamon
- 2¼ teaspoons bread machine yeast

Directions:

1. Choose the size of loaf you would like to make and measure your ingredients.

2. Add the ingredients to the bread pan in the order listed above.

3. Place the pan in the bread machine and close the lid.

4. Turn on the bread maker. Select the White/Basic setting, then the loaf size, and finally the crust color. Start the cycle.

5. When the cycle is finished and the bread is baked, carefully remove the pan from the machine. Use a potholder as the handle will be very hot. Let rest for a few minutes.

6. Remove the bread from the pan and allow to cool on a wire rack for at least 10 minutes before slicing.

Apple Pie Bread

Ingredients:
- 8 slices (1 pound)
- 1½ teaspoons active dry yeast
- 1½ teaspoons ground cinnamon
- 3¼ cups bread flour
- 1½ teaspoons salt
- 3 tablespoons powdered buttermilk
- 1¼ cups apple pie filling
- 1½ tablespoons butter, soft
- ½ cup water
- 12 slices (1 ½ pounds)
- 2 1/4 teaspoons active dry yeast
- 2 1/4 teaspoons ground cinnamon
- 4 7/8 cups bread flour
- 2 1/4 teaspoons salt
- 4 1/2 tablespoons powdered buttermilk
- 1 7/8 cups apple pie filling
- 2 1/4 tablespoons butter, soft
- 3/4 cup water
- 16 slices (2 pounds)
- 3 teaspoons active dry yeast
- 3 teaspoons ground cinnamon
- 6 1/2 cups bread flour
- 3 teaspoons salt
- 6 tablespoons powdered buttermilk
- 2 1/2 cups apple pie filling
- 3 tablespoons butter, soft

- 1 cup water

Directions:
1.   Choose the size of loaf you would like to make and measure your ingredients.
2.   Add the ingredients to the bread pan in the order listed above.
3.   Place the pan in the bread machine and close the lid.
4.   Turn on the bread maker. Select the White/Basic setting, then the loaf size, and finally the crust color. Start the cycle.
5.   When the cycle is finished and the bread is baked, carefully remove the pan from the machine. Use a potholder as the handle will be very hot. Let rest for a few minutes.
6.   Remove the bread from the pan and allow to cool on a wire rack for at least 10 minutes before slicing.

Herb Garlic Cream Cheese Bread

Ingredients:
- 8 slices (1 pound)
- 1/3 cup water, at room temperature
- 1/3 cup herb and garlic cream cheese mixture
- 1 whole egg
- 4 teaspoons melted butter, cooled
- 1 tablespoon sugar
- 2/3 teaspoon salt
- 2 cups white bread flour
- 1 teaspoon bread machine yeast
- 12 slices (1 ½ pounds)
- 1/2 cup water, at room temperature
- 1/2 cup herb and garlic cream cheese mixture
- 1 1/2 whole eggs
- 6 teaspoons melted butter, cooled
- 1 1/2 tablespoons sugar
- 1 teaspoon salt
- 3 cups white bread flour
- 1 1/2 teaspoons bread machine yeast
- 16 slices (2 pounds)
- 2/3 cup water, at room temperature
- 2/3 cup herb and garlic cream cheese mixture
- 2 whole eggs
- 8 teaspoons melted butter, cooled
- 2 tablespoons sugar

- 1 1/3 teaspoons salt
- 4 cups white bread flour
- 2 teaspoons bread machine yeast

Directions:
1.   Choose the size of loaf you would like to make and measure your ingredients.
2.   Add the ingredients to the bread pan in the order listed above.
3.   Place the pan in the bread machine and close the lid.
4.   Turn on the bread maker. Select the White/Basic setting, then the loaf size, and finally the crust color. Start the cycle.
5.   When the cycle is finished and the bread is baked, carefully remove the pan from the machine. Use a potholder as the handle will be very hot. Let rest for a few minutes.
6.   Remove the bread from the pan and allow to cool on a wire rack for at least 10 minutes before slicing.

Cinnamon & Dried Fruits Bread

Ingredients:
- 8 slices (1 pound)
- 1 3/8 cups flour
- 3/4 cups dried fruits
- 2 tablespoons sugar
- 1 1/4 tablespoons butter
- 1/2 tablespoon milk powder
- 1/2 teaspoon cinnamon
- 1/4 teaspoon ground nutmeg
- 1/8 teaspoon vanillin
- 1/4 cup peanuts
- powdered sugar, for sprinkling
- 1/2 teaspoon salt
- 3/4 bread machine yeast
- 12 slices (1 ½ pounds)
- 2 1/16 cups flour
- 1 1/8 cups dried fruits
- 3 tablespoons sugar
- 1 7/8 tablespoons butter
- 3/4 tablespoon milk powder
- 3/4 teaspoon cinnamon
- 3/8 teaspoon ground nutmeg
- 3/16 teaspoon vanillin

- 3/8 cup peanuts
- powdered sugar, for sprinkling
- 3/4 teaspoon salt
- 1 1/8 bread machine yeast
- 16 slices (2 pounds)
- 2¾ cups flour
- 1½ cups dried fruits
- 4 tablespoons sugar
- 2½ tablespoons butter
- 1 tablespoon milk powder
- 1 teaspoon cinnamon
- ½ teaspoon ground nutmeg
- ¼ teaspoon vanillin
- ½ cup peanuts
- powdered sugar, for sprinkling
- 1 teaspoon salt
- 1½ bread machine yeast

Directions:

1. Choose the size of loaf you would like to make and measure your ingredients.

2. Add the ingredients to the bread pan in the order listed above (except peanuts and powdered sugar).

3. Place the pan in the bread machine and close the lid.

4. Turn on the bread maker. Select the White/Basic setting, then the loaf size, and finally the crust color. Start the cycle.

5. Once the bread maker beeps, moisten dough with a bit of water and add peanuts.

6. When the cycle is finished and the bread is baked, carefully remove the pan from the machine. Use a potholder as the handle will be very hot. Let rest for a few minutes.

7. Sprinkle with powdered sugar.

8. Remove the bread from the pan and allow to cool on a wire rack for at least 10 minutes before slicing.

Anise Honey Bread

Ingredients:

- 8 slices (1 pound)
- 1/2 cup + 1/2 tablespoon lukewarm water
- 1/2 egg, at room temperature
- 1/6 cup butter, melted and cooled
- 1/6 cup honey
- 1/3 teaspoon table salt
- 2 cups white bread flour
- 2/3 teaspoon anise seed
- 2/3 teaspoon lemon zest
- 1 1/4 teaspoons bread machine yeast
- 12 slices (1 ½ pounds)
- ¾ cup lukewarm water
- 1 egg, at room temperature
- ¼ cup butter, melted and cooled
- ¼ cup honey
- ½ teaspoon table salt
- 3 cups white bread flour
- 1 teaspoon anise seed
- 1 teaspoon lemon zest
- 2 teaspoons bread machine yeast
- 16 slices (2 pounds)
- 1 cup + 1 tablespoon lukewarm water
- 1 egg, at room temperature
- ⅓ cup butter, melted and cooled
- ⅓ cup honey
- ⅔ teaspoon table salt
- 4 cups white bread flour
- 1⅓ teaspoons anise seed
- 1⅓ teaspoons lemon zest
- 2½ teaspoons bread machine yeast

Directions:

1. Choose the size of loaf you would like to make and measure your ingredients.

2. Add the ingredients to the bread pan in the order listed above.

3. Place the pan in the bread machine and close the lid.

4. Turn on the bread maker. Select the White/Basic setting, then the loaf size, and finally the crust color. Start the cycle.

5. When the cycle is finished and the bread is baked, carefully remove the pan from the machine. Use a potholder as the handle will be very hot. Let rest for a few minutes.

6. Remove the bread from the pan and allow to cool on a wire rack for at least 10 minutes before slicing.

Cinnamon Rolls

Ingredients:

- 8 slices (1 pound)
- 2/3 cups warm water
- 1/2 stick of butter, cut into small chunks
- 2 1/2 tablespoons sugar
- 1/2 egg
- 1/2 teaspoon salt
- 1 1/2 cups all-purpose flour
- 3/4 cup bread flour
- 1/8 cup powdered milk
- 1/2 tablespoon dry active yeast
- For the Filling:
- 1/2 cup sugar
- 3/4 tablespoons ground cinnamon
- 1/4 cup butter, softened
- For the Icing:
- 2 cups powdered sugar
- 1 tablespoon melted butter
- 1/4 teaspoon vanilla extract
- 2 tablespoons milk
- 12 slices (1 ½ pounds)
- 1 cup warm water
- 3/4 stick of butter, cut into small chunks
- 3 3/4 tablespoons sugar
- 3/4 egg
- 3/4 teaspoon salt
- 2 1/4 cups all-purpose flour
- 1 1/8 cups bread flour
- 1/4 cup powdered milk
- 3/4 tablespoon dry active yeast
- For the Filling:
- 3/4 cup sugar
- 1 1/8 tablespoons ground cinnamon
- 1/4 cup butter, softened
- For the Icing:
- 3 cups powdered sugar
- 1 1/2 tablespoons melted butter
- 3/8 teaspoon vanilla extract
- 3 tablespoons milk
- 16 slices (2 pounds)
- 1 1/3 cups warm water
- 1 stick of butter, cut into small chunks
- 5 tablespoons sugar
- 1 egg
- 1 teaspoon salt
- 3 cups all-purpose flour
- 1 1/2 cups bread flour
- 1/4 cup powdered milk
- 1 tablespoon dry active yeast
- For the Filling:
- 1 cup sugar
- 1 1/2 tablespoons ground cinnamon
- 1/2 cup butter, softened
- For the Icing:
- 4 cups powdered sugar
- 2 tablespoons melted butter
- 1/2 teaspoon vanilla extract
- 4 tablespoons milk

Directions:

1. Place the ingredients (except yeast) for the dough in your bread machine in the order listed.

2. Make a well in the center of the dry ingredients and add the yeast.

3. Select Dough cycle and press Start.

4. Split kneaded dough into two mounds.

5. On a lightly floured surface, roll one mound of your dough out into a rectangle.

6. Baste with half of the melted butter.

7. Sprinkle half of the cinnamon sugar over the melted butter making sure to cover as much surface with the filling as you can.

8. Starting at one of the short ends of your rectangle of dough, roll it up and brush the outside of roll with melted butter.

9. Slice the dough into about 1-inch pieces.

10. Place pinwheels on greased baking sheet next to one another.

11. Repeat the steps above with the second mound of dough.

12. Cover assembled dough with a light towel and let rise for 25-30 minutes.

13. Bake at 350°F for 17 minutes or until lightly brown on top.

14. Combine icing ingredients and cover rolls when removed from the oven; allow to cool 10 minutes before serving.

Mixed Herb Cheese Bread

Ingredients:

- 8 slices (1 pound)
- 2/3 cup lukewarm water
- 1 tablespoon olive oil
- 1/2 teaspoon table salt
- 1/2 tablespoon sugar
- 1 cloves garlic, crushed
- 11/2 tablespoons mixed fresh herbs (basil, chives, oregano, rosemary, etc.)
- 1/8 cup Parmesan cheese, grated
- 2 cups white bread flour
- 11/8 teaspoons bread machine yeast
- 12 slices (1 ½ pounds)
- 1 cup lukewarm water
- 1½ tablespoons olive oil
- ¾ teaspoon table salt
- ¾ tablespoon sugar
- 2 cloves garlic, crushed
- 2 tablespoons mixed fresh herbs (basil, chives, oregano, rosemary, etc.)
- 3 tablespoons Parmesan cheese, grated
- 3 cups white bread flour
- 1⅔ teaspoons bread machine yeast
- 16 slices (2 pounds)
- 1⅓ cups lukewarm water
- 2 tablespoons olive oil
- 1 teaspoon table salt
- 1 tablespoon sugar
- 2 cloves garlic, crushed
- 3 tablespoons mixed fresh herbs (basil, chives, oregano, rosemary, etc.)
- ¼ cup Parmesan cheese, grated
- 4 cups white bread flour
- 2¼ teaspoons bread machine yeast

Directions:

1. Choose the size of loaf you would like to make and measure your ingredients.
2. Add the ingredients to the bread pan in the order listed above.
3. Place the pan in the bread machine and close the lid.
4. Turn on the bread maker. Select the White/Basic setting, then the loaf size, and finally the crust color. Start the cycle.
5. When the cycle is finished and the bread is baked, carefully remove the pan from the machine. Use a potholder as the handle will be very hot. Let rest for a few minutes.
6. Remove the bread from the pan and allow to cool on a wire rack for at least 10 minutes before slicing.

Fragrant Cardamom Bread

Ingredients:

- 8 slices (1 pound)
- ½ cup milk at 80 degrees F
- 1 egg, at room temperature
- 1 teaspoon melted butter, cooled
- 4 teaspoons honey
- ⅔ teaspoon salt
- ⅔ teaspoon ground cardamom
- 2 cups white bread flour
- ¾ teaspoon instant yeast
- 12 slices (1 ½ pounds)
- 3/4 cup milk at 80 degrees F
- 1 1/2 eggs, at room temperature
- 1 1/2 teaspoons melted butter, cooled
- 6 teaspoons honey
- 1 teaspoon salt
- 1 teaspoon ground cardamom
- 3 cups white bread flour
- 1 1/8 teaspoons instant yeast
- 16 slices (2 pounds)
- 1 cup milk at 80 degrees F
- 2 eggs, at room temperature
- 2 teaspoons melted butter, cooled
- 8 teaspoons honey
- 1 1/3 teaspoons salt
- 1 1/3 teaspoons ground cardamom
- 4 cups white bread flour
- 1 1/2 teaspoons instant yeast

Directions:

1. Choose the size of loaf you would like to make and measure your ingredients.

2. Add the ingredients to the bread pan in the order listed above.

3. Place the pan in the bread machine and close the lid.

4. Turn on the bread maker. Select the White/Basic setting, then the loaf size, and finally the crust color. Start the cycle.

5. When the cycle is finished and the bread is baked, carefully remove the pan from the machine. Use a potholder as the handle will be very hot. Let rest for a few minutes.

6. Remove the bread from the pan and allow to cool on a wire rack for at least 10 minutes before slicing.

Fresh Herb Bread

Ingredients:
- 8 slices (1 pound)
- 2/3 cup plus 1 1/3 tablespoons water (for 9 1/3-ounce mix) or 1 10/12 cups water (for 2/3-pound mix)
- One9 1/3-ounce or 1-pound box white or whole wheat bread machine mix
- 1/3 cup chopped fresh herbs, any combination of parsley, chervil, basil, marjoram, sage, chives, mint, thyme, or lovage
- 1/6 cup chopped hazelnuts
- Grated zest of 2/3 lemon
- 1 1/3 teaspoons gluten
- 2/3 yeast packet (included in mix)
- 12 slices (1½ pounds)
- 1 cup plus 2 tablespoons water (for 14-ounce mix) or 11/4 cups water (for 1-pound mix)
- One 14-ounce or 1-pound box white or whole wheat bread machine mix
- 1/2 cup chopped fresh herbs, any combination of parsley, chervil, basil, marjoram, sage, chives, mint, thyme, or lovage
- 1/4 cup chopped hazelnuts
- Grated zest of 1 lemon
- 2 teaspoons gluten
- 1 yeast packet (included in mix)
- 16 slices (2 pounds)
- 1 1/3 cup plus 2 2/3 tablespoons water (for 18 2/3-ounce mix) or 3 4/6 cups water (for 1 1/3-pound mix)
- One 18 2/3-ounce or 2-pound box white or whole wheat bread machine mix
- 2/3 cup chopped fresh herbs, any combination of parsley, chervil, basil, marjoram, sage, chives, mint, thyme, or lovage
- 1/3 cup chopped hazelnuts
- Grated zest of 1 1/3 lemon
- 2 2/3 teaspoons gluten
- 1 1/3 yeast packet (included in mix)

Directions:
1. Choose the size of loaf you would like to make and measure your ingredients.

2. Add the ingredients to the bread pan in the order listed above.

3. Place the pan in the bread machine and close the lid.

4. Turn on the bread maker. Select the Basic setting, then the loaf size, and finally the crust color. Start the cycle.

5. When the cycle is finished and the bread is baked, carefully remove the pan from the machine. Use a potholder as the handle will be very hot. Let rest for a few minutes.

6. Remove the bread from the pan and allow to cool on a wire rack for at least 10 minutes before slicing.

Mountain Herb Bread

Ingredients:
- 8 slices (1 pound)
- 5/6 cup water
- 2 1/2 tablespoons olive oil
- 1/4 cup wildflower honey
- 2 3/4 cups bread flour
- 1 1/4 cups whole wheat flour
- 1/4 cup light brown sugar
- 1/4 cup nonfat dry milk
- 1 tablespoon plus 1 teaspoon gluten
- 2 tablespoons minced fresh parsley
- 2 teaspoons dried basil
- 1 1/4 teaspoons dried dill weed
- 1 1/4 teaspoons dried summer savory
- 1 teaspoon dried marjoram
- 3/4 teaspoon dried tarragon
- 1/3 teaspoon dried thyme

- 2 teaspoons salt
- 21/4 teaspoons SAF yeast or 23/4 teaspoons bread machine yeast
- 12 slices (1½ pounds)
- 11/4 cups water
- 2 tablespoons olive oil
- 1/4 cup wildflower honey
- 2 cups bread flour
- 1 cup whole wheat flour
- 3 tablespoons light brown sugar
- 3 tablespoons nonfat dry milk
- 1 tablespoon gluten
- 11/2 tablespoons minced fresh parsley
- 11/2 teaspoons dried basil
- 1 teaspoon dried dill weed
- 1 teaspoons dried summer savory
- 3/4 teaspoon dried marjoram
- 1/2 teaspoon dried tarragon
- 1/4 teaspoon dried thyme
- 11/2 teaspoons salt
- 2 teaspoons SAF yeast or 21/2 teaspoons bread machine yeast
- 16 slices (2 pounds)
- 12/3 cups water
- 21/2 tablespoons olive oil
- 1/4 cup wildflower honey
- 23/4 cups bread flour
- 11/4 cups whole wheat flour
- 1/4 cup light brown sugar
- 1/4 cup nonfat dry milk
- 1 tablespoon plus 1 teaspoon gluten
- 2 tablespoons minced fresh parsley
- 2 teaspoons dried basil
- 11/4 teaspoons dried dill weed
- 11/4 teaspoons dried summer savory
- 1 teaspoon dried marjoram
- 3/4 teaspoon dried tarragon
- 1/3 teaspoon dried thyme
- 2 teaspoons salt
- 21/4 teaspoons SAF yeast or 23/4 teaspoons bread machine yeast

Directions:

1. Choose the size of loaf you would like to make and measure your ingredients.
2. Add the ingredients to the bread pan in the order listed above.
3. Place the pan in the bread machine and close the lid.
4. Turn on the bread maker. Select the Basic setting, then the loaf size, and finally the crust color. Start the cycle.
5. When the cycle is finished and the bread is baked, carefully remove the pan from the machine. Use a potholder as the handle will be very hot. Let rest for a few minutes.
6. Remove the bread from the pan and allow to cool on a wire rack for at least 10 minutes before slicing.

Inspiring Cinnamon Bread

Ingredients:

- 8 slices (1 pound)
- ⅔ cup milk at 80 degrees F
- 1 whole egg, beaten
- 3 tablespoons melted butter, cooled
- ⅓ cup sugar
- ⅓ teaspoon salt
- 1 teaspoon ground cinnamon
- 2 cups white bread flour
- 1⅓ teaspoons active dry yeast
- 12 slices (1 ½ pounds)
- 1 cup milk at 80 degrees F
- 1 1/2 whole eggs, beaten
- 4 1/2 tablespoons melted butter, cooled
- 1/2 cup sugar
- 1/2 teaspoon salt
- 1 1/2 teaspoons ground cinnamon
- 3 cups white bread flour
- 2 teaspoons active dry yeast
- 16 slices (2 pounds)
- 1 1/3 cups milk at 80 degrees F
- 2 whole eggs, beaten
- 6 tablespoons melted butter, cooled
- 2/3 cup sugar
- 2/3 teaspoon salt
- 2 teaspoons ground cinnamon
- 4 cups white bread flour

- 2 2/3 teaspoons active dry yeast

Directions:

1. Choose the size of loaf you would like to make and measure your ingredients.

2. Add the ingredients to the bread pan in the order listed above.

3. Place the pan in the bread machine and close the lid.

4. Turn on the bread maker. Select the White/Basic setting, then the loaf size, and finally the crust color. Start the cycle.

5. When the cycle is finished and the bread is baked, carefully remove the pan from the machine. Use a potholder as the handle will be very hot. Let rest for a few minutes.

6. Remove the bread from the pan and allow to cool on a wire rack for at least 10 minutes before slicing.

Lemon Flavored Poppy Loaf

Ingredients:

- 8 slices (1 pound)
- 1 and 1/3 cups hot water
- 3 tablespoons powdered milk
- 2 tablespoons Crisco shortening
- 2 tablespoons sugar
- 1½ teaspoon salt
- 1 tablespoon lemon juice
- 4¼ cups bread flour
- ½ teaspoon nutmeg
- 2 teaspoons grated lemon rind
- 2 tablespoons poppy seeds
- 1¼ teaspoon bread machine yeast
- 2 teaspoons wheat gluten
- 12 slices (1 ½ pounds)
- 1 1/2 and 1/2 cups hot water
- 4 1/2 tablespoons powdered milk
- 3 tablespoons Crisco shortening
- 3 tablespoons sugar
- 2 1/4 teaspoons salt
- 1 1/2 tablespoons lemon juice
- 6 3/8 cups bread flour
- 3/4 teaspoon nutmeg
- 3 teaspoons grated lemon rind
- 3 tablespoons poppy seeds

- 1 7/8 teaspoons bread machine yeast
- 3 teaspoons wheat gluten
- 16 slices (2 pounds)
- 2 and 2/3 cups hot water
- 6 tablespoons powdered milk
- 4 tablespoons Crisco shortening
- 4 tablespoons sugar
- 3 teaspoons salt
- 2 tablespoons lemon juice
- 8 1/2 cups bread flour
- 1 teaspoon nutmeg
- 4 teaspoons grated lemon rind
- 4 tablespoons poppy seeds
- 8 1/2 teaspoons bread machine yeast
- 4 teaspoons wheat gluten

Directions:

1. Choose the size of loaf you would like to make and measure your ingredients.

2. Add the ingredients to the bread pan in the order listed above.

3. Place the pan in the bread machine and close the lid.

4. Turn on the bread maker. Select the White/Basic setting, then the loaf size, and finally the crust color. Start the cycle.

5. When the cycle is finished and the bread is baked, carefully remove the pan from the machine. Use a potholder as the handle will be very hot. Let rest for a few minutes.

6. Remove the bread from the pan and allow to cool on a wire rack for at least 10 minutes before slicing.

Spice Pumpkin Bread

Ingredients:

- 8 slices (1 pound)
- Butter for grease
- 1½ cups pumpkin puree
- 3 whole eggs
- 1/3 cup butter, melted
- 1 cup sugar
- 3 cups all-purpose flour
- 1½ teaspoons baking powder
- ¾ teaspoon ground cinnamon
- ½ teaspoon baking soda

- ¼ teaspoon ground nutmeg
- ¼ teaspoon ground ginger
- ¼ teaspoon salt
- Pinch of ground cloves
- 12 slices (1 ½ pounds)
- Butter for grease
- 2 1/4 cups pumpkin puree
- 4 1/2 whole eggs
- 1/2 cup butter, melted
- 1 1/2 cups sugar
- 4 1/2 cups all-purpose flour
- 2 1/4 teaspoons baking powder
- 1 1/8 teaspoons ground cinnamon
- 3/4 teaspoon baking soda
- 3/8 teaspoon ground nutmeg
- 3/8 teaspoon ground ginger
- 3/8 teaspoon salt
- Pinch of ground cloves
- 16 slices (2 pounds)
- Butter for grease
- 3 cups pumpkin puree
- 6 whole eggs
- 2/3 cup butter, melted
- 2 cups sugar
- 6 cups all-purpose flour
- 3 teaspoons baking powder
- 1 1/2 teaspoons ground cinnamon
- 2 teaspoons baking soda
- 1/2 teaspoon ground nutmeg
- 1/2 teaspoon ground ginger
- 1/2 teaspoon salt
- Pinch of ground cloves

Directions:

1. Choose the size of loaf you would like to make and measure your ingredients.
2. Grease the bread pan with butter.
3. Add pumpkin, eggs, butter, and sugar to the bread pan.
4. Place the pan in the bread machine and close the lid.
5. Turn on the bread maker. Select the Quick/Rapid Bread setting, then the loaf size, and finally the crust color. Start the cycle.

6. Take a bowl, add flour, baking powder, cinnamon, baking soda, nutmeg, ginger, salt, cloves, and add the mixture to the machine once the machine beeps.
7. When the cycle is finished and the bread is baked, carefully remove the pan from the machine. Use a potholder as the handle will be very hot. Let rest for a few minutes.
8. Remove the bread from the pan and allow to cool on a wire rack for at least 10 minutes before slicing.

Cardamom Honey Bread

Ingredients:

- 8 slices (1 pound)
- 9/16 cup lukewarm milk
- 1/2 egg, at room temperature
- 1 teaspoon unsalted butter, melted
- 1/8 cup honey
- 2/3 teaspoon table salt
- 2 cups white bread flour
- 2/3 teaspoon ground cardamom
- 5/6 teaspoon bread machine yeast
- 12 slices (1 ½ pounds)
- ¾ cup lukewarm milk
- 1 egg, at room temperature
- 1½ teaspoons unsalted butter, melted
- 3 tablespoons honey
- 1 teaspoon table salt
- 3 cups white bread flour
- 1 teaspoon ground cardamom
- 1¼ teaspoons bread machine yeast
- 16 slices (2 pounds)
- 1⅛ cups lukewarm milk
- 1 egg, at room temperature
- 2 teaspoons unsalted butter, melted
- ¼ cup honey
- 1⅓ teaspoons table salt
- 4 cups white bread flour
- 1⅓ teaspoons ground cardamom
- 1⅔ teaspoons bread machine yeast

Directions:

1. Choose the size of loaf you would like to make and measure your ingredients.

2. Add the ingredients to the bread pan in the order listed above.

3. Place the pan in the bread machine and close the lid.

4. Turn on the bread maker. Select the White/Basic setting, then the loaf size, and finally the crust color. Start the cycle.

5. When the cycle is finished and the bread is baked, carefully remove the pan from the machine. Use a potholder as the handle will be very hot. Let rest for a few minutes.

6. Remove the bread from the pan and allow to cool on a wire rack for at least 10 minutes before slicing.

VEGETABLE BREAD RECIPES

Carrot Bread With Crystallized Ginger

Ingredients:
- 8 slices (1 pound)
- 1/8 cup fat-free milk
- One 3-ounce jar junior baby food strained carrots or 3/8 cup pureed carrots
- 1 large eggs
- 1 1/2 tablespoons unsalted butter, cut into pieces
- 2 cups bread flour
- 1/6 cup chopped crystallized ginger
- 1/2 tablespoon plus 1/2 teaspoon gluten
- 1 teaspoon salt
- 1 teaspoon SAF yeast or 1 1/4 teaspoons bread machine yeast
- 12 slices (1½ pounds)
- 3 tablespoons fat-free milk
- One 6-ounce jar junior baby food strained carrots or 3/4 cup pureed carrots
- 2 large eggs
- 2 tablespoons unsalted butter, cut into pieces
- 3 cups bread flour
- 1/4 cup chopped crystallized ginger
- 1 tablespoon gluten
- 11/2 teaspoons salt
- 13/4 teaspoons SAF yeast or 21/4 teaspoons bread machine yeast
- 16 slices (2 pounds)
- 1/4 cup fat-free milk
- One 6-ounce jar junior baby food strained carrots or 3/4 cup pureed carrots
- 2 large eggs
- 3 tablespoons unsalted butter, cut into pieces
- 4 cups bread flour
- 1/3 cup chopped crystallized ginger
- 1 tablespoon plus 1 teaspoon gluten
- 2 teaspoons salt
- 2 teaspoons SAF yeast or 21/2 teaspoons bread machine yeast

Directions:

1. Choose the size of loaf you would like to make and measure your ingredients.
2. Add the ingredients to the bread pan in the order listed above.
3. Place the pan in the bread machine and close the lid.
4. Turn on the bread maker. Select the Basic setting, then the loaf size, and finally the crust color. Start the cycle.
5. When the cycle is finished and the bread is baked, carefully remove the pan from the machine. Use a potholder as the handle will be very hot. Let rest for a few minutes.
6. Remove the bread from the pan and allow to cool on a wire rack for at least 10 minutes before slicing.

Caraway Potato Bread

Ingredients:
- 8 slices (1 pound)
- 1¼ cups water
- 2 tablespoons butter, at room temperature
- 3 cups bread flour
- 2 teaspoons caraway seeds
- ½ cup instant mashed potatoes
- 1 tablespoon white sugar
- 1½ teaspoon salt
- 2 teaspoons bread machine yeast
- 12 slices (1 ½ pounds)
- 1 7/8 cups water
- 3 tablespoons butter, at room temperature
- 4 1/2 cups bread flour
- 3 teaspoons caraway seeds
- 3/4 cup instant mashed potatoes
- 1 1/2 tablespoons white sugar
- 2 1/4 teaspoons salt
- 3 teaspoons bread machine yeast
- 16 slices (2 pounds)
- 2 1/2 cups water
- 4 tablespoons butter, at room temperature
- 6 cups bread flour
- 4 teaspoons caraway seeds
- 1 cup instant mashed potatoes

- 2 tablespoons white sugar
- 3 teaspoons salt
- 4 teaspoons bread machine yeast

Directions:

1. Choose the size of loaf you would like to make and measure your ingredients.

2. Add the ingredients to the bread pan in the order listed above.

3. Place the pan in the bread machine and close the lid.

4. Turn on the bread maker. Select the White/Basic setting, then the loaf size, and finally the crust color. Start the cycle.

5. When the cycle is finished and the bread is baked, carefully remove the pan from the machine. Use a potholder as the handle will be very hot. Let rest for a few minutes.

6. Remove the bread from the pan and allow to cool on a wire rack for at least 10 minutes before slicing.

Spicy Hot Red Pepper Bread

Ingredients:

- 8 slices (1 pound)
- ¾ cup + 1 tablespoons milk at room temperature
- 2 and 2/3 tablespoons red pepper relish
- 4 teaspoons chopped roasted red pepper
- 2 tablespoons melted butter, cooled
- 2 tablespoons light brown sugar
- 2/3 teaspoon salt
- 2 cups white bread flour
- 1 teaspoon bread machine yeast
- 12 slices (1 ½ pounds)
- 1 1/8 cups + 1 1/2 tablespoons milk at room temperature
- 3 and 1 tablespoons red pepper relish
- 6 teaspoons chopped roasted red pepper
- 3 tablespoons melted butter, cooled
- 3 tablespoons light brown sugar
- 1 teaspoon salt
- 3 cups white bread flour
- 1 1/2 teaspoons bread machine yeast
- 16 slices (2 pounds)
- 1 1/2 cups + 2 tablespoons milk at room temperature
- 4 and 1 1/3 tablespoons red pepper relish

- 8 teaspoons chopped roasted red pepper
- 4 tablespoons melted butter, cooled
- 4 tablespoons light brown sugar
- 1 1/3 teaspoons salt
- 4 cups white bread flour
- 2 teaspoons bread machine yeast

Directions:

1. Choose the size of loaf you would like to make and measure your ingredients.

2. Add the ingredients to the bread pan in the order listed above.

3. Place the pan in the bread machine and close the lid.

4. Turn on the bread maker. Select the White/Basic setting, then the loaf size, and finally the crust color. Start the cycle.

5. When the cycle is finished and the bread is baked, carefully remove the pan from the machine. Use a potholder as the handle will be very hot. Let rest for a few minutes.

6. Remove the bread from the pan and allow to cool on a wire rack for at least 10 minutes before slicing.

Zucchini Herbed Bread

Ingredients:

- 8 slices (1 pound)
- ½ cup water
- 2 teaspoon honey
- 1 tablespoons oil
- ¾ cup zucchini, grated
- ¾ cup whole wheat flour
- 2 cups bread flour
- 1 tablespoon fresh basil, chopped
- 2 teaspoon sesame seeds
- 1 teaspoon salt
- 1½ teaspoon active dry yeast
- 12 slices (1 ½ pounds)
- 3/4 cup water
- 3 teaspoons honey
- 1 1/2 tablespoons oil
- 1 1/8 cups zucchini, grated
- 1 1/8 cups whole wheat flour
- 3 cups bread flour
- 1 1/2 tablespoons fresh basil, chopped

- 3 teaspoons sesame seeds
- 1 1/2 teaspoons salt
- 2 1/4 teaspoons active dry yeast
- 16 slices (2 pounds)
- 1 cup water
- 4 teaspoons honey
- 2 tablespoons oil
- 1 1/2 cups zucchini, grated
- 1 1/2 cups whole wheat flour
- 4 cups bread flour
- 2 tablespoons fresh basil, chopped
- 4 teaspoons sesame seeds
- 2 teaspoons salt
- 3 teaspoons active dry yeast

Directions:

1. Choose the size of loaf you would like to make and measure your ingredients.
2. Add the ingredients to the bread pan in the order listed above.
3. Place the pan in the bread machine and close the lid.
4. Turn on the bread maker. Select the White/Basic setting, then the loaf size, and finally the crust color. Start the cycle.
5. When the cycle is finished and the bread is baked, carefully remove the pan from the machine. Use a potholder as the handle will be very hot. Let rest for a few minutes.
6. Remove the bread from the pan and allow to cool on a wire rack for at least 10 minutes before slicing.

Pain D'ail

Ingredients:

- 8 slices (1 pound)
- 2 cloves garlic
- 1 1/2 tablespoons unsalted butter, softened
- 3/4 cup water
- 2 cups bread flour
- 1/2 tablespoon plus 1/2 teaspoon gluten
- 3/4 tablespoon sugar
- 7/8 teaspoon salt
- 1 1/4 teaspoons SAF yeast or 1/2 tablespoon bread machine yeast
- 12 slices (1½ pounds)

- 3 cloves garlic
- 2 tablespoons unsalted butter, softened
- 11/4 cups water
- 31/8 cups bread flour
- 1 tablespoon gluten
- 1 tablespoon sugar
- 11/2 teaspoons salt
- 2 teaspoons SAF yeast or 21/2 teaspoons bread machine yeast
- 16 slices (2 pounds)
- 4 cloves garlic
- 3 tablespoons unsalted butter, softened
- 11/2 cups water
- 4 cups bread flour
- 1 tablespoon plus 1 teaspoon gluten
- 11/2 tablespoons sugar
- 13/4 teaspoons salt
- 21/2 teaspoons SAF yeast or 1 tablespoon bread machine yeast

Directions:

1. Choose the size of loaf you would like to make and measure your ingredients.
2. Peel the garlic cloves and press into the butter. Mash together.
3. Add the ingredients to the bread pan in the order listed above.
4. Add the garlic butter with the liquid ingredients.
5. Place the pan in the bread machine and close the lid.
6. Turn on the bread maker. Select the French setting, then the loaf size, and finally the crust color. Start the cycle.
7. When the cycle is finished and the bread is baked, carefully remove the pan from the machine. Use a potholder as the handle will be very hot. Let rest for a few minutes.
8. Remove the bread from the pan and allow to cool on a wire rack for at least 10 minutes before slicing.

Cornmeal Stuffing Bread

Ingredients:

- 8 slices (1 pound)
- One 5 1/2-ounce can of corn with liquid
- 1/6 cup buttermilk

- 1 1/2 tablespoons canola or olive oil
- 1 1/2 tablespoons honey
- 1 3/8 cups bread flour
- 5/8 cup yellow cornmeal
- 1/6 cup minced fresh parsley
- 7/8 tablespoon poultry seasoning
- 3/8 teaspoon garlic powder
- 1/2 tablespoon plus 1 teaspoons gluten
- 3/4 teaspoon salt
- 1 1/4 teaspoons SAF yeast or 1/2 tablespoon bread machine yeast
- 12 slices (1½ pounds)
- One 11-ounce can of corn with liquid
- 1/4 cup buttermilk
- 2 tablespoons canola or olive oil
- 2 tablespoons honey
- 2 cups bread flour
- 1 cup yellow cornmeal
- 1/4 cup minced fresh parsley
- 11/2 tablespoons poultry seasoning
- 1/2 teaspoon garlic powder
- 1 tablespoon plus 1 teaspoon gluten
- 11/4 teaspoons salt
- 2 teaspoons SAF yeast or 21/2 teaspoons bread machine yeast
- 16 slices (2 pounds)
- One 11-ounce can of corn with liquid
- 1/3 cup buttermilk
- 3 tablespoons canola or olive oil
- 3 tablespoons honey
- 23/4 cups bread flour
- 11/4 cups yellow cornmeal
- 1/3 cup minced fresh parsley
- 13/4 tablespoons poultry seasoning
- 3/4 teaspoon garlic powder
- 1 tablespoon plus 2 teaspoons gluten
- 11/2 teaspoons salt
- 21/2 teaspoons SAF yeast or 1 tablespoon bread machine yeast

Directions:

1. Choose the size of loaf you would like to make and measure your ingredients.

2. Add the ingredients to the bread pan in the order listed above.

3. Place the pan in the bread machine and close the lid.

4. Turn on the bread maker. Select the Basic setting, then the loaf size, and finally the crust color. Start the cycle.

5. When the cycle is finished and the bread is baked, carefully remove the pan from the machine. Use a potholder as the handle will be very hot. Let rest for a few minutes.

6. Remove the bread from the pan and allow to cool on a wire rack for at least 10 minutes before slicing.

Prosciutto Stuffing Bread

Ingredients:

- 8 slices (1 pound)
- 5/8 cup water
- 1/6 cup olive oil
- 2 cups bread flour
- 2 ounces prosciutto, coarsely chopped
- 1/2 tablespoon plus 1/2 teaspoon gluten
- 1/2 tablespoon plus 1/2 teaspoon sugar
- 5/8 teaspoon ground black pepper
- 3/8 teaspoon salt
- 1 teaspoon SAF yeast or 1 1/4 teaspoons bread machine yeast
- 12 slices (1½ pounds)
- 7/8 cup water
- 1/4 cup olive oil
- 3 cups bread flour
- 3 ounces prosciutto, coarsely chopped
- 1 tablespoon gluten
- 1 tablespoon sugar
- 1 teaspoon ground black pepper
- 1/2 teaspoon salt
- 11/2 teaspoons SAF yeast or 2 teaspoons bread machine yeast
- 16 slices (2 pounds)
- 11/4 cups water
- 1/3 cup olive oil
- 4 cups bread flour
- 4 ounces prosciutto, coarsely chopped
- 1 tablespoon plus 1 teaspoon gluten

- 1 tablespoon plus 1 teaspoon sugar
- 11/4 teaspoons ground black pepper
- 3/4 teaspoon salt
- 2 teaspoons SAF yeast or 21/2 teaspoons bread machine yeast

Directions:

1. Choose the size of loaf you would like to make and measure your ingredients.
2. Add the ingredients to the bread pan in the order listed above.
3. Place the pan in the bread machine and close the lid.
4. Turn on the bread maker. Select the Basic setting, then the loaf size, and finally the crust color. Start the cycle.
5. When the cycle is finished and the bread is baked, carefully remove the pan from the machine. Use a potholder as the handle will be very hot. Let rest for a few minutes.
6. Remove the bread from the pan and allow to cool on a wire rack for at least 10 minutes before slicing.

Zucchini Spice Bread

Ingredients:
- 8 slices (1 pound)
- 1 eggs, at room temperature
- 1/3 cup unsalted butter, melted
- 1/3 teaspoon table salt
- 1/2 cup shredded zucchini
- 1/3 cup light brown sugar
- 1 1/2tablespoons sugar
- 1 cups all-purpose flour
- 1/3 teaspoon baking powder
- 1/3 teaspoon baking soda
- 1/6 teaspoon ground allspice
- 2/3 teaspoons ground cinnamon
- 1/3 cup chopped pecans
- 12 slices (1 ½ pounds)
- 2 eggs, at room temperature
- ½ cup unsalted butter, melted
- ½ teaspoon table salt
- ¾ cup shredded zucchini
- ½ cup light brown sugar
- 2 tablespoons sugar

- 1½ cups all-purpose flour
- ½ teaspoon baking powder
- ½ teaspoon baking soda
- ¼ teaspoon ground allspice
- 1 teaspoon ground cinnamon
- ½ cup chopped pecans
- 16 slices (2 pounds)
- 2 eggs, at room temperature
- ⅔ cup unsalted butter, melted
- ⅔ teaspoon table salt
- 1 cup shredded zucchini
- ⅔ cup light brown sugar
- 3 tablespoons sugar
- 2 cups all-purpose flour
- ⅔ teaspoon baking powder
- ⅔ teaspoon baking soda
- ⅓ teaspoon ground allspice
- 1⅓ teaspoons ground cinnamon
- ⅔ cup chopped pecans

Directions:

1. Choose the size of loaf you would like to make and measure your ingredients.
2. Add the ingredients to the bread pan in the order listed above.
3. Place the pan in the bread machine and close the lid.
4. Turn on the bread maker. Select the Quick/Rapid setting, then the loaf size, and finally the crust color. Start the cycle.
5. When the cycle is finished and the bread is baked, carefully remove the pan from the machine. Use a potholder as the handle will be very hot. Let rest for a few minutes.
6. Remove the bread from the pan and allow to cool down on a wire rack for at least 10 minutes or more before slicing.

Fresh Herb And Nut Stuffing Bread

Ingredients:
- 8 slices (1 pound)
- 3/4 cup plus 1/2 tablespoon water
- 1 tablespoon walnut oil
- 2 cups bread flour
- 3/4 tablespoon light brown sugar

- 3/8 cup mixed fresh herbs, minced
- 1/6 cup walnuts
- 1/2 tablespoon plus 1/2 teaspoon gluten
- 1 teaspoon salt
- 1 1/4 teaspoons SAF yeast or 1/2 tablespoon bread machine yeast
- 12 slices (1½ pounds)
- 1 cup plus 3 tablespoons water
- 11/2 tablespoons walnut oil
- 3 cups bread flour
- 1 tablespoon light brown sugar
- 1/2 cup mixed fresh herbs, minced
- 1/4 cup walnuts
- 1 tablespoon gluten
- 11/2 teaspoons salt
- 2 teaspoons SAF yeast or 21/2 teaspoons bread machine yeast
- 16 slices (2 pounds)
- 11/2 cups plus 1 tablespoon water
- 2 tablespoons walnut oil
- 4 cups bread flour
- 11/2 tablespoons light brown sugar
- 3/4 cup mixed fresh herbs, minced
- 1/3 cup walnuts
- 1 tablespoon plus 1 teaspoon gluten
- 2 teaspoons salt
- 21/2 teaspoons SAF yeast or 1 tablespoon bread machine yeast

Directions:

1. Choose the size of loaf you would like to make and measure your ingredients.

2. Add the ingredients to the bread pan in the order listed above.

3. Place the pan in the bread machine and close the lid.

4. Turn on the bread maker. Select the Basic setting, then the loaf size, and finally the crust color. Start the cycle.

5. When the cycle is finished and the bread is baked, carefully remove the pan from the machine. Use a potholder as the handle will be very hot. Let rest for a few minutes.

6. Remove the bread from the pan and allow to cool on a wire rack for at least 10 minutes before slicing.

Zucchini Bread

Ingredients:

- 8 slices (1 pound)
- 2 large eggs
- 1/2 cup vegetable oil
- 11/2 teaspoons vanilla extract
- 1 cup sugar
- 11/4 cups lightly packed shredded zucchini (about 2 medium)
- 11/2 cups unbleached all-purpose flour
- 1 teaspoon baking soda
- 3/4 teaspoon baking powder
- 11/4 teaspoons ground cinnamon or apple pie spice
- 1/4 teaspoon salt
- 1/2 cup coarsely chopped walnuts
- 12 slices (1 ½ pounds)
- 3 large eggs
- 3/4 cup vegetable oil
- 2 1/4 teaspoons vanilla extract
- 1 1/2 cups sugar
- 1 7/8 cups lightly packed shredded zucchini (about 2 medium)
- 2 1/4 cups unbleached all-purpose flour
- 1 1/2 teaspoons baking soda
- 1 1/8 teaspoons baking powder
- 1 7/8 teaspoons ground cinnamon or apple pie spice
- 3/8 teaspoon salt
- 3/4 cup coarsely chopped walnuts
- 16 slices (2 pounds)
- 4 large eggs
- 1 cup vegetable oil
- 3 teaspoons vanilla extract
- 2 cups sugar
- 2 1/2 cups lightly packed shredded zucchini (about 2 medium)
- 3 cups unbleached all-purpose flour
- 2 teaspoons baking soda
- 1 1/2 teaspoons baking powder
- 2 1/2 teaspoons ground cinnamon or apple pie spice
- 1/2 teaspoon salt
- 1 cup coarsely chopped walnuts

Directions:

1. Choose the size of loaf you would like to make and measure your ingredients.

2. Add the ingredients to the bread pan in the order listed above.

3. Place the pan in the bread machine and close the lid.

4. Turn on the bread maker. Select the Quick Bread/Cake setting, then the loaf size, and finally the crust color. Start the cycle.

5. When the cycle is finished and the bread is baked, carefully remove the pan from the machine. Use a potholder as the handle will be very hot. Let rest for a few minutes.

6. Remove the bread from the pan and allow to cool on a wire rack for at least 10 minutes before slicing.

Pumpkin Coconut Almond Bread

Ingredients:
- 8 slices (1 pound)
- 1/4 cup vegetable oil
- 2 large eggs
- 1 cups canned pumpkin puree
- 2/3 cup sugar
- 1 teaspoons baking powder
- 1/3 teaspoon baking soda
- 1/6 teaspoon salt
- 2/3 tablespoon allspice
- 2 cups all-purpose flour
- 1/3 cup coconut flakes, plus a small handful for the topping
- 1/2 cup slivered almonds, plus a tablespoonful for the topping
- Non-stick cooking spray
- 12 slices (1 ½ pounds)
- 1/3 cup vegetable oil
- 3 large eggs
- 1 1/2 cups canned pumpkin puree
- 1 cup sugar
- 1 1/2 teaspoons baking powder
- 1/2 teaspoon baking soda
- 1/4 teaspoon salt
- 1 tablespoon allspice
- 3 cups all-purpose flour
- 1/2 cup coconut flakes, plus a small handful for the topping
- 2/3 cup slivered almonds, plus a tablespoonful for the topping
- Non-stick cooking spray
- 16 slices (2 pounds)
- 1/2 cup vegetable oil
- 4 large eggs
- 2 cups canned pumpkin puree
- 1 1/3 cups sugar
- 1 teaspoon baking powder
- 2/3 teaspoon baking soda
- 1/3 teaspoon salt
- 1 1/3 tablespoons allspice
- 4 cups all-purpose flour
- 2/3 cup coconut flakes, plus a small handful for the topping
- 1 cup slivered almonds, plus a tablespoonful for the topping
- Non-stick cooking spray

Directions:
1. Choose the size of loaf you would like to make and measure your ingredients.

2. Spray bread maker pan with non-stick cooking spray.

3. Mix oil, eggs, and pumpkin in a large mixing bowl.

4. Mix remaining ingredients together in a separate mixing bowl.

5. Add wet ingredients to bread pan, and dry ingredients on top.

6. Place the pan in the bread machine and close the lid.

7. Turn on the bread maker. Select the Dough/Rapid setting, then the loaf size, and finally the crust color. Start the cycle.

8. Open lid and sprinkle top of bread with reserved coconut and almonds.

9. When the cycle is finished and the bread is baked, carefully remove the pan from the machine. Use a potholder as the handle will be very hot. Let rest for a few minutes.

10. Remove the bread from the pan and allow to cool on a wire rack for at least 10 minutes before slicing.

Honey Potato Flakes Bread

Ingredients:

- 8 slices (1 pound)
- 5/6 cup lukewarm milk
- 1 1/3 tablespoons unsalted butter, melted
- 2 teaspoons honey
- 1 teaspoon table salt
- 2 cups white bread flour
- 3/4 teaspoon dried thyme
- 1/3 cup instant potato flakes
- 1 1/4 teaspoons bread machine yeast
- 12 slices (1 ½ pounds)
- 1¼ cups lukewarm milk
- 2 tablespoons unsalted butter, melted
- 1 tablespoon honey
- 1½ teaspoons table salt
- 3 cups white bread flour
- 1 teaspoon dried thyme
- ½ cup instant potato flakes
- 2 teaspoons bread machine yeast
- 16 slices (2 pounds)
- 1⅔ cups lukewarm milk
- 2⅔ tablespoons unsalted butter, melted
- 4 teaspoons honey
- 2 teaspoons table salt
- 4 cups white bread flour
- 1½ teaspoons dried thyme
- ⅔ cup instant potato flakes
- 2½ teaspoons bread machine yeast

Directions:

1. Choose the size of loaf you would like to make and measure your ingredients.

2. Add the ingredients to the bread pan in the order listed above.

3. Place the pan in the bread machine and close the lid.

4. Turn on the bread maker. Select the White/Basic setting, then the loaf size, and finally the crust color. Start the cycle.

5. When the cycle is finished and the bread is baked, carefully remove the pan from the machine. Use a potholder as the handle will be very hot. Let rest for a few minutes.

6. Remove the bread from the pan and allow to cool on a wire rack for at least 10 minutes before slicing.

Veggie Bread

Ingredients:

- 8 slices (1 pound)
- ½ cup warm buttermilk
- 3 tablespoons water, at room temperature
- 1 tablespoon canola oil
- 2/3 cup zucchini, shredded
- 2 tablespoons green onions, chopped
- ¼ cup red bell pepper, chopped
- 2 tablespoons Parmesan cheese, grated
- 2 tablespoons sugar
- 1 teaspoon salt
- ½ teaspoon lemon-pepper seasoning
- ½ cup old fashioned oats
- 2½ cups bread flour
- 1½ teaspoon dry yeast
- 12 slices (1 ½ pounds)
- 3/4 cup warm buttermilk
- 4 1/2 tablespoons water, at room temperature
- 1 1/2 tablespoons canola oil
- 1 cup zucchini, shredded
- 3 tablespoons green onions, chopped
- 3/8 cup red bell pepper, chopped
- 3 tablespoons Parmesan cheese, grated
- 3 tablespoons sugar
- 1 1/2 teaspoons salt
- 3/4 teaspoon lemon-pepper seasoning
- 3/4 cup old fashioned oats
- 3 3/4 cups bread flour
- 2 1/4 teaspoons dry yeast
- 16 slices (2 pounds)
- 1 cup warm buttermilk
- 6 tablespoons water, at room temperature
- 2 tablespoons canola oil
- 1 1/3 cups zucchini, shredded
- 4 tablespoons green onions, chopped
- 1/2 cup red bell pepper, chopped
- 4 tablespoons Parmesan cheese, grated
- 4 tablespoons sugar
- 2 teaspoons salt

- 1 teaspoon lemon-pepper seasoning
- 1 cup old fashioned oats
- 5 cups bread flour
- 3 teaspoons dry yeast

Directions:

1. Choose the size of loaf you would like to make and measure your ingredients.

2. Add the ingredients to the bread pan in the order listed above.

3. Place the pan in the bread machine and close the lid.

4. Turn on the bread maker. Select the White/Basic setting, then the loaf size, and finally the crust color. Start the cycle.

5. When the cycle is finished and the bread is baked, carefully remove the pan from the machine. Use a potholder as the handle will be very hot. Let rest for a few minutes.

6. Remove the bread from the pan and allow to cool on a wire rack for at least 10 minutes before slicing.

Onion Chive Bread

Ingredients:
- 8 slices (1 pound)
- 5/8 cup lukewarm water
- 1/8 cup unsalted butter, melted
- 1 tablespoon sugar
- 3/4 teaspoon table salt
- 2 1/8 cups white bread flour
- 1/8 cup dried minced onion
- 1 tablespoon fresh chives, chopped
- 1 1/8 teaspoons bread machine yeast
- 12 slices (1 ½ pounds)
- 1 cup lukewarm water
- 3 tablespoons unsalted butter, melted
- 1½ tablespoons sugar
- 1⅛ teaspoons table salt
- 3⅛ cups white bread flour
- 3 tablespoons dried minced onion
- 1½ tablespoons fresh chives, chopped
- 1⅔ teaspoons bread machine yeast
- 16 slices (2 pounds)
- 1¼ cups lukewarm water
- ¼ cup unsalted butter, melted

- 2 tablespoons sugar
- 1½ teaspoons table salt
- 4¼ cups white bread flour
- ¼ cup dried minced onion
- 2 tablespoons fresh chives, chopped
- 2¼ teaspoons bread machine yeast

Directions:

1. Choose the size of loaf you would like to make and measure your ingredients.

2. Add the ingredients to the bread pan in the order listed above.

3. Place the pan in the bread machine and close the lid.

4. Turn on the bread maker. Select the White/Basic setting, then the loaf size, and finally the crust color. Start the cycle.

5. When the cycle is finished and the bread is baked, carefully remove the pan from the machine. Use a potholder as the handle will be very hot. Let rest for a few minutes.

6. Remove the bread from the pan and allow to cool on a wire rack for at least 10 minutes before slicing.

Beetroot Bread

Ingredients:
- 8 slices (1 pound)
- 1/2 cup lukewarm water
- 1/2 cup grated raw beetroot
- 1 tablespoon unsalted butter, melted
- 1 tablespoon sugar
- 1 teaspoon table salt
- 2 cups white bread flour
- 5/6 teaspoon bread machine yeast
- 12 slices (1 ½ pounds)
- ¾ cups lukewarm water
- ¾ cup grated raw beetroot
- 1½ tablespoons unsalted butter, melted
- 1½ tablespoons sugar
- 1¼ teaspoons table salt
- 3 cups white bread flour
- 1¼ teaspoons bread machine yeast
- 16 slices (2 pounds)
- 1 cup lukewarm water
- 1 cup grated raw beetroot

- 2 tablespoons unsalted butter, melted
- 2 tablespoons sugar
- 2 teaspoons table salt
- 4 cups white bread flour
- 1⅔ teaspoons bread machine yeast

Directions:

1. Choose the size of loaf you would like to make and measure your ingredients.

2. Add the ingredients to the bread pan in the order listed above.

3. Place the pan in the bread machine and close the lid.

4. Turn on the bread maker. Select the White/Basic setting, then the loaf size, and finally the crust color. Start the cycle.

5. When the cycle is finished and the bread is baked, carefully remove the pan from the machine. Use a potholder as the handle will be very hot. Let rest for a few minutes.

6. Remove the bread from the pan and allow to cool on a wire rack for at least 10 minutes before slicing.

Zucchini Lemon Bread

Ingredients:

- 8 slices (1 pound)
- 1/3 cup lukewarm milk
- 1/2 cup finely shredded zucchini
- 1/6 teaspoon lemon juice, at room temperature
- 2 teaspoons olive oil
- 2 teaspoons sugar
- 2/3 teaspoon table salt
- 1/2 cup whole-wheat flour
- 1 cup white bread flour
- 1/2 cup quick oats
- 1 1/8 teaspoons bread machine yeast
- 12 slices (1 ½ pounds)
- ½ cup lukewarm milk
- ¾ cup finely shredded zucchini
- ¼ teaspoon lemon juice, at room temperature
- 1 tablespoon olive oil
- 1 tablespoon sugar
- 1 teaspoon table salt
- ¾ cup whole-wheat flour
- 1½ cups white bread flour

- ¾ cup quick oats
- 2¼ teaspoons bread machine yeast
- 16 slices (2 pounds)
- ⅔ cup lukewarm milk
- 1 cup finely shredded zucchini
- ⅓ teaspoon lemon juice, at room temperature
- 4 teaspoons olive oil
- 4 teaspoons sugar
- 1⅓ teaspoons table salt
- 1 cup whole-wheat flour
- 2 cups white bread flour
- 1 cup quick oats
- 2¼ teaspoons bread machine yeast

Directions:

1. Choose the size of loaf you would like to make and measure your ingredients.

2. Add the ingredients to the bread pan in the order listed above.

3. Place the pan in the bread machine and close the lid.

4. Turn on the bread maker. Select the White/Basic setting, then the loaf size, and finally the crust color. Start the cycle.

5. When the cycle is finished and the bread is baked, carefully remove the pan from the machine. Use a potholder as the handle will be very hot. Let rest for a few minutes.

6. Remove the bread from the pan and allow to cool on a wire rack for at least 10 minutes before slicing.

Sweet Potato Bread

Ingredients:

- 8 slices (1 pound)
- 5/16 cup lukewarm water
- 1/2 cup plain sweet potatoes, peeled and mashed
- 1 tablespoon unsalted butter, melted
- 1/6 cup dark brown sugar
- 3/4 teaspoon table salt
- 2 cups bread flour
- 1/8 teaspoon ground nutmeg
- 1/8 teaspoon cinnamon
- 1/2 teaspoon vanilla extract
- 1 tablespoon dry milk powder
- 1 teaspoon bread machine yeast

- 12 slices (1 ½ pounds)
- ⅓ cup + 2 tablespoons lukewarm water
- ¾ cup plain sweet potatoes, peeled and mashed
- 1½ tablespoons unsalted butter, melted
- ¼ cup dark brown sugar
- 1 teaspoon table salt
- 3 cups bread flour
- ⅛ teaspoon ground nutmeg
- ⅛ teaspoon cinnamon
- ¾ teaspoon vanilla extract
- 1½ tablespoons dry milk powder
- 1½ teaspoons bread machine yeast
- 16 slices (2 pounds)
- ⅝ cup lukewarm water
- 1 cup plain sweet potatoes, peeled and mashed
- 2 tablespoons unsalted butter, melted
- ⅓ cup dark brown sugar
- 1½ teaspoons table salt
- 4 cups bread flour
- ¼ teaspoon ground nutmeg
- ¼ teaspoon cinnamon
- 1 teaspoon vanilla extract
- 2 tablespoons dry milk powder
- 2 teaspoons bread machine yeast

Directions:

1. Choose the size of loaf you would like to make and measure your ingredients.
2. Add the ingredients to the bread pan in the order listed above.
3. Place the pan in the bread machine and close the lid.
4. Turn on the bread maker. Select the White/Basic setting, then the loaf size, and finally the crust color. Start the cycle.
5. When the cycle is finished, and the bread is baked, carefully remove the pan from the machine. Use a potholder as the handle will be very hot. Let rest for a few minutes.
6. Remove the bread from the pan and allow to cool on a wire rack for at least 10 minutes before slicing.

Hot Paprika Onion Bread

Ingredients:

- 8 slices (1 pound)
- 1 cup water at room temperature
- 2 tablespoons butter, soft
- 1/3 cup onion, finely chopped
- 1½ teaspoon salt
- 1 teaspoon sugar
- 1 teaspoon paprika
- 3 cups bread flour
- 1 pack active dry yeast
- 12 slices (1 ½ pounds)
- 1 1/2 cups water at room temperature
- 3 tablespoons butter, soft
- 1/2 cup onion, finely chopped
- 2 1/4 teaspoons salt
- 1 1/2 teaspoons sugar
- 1 1/2 teaspoons paprika
- 4 1/2 cups bread flour
- 1 1/2 packs active dry yeast
- 16 slices (2 pounds)
- 2 cups water at room temperature
- 4 tablespoons butter, soft
- 2/3 cup onion, finely chopped
- 3 teaspoons salt
- 2 teaspoons sugar
- 2 teaspoons paprika
- 6 cups bread flour
- 2 packs active dry yeast

Directions:

1. Choose the size of loaf you would like to make and measure your ingredients.
2. Add the ingredients to the bread pan in the order listed above.
3. Place the pan in the bread machine and close the lid.
4. Turn on the bread maker. Select the White/Basic setting, then the loaf size, and finally the crust color. Start the cycle.
5. When the cycle is finished and the bread is baked, carefully remove the pan from the machine. Use a potholder as the handle will be very hot. Let rest for a few minutes.
6. Remove the bread from the pan and allow to cool on a wire rack for at least 10 minutes before slicing.

Cornbread

Ingredients:

- 8 slices (1 pound)
- 1 large egg
- 11/4 cups buttermilk
- 6 tablespoons unsalted butter, melted
- 1/3 cup sugar
- 1 cup fine-grind yellow cornmeal, preferably stone-ground
- 1 cup unbleached all-purpose flour
- 2 tablespoons toasted wheat germ
- 1 teaspoon baking soda
- 1/2 teaspoon baking powder
- 1/2 teaspoon salt
- 12 slices (1 ½ pounds)
- 1 1/2 large eggs
- 1 7/8 cups buttermilk
- 9 tablespoons unsalted butter, melted
- 1/2 cup sugar
- 1 1/2 cup fine-grind yellow cornmeal, preferably stone-ground
- 1 1/2 cups unbleached all-purpose flour
- 3 tablespoons toasted wheat germ
- 1 1/2 teaspoons baking soda
- 3/4 teaspoon baking powder
- 3/4 teaspoon salt
- 16 slices (2 pounds)
- 2 large eggs
- 2 1/2 cups buttermilk
- 12 tablespoons unsalted butter, melted
- 2/3 cup sugar
- 2 cups fine-grind yellow cornmeal, preferably stone-ground
- 2 cups unbleached all-purpose flour
- 4 tablespoons toasted wheat germ
- 2 teaspoons baking soda
- 1 teaspoon baking powder
- 1 teaspoon salt

Directions:

1. Place the ingredients in the pan according to the order in the manufacturer's instructions. Set the crust for medium, if your machine offers crust control for this cycle, and program for the Quick Bread/Cake cycle; press Start. The batter will be thick. When the machine beeps at the end of the cycle, check the loaf for doneness. The cornbread is done when it shrinks slightly from the sides of the pan, the sides are dark brown, and the top is firm to a gentle pressure when touched with your finger. A toothpick or metal skewer will come out clean when inserted into the center of the bread.

2. When the bread is done baking, immediately remove the pan from the machine. Let the bread stand in the pan for 15 minutes before gently turning it out, right side up, to cool on a rack. Serve warm or at room temperature, the day it is baked, cut into thick slices.

Cheesy Broccoli & Cauliflower Bread

Ingredients:

- 8 slices (1 pound)
- ¼ cup water
- 4 tablespoons olive oil
- 1 egg white
- 1 teaspoon lemon juice
- 2/3 cup grated cheddar cheese
- 3 tablespoons green onion
- ½ cup broccoli, chopped
- ½ cup cauliflower, chopped
- ½ teaspoon lemon pepper seasoning
- 2 cups bread flour
- 1 teaspoon bread machine yeast
- 12 slices (1 ½ pounds)
- 3/8 cup water
- 6 tablespoons olive oil
- 1 1/2 egg whites
- 1 1/2 teaspoons lemon juice
- 1 cup grated cheddar cheese
- 4 1/2 tablespoons green onion
- 3/4 cup broccoli, chopped
- 3/4 cup cauliflower, chopped
- 3/4 teaspoon lemon pepper seasoning
- 3 cups bread flour
- 1 1/2 teaspoons bread machine yeast
- 16 slices (2 pounds)
- 1/2 cup water
- 8 tablespoons olive oil
- 2 egg whites

- 2 teaspoons lemon juice
- 1 1/3 cups grated cheddar cheese
- 6 tablespoons green onion
- 1 cup broccoli, chopped
- 1 cup cauliflower, chopped
- 1 teaspoon lemon pepper seasoning
- 4 cups bread flour
- 2 teaspoons bread machine yeast

Directions:

1. Choose the size of loaf you would like to make and measure your ingredients.

2. Add the ingredients to the bread pan in the order listed above.

3. Place the pan in the bread machine and close the lid.

4. Turn on the bread maker. Select the White/Basic setting, then the loaf size, and finally the crust color. Start the cycle.

5. When the cycle is finished and the bread is baked, carefully remove the pan from the machine. Use a potholder as the handle will be very hot. Let rest for a few minutes.

6. Remove the bread from the pan and allow to cool on a wire rack for at least 10 minutes before slicing.

Celery Bread

Ingredients:
- 8 slices (1 pound)
- 1 can (10 ounces) cream of celery soup
- 3 tablespoons low-fat milk, heated
- 1 tablespoon vegetable oil
- 1¼ teaspoons celery salt
- ¾ cup celery, fresh/sliced thin
- 1 tablespoon celery leaves, fresh, chopped
- 1 whole egg
- ¼ teaspoon sugar
- 3 cups bread flour
- ¼ teaspoon ginger
- ½ cup quick-cooking oats
- 2 tablespoons gluten
- 2 teaspoons celery seeds
- 1 pack of active dry yeast
- 12 slices (1 ½ pounds)
- 1 1/2 cans (15 ounces) cream of celery soup
- 4 1/2 tablespoons low-fat milk, heated
- 1 1/2 tablespoons vegetable oil
- 1 7/8 teaspoons celery salt
- 1 1/8 cups celery, fresh/sliced thin
- 1 1/2 tablespoons celery leaves, fresh, chopped
- 1 1/2 whole eggs
- 3/8 teaspoon sugar
- 4 1/2 cups bread flour
- 3/8 teaspoon ginger
- 3/4 cup quick-cooking oats
- 3 tablespoons gluten
- 3 teaspoons celery seeds
- 1 1/2 pack of active dry yeast
- 16 slices (2 pounds)
- 2 cans (10 ounces) cream of celery soup
- 6 tablespoons low-fat milk, heated
- 2 tablespoons vegetable oil
- 2 1/2 teaspoons celery salt
- 1 1/2 cups celery, fresh/sliced thin
- 2 tablespoons celery leaves, fresh, chopped
- 2 whole eggs
- 1/2 teaspoon sugar
- 6 cups bread flour
- 1/2 teaspoon ginger
- 1 cup quick-cooking oats
- 4 tablespoons gluten
- 4 teaspoons celery seeds
- 2 pack of active dry yeast

Directions:

1. Choose the size of loaf you would like to make and measure your ingredients.

2. Add the ingredients to the bread pan in the order listed above.

3. Place the pan in the bread machine and close the lid.

4. Turn on the bread maker. Select the White/Basic setting, then the loaf size, and finally the crust color. Start the cycle.

5. When the cycle is finished and the bread is baked, carefully remove the pan from the machine. Use a potholder as the handle will be very hot. Let rest for a few minutes.

6. Remove the bread from the pan and allow to cool on a wire rack for at least 10 minutes before slicing.

Italian Onion Bread

Ingredients:

- 8 slices (1 pound)
- 1 cup warm milk, at room temperature
- 1 large whole egg
- 2 tablespoons butter, soft
- ¼ cup dried onion, minced
- 1½ teaspoons salt
- 2 tablespoons dried parsley flakes
- 1 teaspoon dried oregano
- 3½ cups bread flour
- 2 teaspoons dry yeast
- 12 slices (1 ½ pounds)
- 1 1/2 cups warm milk, at room temperature
- 1 1/2 large whole eggs
- 3 tablespoons butter, soft
- 3/8 cup dried onion, minced
- 2 1/4 teaspoons salt
- 3 tablespoons dried parsley flakes
- 1 1/2 teaspoons dried oregano
- 5 1/4 cups bread flour
- 3 teaspoons dry yeast
- 16 slices (2 pounds)
- 2 cups warm milk, at room temperature
- 2 large whole eggs
- 4 tablespoons butter, soft
- 1/2 cup dried onion, minced
- 3 teaspoons salt
- 4 tablespoons dried parsley flakes
- 2 teaspoons dried oregano
- 7 cups bread flour
- 4 teaspoons dry yeast

Directions:

1. Choose the size of loaf you would like to make and measure your ingredients.

2. Add the ingredients to the bread pan in the order listed above.

3. Place the pan in the bread machine and close the lid.

4. Turn on the bread maker. Select the White/Basic setting, then the loaf size, and finally the crust color. Start the cycle.

5. When the cycle is finished and the bread is baked, carefully remove the pan from the machine. Use a potholder as the handle will be very hot. Let rest for a few minutes.

6. Remove the bread from the pan and allow to cool on a wire rack for at least 10 minutes before slicing.

Potato Honey Bread

Ingredients:

- 8 slices (1 pound)
- 1/2 cup lukewarm water
- 1/3 cup finely mashed potatoes, at room temperature
- 1/2 egg, at room temperature
- 1/4 cup unsalted butter, melted
- 1 1/3 tablespoons honey
- 2/3 teaspoon table salt
- 2 cups white bread flour
- 1 1/8 teaspoons bread machine yeast
- 12 slices (1 ½ pounds)
- ¾ cup lukewarm water
- ½ cup finely mashed potatoes, at room temperature
- 1 egg, at room temperature
- ¼ cup unsalted butter, melted
- 2 tablespoons honey
- 1 teaspoon table salt
- 3 cups white bread flour
- 2 teaspoons bread machine yeast
- 16 slices (2 pounds)
- 1 cup lukewarm water
- ⅔ cup finely mashed potatoes, at room temperature
- 1 egg, at room temperature
- ½ cup unsalted butter, melted
- 2⅔ tablespoons honey
- 1⅓ teaspoons table salt
- 4 cups white bread flour
- 2¼ teaspoons bread machine yeast

Directions:

1. Choose the size of loaf you would like to make and measure your ingredients.

2. Add the ingredients to the bread pan in the order listed above.

3. Place the pan in the bread machine and close the lid.

4. Turn on the bread maker. Select the White/Basic setting, then the loaf size, and finally the crust color. Start the cycle.

5.   When the cycle is finished and the bread is baked, carefully remove the pan from the machine. Use a potholder as the handle will be very hot. Let rest for a few minutes.

6.   Remove the bread from the pan and allow to cool on a wire rack for at least 10 minutes before slicing.

Sauerkraut Rye Bread

Ingredients:

- 8 slices (1 pound)
- 1 cup sauerkraut, rinsed and drained
- ¾ cup warm water
- 1½ tablespoons molasses
- 1½ tablespoons butter
- 1½ tablespoons brown sugar
- 1 teaspoon caraway seeds
- 1½ teaspoons salt
- 1 cup rye flour
- 2 cups bread flour
- 1½ teaspoons active dry yeast
- 12 slices (1 ½ pounds)
- 1 1/2 cups sauerkraut, rinsed and drained
- 1 1/8 cups warm water
- 2 1/4 tablespoons molasses
- 2 1/4 tablespoons butter
- 2 1/4 tablespoons brown sugar
- 1 1/2 teaspoons caraway seeds
- 2 1/4 teaspoons salt
- 1 1/2 cups rye flour
- 3 cups bread flour
- 2 1/4 teaspoons active dry yeast
- 16 slices (2 pounds)
- 2 cups sauerkraut, rinsed and drained
- 1 1/2 cups warm water
- 3 tablespoons molasses
- 3 tablespoons butter
- 3 tablespoons brown sugar
- 2 teaspoons caraway seeds
- 3 teaspoons salt
- 2 cups rye flour
- 4 cups bread flour
- 3 teaspoons active dry yeast

Directions:

1.   Choose the size of loaf you would like to make and measure your ingredients.

2.   Add the ingredients to the bread pan in the order listed above.

3.   Place the pan in the bread machine and close the lid.

4.   Turn on the bread maker. Select the White/Basic setting, then the loaf size, and finally the crust color. Start the cycle.

5.   When the cycle is finished and the bread is baked, carefully remove the pan from the machine. Use a potholder as the handle will be very hot. Let rest for a few minutes.

6.   Remove the bread from the pan and allow to cool on a wire rack for at least 10 minutes before slicing.

Fresh Herb Stuffing Bread With Fennel Seed And Pepper

Ingredients:

- 8 slices (1 pound)
- 3/4 cup water
- 1 1/2 tablespoons olive oil
- 1 1/2 cups bread flour
- 1/2 cup whole wheat flour
- 1/4 cup chopped fresh herbs
- 2 tablespoons chopped walnuts or pine nuts
- 1 tablespoon sugar
- 1 tablespoon dry buttermilk powder
- 1/2 tablespoon gluten
- 3/4 teaspoon salt
- 5/8 teaspoon fennel seed
- 3/8 teaspoon grated lemon zest
- 3/8 teaspoon ground black, white, or red peppercorns
- 1 1/8 teaspoons SAF yeast or 1 3/8 teaspoons bread machine yeast
- 12 slices (1½ pounds)
- 11/8 cups water
- 2 tablespoons olive oil
- 21/2 cups bread flour
- 1/2 cup whole wheat flour
- 1/3 cup chopped fresh herbs
- 3 tablespoons chopped walnuts or pine nuts
- 11/2 tablespoons sugar

- 11/2 tablespoons dry buttermilk powder
- 2 teaspoons gluten
- 11/4 teaspoons salt
- 1 teaspoon fennel seed
- 1/2 teaspoon grated lemon zest
- 1/2 teaspoon ground black, white, or red peppercorns
- 2 teaspoons SAF yeast or 21/2 teaspoons bread machine yeast
- 16 slices (2 pounds)
- 11/2 cups water
- 3 tablespoons olive oil
- 3 cups bread flour
- 1 cup whole wheat flour
- 1/2 cup chopped fresh herbs
- 4 tablespoons chopped walnuts or pine nuts
- 2 tablespoons sugar
- 2 tablespoons dry buttermilk powder
- 1 tablespoon gluten
- 11/2 teaspoons salt
- 11/4 teaspoons fennel seed
- 3/4 teaspoon grated lemon zest
- 3/4 teaspoon ground black, white, or red peppercorns
- 21/4 teaspoons SAF yeast or 23/4 teaspoons bread machine yeast

Directions:

1. Choose the size of loaf you would like to make and measure your ingredients.

2. Add the ingredients to the bread pan in the order listed above.

3. Place the pan in the bread machine and close the lid.

4. Turn on the bread maker. Select the Basic setting, then the loaf size, and finally the crust color. Start the cycle.

5. When the cycle is finished and the bread is baked, carefully remove the pan from the machine. Use a potholder as the handle will be very hot. Let rest for a few minutes.

6. Remove the bread from the pan and allow to cool on a wire rack for at least 10 minutes before slicing.

Chocolate Chip Bread

Ingredients:

- 8 slices (1 pound)
- 2/3 cup sour cream
- 1 1/2 eggs, at room temperature
- 2/3 cup sugar
- 3/8 cup unsalted butter, melted
- 1/6 cup plain Greek yogurt
- 1 1/8 cups all-purpose flour
- 1/3 cup unsweetened cocoa powder
- 1/3 teaspoon baking powder
- 1/3 teaspoon table salt
- 2/3 cup milk chocolate chips
- 12 slices (1 ½ pounds)
- 1 cup sour cream
- 2 eggs, at room temperature
- 1 cup sugar
- ½ cup unsalted butter, melted
- ¼ cup plain Greek yogurt
- 1¾ cups all-purpose flour
- ½ cup unsweetened cocoa powder
- ½ teaspoon baking powder
- ½ teaspoon table salt
- 1 cup milk chocolate chips
- 16 slices (2 pounds)
- 1⅓ cups sour cream
- 3 eggs, at room temperature
- 1⅓ cups sugar
- ¾ cup unsalted butter, melted
- ⅓ cup plain Greek yogurt
- 2¼ cups all-purpose flour
- ⅔ cup unsweetened cocoa powder
- ⅔ teaspoon baking powder
- ⅔ teaspoon table salt
- 1⅓ cups milk chocolate chips

Directions:

1. Choose the size of loaf you would like to make and measure your ingredients.
2. Add the ingredients to the bread pan in the order listed above.
3. Place the pan in the bread machine and close the lid.
4. Turn on the bread maker. Select the Quick/Rapid setting, then the loaf size, and finally the crust color. Start the cycle.
5. When the cycle is finished and the bread is baked, carefully remove the pan from the machine. Use a potholder as the handle will be very hot. Let rest for a few minutes.
6. Remove the bread from the pan and allow to cool on a wire rack for at least 10 minutes before slicing.

Sweet Vanilla Bread

Ingredients:

- 8 slices (1 pound)
- 3/8 cup lukewarm milk
- 1/8 cup unsalted butter, melted
- 1/8 cup sugar
- 1/2 egg, at room temperature
- 1 teaspoon pure vanilla extract
- 1/4 teaspoon almond extract
- 1 2/3 cups white bread flour
- 1 teaspoon bread machine yeast
- 12 slices (1 ½ pounds)
- ½ cup + 1 tablespoon lukewarm milk
- 3 tablespoons unsalted butter, melted
- 3 tablespoons sugar
- 1 egg, at room temperature
- 1½ teaspoons pure vanilla extract
- ⅓ teaspoon almond extract
- 2½ cups white bread flour
- 1½ teaspoons bread machine yeast
- 16 slices (2 pounds)
- ¾ cup lukewarm milk
- ¼ cup unsalted butter, melted
- ¼ cup sugar
- 1 egg, at room temperature
- 2 teaspoons pure vanilla extract
- ½ teaspoon almond extract
- 3⅓ cups white bread flour
- 2 teaspoons bread machine yeast

Directions:

1. Choose the size of loaf you would like to make and measure your ingredients.
2. Add the ingredients to the bread pan in the order listed above.
3. Place the pan in the bread machine and close the lid.
4. Turn on the bread maker. Select the White/Basic setting, then the loaf size, and finally the crust color. Start the cycle.
5. When the cycle is finished and the bread is baked, carefully remove the pan from the machine. Use a potholder as the handle will be very hot. Let rest for a few minutes.
6. Remove the bread from the pan and allow to cool on a wire rack for at least 10 minutes before slicing.

Buttermilk Pecan Bread

Ingredients:
- 8 slices (1 pound)
- 1/2 cup buttermilk, at room temperature
- 1/2 cup butter, at room temperature
- 2/3 tablespoon instant coffee granules
- 1 1/2 eggs, at room temperature
- 1/2 cup sugar
- 1 1/2cups all-purpose flour
- 1/3 tablespoon baking powder
- 1/3 teaspoon table salt
- 2/3 cup chopped pecans
- 12 slices (1 ½ pounds)
- ¾ cup buttermilk, at room temperature
- ¾ cup butter, at room temperature
- 1 tablespoon instant coffee granules
- 3 eggs, at room temperature
- ¾ cup sugar
- 2 cups all-purpose flour
- ½ tablespoon baking powder
- ½ teaspoon table salt
- 1 cup chopped pecans
- 16 slices (2 pounds)
- 1 cup buttermilk, at room temperature
- 1 cup butter, at room temperature
- 1⅓ tablespoons instant coffee granules
- 3 eggs, at room temperature
- 1 cup sugar

- 3 cups all-purpose flour
- ⅔ tablespoon baking powder
- ⅔ teaspoon table salt
- 1⅓ cups chopped pecans

Directions:
1. Choose the size of loaf you would like to make and measure your ingredients.
2. Add the ingredients to the bread pan in the order listed above.
3. Place the pan in the bread machine and close the lid.
4. Turn on the bread maker. Select the Quick/Rapid setting, then the loaf size, and finally the crust color. Start the cycle.
5. When the cycle is finished and the bread is baked, carefully remove the pan from the machine. Use a potholder as the handle will be very hot. Let rest for a few minutes.
6. Remove the bread from the pan and allow to cool on a wire rack for at least 10 minutes before slicing.

White And Dark Chocolate Tea Cake

Ingredients:
- 8 slices (1 pound)
- 1 cup plain yogurt
- 1/4 cup buttermilk
- 2 large eggs
- 1/4 cup vegetable oil
- 2 teaspoons vanilla extract
- 2/3 cup light brown sugar
- 21/2 cups unbleached all-purpose flour
- 1/3 cup unsweetened Dutch-process cocoa powder
- 1/2 teaspoon baking powder
- 11/2 teaspoons baking soda
- 1/2 teaspoon instant espresso powder
- 1/4 teaspoon salt
- 1 cup white chocolate chips or chunks broken off a bar of white chocolate
- 12 slices (1 ½ pounds)
- 1 1/2 cups plain yogurt
- 3/8 cup buttermilk
- 3 large eggs
- 3/8 cup vegetable oil
- 3 teaspoons vanilla extract

- 1 cup light brown sugar
- 3 3/4 cups unbleached all-purpose flour
- 1/2 cup unsweetened Dutch-process cocoa powder
- 3/4 teaspoon baking powder
- 2 1/4 teaspoons baking soda
- 3/4 teaspoon instant espresso powder
- 3/8 teaspoon salt
- 1 1/2 cups white chocolate chips or chunks broken off a bar of white chocolate
- 16 slices (2 pounds)
- 2 cups plain yogurt
- 1/2 cup buttermilk
- 4 large eggs
- 1/2 cup vegetable oil
- 4 teaspoons vanilla extract
- 1 1/3 cups light brown sugar
- 5 cups unbleached all-purpose flour
- 2/3 cup unsweetened Dutch-process cocoa powder
- 1 teaspoon baking powder
- 3 teaspoons baking soda
- 1 teaspoon instant espresso powder
- 1/2 teaspoon salt
- 2 cups white chocolate chips or chunks broken off a bar of white chocolate

Directions:

1. Choose the size of loaf you would like to make and measure your ingredients.

2. Add the ingredients to the bread pan in the order listed above.

3. Place the pan in the bread machine and close the lid.

4. Turn on the bread maker. Select the Quick Bread/Cake setting, then the loaf size, and finally the crust color. Start the cycle.

5. When the cycle is finished and the bread is baked, carefully remove the pan from the machine. Use a potholder as the handle will be very hot. Let rest for a few minutes.

6. Remove the bread from the pan and allow to cool on a wire rack for at least 10 minutes before slicing.

Allspice Currant Bread

Ingredients:
- 8 slices (1 pound)

- 3/4 cup lukewarm water
- 1 tablespoon unsalted butter, melted
- 1/8 cup sugar
- 1/8 cup skim milk powder
- 1 teaspoon table salt
- 2 cups white bread flour
- 3/4 teaspoon dried lemon zest
- 3/8 teaspoon ground allspice
- 1/8 teaspoon ground nutmeg
- 1 1/4 teaspoons bread machine yeast
- 1/2 cup dried currants
- 12 slices (1 ½ pounds)
- 1⅛ cups lukewarm water
- 1½ tablespoons unsalted butter, melted
- 3 tablespoons sugar
- 3 tablespoons skim milk powder
- 1½ teaspoons table salt
- 3 cups white bread flour
- 1 teaspoon dried lemon zest
- ½ teaspoon ground allspice
- ¼ teaspoon ground nutmeg
- 2½ teaspoons bread machine yeast
- ¾ cup dried currants
- 16 slices (2 pounds)
- 1½ cups lukewarm water
- 2 tablespoons unsalted butter, melted
- ¼ cup sugar
- ¼ cup skim milk powder
- 2 teaspoons table salt
- 4 cups white bread flour
- 1½ teaspoons dried lemon zest
- ¾ teaspoon ground allspice
- ¼ teaspoon ground nutmeg
- 2½ teaspoons bread machine yeast
- 1 cup dried currants

Directions:

1. Choose the size of loaf you would like to make and measure your ingredients.

2. Add all of the ingredients except for the dried currants to the bread pan in the order listed above.

3. Place the pan in the bread machine and close the lid.

4. Turn on the bread maker. Select the White/Basic or Fruit/Nut (if your machine has this setting) setting, then the loaf size, and finally the crust color. Start the cycle.

5. When the machine signals to add ingredients, add the dried currants. (Some machines have a fruit/nut hopper where you can add the dried currants when you start the machine. The machine will automatically add them to the dough during the baking process.)

6. When the cycle is finished and the bread is baked, carefully remove the pan from the machine. Use a potholder as the handle will be very hot. Let rest for a few minutes.

7. Remove the bread from the pan and allow to cool on a wire rack for at least 10 minutes before slicing.

Choco Banana Oatmeal Bread

Ingredients:
- 8 slices (1 pound)
- 3 bananas, mashed
- 2 whole eggs, at room temperature
- ¾ cup packed light brown sugar
- 1/2 cup butter
- ½ cup sour cream
- ¼ cup sugar
- 1½ teaspoons vanilla extract
- 1 cup all-purpose flour
- ½ cup quick oats
- 2 tablespoons unsweetened cocoa powder
- 1 teaspoon baking soda
- 12 slices (1 ½ pounds)
- 4 1/2 bananas, mashed
- 3 whole eggs, at room temperature
- 1 1/8 cups packed light brown sugar
- 3/4 cup butter
- 3/4 cup sour cream
- 3/8 cup sugar
- 2 1/4 teaspoons vanilla extract
- 1 1/2 cups all-purpose flour
- 3/4 cup quick oats
- 3 tablespoons unsweetened cocoa powder
- 1 1/2 teaspoons baking soda
- 16 slices (2 pounds)
- 6 bananas, mashed

- 4 whole eggs, at room temperature
- 1 1/2 cups packed light brown sugar
- 1 cup butter
- 1 cup sour cream
- 1/2 cup sugar
- 3 teaspoons vanilla extract
- 2 cups all-purpose flour
- 1 cup quick oats
- 4 tablespoons unsweetened cocoa powder
- 2 teaspoons baking soda

Directions:
1. Choose the size of loaf you would like to make and measure your ingredients.

2. Add the banana, eggs, brown sugar, butter, sour cream, vanilla and sugar to the bread pan in the order listed above.

3. Place the pan in the bread machine and close the lid.

4. Turn on the bread maker. Select the Quick/Rapid setting, then the loaf size, and finally the crust color. Start the cycle.

5. Mix the dry ingredients in a bowl and add the dry ingredients to the bread machine once the machine beeps.

6. When the cycle is finished and the bread is baked, carefully remove the pan from the machine. Use a potholder as the handle will be very hot. Let rest for a few minutes.

7. Remove the bread from the pan and allow to cool on a wire rack for at least 10 minutes before slicing.

Pumpkin Spice Cake

Ingredients:
- 8 slices (1 pound)
- 1 cup sugar
- 1 cup canned pumpkin
- 1/3 cup vegetable oil
- 1 teaspoon vanilla extract
- 2 eggs
- 1 1/2 cups all-purpose flour
- 2 teaspoons baking powder
- 1/4 teaspoon salt
- 1 teaspoon ground cinnamon
- 1/4 teaspoon ground nutmeg

- 1/8 teaspoon ground cloves
- Shortening, for greasing pan
- 12 slices (1 ½ pounds)
- 1 1/2 cups sugar
- 1 1/2 cups canned pumpkin
- 1/2 cup vegetable oil
- 1 1/2 teaspoons vanilla extract
- 3 eggs
- 2 1/4 cups all-purpose flour
- 4 teaspoons baking powder
- 1/2 teaspoon salt
- 2 teaspoons ground cinnamon
- 1/2 teaspoon ground nutmeg
- 1/4 teaspoon ground cloves
- Shortening, for greasing pan
- 16 slices (2 pounds)
- 2 cups sugar
- 2 cups canned pumpkin
- 2/3 cup vegetable oil
- 2 teaspoons vanilla extract
- 4 eggs
- 3 cups all-purpose flour
- 4 teaspoons baking powder
- 1/2 teaspoon salt
- 2 teaspoons ground cinnamon
- 1/2 teaspoon ground nutmeg
- 1/4 teaspoon ground cloves
- Shortening, for greasing pan

Directions:

1. Choose the size of loaf you would like to make and measure your ingredients.
2. Grease bread pan and kneading blade generously with shortening.
3. Add the ingredients to the bread pan in the order listed above.
4. Place the pan in the bread machine and close the lid.
5. Turn on the bread maker. Select the Rapid setting, then the loaf size, and finally the crust color. Start the cycle.
6. Open the lid three minutes into the cycle and carefully scrape down sides of pan with a rubber spatula; close lid to continue cycle.

7. When the cycle is finished and the bread is baked, carefully remove the pan from the machine. Use a potholder as the handle will be very hot. Let rest for a few minutes.
8. Remove the bread from the pan and allow to cool on a wire rack for at least 10 minutes before slicing.

Honey Pound Cake

Ingredients:

- 8 slices (1 pound)
- 1 cup butter, unsalted
- 1/4 cup honey
- 2 tablespoons whole milk
- 4 eggs, beaten
- 1 cup sugar
- 2 cups flour
- 12 slices (1 ½ pounds)
- 1 1/2 cups butter, unsalted
- 3/8 cup honey
- 3 tablespoons whole milk
- 6 eggs, beaten
- 1 1/2 cups sugar
- 3 cups flour
- 16 slices (2 pounds)
- 2 cups butter, unsalted
- 1/2 cup honey
- 4 tablespoons whole milk
- 8 eggs, beaten
- 2 cups sugar
- 4 cups flour

Directions:

1. Choose the size of loaf you would like to make and measure your ingredients.
2. Bring the butter to room temperature and cut into 1/2-inch cubes.
3. Add the ingredients to the bread pan in the order listed above.
4. Place the pan in the bread machine and close the lid.
5. Turn on the bread maker. Select the Sweet Bread setting, then the loaf size, and finally the crust color. Start the cycle.
6. When the cycle is finished and the bread is baked, carefully remove the pan from the machine. Use a

potholder as the handle will be very hot. Let rest for a few minutes.

7.　Remove the bread from the pan and allow to cool on a wire rack for at least 10 minutes before slicing.

White Chocolate Bread

Ingredients:

- 8 slices (1 pound)
- 2/3 cup lukewarm milk
- 1/2 egg, at room temperature
- 1 1/3 tablespoons unsalted butter, melted
- 1 teaspoon pure vanilla extract
- 1/8 cup light brown sugar
- 1 tablespoon cocoa powder, unsweetened
- 1/2 teaspoon table salt
- 2 cups white bread flour
- 5/6 teaspoon bread machine yeast
- 1/4 cup semisweet chocolate chips
- 1/4 cup white chocolate chips
- 12 slices (1 ½ pounds)
- 1 cup lukewarm milk
- 1 egg, at room temperature
- 2 tablespoons unsalted butter, melted
- 1½ teaspoons pure vanilla extract
- 3 tablespoons light brown sugar
- 4 teaspoons cocoa powder, unsweetened
- ¾ teaspoon table salt
- 3 cups white bread flour
- 1¼ teaspoons bread machine yeast
- ⅓ cup semisweet chocolate chips
- ⅓ cup white chocolate chips
- 16 slices (2 pounds)
- 1⅓ cups lukewarm milk
- 1 egg, at room temperature
- 2⅔ tablespoons unsalted butter, melted
- 2 teaspoons pure vanilla extract
- ¼ cup light brown sugar
- 2 tablespoons cocoa powder, unsweetened
- 1 teaspoon table salt
- 4 cups white bread flour
- 1⅔ teaspoons bread machine yeast
- ½ cup semisweet chocolate chips
- ½ cup white chocolate chips

Directions:

1.　Choose the size of loaf you would like to make and measure your ingredients.

2.　Take the bread pan; add the ingredients except both the chocolate chips to the bread pan in the order listed above.

3.　Place the pan in the bread machine and close the lid.

4.　Turn on the bread maker. Select the White/Basic or Fruit/Nut (if your machine has this setting) setting, then the loaf size, and finally the crust color. Start the cycle.

5.　When the machine signals to add ingredients, add both the chocolate chips. (Some machines have a fruit/nut hopper where you can add both the chocolate chips when you start the machine. The machine will automatically add them to the dough during the baking process.)

6.　When the cycle is finished and the bread is baked, carefully remove the pan from the machine. Use a potholder as the handle will be very hot. Let rest for a few minutes.

7.　Remove the bread from the pan and allow to cool on a wire rack for at least 10 minutes before slicing.

Shortcut Vanilla Pound Cake

Ingredients:

- 11/2- or 2-pound-loaf machines
- 3 large eggs
- 11/4 cups buttermilk
- 2 teaspoons vanilla powder or 1 teaspoon vanilla extract
- 1/2 teaspoon ground mace
- One and a half 16-ounce boxes commercial pound cake mix (a half box is 12/3 cups)

Directions:

1.　According to the order in the manufacturer's instructions, place the eggs, buttermilk, vanilla, and mace in the pan and sprinkle in the cake mix. Set the crust for dark, if your machine offers crust control for this setting, and program for the Quick Bread/Cake cycle; press Start. The batter will be smooth.

2.　When the machine beeps at the end of the cycle, press Stop/Reset and program for the Bake Only cycle for an additional 50 minutes. The cake is done when it shrinks slightly from the sides of the pan, the sides are dark brown, and the top is firm to a gentle pressure when touched with your finger. A toothpick will come out clean when inserted into the center of the cake.

3. When the bread is done, immediately remove the pan from the machine. Let the bread stand in the pan for 5 minutes before turning it out, right side up, to cool completely on a rack. Wrap tightly in plastic wrap and store at room temperature.

Cashew Butter/peanut Butter Bread

Ingredients:
- 8 slices (1 pound)
- 2/3 cup peanut butter or cashew butter
- 2/3 cup lukewarm milk
- 1/3 cup packed light brown sugar
- 1/6 cup sugar
- 1/6 cup butter, at room temperature
- 1/2 egg, at room temperature
- 1 1/2 teaspoons pure vanilla extract
- 1 1/2 cups all-purpose flour
- 2/3 tablespoon baking powder
- 3/8 teaspoon table salt
- 12 slices (1 ½ pounds)
- 1 cup peanut butter or cashew butter
- 1 cup lukewarm milk
- ½ cup packed light brown sugar
- ¼ cup sugar
- ¼ cup butter, at room temperature
- 1 egg, at room temperature
- 2 teaspoons pure vanilla extract
- 2 cups all-purpose flour
- 1 tablespoon baking powder
- ½ teaspoon table salt
- 16 slices (2 pounds)
- 1⅓ cups peanut butter or cashew butter
- 1⅓ cups lukewarm milk
- ⅔ cup packed light brown sugar
- ⅓ cup sugar
- ⅓ cup butter, at room temperature
- 1 egg, at room temperature
- 3 teaspoons pure vanilla extract
- 3 cups all-purpose flour

- 1⅓ tablespoons baking powder
- ¾ teaspoon table salt

Directions:
1. Choose the size of loaf you would like to make and measure your ingredients.
2. Add the ingredients to the bread pan in the order listed above.
3. Place the pan in the bread machine and close the lid.
4. Turn on the bread maker. Select the Quick/Rapid setting, then the loaf size, and finally the crust color. Start the cycle.
5. When the cycle is finished and the bread is baked, carefully remove the pan from the machine. Use a potholder as the handle will be very hot. Let rest for a few minutes.
6.. Remove the bread from the pan and allow to cool down on a wire rack for at least 10 minutes or more before slicing.

Milk Sweet Bread

Ingredients:
- 8 slices (1 pound)
- 2/3 cup lukewarm milk
- 1/2 egg, at room temperature
- 1 1/3 tablespoons butter, softened
- 1/3 cup sugar
- 2/3 teaspoon table salt
- 2 cups white bread flour
- 1 1/8 teaspoons bread machine yeast
- 12 slices (1 ½ pounds)
- 1 cup lukewarm milk
- 1 egg, at room temperature
- 2 tablespoons butter, softened
- ½ cup sugar
- 1 teaspoon table salt
- 3 cups white bread flour
- 2¼ teaspoons bread machine yeast
- 16 slices (2 pounds)
- 1⅓ cups lukewarm milk
- 1 egg, at room temperature
- 2⅔ tablespoons butter, softened
- ⅔ cup sugar
- 1⅓ teaspoons table salt

- 4 cups white bread flour
- 2¼ teaspoons bread machine yeast

Directions:

1. Choose the size of loaf you would like to make and measure your ingredients.
2. Add the ingredients to the bread pan in the order listed above.
3. Place the pan in the bread machine and close the lid.
4. Turn on the bread maker. Select the Sweet setting, then the loaf size, and finally the crust color. Start the cycle.
5. When the cycle is finished and the bread is baked, carefully remove the pan from the machine. Use a potholder as the handle will be very hot. Let rest for a few minutes.
6. Remove the bread from the pan and allow to cool on a wire rack for at least 10 minutes before slicing.

Cocoa Banana Bread

Ingredients:
- 8 slices (1 pound)
- 2 bananas, mashed
- 1 1/2 eggs, at room temperature
- 1/2 cup packed light brown sugar
- 3/8 cup unsalted butter, melted
- 3/8 cup sour cream, at room temperature
- 1/6 cup sugar
- 1 teaspoon pure vanilla extract
- 2/3 cup all-purpose flour
- 1/3 cup quick oats
- 1 1/2 tablespoons unsweetened cocoa powder
- 2/3 teaspoon baking soda
- 12 slices (1 ½ pounds)
- 3 bananas, mashed
- 2 eggs, at room temperature
- ¾ cup packed light brown sugar
- ½ cup unsalted butter, melted
- ½ cup sour cream, at room temperature
- ¼ cup sugar
- 1½ teaspoons pure vanilla extract
- 1 cup all-purpose flour
- ½ cup quick oats
- 2 tablespoons unsweetened cocoa powder

- 1 teaspoon baking soda
- 16 slices (2 pounds)
- 4 bananas, mashed
- 3 eggs, at room temperature
- 1 cup packed light brown sugar
- ¾ cup unsalted butter, melted
- ¾ cup sour cream, at room temperature
- ⅓ cup sugar
- 2 teaspoons pure vanilla extract
- 1⅓ cups all-purpose flour
- ⅔ cup quick oats
- 3 tablespoons unsweetened cocoa powder
- 1⅓ teaspoons baking soda

Directions:

1. Choose the size of loaf you would like to make and measure your ingredients.
2. Add the ingredients to the bread pan in the order listed above.
3. Place the pan in the bread machine and close the lid.
4. Turn on the bread maker. Select the Quick/Rapid setting, then the loaf size, and finally the crust color. Start the cycle.
5. When the cycle is finished and the bread is baked, carefully remove the pan from the machine. Use a potholder as the handle will be very hot. Let rest for a few minutes.
6. Remove the bread from the pan and allow to cool on a wire rack for at least 10 minutes before slicing.

Honey Bread

Ingredients:
- 8 slices (1 pound)
- ¾ cups milk, at 80 degrees F
- 2 tablespoons honey
- 1 tablespoon butter, melted and cooled
- ¾ teaspoon salt
- ½ cup whole wheat flour
- ½ cup prepared granola crushed
- 1¼ cups white bread flour
- 1 teaspoon bread machine yeast
- 12 slices (1 ½ pounds)
- 1 1/8 cups milk, at 80 degrees F
- 3 tablespoons honey

- 1 1/2 tablespoons butter, melted and cooled
- 1 1/8 teaspoons salt
- 3/4 cup whole wheat flour
- 3/4 cup prepared granola crushed
- 1 7/8 cups white bread flour
- 1 1/2 teaspoons bread machine yeast
- 16 slices (2 pounds)
- 1 1/2 cups milk, at 80 degrees F
- 4 tablespoons honey
- 2 tablespoons butter, melted and cooled
- 1 1/2 teaspoons salt
- 1 cup whole wheat flour
- 1 cup prepared granola crushed
- 2 1/2cups white bread flour
- 2 teaspoons bread machine yeast

Directions:

1. Choose the size of loaf you would like to make and measure your ingredients.

2. Add the ingredients to the bread pan in the order listed above.

3. Place the pan in the bread machine and close the lid.

4. Turn on the bread maker. Select the White/Basic setting, then the loaf size, and finally the crust color. Start the cycle.

5. When the cycle is finished and the bread is baked, carefully remove the pan from the machine. Use a potholder as the handle will be very hot. Let rest for a few minutes.

6. Remove the bread from the pan and allow to cool on a wire rack for at least 10 minutes before slicing.

Carrot Cake Bread

Ingredients:
- 8 slices (1 pound)
- Non-stick cooking spray
- 1/4 cup vegetable oil
- 2 large eggs, room temperature
- 1/2 teaspoon pure vanilla extract
- 1/2 cup sugar
- 1/4 cup light brown sugar
- 1/4 cup crushed pineapple with juice (from can or fresh)
- 1 1/4 cups unbleached, all-purpose flour
- 1 teaspoon baking powder
- 1/4 teaspoon baking soda
- 1/4 teaspoon salt
- 1 teaspoon ground cloves
- 3/4 teaspoon ground cinnamon
- 1 cup freshly grated carrots
- 1/3 cup chopped pecans
- 1/3 cup golden raisins
- 12 slices (1 ½ pounds)
- Non-stick cooking spray
- 3/8 cup vegetable oil
- 3 large eggs, room temperature
- 3/4 teaspoon pure vanilla extract
- 3/4 cup sugar
- 3/8 cup light brown sugar
- 3/8 cup crushed pineapple with juice (from can or fresh)
- 1 7/8 cups unbleached, all-purpose flour
- 1 1/2 teaspoons baking powder
- 3/8 teaspoon baking soda
- 3/8 teaspoon salt
- 1 1/2 teaspoons ground cloves
- 1 1/8 teaspoons ground cinnamon
- 1 1/2 cups freshly grated carrots
- 1/2 cup chopped pecans
- 1/2 cup golden raisins
- 16 slices (2 pounds)
- Non-stick cooking spray
- 1/2 cup vegetable oil
- 4 large eggs, room temperature
- 1 teaspoon pure vanilla extract
- 1 cup sugar
- 1/2 cup light brown sugar
- 1/2 cup crushed pineapple with juice (from can or fresh)
- 2 1/2 cups unbleached, all-purpose flour
- 2 teaspoons baking powder
- 1/2 teaspoon baking soda
- 1/2 teaspoon salt
- 2 teaspoons ground cloves
- 1 1/2 teaspoons ground cinnamon
- 2 cups freshly grated carrots
- 2/3 cup chopped pecans
- 2/3 cup golden raisins

Directions:

1. Choose the size of loaf you would like to make and measure your ingredients.

2. Coat the inside of the bread pan with non-stick cooking spray.

3. Add the ingredients to the bread pan in the order listed above.

4. Place the pan in the bread machine and close the lid.

5. Turn on the bread maker. Select the Express Bake setting, then the loaf size, and finally the crust color. Start the cycle.

6. While the batter is mixing, scrape the sides of the bread pan with a rubber spatula to fully incorporate ingredients.

7. When the cycle is finished and the bread is baked, carefully remove the pan from the machine. Use a potholder as the handle will be very hot. Let rest for a few minutes.

8. Remove the bread from the pan and allow to cool on a wire rack for at least 10 minutes before slicing.

Rainbow Swirl Cake

Ingredients:
- 8 slices (1 pound)
- 2/3 cup milk plus 2/3 egg yolk
- 2 cups unbleached all-purpose flour
- 1 2/3 tablespoons sugar
- 1 1/2teaspoons active dry yeast
- 1 tablespoon unsalted butter, softened
- 1 1/3 teaspoons salt
- Red, yellow, green and blue food coloring
- Flour, for surface
- 12 slices (1 ½ pounds)
- 1 cup milk plus 1 egg yolk
- 3 cups unbleached all-purpose flour
- 2 1/2 tablespoons sugar
- 2 1/4 teaspoons active dry yeast
- 1 1/2 tablespoons unsalted butter, softened
- 2 teaspoons salt
- Red, yellow, green and blue food coloring
- Flour, for surface
- 16 slices (2 pounds)
- 1 1/3 cups milk plus 1 1/3 egg yolks

- 4 cups unbleached all-purpose flour
- 3 1/3 tablespoons sugar
- 3teaspoons active dry yeast
- 2 tablespoons unsalted butter, softened
- 2 2/3 teaspoons salt
- Red, yellow, green and blue food coloring
- Flour, for surface

Directions:

1. Choose the size of loaf you would like to make and measure your ingredients.

2. Whisk milk and egg yolk together in a microwave safe bowl and microwave 30 seconds and add to the bread pan.

3. Whisk together flour, sugar and yeast in a large mixing bowl and add to the bread pan.

4. Add milk mixture, butter, salt, and stir to combine and add to the bread pan.

5. Place the pan in the bread machine and close the lid.

6. Turn on the bread maker. Select the Dough setting, then the loaf size, and finally the crust color. Start the cycle.

7. When kneading is finished, divide dough into 5 equal dough balls and place each one in a small bowl and cover with a tea towel.

8. Remove one piece from a bowl and place it on a plastic cutting board. Add several drops of food coloring and knead the food coloring into the dough with gloved hands, adding more food coloring until it is fully incorporated.

9. Shape dough into a ball and return to its bowl. Repeat with remaining pieces of dough, dying each a different color; be sure to wash your hands and your work surface between each color.

10. Cover each bowl with plastic wrap and let rise until doubled; about 2 hours.

11. Punch down each dough ball when risen.

12. Roll the red dough ball out on a lightly floured surface into an 8-by-4-inch rectangle. Roll out yellow piece of dough into an 8-by-4-inch rectangle and place directly on top of the red dough. Repeat with green, blue, and purple dough balls until you have a stack of 8-by-4-inch rectangles.

13. Roll up dough tightly from the short end into a loaf.

14. Place loaf in a lightly greased 9-by-5-inch loaf pan. Cover with a tea towel or plastic wrap and let rise until doubled, about 1 hour.

15. Preheat oven to 375°F and bake until browned on top and a thermometer inserted in the bottom center reads 190°F, about 30 minutes.

16. When the bread is baked, carefully remove the pan from the machine. Use a potholder as the handle will be very hot. Let rest for a few minutes.

17. Remove the bread from the pan and allow to cool on a wire rack for at least 10 minutes before slicing.

Sweet Almond Anise Bread

Ingredients:
- 8 slices (1 pound)
- ¾ cup lukewarm water
- ¼ cup butter
- ¼ cup sugar
- ½ teaspoon salt
- 3 cups bread flour
- 1 teaspoon anise seed
- 2 teaspoons active dry yeast
- ½ cup almonds, chopped
- 12 slices (1 ½ pounds)
- 1 1/8 cups lukewarm water
- 3/8 cup butter
- 3/8 cup sugar
- 3/4 teaspoon salt
- 4 1/2 cups bread flour
- 1 1/2 teaspoons anise seed
- 3 teaspoons active dry yeast
- 3/4 cup almonds, chopped
- 16 slices (2 pounds)
- 1 1/2 cups lukewarm water
- 1/2 cup butter
- 1/2 cup sugar
- 1 teaspoon salt
- 6 cups bread flour
- 2 teaspoons anise seed
- 4 teaspoons active dry yeast
- 1 cup almonds, chopped

Directions:

1. Choose the size of loaf you would like to make and measure your ingredients.

2. Add the ingredients to the bread pan in the order listed above (except almonds) .

3. Place the pan in the bread machine and close the lid.

4. Turn on the bread maker. Select the White/Basic setting, then the loaf size, and finally the crust color. Start the cycle.

5. When the cycle is finished and the bread is baked, carefully remove the pan from the machine. Use a potholder as the handle will be very hot. Let rest for a few minutes.

6. Remove the bread from the pan and allow to cool on a wire rack for at least 10 minutes before slicing.

Insane Coffee Cake

Ingredients:
- 8 slices (1 pound)
- 7/8 cup of milk
- 1/4 cup of sugar
- 1 teaspoon salt
- 1 egg yolk
- 1 tablespoon butter
- 2 1/4 cups bread flour
- 2 teaspoons of active dry yeast
- For the topping:
- 2 tablespoons butter, melted
- 2 tablespoons brown sugar
- 1 teaspoon cinnamon
- 12 slices (1 ½ pounds)
- 1 3/8 cups of milk
- 3/8 cup of sugar
- 1 1/2 teaspoons salt
- 1 1/2 egg yolks
- 1 1/2 tablespoons butter
- 3 3/8 cups bread flour
- 3 teaspoons of active dry yeast
- For the topping:
- 3 tablespoons butter, melted
- 3 tablespoons brown sugar
- 1 1/2 teaspoons cinnamon
- 16 slices (2 pounds)
- 1 3/4 cups of milk

- 1/2 cup of sugar
- 2 teaspoons salt
- 2 egg yolks
- 2 tablespoons butter
- 1 1/8 cups bread flour
- 4 teaspoons of active dry yeast
- For the topping:
- 4 tablespoons butter, melted
- 4 tablespoons brown sugar
- 2 teaspoons cinnamon

Directions:

1. Choose the size of loaf you would like to make and measure your ingredients.
2. Add the ingredients to the bread pan in the order listed above (except the topping ingredients).
3. Place the pan in the bread machine and close the lid.
4. Turn on the bread maker. Select the Dough setting, then the loaf size, and finally the crust color. Start the cycle.
5. Butter a 9-by-9-inch glass baking dish and pour the dough into the dish. Cover with a towel and let rise for about 10 minutes.
6. Preheat an oven to 375°F.
7. Brush the dough with the melted butter.
8. Mix the brown sugar and cinnamon in a bowl and sprinkle on top of the coffee cake.
9. Let the topped dough rise, uncovered, for another 30 minutes.
10. Place in oven and bake for 30 to 35 minutes or until a wooden toothpick inserted into the center comes out clean and dry.

Lemon Cake

Ingredients:
- 8 slices (1 pound)
- 3 large eggs, beaten
- 1/3 cup 2% milk
- 1/2 cup butter, melted
- 2 cups all-purpose flour
- 3 teaspoons baking powder
- 1 1/3 cup sugar
- 1 teaspoon vanilla extract
- 2 lemons, zested
- For the glaze:
- 1 cup powdered sugar
- 2 tablespoons lemon juice, freshly squeezed
- 12 slices (1 ½ pounds)
- 4 1/2 large eggs, beaten
- 1/2 cup 2% milk
- 3/4 cup butter, melted
- 3 cups all-purpose flour
- 4 1/2 teaspoons baking powder
- 2 cups sugar
- 1 1/2 teaspoons vanilla extract
- 3 lemons, zested
- For the glaze:
- 1 1/2 cups powdered sugar
- 3 tablespoons lemon juice, freshly squeezed
- 16 slices (2 pounds)
- 6 large eggs, beaten
- 2/3 cup 2% milk
- 1 cup butter, melted
- 4 cups all-purpose flour
- 6 teaspoons baking powder
- 2 2/3 cups sugar
- 2 teaspoons vanilla extract
- 4 lemons, zested
- For the glaze:
- 2 cups powdered sugar
- 4 tablespoons lemon juice, freshly squeezed

Directions:

1. Choose the size of loaf you would like to make and measure your ingredients.
2. Prepare the glaze by whisking the powdered sugar and lemon juice together in a small mixing bowl and set aside.
3. Add the ingredients to the bread pan in the order listed above.
4. Place the pan in the bread machine and close the lid.
5. Turn on the bread maker. Select the Sweet Bread setting, then the loaf size, and finally the crust color. Start the cycle.
6. When the cycle is finished and the bread is baked, carefully remove the pan from the machine. Use a potholder as the handle will be very hot. Let rest for a few minutes.
7. Remove the bread from the pan and allow to cool on a wire rack for at least 10 minutes before slicing.

Crunchy Raisin Bread

Ingredients:

- 8 slices (1 pound)
- 1/3 cup milk, at 80 degrees F
- 2 whole eggs, at room temperature
- 4 teaspoons butter, melted and cooled
- 2 2/3 tablespoons sugar
- 2/3 teaspoons salt
- 1 1/3 teaspoons lemon zest
- 2 cups white bread flour
- 1 1/3 teaspoons bread machine yeast
- ¼ cup slivered almonds
- ¼ cup golden raisins
- 12 slices (1 ½ pounds)
- 1/2 cup milk, at 80 degrees F
- 3 whole eggs, at room temperature
- 6 teaspoons butter, melted and cooled
- 4 tablespoons sugar
- 1 teaspoon salt
- 2 teaspoons lemon zest
- 3 cups white bread flour
- 2 teaspoons bread machine yeast
- 3/8 cup slivered almonds
- 3/8 cup golden raisins
- 16 slices (2 pounds)
- 2/3 cup milk, at 80 degrees F
- 4 whole eggs, at room temperature
- 8 teaspoons butter, melted and cooled
- 5 1/3 tablespoons sugar
- 1 1/3 teaspoons salt
- 2 2/3 teaspoons lemon zest
- 4 cups white bread flour
- 2 2/3 teaspoons bread machine yeast
- 1/2 cup slivered almonds
- 1/2 cup golden raisins

Directions:

1. Choose the size of loaf you would like to make and measure your ingredients.
2. Add the ingredients to the bread pan in the order listed above (except almonds and raisins).
3. Place the pan in the bread machine and close the lid.
4. Turn on the bread maker. Select the White/Basic setting, then the loaf size, and finally the crust color. Start the cycle.
5. Once the machine signals, add nuts and raisins.
6. When the cycle is finished and the bread is baked, carefully remove the pan from the machine. Use a potholder as the handle will be very hot. Let rest for a few minutes.
7. Remove the bread from the pan and allow to cool on a wire rack for at least 10 minutes before slicing.

Sweet Applesauce Bread

Ingredients:

- 8 slices (1 pound)
- 1/2 cup lukewarm milk
- 1/6 cup unsweetened applesauce, at room temperature
- 2 teaspoons unsalted butter, melted
- 2 teaspoons sugar
- 2/3 teaspoon table salt
- 1/6 cup quick oats
- 1 1/2 cups white bread flour
- 3/8 teaspoon ground cinnamon
- Pinch ground nutmeg
- 1 1/8 teaspoons bread machine yeast
- 12 slices (1 ½ pounds)
- ⅔ cup lukewarm milk
- ¼ cup unsweetened applesauce, at room temperature
- 1 tablespoon unsalted butter, melted
- 1 tablespoon sugar
- 1 teaspoon table salt
- ¼ cup quick oats
- 2¼ cups white bread flour
- ½ teaspoon ground cinnamon
- Pinch ground nutmeg
- 2¼ teaspoons bread machine yeast
- 16 slices (2 pounds)
- 1 cup lukewarm milk
- ⅓ cup unsweetened applesauce, at room temperature
- 4 teaspoons unsalted butter, melted
- 4 teaspoons sugar
- 1⅓ teaspoons table salt
- ⅓ cup quick oats

- 3 cups white bread flour
- ¾ teaspoon ground cinnamon
- Pinch ground nutmeg
- 2¼ teaspoons bread machine yeast

Directions:
1. Choose the size of loaf you would like to make and measure your ingredients.
2. Add the ingredients to the bread pan in the order listed above.
3. Place the pan in the bread machine and close the lid.
4. Turn on the bread maker. Select the White/Basic setting, then the loaf size, and finally the crust color. Start the cycle.
5. When the cycle is finished and the bread is baked, carefully remove the pan from the machine. Use a potholder as the handle will be very hot. Let rest for a few minutes.
6. Remove the bread from thc pan and allow to cool on a wire rack for at least 10 minutes before slicing.

Chocolate Marble Cake

Ingredients:
- 8 slices (1 pound)
- 1 cup water
- 1 teaspoon vanilla extract
- 1 teaspoon salt
- 2 1/3 cups bread flour
- 1 teaspoon instant yeast
- 2/3 cup semi-sweet chocolate chips
- 12 slices (1 ½ pounds)
- 1 1/2 cups water
- 1 1/2 teaspoons vanilla extract
- 1 1/2 teaspoons salt
- 3 1/2 cups bread flour
- 1 1/2 teaspoons instant yeast
- 1 cup semi-sweet chocolate chips
- 16 slices (2 pounds)
- 2 cups water
- 2 teaspoons vanilla extract
- 2 teaspoons salt
- 4 2/3 cups bread flour
- 2 teaspoons instant yeast
- 1 1/3 cups semi-sweet chocolate chips

Directions:
1. Choose the size of loaf you would like to make and measure your ingredients.
2. Add the ingredients to the bread pan in the order listed above (except the chocolate chips).
3. Place the pan in the bread machine and close the lid.
4. Turn on the bread maker. Select the Sweet Bread setting, then the loaf size, and finally the crust color. Start the cycle.
5. Check the dough after 10 to 15 minutes of kneading.
6. Add the chocolate chips about 3 minutes before the end of the second kneading cycle.
7. When the cycle is finished and the bread is baked, carefully remove the pan from the machine. Use a potholder as the handle will be very hot. Let rest for a few minutes.
8. Remove the bread from the pan and allow to cool on a wire rack for at least 10 minutes before slicing.

Sweet Challah

Ingredients:
- 8 slices (1 pound)
- ¾ cup milk
- 2 whole eggs
- 3 tablespoons margarine
- 3 cups bread flour
- ¼ cup white sugar
- 1½ teaspoons salt
- 1½ teaspoons active dry yeast
- 12 slices (1 ½ pounds)
- 1 1/8 cups milk
- 3 whole eggs
- 4 1/2 tablespoons margarine
- 4 1/2 cups bread flour
- 3/8 cup white sugar
- 2 1/4 teaspoons salt
- 2 1/4 teaspoons active dry yeast
- 16 slices (2 pounds)
- 1 1/2 cups milk
- 4 whole eggs
- 6 tablespoons margarine
- 6 cups bread flour
- 1/2 cup white sugar

- 3 teaspoons salt
- 3 teaspoons active dry yeast

Directions:

1. Choose the size of loaf you would like to make and measure your ingredients.

2. Add the ingredients to the bread pan in the order listed above.

3. Place the pan in the bread machine and close the lid.

4. Turn on the bread maker. Select the White/Basic setting, then the loaf size, and finally the crust color. Start the cycle.

5. When the cycle is finished and the bread is baked, carefully remove the pan from the machine. Use a potholder as the handle will be very hot. Let rest for a few minutes.

6. Remove the bread from the pan and allow to cool on a wire rack for at least 10 minutes before slicing.

German Butter Cake

Ingredients:
- 8 slices (1 pound)
- 2 teaspoons active dry yeast
- 1/4 cup sugar
- 2 1/4 cups all-purpose flour
- 1 teaspoon salt
- 7/8 cup whole milk, lukewarm
- 1 egg yolk
- 1 tablespoon butter, softened
- For the topping:
- 3 tablespoons butter, cold
- 1/2 cup almonds, sliced
- 1/3 cup sugar
- 12 slices (1 ½ pounds)
- 3 teaspoons active dry yeast
- 3/8 cup sugar
- 3 3/8 cups all-purpose flour
- 1 1/2 teaspoon salt
- 1 3/8 cup whole milk, lukewarm
- 1 1/2 egg yolk
- 1 1/2 tablespoon butter, softened
- For the topping:
- 3 tablespoons butter, cold
- 1/2 cup almonds, sliced

- 1/3 cup sugar
- 16 slices (2 pounds)
- 4 teaspoons active dry yeast
- 1/2 cup sugar
- 4 1/2 cups all-purpose flour
- 2 teaspoons salt
- 1 3/4 cups whole milk, lukewarm
- 2 egg yolks
- 2 tablespoons butter, softened
- For the topping:
- 3 tablespoons butter, cold
- 1/2 cup almonds, sliced
- 1/3 cup sugar

Directions:

1. Choose the size of loaf you would like to make and measure your ingredients.

2. Grease a 10-inch springform pan; when the dough cycle is finished, pat the dough into the pan.

3. Add the ingredients to the bread pan in the order listed above.

4. Place the pan in the bread machine and close the lid.

5. Turn on the bread maker. Select the Dough setting, then the loaf size, and finally the crust color. Start the cycle.

6. Prepare the topping by cutting the butter into - inch squares and place them sporadically over the surface of the dough, slightly pushing each into the dough.

7. Sprinkle with almond slices, then sprinkle evenly with sugar.

8. Cover with a towel and let stand in a warm place for 30 minutes.

9. Preheat an oven to 375 F.

10. Bake for 20 to 25 minutes or until golden brown.

11. Remove the bread from the pan and allow to cool on a wire rack for at least 10 minutes before slicing.

Cinnabun Coffee Cake

Ingredients:
- 8 slices (1 pound)
- For the dough:
- 7/12 cup milk
- 1 teaspoon vanilla extract
- 2/3 large egg yolk

- 1 1/3 tablespoons unsalted butter, cut into pieces
- 1 1/2 cups unbleached all-purpose flour
- 1/6 cup sugar
- 2/3 teaspoon salt
- 1 1/3 teaspoons SAF yeast or 1 2/3 teaspoons bread machine yeast
- For the oat crumb topping:
- 3/4 cup unbleached all-purpose flour
- 3/4 cup light brown sugar
- 1/2 cup rolled oats
- 1/2 cup chopped pecans
- 11/2 teaspoons ground cinnamon or apple pie spice
- 1/2 cup (1 stick) unsalted butter, at room temperature
- Confectioners' Sugar Icing
- 12 slices (1 ½ pounds)
- For the dough:
- 7/8 cup milk
- 11/2 teaspoons vanilla extract
- 1 large egg yolk
- 2 tablespoons unsalted butter, cut into pieces
- 21/4 cups unbleached all-purpose flour
- 1/4 cup sugar
- 1 teaspoon salt
- 2 teaspoons SAF yeast or 21/2 teaspoons bread machine yeast
- For the oat crumb topping:
- 3/4 cup unbleached all-purpose flour
- 3/4 cup light brown sugar
- 1/2 cup rolled oats
- 1/2 cup chopped pecans
- 11/2 teaspoons ground cinnamon or apple pie spice
- 1/2 cup (1 stick) unsalted butter, at room temperature
- Confectioners' Sugar Icing
- 16 slices (2 pounds)
- For the dough:
- 1 1/6 cups milk
- 2 teaspoons vanilla extract
- 1 1/3 large egg yolks
- 2 2/3 tablespoons unsalted butter, cut into pieces
- 3 cups unbleached all-purpose flour
- 1/3 cup sugar
- 1 1/3 teaspoons salt
- 2 2/3 teaspoons SAF yeast or 3 1/3 teaspoons bread machine yeast
- For the oat crumb topping:
- 3/4 cup unbleached all-purpose flour
- 3/4 cup light brown sugar
- 1/2 cup rolled oats
- 1/2 cup chopped pecans
- 11/2 teaspoons ground cinnamon or apple pie spice
- 1/2 cup (1 stick) unsalted butter, at room temperature
- Confectioners' Sugar Icing

Directions:

1. Choose the size of loaf you would like to make and measure your ingredients.

2. Add all the dough ingredients to the bread pan in the order listed above.

3. Place the pan in the bread machine and close the lid.

4. Turn on the bread maker. Select the Dough setting, then the loaf size, and finally the crust color. Start the cycle.

5. While the Dough cycle is running, prepare the topping. Combine the flour, sugar, oats, pecans, and cinnamon in a small bowl. Rub the butter in with your fingers to make clumped crumbs. You can also do this quickly in a food processor.

6. Grease a 13-by-9-inch metal or Pyrex baking dish.

7. When the cycle is finished and the bread is baked, with a large rubber spatula, scrape the batter into the pan. Using floured fingers, spread the batter evenly to fill the pan to the edges. Sprinkle with the topping. Cover loosely with plastic wrap and let rest at room temperature for 30 minutes.

8. Meanwhile, preheat the oven to 375°F (350°F if using a glass pan).

9. Bake for 20 to 25 minutes, or until the edges are golden brown and a cake tester inserted into the center comes out clean. Place the pan on a wire rack and prepare the icing. With a large spoon, drizzle the top in a back-and-forth pattern. Serve warm, out of the pan.

HOLIDAY BREAD RECIPES

Cherry Christmas Bread

Ingredients:
- 8 slices (1 pound)
- 1/2 cup + 1/2 tablespoon lukewarm milk
- 1/2 egg, at room temperature
- 1 tablespoon unsalted butter, melted
- 1 1/2 tablespoons light brown sugar
- 1/16 teaspoon ground cinnamon
- 2 cups white bread flour, divided
- 3/4 teaspoon bread machine yeast
- 1/3 cup candied cherries
- 1/4 cup chopped almonds
- 1/4 cup raisins, chopped
- 12 slices (1 ½ pounds)
- ¾ cup lukewarm milk
- 1 egg, at room temperature
- 1½ tablespoons unsalted butter, melted
- 2¼ tablespoons light brown sugar
- ⅛ teaspoon ground cinnamon
- 3 cups white bread flour, divided
- 1⅛ teaspoons bread machine yeast
- ½ cup candied cherries
- ⅓ cup chopped almonds
- ⅓ cup raisins, chopped
- 16 slices (2 pounds)
- 1 cup + 1 tablespoon lukewarm milk
- 1 egg, at room temperature
- 2 tablespoons unsalted butter, melted
- 3 tablespoons light brown sugar
- ⅛ teaspoon ground cinnamon
- 4 cups white bread flour, divided
- 1½ teaspoons bread machine yeast
- ⅔ cup candied cherries
- ½ cup chopped almonds
- ½ cup raisins, chopped

Directions:
1. Choose the size of loaf you would like to make and measure your ingredients.

2. Add all of the ingredients except for the cherries, raisins, and almonds to the bread pan in the order listed above.

3. Place the pan in the bread machine and close the lid.

4. Turn on the bread maker. Select the White/Basic or Fruit/Nut (if your machine has this setting) setting, then the loaf size, and finally the crust color. Start the cycle.

5. When the machine signals to add ingredients, add the cherries, raisins, and almonds. (Some machines have a fruit/nut hopper where you can add the cherries, raisins, and almonds when you start the machine. The machine will automatically add them to the dough during the baking process.)

6. When the cycle is finished and the bread is baked, carefully remove the pan from the machine. Use a potholder as the handle will be very hot. Let rest for a few minutes.

7. Remove the bread from the pan and allow to cool on a wire rack for at least 10 minutes before slicing.

French Butter Bread

Ingredients:
- 8 slices (1 pound)
- 3/8 cup lukewarm milk
- 2 eggs, at room temperature
- 1 1/3 tablespoons sugar
- 1/2 teaspoon table salt
- 1/4 cup + 1 2/3 tablespoons unsalted butter, melted
- 2 cups white bread flour
- 1 teaspoon bread machine yeast
- 12 slices (1 ½ pounds)
- ½ cup + 1 tablespoon lukewarm milk
- 3 eggs, at room temperature
- 2 tablespoons sugar
- ¾ teaspoon table salt
- ½ cup unsalted butter, melted
- 3 cups white bread flour
- 1½ teaspoons bread machine yeast
- 16 slices (2 pounds)
- ¾ cup lukewarm milk
- 4 eggs, at room temperature

- 2⅔ tablespoons sugar
- 1 teaspoon table salt
- ½ cup + 3⅓ tablespoons unsalted butter, melted
- 4 cups white bread flour
- 2 teaspoons bread machine yeast

Directions:

1. Choose the size of loaf you would like to make and measure your ingredients.
2. Add the ingredients to the bread pan in the order listed above.
3. Place the pan in the bread machine and close the lid.
4. Turn on the bread maker. Select the White/Basic setting, then the loaf size, and finally the crust color. Start the cycle.
5. When the cycle is finished and the bread is baked, carefully remove the pan from the machine. Use a potholder as the handle will be very hot. Let rest for a few minutes.
6. Remove the bread from the pan and allow to cool on a wire rack for at least 10 minutes before slicing.

St. Patrick's Rum Bread

Ingredients:
- 8 slices (1 pound)
- 1 whole egg
- 1 tablespoon rum extract
- 3 tablespoons bread flour
- 3 tablespoons packed brown sugar
- 1¼ teaspoons salt
- ½ teaspoon ground cinnamon
- ¼ teaspoon ground nutmeg
- ¼ teaspoon ground cardamom
- 1 teaspoon bread machine yeast
- Topping
- 1 egg yolk, beaten
- 1½ teaspoon pecans, chopped
- 1½ teaspoon brown sugar
- 12 slices (1 ½ pounds)
- 1 1/2 whole eggs
- 1 1/2tablespoons rum extract
- 4 1/2 tablespoons bread flour
- 4 1/2 tablespoons packed brown sugar
- 1 7/8 teaspoons salt

- 3/4 teaspoon ground cinnamon
- 3/8 teaspoon ground nutmeg
- 3/8 teaspoon ground cardamom
- 1 1/2 teaspoons bread machine yeast
- 16 slices (2 pounds)
- 2 whole eggs
- 2 tablespoons rum extract
- 6 tablespoons bread flour
- 6 tablespoons packed brown sugar
- 2 1/2 teaspoons salt
- 1 teaspoon ground cinnamon
- 1/2 teaspoon ground nutmeg
- 1/2 teaspoon ground cardamom
- 2 teaspoons bread machine yeast

Directions:

1. Choose the size of loaf you would like to make and measure your ingredients.
2. Break an egg into 1 cup and add water to fill out a measuring cup.
3. Add egg mixture to the machine.
4. Add the ingredients to the bread pan in the order listed above.
5. Place the pan in the bread machine and close the lid.
6. Turn on the bread maker. Select the White/Basic setting, then the loaf size, and finally the crust color. Start the cycle.
7. When just 40 minutes of the cycle remains, make the topping mixture and brush the top of the bread.
8. When the cycle is finished and the bread is baked, carefully remove the pan from the machine. Use a potholder as the handle will be very hot. Let rest for a few minutes.
9. Remove the bread from the pan and allow to cool on a wire rack for at least 10 minutes before slicing.

Easter Rye Bread With Fruit

Ingredients:
- 8 slices (1 pound)
- 1/2 cup water
- 1 1/2 tablespoons brandy
- 1/2 large egg
- 1/8 cup vegetable oil
- 11/2 cups bread flour

- 1/2 cup light or medium rye flour
- 1/3 cup chopped almonds
- 1/8 cup dark brown sugar
- 2/3 tablespoon gluten
- 1 teaspoon crushed cardamom seeds
- Grated zest of 1/2 lemon
- Grated zest of 1/2 orange
- 3/4 teaspoon salt
- 1/2 tablespoon SAF yeast or 1/2 tablespoon plus 1/4 teaspoon bread machine yeast
- 5/8 cup golden raisins
- 12 slices (1½ pounds)
- 3/4 cup water
- 3 tablespoons brandy
- 1 large egg
- 3 tablespoons vegetable oil
- 21/4 cups bread flour
- 3/4 cup light or medium rye flour
- 1/2 cup chopped almonds
- 3 tablespoons dark brown sugar
- 1 tablespoon gluten
- 11/2 teaspoons crushed cardamom seeds
- Grated zest of 1 lemon
- Grated zest of 1 orange
- 11/4 teaspoons salt
- 21/2 teaspoons SAF yeast or 1 tablespoon bread machine yeast
- 1 cup golden raisins
- 16 slices (2 pounds)
- 1 cup water
- 3 tablespoons brandy
- 1 large egg
- 1/4 cup vegetable oil
- 3 cups bread flour
- 1 cup light or medium rye flour
- 2/3 cup chopped almonds
- 1/4 cup dark brown sugar
- 1 tablespoon plus 1 teaspoon gluten
- 2 teaspoons crushed cardamom seeds
- Grated zest of 1 lemon
- Grated zest of 1 orange
- 11/2 teaspoons salt
- 1 tablespoon SAF yeast or 1 tablespoon plus 1/2 teaspoon bread machine yeast

- 11/4 cups golden raisins

Directions:

1. Choose the size of loaf you would like to make and measure your ingredients.

2. Add the ingredients to the bread pan in the order listed above (except the raisins).

3. Place the pan in the bread machine and close the lid.

4. Turn on the bread maker. Select the Sweet Bread or Fruit and Nut setting, then the loaf size, and finally the crust color. Start the cycle. (This recipe is not suitable for use with the Delay Timer.)

5. When the machine beeps, or between Knead 1 and Knead 2, add the raisins.

6. When the cycle is finished and the bread is baked, carefully remove the pan from the machine. Use a potholder as the handle will be very hot. Let rest for a few minutes.

7. Remove the bread from the pan and allow to cool on a wire rack for at least 10 minutes before slicing.

Hungarian Spring Bread

Ingredients:

- 8 slices (1 pound)
- For the dough:
- 1/2 cup sour cream, at room temperature
- 1/4 cup buttermilk
- 2/3 large egg plus 2/3 egg yolk
- 1 teaspoon vanilla extract
- 1/3 teaspoon almond extract
- 2 tablespoons unsalted butter or margarine, cut into pieces and softened
- 2 cups bread flour
- 1/6 cup sugar
- 1 teaspoon salt
- 1 2/3 teaspoons SAF yeast or 2/3 tablespoon bread machine yeast
- 1/4 cup golden raisins
- 1/4 cup diced lemon confit (shown here) or candied lemon peel
- 1/6 cup pecan pieces
- 2/3 tablespoon unbleached all-purpose flour
- For the lemon icing:
- 3/4 cup sifted confectioners' sugar

- 1 teaspoon grated lemon zest
- 1 teaspoon fresh lemon juice or syrup from the lemon confit
- 1 to 11/2 tablespoons warm milk
- 1 teaspoon soft butter
- 12 slices (1 ½ pounds)
- For the dough:
- 3/4 cup sour cream, at room temperature
- 1/3 cup buttermilk
- 1 large egg plus 1 egg yolk
- 11/2 teaspoons vanilla extract
- 1/2 teaspoon almond extract
- 3 tablespoons unsalted butter or margarine, cut into pieces and softened
- 3 cups bread flour
- 1/4 cup sugar
- 11/2 teaspoons salt
- 21/2 teaspoons SAF yeast or 1 tablespoon bread machine yeast
- 1/3 cup golden raisins
- 1/3 cup diced lemon confit (shown here) or candied lemon peel
- 1/4 cup pecan pieces
- 1 tablespoon unbleached all-purpose flour
- For the lemon icing:
- 3/4 cup sifted confectioners' sugar
- 1 teaspoon grated lemon zest
- 1 teaspoon fresh lemon juice or syrup from the lemon confit
- 1 to 11/2 tablespoons warm milk
- 1 teaspoon soft butter
- 16 slices (2 pounds)
- For the dough:
- 1 cup sour cream, at room temperature
- 1/2 cup buttermilk
- 1 1/3 large eggs plus 1 1/3 egg yolks
- 2 teaspoons vanilla extract
- 2/3 teaspoon almond extract
- 4 tablespoons unsalted butter or margarine, cut into pieces and softened
- 4 cups bread flour
- 1/3 cup sugar
- 2 teaspoons salt

- 3 1/3 teaspoons SAF yeast or 1 1/3 tablespoons bread machine yeast
- 1/2 cup golden raisins
- 1/2 cup diced lemon confit (shown here) or candied lemon peel
- 1/3 cup pecan pieces
- 1 1/3 tablespoons unbleached all-purpose flour
- For the lemon icing:
- 3/4 cup sifted confectioners' sugar
- 1 teaspoon grated lemon zest
- 1 teaspoon fresh lemon juice or syrup from the lemon confit
- 1 to 11/2 tablespoons warm milk
- 1 teaspoon soft butter

Directions:

1. Choose the size of loaf you would like to make and measure your ingredients.
2. To make the dough, add the dough ingredients to the bread pan in the order listed above (except the raisins, lemon peel, and pecans).
3. Place the pan in the bread machine and close the lid.
4. Turn on the bread maker. Select the Sweet Bread setting, then the loaf size, and finally the crust color. Start the cycle. (This recipe is not suitable for use with the Delay Timer.)
5. Sprinkle the fruit and nuts with the tablespoon of flour.
6. When the machine beeps, or between Knead 1 and Knead 2, add the raisins, lemon peel, and nuts. The dough ball will look dry at first and take about 7 minutes to smooth out.
7. To make the icing, combine the icing ingredients in a small bowl and whisk until smooth. Adjust the consistency by adding more milk, a few drops at a time.
8. When the cycle is finished and the bread is baked, carefully remove the pan from the machine. Use a potholder as the handle will be very hot. Let rest for a few minutes.
9. Remove the bread from the pan and allow to cool on a wire rack for at least 10 minutes before slicing. Using an oversized spoon, drizzle the icing over the top of the loaf in a back and forth motion. As the glaze cools, it will set.

Champagne-soaked Baba

Ingredients:

- 8 slices (1 pound)
- For the dough:
- 1/4 cup water
- 1 1/2 large eggs
- 1/4 cup (1/2 stick) unsalted butter, melted
- 1 1/2 cups bread flour
- 1 tablespoons sugar
- 3/8 teaspoon grated lemon zest
- 3/8 teaspoon salt
- 7/8 teaspoons SAF yeast or 1 1/8 teaspoons bread machine yeast
- For the soaking syrup:
- 3/8 cup sugar
- 3/8 cup water
- 1/4 cup sweet champagne or Asti Spumante
- For apricot glaze:
- 1/6 cup apricot jam
- 12 slices (1½ pounds)
- For the dough:
- 1/3 cup water
- 3 large eggs
- 6 tablespoons unsalted butter, melted
- 2 cups bread flour
- 11/2 tablespoons sugar
- 1/2 teaspoon grated lemon zest
- 1/2 teaspoon salt
- 11/4 teaspoons SAF yeast or 13/4 teaspoons bread machine yeast
- For the soaking syrup:
- 3/4 cup sugar
- 3/4 cup water
- 1/2 cup sweet champagne or Asti Spumante
- For apricot glaze:
- 1/3 cup apricot jam
- 16 slices (2 pounds)
- For the dough:
- 1/2 cup water
- 3 large eggs
- 1/2 cup (1 stick) unsalted butter, melted
- 3 cups bread flour
- 2 tablespoons sugar

- 3/4 teaspoon grated lemon zest
- 3/4 teaspoon salt
- 13/4 teaspoons SAF yeast or 21/4 teaspoons bread machine yeast
- For the soaking syrup:
- 3/4 cup sugar
- 3/4 cup water
- 1/2 cup sweet champagne or Asti Spumante
- For apricot glaze:
- 1/3 cup apricot jam

Directions:

1. Choose the size of loaf you would like to make and measure your ingredients.

2. Add all the dough ingredients to the bread pan in the order listed above.

3. Place the pan in the bread machine and close the lid.

4. Turn on the bread maker. Select the Sweet Bread setting, then the loaf size, and finally the crust color. Start the cycle. (This recipe is not suitable for use with the Delay Timer.)

5. Meanwhile make the soaking syrup. Combine the sugar and water in a small pan and heat until sugar is dissolved, about 5 minutes. Cool until warm. Add the champagne; set aside.

6. When the baking cycle is finished and the bread is baked, carefully remove the pan from the machine. Use a potholder as the handle will be very hot. Let rest for a few minutes.

7. Pierce the top of the baba in a few places with a bamboo skewer. Turn out of the pan onto a deep plate. Slowly pour the champagne soaking syrup all over the cake and let it stand to absorb the puddle that collects at the base. Cover with plastic wrap.

8. To prepare the apricot glaze, place the jam in a small saucepan and boil for 2 minutes to liquify. Drain off any extra soaking syrup from the plate. Brush the cake all over with hot glaze to seal in moisture. Cool and transfer to a clean serving plate before serving, turning the baba on its side to cut into round slices. Store the baba in the refrigerator.

Cocoa Holiday Bread

Ingredients:

- 8 slices (1 pound)
- 1/2 cup brewed coffee, lukewarm
- 1/4 cup evaporated milk, lukewarm
- 1 tablespoon unsalted butter, melted
- 1 1/2 tablespoons honey
- 1/2 tablespoon dark molasses
- 1/2 tablespoon sugar
- 2 teaspoons unsweetened cocoa powder
- 1/2 tcaspoon table salt
- 1 1/8 cups whole-wheat bread flour
- 1 1/8 cups white bread flour
- 1 1/8 teaspoons bread machine yeast
- 12 slices (1 ½ pounds)
- ¾ cup brewed coffee, lukewarm
- ⅓ cup evaporated milk, lukewarm
- 1½ tablespoons unsalted butter, melted
- 2¼ tablespoons honey
- ¾ tablespoon dark molasses
- ¾ tablespoon sugar
- 1 tablespoon unsweetened cocoa powder
- ¾ teaspoon table salt
- 1⅔ cups whole-wheat bread flour
- 1⅔ cups white bread flour
- 1⅔ teaspoons bread machine yeast
- 16 slices (2 pounds)
- 1 cup brewed coffee, lukewarm
- ½ cup evaporated milk, lukewarm
- 2 tablespoons unsalted butter, melted
- 3 tablespoons honey
- 1 tablespoon dark molasses
- 1 tablespoon sugar
- 4 teaspoons unsweetened cocoa powder
- 1 teaspoon table salt
- 2¼ cups whole-wheat bread flour
- 2¼ cups white bread flour
- 2¼ teaspoons bread machine yeast

Directions:

1. Choose the size of loaf you would like to make and measure your ingredients.
2. Add the ingredients to the bread pan in the order listed above.
3. Place the pan in the bread machine and close the lid.
4. Turn on the bread maker. Select the Sweet setting, then the loaf size, and finally the crust color. Start the cycle.
5. When the cycle is finished and the bread is baked, carefully remove the pan from the machine. Use a potholder as the handle will be very hot. Let rest for a few minutes.
6. Remove the bread from the pan and allow to cool on a wire rack for at least 10 minutes before slicing.

Cinnamon Beer Bread

Ingredients:

- 8 slices (1 pound)
- 1 cup beer, at room temperature
- 1/2 cup unsalted butter, melted
- 1/6 cup honey
- 2 cups all-purpose flour
- 2/3 teaspoon table salt
- 1/6 teaspoon ground cinnamon
- 2/3 tablespoon baking powder
- 12 slices (1 ½ pounds)
- 1½ cups beer, at room temperature
- ⅓ cup unsalted butter, melted
- ¼ cup honey
- 3 cups all-purpose flour
- 1 teaspoon table salt
- ¼ teaspoon ground cinnamon
- 1 tablespoon baking powder
- 16 slices (2 pounds)
- 2 cups beer, at room temperature
- 1 cup unsalted butter, melted
- ⅓ cup honey
- 4 cups all-purpose flour
- 1⅓ teaspoons table salt
- ⅓ teaspoon ground cinnamon
- 1⅓ tablespoons baking powder

Directions:

1. Choose the size of loaf you would like to make and measure your ingredients.
2. Add the ingredients to the bread pan in the order listed above.
3. Place the pan in the bread machine and close the lid.

4. Turn on the bread maker. Select the Quick/Rapid setting, then the loaf size, and finally the crust color. Start the cycle.

5. When the cycle is finished and the bread is baked, carefully remove the pan from the machine. Use a potholder as the handle will be very hot. Let rest for a few minutes.

6. Remove the bread from the pan and allow to cool on a wire rack for at least 10 minutes before slicing.

Anise Christmas Bread

Ingredients:
- 8 slices (1 pound)
- 9/16 cup water
- 1/2 large egg plus 1/2 egg yolk
- 1 1/2 tablespoons unsalted butter, cut into pieces
- 1/2 teaspoon anise extract
- 1 3/4 cups bread flour
- 1/8 cup sugar
- 1 1/2 tablespoons dry buttermilk powder
- 2/3 tablespoon gluten
- 3/4 teaspoon salt
- 1 1/4 teaspoons SAF yeast or 1/2 tablespoon bread machine yeast
- 1/2 cup whole glacéed cherries or chopped glacéed apricots (shown here)
- 12 slices (1½ pounds)
- 7/8 cup water
- 1 large egg
- 2 tablespoons unsalted butter, cut into pieces
- 3/4 teaspoon anise extract
- 21/2 cups bread flour
- 3 tablespoons sugar
- 2 tablespoons dry buttermilk powder
- 1 tablespoon gluten
- 11/4 teaspoons salt
- 21/4 teaspoons SAF yeast or 23/4 teaspoons bread machine yeast
- 3/4 cup whole glacéed cherries or chopped glacéed apricots (shown here)
- 16 slices (2 pounds)
- 11/8 cups water
- 1 large egg plus 1 egg yolk
- 3 tablespoons unsalted butter, cut into pieces
- 1 teaspoon anise extract
- 31/2 cups bread flour
- 1/4 cup sugar
- 3 tablespoons dry buttermilk powder
- 1 tablespoon plus 1 teaspoon gluten
- 1 1/2 teaspoons salt
- 2 1/2 teaspoons SAF yeast or 1 tablespoon bread machine yeast
- 1 cup whole glacéed cherries or chopped glacéed apricots (shown here)

Directions:
1. Choose the size of loaf you would like to make and measure your ingredients.

2. Add the ingredients to the bread pan in the order listed above (except the cherries or apricots).

3. Place the pan in the bread machine and close the lid.

4. Turn on the bread maker. Select the Sweet Bread/Fruit and Nut cycle setting, then the loaf size, and finally the crust color. Start the cycle.

5. When the machine beeps, or between Knead 1 and Knead 2, add the fruit.

6. When the cycle is finished and the bread is baked, carefully remove the pan from the machine. Use a potholder as the handle will be very hot. Let rest for a few minutes.

7. Remove the bread from the pan and allow to cool on a wire rack for at least 10 minutes before slicing.

Holiday Chocolate Bread

Ingredients:
- 8 slices (1 pound)
- 1/2 cup + 1 1/2 tablespoons lukewarm milk
- 1/2 egg, at room temperature
- 1 tablespoon unsalted butter, melted
- 3/4 teaspoon pure vanilla extract
- 1 1/3 tablespoons sugar
- 1/2 teaspoon table salt
- 2 cups white bread flour
- 2/3 teaspoon bread machine yeast
- 1/3 cup white chocolate chips
- 1/4 cup dried cranberries
- 12 slices (1 ½ pounds)

- ⅞ cup lukewarm milk
- 1 egg, at room temperature
- 1½ tablespoons unsalted butter, melted
- 1 teaspoon pure vanilla extract
- 2 tablespoons sugar
- ¾ teaspoon table salt
- 3 cups white bread flour
- 1 teaspoon bread machine yeast
- ½ cup white chocolate chips
- ⅓ cup dried cranberries
- 16 slices (2 pounds)
- 1 cup + 3 tablespoons lukewarm milk
- 1 egg, at room temperature
- 2 tablespoons unsalted butter, melted
- 1½ teaspoons pure vanilla extract
- 2⅔ tablespoons sugar
- 1 teaspoon table salt
- 4 cups white bread flour
- 1⅓ teaspoons bread machine yeast
- ⅔ cup white chocolate chips
- ½ cup dried cranberries

Directions:

1. Choose the size of loaf you would like to make and measure your ingredients.
2. Add all of the ingredients except for the chocolate chips and cranberries to the bread pan in the order listed above.
3. Place the pan in the bread machine and close the lid.
4. Turn on the bread maker. Select the White/Basic or Fruit/Nut (if your machine has this setting) setting, then the loaf size, and finally the crust color. Start the cycle.
5. When the machine signals to add ingredients, add the chocolate chips and cranberries. (Some machines have a fruit/nut hopper where you can add the chocolate chips and cranberries when you start the machine. The machine will automatically add them to the dough during the baking process.)
6. When the cycle is finished and the bread is baked, carefully remove the pan from the machine. Use a potholder as the handle will be very hot. Let rest for a few minutes.
7. Remove the bread from the pan and allow to cool on a wire rack for at least 10 minutes before slicing.

Challah Bread

Ingredients:

- 8 slices (1 pound)
- 1/2 cup + 3/8 teaspoon water, lukewarm between 80 and 90⁰F
- 1 1/4 tablespoons unsalted butter, melted
- 1 small egg, beaten
- 1 1/4 tablespoons sugar
- 7/8 teaspoon salt
- 2 1/4 cups white bread flour
- 1 teaspoon bread machine yeast or rapid rise yeast
- For oven baking:
- 1 egg yolk
- 2 tablespoons cold water
- 1 tablespoon poppy seed (optional)
- 12 slices (1 ½ pounds)
- ¾ cup +1 tablespoon water, lukewarm between 80 and 90⁰F
- 2 tablespoons unsalted butter, melted
- 1 egg, beaten
- 2 tablespoons sugar
- 1 ½ teaspoons salt
- 3 ¼ cups white bread flour
- 1 ½ teaspoons bread machine yeast or rapid rise yeast
- For oven baking:
- 1 egg yolk
- 2 tablespoons cold water
- 1 tablespoon poppy seed (optional)
- 16 slices (2 pounds)
- 1 cup +¾ teaspoon water, lukewarm between 80 and 90⁰F
- 2 ½ tablespoons unsalted butter, melted
- 2 small eggs, beaten
- 2 ½ tablespoons sugar
- 1 ¾ teaspoons salt
- 4 ½ cups white bread flour
- 2 teaspoons bread machine yeast or rapid rise yeast
- For oven baking:
- 1 egg yolk
- 2 tablespoons cold water
- 1 tablespoon poppy seed (optional)

Directions:

1. Choose the size of loaf you would like to make and measure your ingredients.

2. Add the ingredients to the bread pan in the order listed above.

3. Place the pan in the bread machine and close the lid.

4. Turn on the bread maker. Select the Dough setting, then the loaf size, and finally the crust color. Start the cycle.

5. Lightly flour a working surface and prepare a large baking sheet by greasing it with cooking spray or vegetable oil or line with parchment paper or a silicone mat.

6. Preheat the oven to 375°F and place the oven rack in the middle position.

7. After the dough cycle is done, carefully remove the dough from the pan and place it on the working surface. Divide dough in three even parts.

8. Roll each part into 13-inch-long cables for the 1 ½ pound Challah bread or 17-inch for the 2-pound loaf. Arrange the dough cables side by side and start braiding from its middle part.

9. In order to make a seal, pinch ends and tuck the ends under the braid.

10. Arrange the loaf onto the baking sheet; cover the sheet with a clean kitchen towel. Let rise for 45-60 minutes or more until it doubles in size.

11. In a mixing bowl, mix the egg yolk and cold water to make an egg wash. Gently brush the egg wash over the loaf. Sprinkle top with the poppy seed, if desired.

12. Bake for about 25-30 minutes or until loaf turns golden brown and is fully cooked.

Portuguese Sweet Bread

Ingredients:
- 8 slices (1 pound)
- 3/8 cup evaporated milk
- 1/6 cup plus 1/2 tablespoon water
- 1 large egg
- 2 tablespoons butter, melted
- 1/4 teaspoon lemon extract
- 1/2 tablespoon plus 1/2 teaspoon vanilla extract or vanilla powder
- 1 7/8 cups bread flour
- 1/4 cup light brown sugar
- 3/4 tablespoon instant potato flakes
- 1/2 tablespoon gluten
- 1 teaspoon salt
- 1 1/2 teaspoons SAF yeast or 1/2 tablespoon plus 1/4 teaspoon bread machine yeast
- 12 slices (1½ pounds)
- 2/3 cup evaporated milk
- 1/4 cup plus 1 tablespoon water
- 2 large eggs
- 3 tablespoons butter, melted
- 1/2 teaspoon lemon extract
- 1 tablespoon vanilla extract or vanilla powder
- 3 cups bread flour
- 1/3 cup light brown sugar
- 1 tablespoon instant potato flakes
- 2 teaspoons gluten
- 11/2 teaspoons salt
- 21/2 teaspoons SAF yeast or 1 tablespoon bread machine yeast
- 16 slices (2 pounds)
- 3/4 cup evaporated milk
- 1/3 cup plus 1 tablespoon water
- 2 large eggs
- 4 tablespoons butter, melted
- 1/2 teaspoon lemon extract
- 1 tablespoon plus 1 teaspoon vanilla extract or vanilla powder
- 33/4 cups bread flour
- 1/2 cup light brown sugar
- 11/2 tablespoons instant potato flakes
- 1 tablespoon gluten
- 2 teaspoons salt
- 3 teaspoons SAF yeast or 1 tablespoon plus 1/2 teaspoon bread machine yeast

Directions:

1. Choose the size of loaf you would like to make and measure your ingredients.

2. Add the ingredients to the bread pan in the order listed above.

3. Place the pan in the bread machine and close the lid.

4. Turn on the bread maker. Select the Basic/Sweet Bread setting, then the loaf size, and finally the crust

color. Start the cycle. (This recipe is not suitable for use with the Delay Timer.)

5. When the cycle is finished and the bread is baked, carefully remove the pan from the machine. Use a potholder as the handle will be very hot. Let rest for a few minutes.

6. Remove the bread from the pan and allow to cool on a wire rack for at least 10 minutes before slicing.

Dry Fruit Cinnamon Bread

Ingredients:
- 8 slices (1 pound)
- 5/6 cup lukewarm milk
- 1/6 cup unsalted butter, melted
- 1/3 teaspoon pure vanilla extract
- 1/8 teaspoon pure almond extract
- 1/6 cup light brown sugar
- 2/3 teaspoon table salt
- 1 teaspoon ground cinnamon
- 2 cups white bread flour
- 5/6 teaspoon bread machine yeast
- 1/3 cup dried mixed fruit
- 1/3 cup golden raisins, chopped
- 12 slices (1 ½ pounds)
- 1¼ cups lukewarm milk
- ¼ cup unsalted butter, melted
- ½ teaspoon pure vanilla extract
- ¼ teaspoon pure almond extract
- 3 tablespoons light brown sugar
- 1 teaspoon table salt
- 2 teaspoons ground cinnamon
- 3 cups white bread flour
- 1 teaspoon bread machine yeast
- ½ cup dried mixed fruit
- ½ cup golden raisins, chopped
- 16 slices (2 pounds)
- 1⅔ cups lukewarm milk
- ⅓ cup unsalted butter, melted
- ⅔ teaspoon pure vanilla extract
- ¼ teaspoon pure almond extract
- ⅓ cup light brown sugar
- 1⅓ teaspoons table salt
- 2 teaspoons ground cinnamon

- 4 cups white bread flour
- 1⅔ teaspoons bread machine yeast
- ⅔ cup dried mixed fruit
- ⅔ cup golden raisins, chopped

Directions:
1. Choose the size of loaf you would like to make and measure your ingredients.
2. Add all of the ingredients except for the mixed fruit and raisins to the bread pan in the order listed above.
3. Place the pan in the bread machine and close the lid.
4. Turn on the bread maker. Select the White/Basic or Fruit/Nut (if your machine has this setting) setting, then the loaf size, and finally the crust color. Start the cycle.
5. When the machine signals to add ingredients, add the mixed fruit and raisins. (Some machines have a fruit/nut hopper where you can add the mixed fruit and raisins when you start the machine. The machine will automatically add them to the dough during the baking process.)
6. When the cycle is finished and the bread is baked, carefully remove the pan from the machine. Use a potholder as the handle will be very hot. Let rest for a few minutes.
7. Remove the bread from the pan and allow to cool on a wire rack for at least 10 minutes before slicing.

Coffee Caraway Seed Bread

Ingredients:
- 8 slices (1 pound)
- 1/2 cup lukewarm water
- 1/4 cup brewed coffee, lukewarm
- 1 tablespoon balsamic vinegar
- 1 tablespoon olive oil
- 1 tablespoon dark molasses
- 1/2 tablespoon light brown sugar
- 1/2 teaspoon table salt
- 1 teaspoon caraway seeds
- 1/8 cup unsweetened cocoa powder
- 1/2 cup dark rye flour
- 1 1/4 cups white bread flour
- 1 teaspoon bread machine yeast
- 12 slices (1 ½ pounds)
- ¾ cup lukewarm water

- ⅓ cup brewed coffee, lukewarm
- 1½ tablespoons balsamic vinegar
- 1½ tablespoons olive oil
- 1½ tablespoons dark molasses
- ¾ tablespoon light brown sugar
- ¾ teaspoon table salt
- 1½ teaspoons caraway seeds
- 3 tablespoons unsweetened cocoa powder
- ¾ cup dark rye flour
- 1¾ cups white bread flour
- 1½ teaspoons bread machine yeast
- 16 slices (2 pounds)
- 1 cup lukewarm water
- ½ cup brewed coffee, lukewarm
- 2 tablespoons balsamic vinegar
- 2 tablespoons olive oil
- 2 tablespoons dark molasses
- 1 tablespoon light brown sugar
- 1 teaspoon table salt
- 2 teaspoons caraway seeds
- ¼ cup unsweetened cocoa powder
- 1 cup dark rye flour
- 2½ cups white bread flour
- 2 teaspoons bread machine yeast

Directions:

1. Choose the size of loaf you would like to make and measure your ingredients.

2. Add the ingredients to the bread pan in the order listed above.

3. Place the pan in the bread machine and close the lid.

4. Turn on the bread maker. Select the Whole Wheat/Wholegrain setting, then the loaf size, and finally the crust color. Start the cycle.

5. When the cycle is finished and the bread is baked, carefully remove the pan from the machine. Use a potholder as the handle will be very hot. Let rest for a few minutes.

6. Remove the bread from the pan and allow to cool down on a wire rack for at least 10 minutes or more before slicing.

Portuguese Holiday Bread

Ingredients:

- 8 slices (1 pound)
- 2/3 cup milk at 80 degrees F
- 1 whole egg, at room temperature
- 4 teaspoons butter, soft
- 1/3 cup sugar
- 2 cups white bread flour
- 1½ teaspoons bread machine yeast
- 12 slices (1 ½ pounds)
- 1 cup milk at 80 degrees F
- 1 1/2 whole eggs, at room temperature
- 6 teaspoons butter, soft
- 1/2 cup sugar
- 3 cups white bread flour
- 2 1/4 teaspoons bread machine yeast
- 16 slices (2 pounds)
- 1 1/3 cups milk at 80 degrees F
- 2 whole eggs, at room temperature
- 8 teaspoons butter, soft
- 2/3 cup sugar
- 4 cups white bread flour
- 3 teaspoons bread machine yeast

Directions:

1. Choose the size of loaf you would like to make and measure your ingredients.

2. Add the ingredients to the bread pan in the order listed above.

3. Place the pan in the bread machine and close the lid.

4. Turn on the bread maker. Select the Sweet Bread setting, then the loaf size, and finally the crust color. Start the cycle.

5. When the cycle is finished and the bread is baked, carefully remove the pan from the machine. Use a potholder as the handle will be very hot. Let rest for a few minutes.

6. Remove the bread from the pan and allow to cool on a wire rack for at least 10 minutes before slicing.

Easter Bread

Ingredients:

- 8 slices (1 pound)
- 1/2 cup lukewarm milk
- 1 egg, at room temperature
- 11/3 tablespoons unsalted butter, melted

- 1/6 cup sugar
- 1/2 teaspoon table salt
- 11/6 teaspoons lemon zest
- 2 cups white bread flour
- 11/8 teaspoons bread machine yeast
- 12 slices (1 ½ pounds)
- ¾ cup lukewarm milk
- 2 eggs, at room temperature
- 2 tablespoons unsalted butter, melted
- ¼ cup sugar
- 1 teaspoon table salt
- 2 teaspoons lemon zest
- 3 cups white bread flour
- 2 teaspoons bread machine yeast
- 16 slices (2 pounds)
- 1 cup lukewarm milk
- 2 eggs, at room temperature
- 2⅔ tablespoons unsalted butter, melted
- ⅓ cup sugar
- 1 teaspoon table salt
- 2⅓ teaspoons lemon zest
- 4 cups white bread flour
- 2¼ teaspoons bread machine yeast

Directions:

1. Choose the size of loaf you would like to make and measure your ingredients.

2. Add the ingredients to the bread pan in the order listed above.

3. Place the pan in the bread machine and close the lid.

4. Turn on the bread maker. Select the White/Basic setting, then the loaf size, and finally the crust color. Start the cycle.

5. When the cycle is finished and the bread is baked, carefully remove the pan from the machine. Use a potholder as the handle will be very hot. Let rest for a few minutes.

6. Remove the bread from the pan and allow to cool on a wire rack for at least 10 minutes before slicing.

Grandma's Favorite Gingerbread

Ingredients:

- 8 slices (1 pound)
- 2/3 cup buttermilk at 80 degrees F
- 1 egg, at room temperature
- 2 2/3 tablespoons dark molasses
- 2 teaspoons melted butter, cooled
- 2 tablespoons honey
- 1 teaspoon salt
- 1 teaspoon ground ginger
- 2/3 teaspoon ground cinnamon
- 1/3 teaspoon ground nutmeg
- 1/8 teaspoon ground cloves
- 2 1/3 cups white bread flour
- 1 1/3 teaspoons bread machine yeast
- 12 slices (1 ½ pounds)
- 1 cup buttermilk at 80 degrees F
- 1 1/2 eggs, at room temperature
- 4 tablespoons dark molasses
- 3 teaspoons melted butter, cooled
- 3 tablespoons honey
- 1 1/2 teaspoons salt
- 1 1/2 teaspoons ground ginger
- 1 teaspoon ground cinnamon
- 1/2 teaspoon ground nutmeg
- 3/16 teaspoon ground cloves
- 3 1/2 cups white bread flour
- 2 teaspoons bread machine yeast
- 16 slices (2 pounds)
- 1 1/3 cups buttermilk at 80 degrees F
- 2 eggs, at room temperature
- 5 1/3 tablespoons dark molasses
- 4 teaspoons melted butter, cooled
- 4 tablespoons honey
- 2 teaspoons salt
- 2 teaspoons ground ginger
- 1 1/3 teaspoons ground cinnamon
- 2/3 teaspoon ground nutmeg
- 1/4 teaspoon ground cloves
- 4 2/3 cups white bread flour
- 2 2/3 teaspoons bread machine yeast

Directions:

1. Choose the size of loaf you would like to make and measure your ingredients.

2. Add the ingredients to the bread pan in the order listed above.

3. Place the pan in the bread machine and close the lid.

4. Turn on the bread maker. Select the Sweet Bread setting, then the loaf size, and finally the crust color. Start the cycle.

5. When the cycle is finished and the bread is baked, carefully remove the pan from the machine. Use a potholder as the handle will be very hot. Let rest for a few minutes.

6. Remove the bread from the pan and allow to cool on a wire rack for at least 10 minutes before slicing.

White Chocolate Cranberry Party Loaf

Ingredients:

- 8 slices (1 pound)
- ½ cup milk, at room temperature
- 1 egg, at room temperature
- 2/3 teaspoons pure vanilla extract
- 4 teaspoons sugar
- ½ teaspoon salt
- 2 cups white bread flour
- ¾ teaspoon instant yeast
- ½ cup white chocolate chips
- ½ cup cranberries
- 12 slices (1 ½ pounds)
- 3/4 cup milk, at room temperature
- 1 1/2 eggs, at room temperature
- 1 teaspoon pure vanilla extract
- 6 teaspoons sugar
- 3/4 teaspoon salt
- 3 cups white bread flour
- 1 1/8 teaspoons instant yeast
- 3/4 cup white chocolate chips
- 3/4 cup cranberries
- 16 slices (2 pounds)
- 1 cup milk, at room temperature
- 2 eggs, at room temperature
- 1 1/3 teaspoons pure vanilla extract
- 8 teaspoons sugar
- 1 teaspoon salt
- 4 cups white bread flour
- 1 1/2 teaspoons instant yeast
- 1 cup white chocolate chips
- 1 cup cranberries

Directions:

1. Choose the size of loaf you would like to make and measure your ingredients.

2. Add the ingredients to the bread pan in the order listed above (except chocolate chips and cranberries).

3. Place the pan in the bread machine and close the lid.

4. Turn on the bread maker. Select the White/Basic setting, then the loaf size, and finally the crust color. Start the cycle.

5. Add chocolate chips and cranberries once the machine beeps.

6. When the cycle is finished and the bread is baked, carefully remove the pan from the machine. Use a potholder as the handle will be very hot. Let rest for a few minutes.

7. Remove the bread from the pan and allow to cool on a wire rack for at least 10 minutes before slicing.

Amaretto Bread

Ingredients:

- 8 slices (1 pound)
- 1/2 cup (2 ounces) whole almonds
- 2/3 cup commercial eggnog
- 1/6 cup amaretto liqueur
- 1 large egg yolk
- 1 1/2 tablespoons unsalted butter, cut into pieces, or almond oil
- 2 cups bread flour
- 1 tablespoon sugar
- 2/3 tablespoon gluten
- 3/4 teaspoon salt
- 1/2 tablespoon SAF yeast or 1/2 tablespoon plus 1/4 teaspoon bread machine yeast
- 1/8 cup Almond Confectioners' Sugar, for dusting (opposite)
- 12 slices (1½ pounds)
- 3/4 cup (3 ounces) whole almonds
- 1 cup plus 1 tablespoon commercial eggnog
- 1/4 cup amaretto liqueur
- 2 large egg yolks
- 2 tablespoons unsalted butter, cut into pieces, or almond oil
- 3 cups bread flour
- 1 tablespoon sugar

- 1 tablespoon gluten
- 11/4 teaspoons salt
- 21/2 teaspoons SAF yeast or 1 tablespoon bread machine yeast
- 1/4 cup Almond Confectioners' Sugar, for dusting (opposite)
- 16 slices (2 pounds)
- 1 cup (4 ounces) whole almonds
- 11/3 cups commercial eggnog
- 1/3 cup amaretto liqueur
- 2 large egg yolks
- 3 tablespoons unsalted butter, cut into pieces, or almond oil
- 4 cups bread flour
- 2 tablespoons sugar
- 1 tablespoon plus 1 teaspoon gluten
- 11/2 teaspoons salt
- 1 tablespoon SAF yeast or 1 tablespoon plus 1/2 teaspoon bread machine yeast
- 1/4 cup Almond Confectioners' Sugar, for dusting (opposite)

Directions:

1. Preheat the oven to 350°F.
2. Coarsely chop the almonds and spread them evenly on a clean baking sheet. Bake until lightly toasted, about 5 to 7 minutes. Remove from the oven and let cool.
3. Choose the size of loaf you would like to make and measure your ingredients.
4. Add the ingredients to the bread pan in the order listed above.
5. Place the pan in the bread machine and close the lid.
6. Turn on the bread maker. Select the Basic setting, then the loaf size, and finally the crust color. Start the cycle.
7. When the machine beeps, or between Knead 1 and Knead 2, add the almonds. Touch and press the dough with your fingers. It should be soft and pliable.
8. When the cycle is finished and the bread is baked, carefully remove the pan from the machine. Use a potholder as the handle will be very hot. Let rest for a few minutes.
9. Remove the bread from the pan and allow to cool on a wire rack for at least 10 minutes, then dust with Almond Confectioners' Sugar before slicing.

Holiday Raisin Bread With Candied Peels

Ingredients:
- 8 slices (1 pound)
- 2/3 cup milk
- 1 1/2 tablespoons honey
- 2 cups bread flour
- 2/3 tablespoon gluten
- 1 teaspoon salt
- 1 1/4 teaspoons SAF yeast or 1/2 tablespoon bread machine yeast
- 1/4 cup rum raisins (shown here)
- 1/6 cup chopped candied grapefruit peel or candied lemon peel (opposite)
- 1/4 cup chopped candied orange peel (opposite)
- 12 slices (1½ pounds)
- 11/8 cups milk
- 2 tablespoons honey
- 3 cups bread flour
- 1 tablespoon gluten
- 11/2 teaspoons salt
- 2 teaspoons SAF yeast or 21/2 teaspoons bread machine yeast
- 1/3 cup rum raisins (shown here)
- 1/4 cup chopped candied grapefruit peel or candied lemon peel (opposite)
- 1/3 cup chopped candied orange peel (opposite)
- 16 slices (2 pounds)
- 11/3 cups milk
- 3 tablespoons honey
- 4 cups bread flour
- 1 tablespoon plus 1 teaspoon gluten
- 2 teaspoons salt
- 21/2 teaspoons SAF yeast or 1 tablespoon bread machine yeast
- 1/2 cup rum raisins (shown here)
- 1/3 cup chopped candied grapefruit peel or candied lemon peel (opposite)
- 1/2 cup chopped candied orange peel (opposite)

Directions:

1. Choose the size of loaf you would like to make and measure your ingredients.

2. Add the ingredients to the bread pan in the order listed above (except the raisins and candied peels).

3. Place the pan in the bread machine and close the lid.

4. Turn on the bread maker. Select the Sweet Bread/Fruit and Nut setting, then the loaf size, and finally the crust color. Start the cycle. (This recipe is not suitable for use with the Delay Timer.)

5. When the machine beeps, or between Knead 1 and Knead 2, add the raisins and candied peels.

6. When the cycle is finished and the bread is baked, carefully remove the pan from the machine. Use a potholder as the handle will be very hot. Let rest for a few minutes.

7. Remove the bread from the pan and allow to cool on a wire rack for at least 10 minutes before slicing.

Holiday Eggnog Bread

Ingredients:

- 8 slices (1 pound)
- 3/4 cup eggnog, at room temperature
- 3/4 tablespoon unsalted butter, melted
- 1 tablespoon sugar
- 5/8 teaspoon table salt
- 1/4 teaspoon ground cinnamon
- 1/4 teaspoon ground nutmeg
- 2 cups white bread flour
- 7/8 teaspoon bread machine yeast
- 12 slices (1 ½ pounds)
- 1⅛ cups eggnog, at room temperature
- 1⅛ tablespoons unsalted butter, melted
- 1½ tablespoons sugar
- 1 teaspoon table salt
- ⅓ teaspoon ground cinnamon
- ⅓ teaspoon ground nutmeg
- 3 cups white bread flour
- 1⅓ teaspoons bread machine yeast
- 16 slices (2 pounds)
- 1½ cups eggnog, at room temperature
- 1½ tablespoons unsalted butter, melted
- 2 tablespoons sugar

- 1¼ teaspoons table salt
- ½ teaspoon ground cinnamon
- ½ teaspoon ground nutmeg
- 4 cups white bread flour
- 1¾ teaspoons bread machine yeast

Directions:

1. Choose the size of loaf you would like to make and measure your ingredients.

2. Add the ingredients to the bread pan in the order listed above.

3. Place the pan in the bread machine and close the lid.

4. Turn on the bread maker. Select the White/Basic setting, then the loaf size, and finally the crust color. Start the cycle.

5. When the cycle is finished and the bread is baked, carefully remove the pan from the machine. Use a potholder as the handle will be very hot. Let rest for a few minutes.

6. Remove the bread from the pan and allow to cool on a wire rack for at least 10 minutes before slicing.

Orange Gingerbread With Orange Whipped Cream

Ingredients:

- 8 slices (1 pound)
- For the gingerbread:
- 4 tablespoons unsalted butter, melted
- 1/2 cup light molasses
- 2 large eggs
- Grated zest of 1 orange
- 1/2 cup light brown sugar
- 3/4 cup buttermilk
- 2 teaspoons baking soda dissolved in 1/4 cup hot water
- 21/2 cups unbleached all-purpose flour
- 1/2 teaspoon baking powder
- 2 teaspoons ground ginger
- 11/2 teaspoons apple pie spice or 1/2 teaspoon ground cinnamon, 1/2 teaspoon allspice, and 1/2 teaspoon cloves
- 3/4 teaspoon salt
- 2 tablespoons chopped candied ginger, optional
- For the orange whipped cream:

- 1 cup heavy cream
- 2 tablespoons confectioners' sugar
- 2 tablespoons Grand Marnier orange liqueur or thawed orange juice concentrate
- 1/2 teaspoon vanilla extract
- 12 slices (1 ½ pounds)
- For the gingerbread:
- 6 tablespoons unsalted butter, melted
- 3/4 cup light molasses
- 3 large eggs
- Grated zest of 1 1/2 oranges
- 3/4 cup light brown sugar
- 1 1/8 cups buttermilk
- 3 teaspoons baking soda dissolved in 3/8 cup hot water
- 3 3/4 cups unbleached all-purpose flour
- 3/4 teaspoon baking powder
- 3 teaspoons ground ginger
- 2 1/4 teaspoons apple pie spice or 3/4 teaspoon ground cinnamon, 3/4 teaspoon allspice, and 3/4 teaspoon cloves
- 1 1/8 teaspoons salt
- 3 tablespoons chopped candied ginger, optional
- For the orange whipped cream:
- 1 cup heavy cream
- 2 tablespoons confectioners' sugar
- 2 tablespoons Grand Marnier orange liqueur or thawed orange juice concentrate
- 1/2 teaspoon vanilla extract
- 16 slices (2 pounds)
- For the gingerbread:
- 8 tablespoons unsalted butter, melted
- 1 cup light molasses
- 4 large eggs
- Grated zest of 2 oranges
- 1 cup light brown sugar
- 1 1/2 cups buttermilk
- 4 teaspoons baking soda dissolved in 1/2 cup hot water
- 5 cups unbleached all-purpose flour
- 1 teaspoon baking powder
- 4 teaspoons ground ginger
- 3 teaspoons apple pie spice or 1 teaspoon ground cinnamon, 1 teaspoon allspice, and 1 teaspoon cloves

- 1 1/2 teaspoons salt
- 4 tablespoons chopped candied ginger, optional
- For the orange whipped cream:
- 1 cup heavy cream
- 2 tablespoons confectioners' sugar
- 2 tablespoons Grand Marnier orange liqueur or thawed orange juice concentrate
- 1/2 teaspoon vanilla extract

Directions:

1. Choose the size of loaf you would like to make and measure your ingredients.

2. To prepare the orange whipped cream, combine all the ingredients in a chilled bowl. Beat with an electric mixer until soft peaks are formed. Cover and chill until needed.

3. To make the gingerbread, add the gingerbread ingredients to the bread pan in the order listed above.

4. Place the pan in the bread machine and close the lid.

5. Turn on the bread maker. Select the Quick Bread/Cake setting, then the loaf size, and finally the crust color. Start the cycle.

6. When the machine beeps at the end of the cycle, check the loaf for doneness. If the indentation remains, press Stop/Reset and program for the Bake Only cycle; check at intervals until the loaf is done.

7. When the cycle is finished and the bread is baked, carefully remove the pan from the machine. Use a potholder as the handle will be very hot. Let rest for a few minutes.

8. Remove the bread from the pan and allow to cool on a wire rack for at least 10 minutes before slicing.

Basil Pizza Dough

Ingredients:
- 8 slices (1 pound)
- 5/8 cup lukewarm water
- 1/8 cup olive oil
- 5/8 teaspoon table salt
- 1 teaspoon sugar
- 1 teaspoon basil, dried
- 2 cups white bread flour or all-purpose flour
- 1 teaspoon bread machine yeast
- 12 slices (1 ½ pounds)

- 1 cup lukewarm water
- 3 tablespoons olive oil
- 1 teaspoon table salt
- 1½ teaspoons sugar
- 1½ teaspoons basil, dried
- 3 cups white bread flour or all-purpose flour
- 1½ teaspoons bread machine yeast
- 16 slices (2 pounds)
- 1¼ cups lukewarm water
- ¼ cup olive oil
- 1¼ teaspoons table salt
- 2 teaspoons sugar
- 2 teaspoons basil, dried
- 4 cups white bread flour or all-purpose flour
- 2 teaspoons bread machine yeast

Directions:

1. Choose the size of dough you would like to make and measure your ingredients.

2. Add the ingredients to the bread pan in the order listed above.

3. Place the pan in the bread machine and close the lid.

4. Turn on the bread maker. Select the Dough setting and then the dough size. Start the machine.

5. When the cycle is finished, carefully remove the dough from the pan.

6. Place the dough on a lightly floured surface and roll to make a pizza crust of your desired thickness. Set aside for 10–15 minutes.

7. Top with your favorite pizza sauce, toppings, cheese, etc.

8. Bake in an oven at 400°F or 204°C for 15–20 minutes or until the edges turn lightly golden.

Granola Breakfast Bread

Ingredients:
- 8 slices (1 pound)
- 3/4 cup milk
- 1/4 cup plain yogurt
- 1/2 cup vegetable or nut oil
- 2 large eggs
- Grated zest of 1 lemon
- 1 teaspoon vanilla extract
- 3/4 cup sugar
- 1 cup whole wheat pastry flour
- 1 cup unbleached all-purpose flour
- 3/4 cup granola
- 1/2 cup chopped dried pineapple or golden raisins
- 1 tablespoon baking powder
- 1/2 teaspoon ground cinnamon or apple pie spice
- 1/2 teaspoon salt
- 12 slices (1 ½ pounds)
- 1 1/8 cups milk
- 3/8 cup plain yogurt
- 3/4 cup vegetable or nut oil
- 3 large eggs
- Grated zest of 1 1/2 lemons
- 1 1/2 teaspoons vanilla extract
- 1 1/8 cups sugar
- 1 1/2 cups whole wheat pastry flour
- 1 1/2 cups unbleached all-purpose flour
- 1 1/8 cups granola
- 3/4 cup chopped dried pineapple or golden raisins
- 1 1/2 tablespoons baking powder
- 3/4 teaspoon ground cinnamon or apple pie spice
- 3/4 teaspoon salt
- 16 slices (2 pounds)
- 1 1/2 cups milk
- 1/2 cup plain yogurt
- 1 cup vegetable or nut oil
- 4 large eggs
- Grated zest of 2 lemons
- 2 teaspoons vanilla extract
- 1 1/2 cups sugar
- 2 cups whole wheat pastry flour
- 2 cups unbleached all-purpose flour
- 1 1/2 cups granola
- 1 cup chopped dried pineapple or golden raisins
- 2 tablespoons baking powder
- 1 teaspoon ground cinnamon or apple pie spice
- 1 teaspoon salt

Directions:

1. Choose the size of loaf you would like to make and measure your ingredients.

2. Add the ingredients to the bread pan in the order listed above.

3. Place the pan in the bread machine and close the lid.

4. Turn on the bread maker. Select the Quick Bread/Cake setting, then the loaf size, and finally the crust color. Start the cycle.

5. When the machine beeps at the end of the cycle, check the loaf for doneness.

6. When the cycle is finished and the bread is baked, carefully remove the pan from the machine. Use a potholder as the handle will be very hot. Let rest for a few minutes.

7. Remove the bread from the pan and allow to cool on a wire rack for at least 10 minutes before slicing.

Christmas Eggnog Bread

Ingredients:
- 8 slices (1 pound)
- 1 cup eggnog
- ½ cup milk
- 4 cups bread flour
- ½ cup dried cranberries
- 1¼ teaspoons salt
- 2 tablespoons sugar
- 1 tablespoon butter
- 1 teaspoon cinnamon
- 1¾ teaspoons bread machine yeast
- 12 slices (1 ½ pounds)
- 1 1/2 cups eggnog
- 3/4 cup milk
- 6 cups bread flour
- 3/4 cup dried cranberries
- 1 7/8 teaspoons salt
- 3 tablespoons sugar
- 1 1/2 tablespoons butter
- 1 1/2 teaspoons cinnamon
- 2 5/8 teaspoons bread machine yeast
- 16 slices (2 pounds)
- 2 cups eggnog
- 1 cup milk
- 8 cups bread flour
- 1 cup dried cranberries
- 2 1/2 teaspoons salt
- 4 tablespoons sugar
- 2 tablespoons butter
- 2 teaspoons cinnamon
- 3 1/2 teaspoons bread machine yeast

Directions:
1. Choose the size of loaf you would like to make and measure your ingredients.

2. Add the ingredients to the bread pan in the order listed above.

3. Place the pan in the bread machine and close the lid.

4. Turn on the bread maker. Select the White/Basic setting, then the loaf size, and finally the crust color. Start the cycle.

5. When the cycle is finished and the bread is baked, carefully remove the pan from the machine. Use a potholder as the handle will be very hot. Let rest for a few minutes.

6. Remove the bread from the pan and allow to cool on a wire rack for at least 10 minutes before slicing.

SOURDOUGH BREAD RECIPES

Classic Sourdough Rye

Ingredients:
- 8 slices (1 pound)
- For the sponge:
- 1/2 cup Next-Day Rye Sourdough Starter
- 3/4 cup water
- 3/4 cup light or medium rye flour
- 1/4 teaspoon SAF or bread machine yeast
- For the dough:
- 3/4 tablespoon unsalted butter, melted
- 11/2 cups bread flour
- 3/4 tablespoon sugar
- 1/2 tablespoon plus 1/2 teaspoon caraway seeds
- 1 teaspoon salt
- 5/8 teaspoon SAF yeast or 1 3/4 teaspoons bread machine yeast
- 12 slices (1 ½ pounds)
- For the sponge:
- 3/4 cup Next-Day Rye Sourdough Starter
- 11/8 cups water
- 11/8 cups light or medium rye flour
- 1/2 teaspoon SAF or bread machine yeast
- For the dough:
- 1 tablespoon unsalted butter, melted
- 21/4 cups bread flour
- 1 tablespoon sugar
- 1 tablespoon caraway seeds
- 11/2 teaspoons salt
- 1 teaspoon SAF yeast or 11/2 teaspoons bread machine yeast
- 16 slices (2 pounds)
- For the sponge:
- 1 cup Next-Day Rye Sourdough Starter
- 11/2 cups water
- 11/2 cups light or medium rye flour
- 1/2 teaspoon SAF or bread machine yeast
- For the dough:
- 11/2 tablespoons unsalted butter, melted
- 3 cups bread flour
- 11/2 tablespoons sugar

- 1 tablespoon plus 1 teaspoon caraway seeds
- 2 teaspoons salt
- 11/4 teaspoons SAF yeast or 13/4 teaspoons bread machine yeast

Directions:
1. Choose the size of loaf you would like to make and measure your ingredients.
2. To make the sponge, place the sponge ingredients in the bread pan. Program for the Dough cycle; press Start. When the machine beeps at the end of the cycle, press Stop and unplug the machine. Let the sponge starter sit in the machine for 8 hours, or as long as overnight.
3. Add all the dough ingredients to the bread pan in the order listed above (including the sponge).
4. Place the pan in the bread machine and close the lid.
5. Turn on the bread maker. Select the Basic or French Bread setting, then the loaf size, and finally the crust color. Start the cycle. (This recipe is not suitable for use with the Delay Timer.)
6. When the cycle is finished and the bread is baked, carefully remove the pan from the machine. Use a potholder as the handle will be very hot. Let rest for a few minutes.
7. Remove the bread from the pan and allow to cool on a wire rack for at least 10 minutes before slicing.

Sourdough Carrot Poppy Seed Bread

Ingredients:
- 8 slices (1 pound)
- 1/2 cup sourdough starter (shown here to here)
- 1/3 cup buttermilk
- 1 tablespoon olive or walnut oil
- 1 2/3 cups bread flour
- 1/3 cup whole wheat flour
- 3/4 cup shredded raw carrots
- 11/2 tablespoons minced dried apricots
- 5/8 tablespoon poppy seeds
- 5/8 tablespoon sugar
- 1 teaspoon salt
- 7/8 teaspoon SAF yeast or 1 1/8 teaspoons bread machine yeast

- 12 slices (1 ½ pounds)
- 3/4 cup sourdough starter (shown here to here)
- 1/2 cup buttermilk
- 11/2 tablespoons olive or walnut oil
- 21/2 cups bread flour
- 1/2 cup whole wheat flour
- 11/4 cups shredded raw carrots
- 2 tablespoons minced dried apricots
- 1 tablespoon poppy seeds
- 1 tablespoon sugar
- 11/2 teaspoons salt
- 11/4 teaspoons SAF yeast or 13/4 teaspoons bread machine yeast
- 16 slices (2 pounds)
- 1 cup sourdough starter (shown here to here)
- 2/3 cup buttermilk
- 2 tablespoons olive or walnut oil
- 31/3 cups bread flour
- 2/3 cup whole wheat flour
- 11/2 cups shredded raw carrots
- 3 tablespoons minced dried apricots
- 11/4 tablespoons poppy seeds
- 11/4 tablespoons sugar
- 2 teaspoons salt
- 13/4 teaspoons SAF yeast or 21/4 teaspoons bread machine yeast

Directions:

1. Choose the size of loaf you would like to make and measure your ingredients.

2. Add the ingredients to the bread pan in the order listed above.

3. Place the pan in the bread machine and close the lid.

4. Turn on the bread maker. Select the Basic setting, then the loaf size, and finally the crust color. Start the cycle.

5. When the cycle is finished and the bread is baked, carefully remove the pan from the machine. Use a potholder as the handle will be very hot. Let rest for a few minutes.

6. Remove the bread from the pan and allow to cool on a wire rack for at least 10 minutes before slicing.

Sourdough Raisin Bread

Ingredients:

- 8 slices (1 pound)
- 7/8 cup raisins
- 3/8 cup sourdough starter (shown here to here)
- 1/3 cup fat-free milk
- 1 large egg
- 1 1/2 tablespoons margarine, cut into pieces
- 2 cups bread flour
- 1 1/4 tablespoons sugar
- 1 teaspoon salt
- 5/8 teaspoon SAF yeast or 7/8 teaspoon bread machine yeast
- 12 slices (1 ½ pounds)
- 11/2 cups raisins
- 1/2 cup sourdough starter (shown here to here)
- 1/2 cup fat-free milk
- 2 large eggs
- 2 tablespoons margarine, cut into pieces
- 3 cups bread flour
- 2 tablespoons sugar
- 11/2 teaspoons salt
- 1 teaspoon SAF yeast or 11/2 teaspoons bread machine yeast
- 16 slices (2 pounds)
- 13/4 cup raisins
- 3/4 cups sourdough starter (shown here to here)
- 2/3 cup fat-free milk
- 2 large eggs
- 3 tablespoons margarine, cut into pieces
- 4 cups bread flour
- 21/2 tablespoons sugar
- 2 teaspoons salt
- 11/4 teaspoons SAF yeast or 13/4 teaspoons bread machine yeast

Directions:

1. Choose the size of loaf you would like to make and measure your ingredients.

2. Place the raisins in a bowl and cover with hot water. Let stand for 11/2 hours at room temperature to soften. Drain the raisins and pat as dry as possible, as any moisture will be incorporated into the dough.

3. Add the ingredients to the bread pan in the order listed above.

4. Place the pan in the bread machine and close the lid.

5. Turn on the bread maker. Select the Basic setting, then the loaf size, and finally the crust color. Start the cycle.

6. Add the raisins during the first 10 minutes of Knead 2. Gradually sprinkle in the raisins while the machine is kneading. If the dough looks too sticky after the raisins are incorporated, sprinkle another 1 to 2 tablespoons of flour around the paddle while the machine is running.

7. When the cycle is finished and the bread is baked, carefully remove the pan from the machine. Use a potholder as the handle will be very hot. Let rest for a few minutes.

8. Remove the bread from the pan and allow to cool on a wire rack for at least 10 minutes before slicing.

Orange Sourdough Bread With Cranberries, Pecans, And Golden Raisins

Ingredients:
- 8 slices (1 pound)
- 3/8 cup French Buttermilk Starter, or any white flour sourdough starter
- 1/2 cup orange juice
- 11/2 tablespoons butter, cut into pieces
- 2 1/8 cups bread flour
- 1/8 cup sugar
- 3/4 teaspoon salt
- 1 teaspoon SAF yeast or 11/4 teaspoons bread machine yeast
- 1/3 cup dried cranberries
- 1/4 cup golden raisins
- 1/4 cup chopped pecans
- 12 slices (1 ½ pounds)
- 1/2 cup French Buttermilk Starter, or any white flour sourdough starter
- 3/4 cup orange juice
- 2 tablespoons butter, cut into pieces
- 31/4 cups bread flour
- 3 tablespoons sugar
- 1 teaspoon salt
- 13/4 teaspoons SAF yeast or 21/4 teaspoons bread machine yeast
- 1/2 cup dried cranberries
- 1/3 cup golden raisins
- 1/3 cup chopped pecans
- 16 slices (2 pounds)
- 3/4 cup French Buttermilk Starter, or any white flour sourdough starter
- 1 cup orange juice
- 3 tablespoons butter, cut into pieces
- 41/4 cups bread flour
- 1/4 cup sugar
- 11/2 teaspoons salt
- 2 teaspoons SAF yeast or 21/2 teaspoons bread machine yeast
- 2/3 cup dried cranberries
- 1/2 cup golden raisins
- 1/2 cup chopped pecans

Directions:

1. Choose the size of loaf you would like to make and measure your ingredients.

2. Add the ingredients to the bread pan in the order listed above (except the fruit and nuts).

3. Place the pan in the bread machine and close the lid.

4. Turn on the bread maker. Select the Basic/Fruit and Nut setting, then the loaf size, and finally the crust color. Start the cycle. (This recipe is not suitable for use with the Delay Timer.)

5. When the machine beeps, or between Knead 1 and Knead 2, add the fruits and nuts.

6. When the cycle is finished and the bread is baked, carefully remove the pan from the machine. Use a potholder as the handle will be very hot. Let rest for a few minutes.

7. Remove the bread from the pan and allow to cool on a wire rack for at least 10 minutes before slicing.

Sourdough Bread With Fresh Pears And Walnuts

Ingredients:
- 8 slices (1 pound)
- 1/2 cup sourdough starter (shown here to here)
- 1/4 cup buttermilk

- 1 teaspoon vanilla extract
- 11 /2 tablespoons butter, cut into pieces
- 2 cups bread flour
- 1/4 cup rolled oats
- 2 tablespoons light brown sugar
- 1/4 cup walnuts
- 1/2 tablespoon apple pie spice
- 1 teaspoon salt
- 7/8 teaspoon SAF yeast or 11/8 teaspoons bread machine yeast
- 1 cup peeled, cored, and chopped fresh pear (about 1 large pear)
- 12 slices (1 ½ pounds)
- 3/4 cup sourdough starter (shown here to here)
- 1/3 cup buttermilk
- 11/2 teaspoons vanilla extract
- 2 tablespoons butter, cut into pieces
- 3 cups bread flour
- 1/3 cup rolled oats
- 3 tablespoons light brown sugar
- 1/3 cup walnuts
- 2 teaspoons apple pie spice
- 11/2 teaspoons salt
- 11/4 teaspoons SAF yeast or 13/4 teaspoons bread machine yeast
- 11/2 cups peeled, cored, and chopped fresh pear (1 to 2 large pears)
- 16 slices (2 pounds)
- 1 cup sourdough starter (shown here to here)
- 1/2 cup buttermilk
- 2 teaspoons vanilla extract
- 3 tablespoons butter, cut into pieces
- 4 cups bread flour
- 1/2 cup rolled oats
- 4 tablespoons light brown sugar
- 1/2 cup walnuts
- 1 tablespoon apple pie spice
- 2 teaspoons salt
- 13/4 teaspoons SAF yeast or 21/4 teaspoons bread machine yeast
- 2 cups peeled, cored, and chopped fresh pear (about 2 large pears)

Directions:

1. Choose the size of loaf you would like to make and measure your ingredients.
2. Add the ingredients to the bread pan in the order listed above (except the pears).
3. Place the pan in the bread machine and close the lid.
4. Turn on the bread maker. Select the Basic or Sweet Bread setting, then the loaf size, and finally the crust color. Start the cycle. (This recipe is not suitable for use with the Delay Timer.)
5. About 5 minutes into the kneading, sprinkle the pears into the dough, a few at a time, until all the pears are added.
6. When the cycle is finished and the bread is baked, carefully remove the pan from the machine. Use a potholder as the handle will be very hot. Let rest for a few minutes.
7. Remove the bread from the pan and allow to cool on a wire rack for at least 10 minutes before slicing.

Sourdough Banana Nut Bread

Ingredients:
- 8 slices (1 pound)
- 3/8 cup sourdough starter
- 1/4 cup buttermilk
- 1/3 cup sliced bananas
- 1/2 large egg
- 1 1/2 tablespoons nut oil
- 1 2/3 cups bread flour
- 1/3 cup whole wheat flour
- 1/3 cup chopped macadamia nuts or pecans
- 2 tablespoons chopped dried pineapple or dates
- 11 /2 tablespoons light brown sugar
- 3/4 teaspoon salt
- 11/8 teaspoons SAF yeast or 1 3/8 teaspoons bread machine yeast
- 12 slices (1 ½ pounds)
- 1/2 cup sourdough starter
- 1/4 cup buttermilk
- 1/2 cup sliced bananas
- 1 large egg
- 2 tablespoons nut oil
- 21/2 cups bread flour
- 1/2 cup whole wheat flour

- 1/2 cup chopped macadamia nuts or pecans
- 3 tablespoons chopped dried pineapple or dates
- 2 tablespoons light brown sugar
- 11/4 teaspoons salt
- 13/4 teaspoons SAF yeast or 21/4 teaspoons bread machine yeast
- 16 slices (2 pounds)
- 3/4 cups sourdough starter
- 1/2 cup buttermilk
- 2/3 cup sliced bananas
- 1 large egg
- 3 tablespoons nut oil
- 31/3 cups bread flour
- 2/3 cup whole wheat flour
- 2/3 cup chopped macadamia nuts or pecans
- 4 tablespoons chopped dried pineapple or dates
- 3 tablespoons light brown sugar
- 11/2 teaspoons salt
- 21/4 teaspoons SAF yeast or 23/4 teaspoons bread machine yeast

Directions:

1. Choose the size of loaf you would like to make and measure your ingredients.

2. Add the ingredients to the bread pan in the order listed above.

3. Place the pan in the bread machine and close the lid.

4. Turn on the bread maker. Select the Basic setting, then the loaf size, and finally the crust color. Start the cycle.

5. When the cycle is finished and the bread is baked, carefully remove the pan from the machine. Use a potholder as the handle will be very hot. Let rest for a few minutes.

6. Remove the bread from the pan and allow to cool on a wire rack for at least 10 minutes before slicing.

Sourdough Pesto Bread

Ingredients:

- 8 slices (1 pound)
- 2/3 cup sourdough starter (shown here to here)
- 1/4 cup fat-free milk
- 1 1/2 tablespoons olive oil
- 1/8 cup pesto
- 2 cups bread flour
- 3/4 tablespoon sugar
- 7/8 teaspoon garlic powder
- 5/8 teaspoon dried marjoram
- 5/8 teaspoon dried basil
- 3/4 teaspoon salt
- 7/8 teaspoon SAF yeast or 1 1/8 teaspoons bread machine yeast
- 12 slices (1 ½ pounds)
- 1 cup sourdough starter (shown here to here)
- 1/3 cup fat-free milk
- 2 tablespoons olive oil
- 3 tablespoons pesto
- 3 cups bread flour
- 1 tablespoon sugar
- 11/2 teaspoons garlic powder
- 1 teaspoon dried marjoram
- 1 teaspoon dried basil
- 1 teaspoon salt
- 11/2 teaspoons SAF yeast or 2 teaspoons bread machine yeast
- 16 slices (2 pounds)
- 11/3 cups sourdough starter (shown here to here)
- 1/2 cup fat-free milk
- 3 tablespoons olive oil
- 1/4 cup pesto
- 4 cups bread flour
- 11/2 tablespoons sugar
- 13/4 teaspoons garlic powder
- 11/4 teaspoons dried marjoram
- 11/4 teaspoons dried basil
- 11/2 teaspoons salt
- 13/4 teaspoons SAF yeast or 21/4 teaspoons bread machine yeast

Directions:

1. Choose the size of loaf you would like to make and measure your ingredients.

2. Add the ingredients to the bread pan in the order listed above.

3. Place the pan in the bread machine and close the lid.

4. Turn on the bread maker. Select the Basic setting, then the loaf size, and finally the crust color. Start the

cycle. (This recipe is not suitable for use with the Delay Timer.)

5. When the cycle is finished and the bread is baked, carefully remove the pan from the machine. Use a potholder as the handle will be very hot. Let rest for a few minutes.

6. Remove the bread from the pan and allow to cool on a wire rack for at least 10 minutes before slicing.

Sourdough Cottage Cheese Bread With Fresh Herbs

Ingredients:
- 8 slices (1 pound)
- 1/2 cup sourdough starter (shown here to here)
- 1/2 cup cottage cheese
- 1 1/2 tablespoons olive oil
- 2 cups bread flour
- 1/8 cup chopped fresh watercress leaves, loosely packed
- 1/2 tablespoon chopped fresh chives
- 1/2 tablespoon chopped fresh basil
- 1/2 tablespoon chopped fresh dill
- 1 teaspoon chopped fresh marjoram
- 1/8 teaspoon dried lemon rind or 1/4 teaspoon fresh lemon zest
- 1 teaspoon salt
- 7/8 teaspoon SAF yeast or 1 1/8 teaspoons bread machine yeast
- 12 slices (1 ½ pounds)
- 3/4 cup sourdough starter (shown here to here)
- 3/4 cup cottage cheese
- 2 tablespoons olive oil
- 3 cups bread flour
- 1/4 cup chopped fresh watercress leaves, loosely packed
- 1 tablespoon chopped fresh chives
- 1 tablespoon chopped fresh basil
- 1 tablespoon chopped fresh dill
- 2 teaspoons chopped fresh marjoram
- 1/4 teaspoon dried lemon rind or 1/2 teaspoon fresh lemon zest
- 11/2 teaspoons salt
- 11/2 teaspoons SAF yeast or 2 teaspoons bread machine yeast
- 16 slices (2 pounds)
- 1 cup sourdough starter (shown here to here)
- 1 cup cottage cheese
- 3 tablespoons olive oil
- 4 cups bread flour
- 1/4 cup chopped fresh watercress leaves, loosely packed
- 1 tablespoon chopped fresh chives
- 1 tablespoon chopped fresh basil
- 1 tablespoon chopped fresh dill
- 2 teaspoons chopped fresh marjoram
- 1/4 teaspoon dried lemon rind or 1/2 teaspoon fresh lemon zest
- 2 teaspoons salt
- 13/4 teaspoons SAF yeast or 21/4 teaspoons bread machine yeast

Directions:
1. Choose the size of loaf you would like to make and measure your ingredients.
2. Add the ingredients to the bread pan in the order listed above.
3. Place the pan in the bread machine and close the lid.
4. Turn on the bread maker. Select the Basic setting, then the loaf size, and finally the crust color. Start the cycle.
5. When the cycle is finished and the bread is baked, carefully remove the pan from the machine. Use a potholder as the handle will be very hot. Let rest for a few minutes.
6. Remove the bread from the pan and allow to cool on a wire rack for at least 10 minutes before slicing.

White Sourdough Bread

Ingredients:
- 8 slices (1 pound)
- 1/2 cup sourdough starter (shown here to here)
- 3/8 cup fat-free milk
- 1 1/2 tablespoons unsalted butter, melted
- 1 tablespoon honey
- 2 cups bread flour
- 1 teaspoon salt

- 7/8 teaspoon SAF yeast or 11/8 teaspoons bread machine yeast
- 12 slices (1 ½ pounds)
- 3/4 cup sourdough starter (shown here to here)
- 1/2 cup fat-free milk
- 2 tablespoons unsalted butter, melted
- 11/2 tablespoons honey
- 3 cups bread flour
- 11/2 teaspoons salt
- 11/2 teaspoons SAF yeast or 2 teaspoons bread machine yeast
- 16 slices (2 pounds)
- 1 cup sourdough starter (shown here to here)
- 3/4 cup fat-free milk
- 3 tablespoons unsalted butter, melted
- 2 tablespoons honey
- 4 cups bread flour
- 2 teaspoons salt
- 13/4 teaspoons SAF yeast or 21/4 teaspoons bread machine yeast

Directions:

1. Choose the size of loaf you would like to make and measure your ingredients.

2. Add the ingredients to the bread pan in the order listed above.

3. Place the pan in the bread machine and close the lid.

4. Turn on the bread maker. Select the Basic setting, then the loaf size, and finally the crust color. Start the cycle.

5. When the cycle is finished and the bread is baked, carefully remove the pan from the machine. Use a potholder as the handle will be very hot. Let rest for a few minutes.

6. Remove the bread from the pan and allow to cool on a wire rack for at least 10 minutes before slicing.

Sourdough Tomato Bread With Feta

Ingredients:
- 8 slices (1 pound)
- 1/2 cup sourdough starter (shown here to here)
- 3/8 cup chopped canned tomatoes with some liquid
- 1 1/2 tablespoons olive oil
- 2 cups bread flour
- 3/8 cup crumbled feta cheese
- 3/8 teaspoon salt
- 7/8 teaspoon SAF yeast or 1 1/8 teaspoons bread machine yeast
- 12 slices (1 ½ pounds)
- 3/4 cup sourdough starter (shown here to here)
- 3/4 cup chopped canned tomatoes with some liquid
- 2 tablespoons olive oil
- 3 cups bread flour
- 2/3 cup crumbled feta cheese
- 1/2 teaspoon salt
- 11/4 teaspoons SAF yeast or 1 3/4 teaspoons bread machine yeast
- 16 slices (2 pounds)
- 1 cup sourdough starter (shown here to here)
- 3/4 cup chopped canned tomatoes with some liquid
- 3 tablespoons olive oil
- 4 cups bread flour
- 3/4 cup crumbled feta cheese
- 3/4 teaspoon salt
- 13/4 teaspoons SAF yeast or 21/4 teaspoons bread machine yeast

Directions:

1. Choose the size of loaf you would like to make and measure your ingredients.

2. Add the ingredients to the bread pan in the order listed above.

3. Place the pan in the bread machine and close the lid.

4. Turn on the bread maker. Select the Basic setting, then the loaf size, and finally the crust color. Start the cycle.

5. When the cycle is finished and the bread is baked, carefully remove the pan from the machine. Use a potholder as the handle will be very hot. Let rest for a few minutes.

6. Remove the bread from the pan and allow to cool on a wire rack for at least 10 minutes before slicing.

Sourdough Cornmeal Bread

Ingredients:
- 8 slices (1 pound)
- 3/4 cup white flour sourdough starter (shown here to here)

- 7/16 cup plus 1/2 tablespoon fat-free milk
- 11/2 tablespoons olive oil or lard
- 2 tablespoons honey or molasses
- 13/4 cups bread flour
- 3/8 cup yellow cornmeal
- 1 teaspoon salt
- 1 teaspoon SAF yeast or 11/4 teaspoons bread machine yeast
- 12 slices (1 ½ pounds)
- 11/4 cups white flour sourdough starter (shown here to here)
- 1/2 cup plus 2 tablespoons fat-free milk
- 2 tablespoons olive oil or lard
- 3 tablespoons honey or molasses
- 21/2 cups bread flour
- 2/3 cup yellow cornmeal
- 11/2 teaspoons salt
- 11/2 teaspoons SAF yeast or 2 teaspoons bread machine yeast
- 16 slices (2 pounds)
- 11/2 cups white flour sourdough starter (shown here to here)
- 7/8 cup plus 1 tablespoon fat-free milk
- 3 tablespoons olive oil or lard
- 4 tablespoons honey or molasses
- 31/2 cups bread flour
- 3/4 cup yellow cornmeal
- 2 teaspoons salt
- 2 teaspoons SAF yeast or 21/2 teaspoons bread machine yeast

Directions:

1. Choose the size of loaf you would like to make and measure your ingredients.

2. Add the ingredients to the bread pan in the order listed above.

3. Place the pan in the bread machine and close the lid.

4. Turn on the bread maker. Select the Basic setting, then the loaf size, and finally the crust color. Start the cycle.

5. When the cycle is finished and the bread is baked, carefully remove the pan from the machine. Use a potholder as the handle will be very hot. Let rest for a few minutes.

6. Remove the bread from the pan and allow to cool on a wire rack for at least 10 minutes before slicing.

Sourdough Sunflower Seed Honey Bread

Ingredients:

- 8 slices (1 pound)
- 2/3 cup sourdough starter
- 1/3 cup fat-free milk
- 1/6 cup margarine, cut into pieces
- 3/4 cup bread flour
- 11/4 cups whole wheat flour
- 1/6 cup dark brown sugar
- 1/4 cup raw sunflower seeds
- 1 1/2 tablespoons chopped walnuts
- 1 teaspoon salt
- 7/8 teaspoon SAF yeast or 11/8 teaspoons bread machine yeast
- 12 slices (1 ½ pounds)
- 1 cup sourdough starter
- 1/2 cup fat-free milk
- 1/4 cup margarine, cut into pieces
- 1 cup bread flour
- 2 cups whole wheat flour
- 1/4 cup dark brown sugar
- 1/3 cup raw sunflower seeds
- 2 tablespoons chopped walnuts
- 11/2 teaspoons salt
- 11/2 teaspoons SAF yeast or 2 teaspoons bread machine yeast
- 16 slices (2 pounds)
- 11/3 cups sourdough starter
- 2/3 cup fat-free milk
- 1/3 cup margarine, cut into pieces
- 11/2 cups bread flour
- 21/2 cups whole wheat flour
- 1/3 cup dark brown sugar
- 1/2 cup raw sunflower seeds
- 3 tablespoons chopped walnuts
- 2 teaspoons salt
- 13/4 teaspoons SAF yeast or 21/4 teaspoons bread machine yeast

Directions:

1. Choose the size of loaf you would like to make and measure your ingredients.

2. Add the ingredients to the bread pan in the order listed above.

3. Place the pan in the bread machine and close the lid.

4. Turn on the bread maker. Select the Whole Wheat setting, then the loaf size, and finally the crust color. Start the cycle.

5. When the cycle is finished and the bread is baked, carefully remove the pan from the machine. Use a potholder as the handle will be very hot. Let rest for a few minutes.

6. Remove the bread from the pan and allow to cool on a wire rack for at least 10 minutes before slicing.

Sourdough Buckwheat Bread

Ingredients:
- 8 slices (1 pound)
- 5/8 cup white flour sourdough starter (shown here to here)
- 1/4 cup buttermilk
- 1/2 large egg
- Grated zest of 1/2 orange
- 1 1/2 tablespoons unsalted butter, melted
- 11/3 cups bread flour
- 1/3 cup whole wheat flour
- 1/3 cup buckwheat flour
- 1 3/4 tablespoons light brown sugar
- 1 teaspoon salt
- 7/8 teaspoon SAF yeast or 11/8 teaspoons bread machine yeast
- 12 slices (1 ½ pounds)
- 1 cup white flour sourdough starter (shown here to here)
- 1/4 cup buttermilk
- 1 large egg
- Grated zest of 1 orange
- 2 tablespoons unsalted butter, melted
- 2 cups bread flour
- 1/2 cup whole wheat flour
- 1/2 cup buckwheat flour
- 3 tablespoons light brown sugar
- 11/2 teaspoons salt
- 11/2 teaspoons SAF yeast or 2 teaspoons bread machine yeast
- 16 slices (2 pounds)
- 11/4 cups white flour sourdough starter (shown here to here)
- 1/2 cup buttermilk
- 1 large egg
- Grated zest of 1 orange
- 3 tablespoons unsalted butter, melted
- 22/3 cups bread flour
- 2/3 cup whole wheat flour
- 2/3 cup buckwheat flour
- 31/2 tablespoons light brown sugar
- 2 teaspoons salt
- 13/4 teaspoons SAF yeast or 21/4 teaspoons bread machine yeast

Directions:
1. Choose the size of loaf you would like to make and measure your ingredients.

2. Add the ingredients to the bread pan in the order listed above.

3. Place the pan in the bread machine and close the lid.

4. Turn on the bread maker. Select the Basic setting, then the loaf size, and finally the crust color. Start the cycle.

5. When the cycle is finished and the bread is baked, carefully remove the pan from the machine. Use a potholder as the handle will be very hot. Let rest for a few minutes.

6. Remove the bread from the pan and allow to cool on a wire rack for at least 10 minutes before slicing.

Sourdough Whole Wheat Bread

Ingredients:
- 8 slices (1 pound)
- 2/3 cup any sourdough starter (shown here to here)
- 1/4 cup fat-free milk
- 13/4 tablespoons canola oil
- 1/6 cup molasses
- 11/4 cups bread flour
- 3/4 cup whole wheat flour
- 1 teaspoon salt

- 7/8 teaspoon SAF yeast or 11/8 teaspoons bread machine yeast
- 12 slices (1 ½ pounds)
- 1 cup any sourdough starter (shown here to here)
- 1/3 cup fat-free milk
- 3 tablespoons canola oil
- 1/4 cup molasses
- 13/4 cups bread flour
- 11/4 cups whole wheat flour
- 11/2 teaspoons salt
- 11/4 teaspoons SAF yeast or 13/4 teaspoons bread machine yeast
- 16 slices (2 pounds)
- 11/3 cups any sourdough starter (shown here to here)
- 1/2 cup fat-free milk
- 31/2 tablespoons canola oil
- 1/3 cup molasses
- 21/2 cups bread flour
- 11/2 cups whole wheat flour
- 2 teaspoons salt
- 13/4 teaspoons SAF yeast or 21/4 teaspoons bread machine yeast

Directions:

1. Choose the size of loaf you would like to make and measure your ingredients.

2. Add the ingredients to the bread pan in the order listed above.

3. Place the pan in the bread machine and close the lid.

4. Turn on the bread maker. Select the Whole Wheat setting, then the loaf size, and finally the crust color. Start the cycle.

5. Check the consistency of the dough during Knead 2 and add a little more milk or flour as needed.

6. When the cycle is finished and the bread is baked, carefully remove the pan from the machine. Use a potholder as the handle will be very hot. Let rest for a few minutes.

7. Remove the bread from the pan and allow to cool on a wire rack for at least 10 minutes before slicing.

GLUTEN-FREE RECIPES

Gluten-free Whole Grain Bread

Ingredients:
- 8 slices (1 pound)
- 2/3 cup sorghum flour
- 1/2 cup buckwheat flour
- 1/2 cup millet flour
- 3/4 cup potato starch
- 2 1/4 teaspoons xanthan gum
- 1 1/4 teaspoons salt
- 3/4 cup skim milk
- 1/2 cup water
- 1 tablespoon instant yeast
- 5 teaspoons agave nectar, separated
- 1 large egg, lightly beaten
- 4 tablespoons extra virgin olive oil
- 1/2 teaspoon cider vinegar
- 1 tablespoon poppy seeds
- 12 slices (1 ½ pounds)
- 1 cup sorghum flour
- 3/4 cup buckwheat flour
- 3/4 cup millet flour
- 1 1/8 cups potato starch
- 3 3/8 teaspoons xanthan gum
- 1 7/8 teaspoons salt
- 1 1/8 cups skim milk
- 3/4 cup water
- 1 1/2 tablespoons instant yeast
- 7 1/2 teaspoons agave nectar, separated
- 1 1/2 large eggs, lightly beaten
- 6 tablespoons extra virgin olive oil
- 3/4 teaspoon cider vinegar
- 1 1/2 tablespoons poppy seeds
- 16 slices (2 pounds)
- 1 1/3 cups sorghum flour
- 1 cup buckwheat flour
- 1 cup millet flour
- 1 1/2 cups potato starch
- 4 1/2 teaspoons xanthan gum
- 2 1/2 teaspoons salt
- 1 1/2 cups skim milk

- 1 cup water
- 2 tablespoons instant yeast
- 10 teaspoons agave nectar, separated
- 2 large eggs, lightly beaten
- 8 tablespoons extra virgin olive oil
- 1 teaspoon cider vinegar
- 2 tablespoons poppy seeds

Directions:
1. Choose the size of loaf you would like to make and measure your ingredients.
2. Whisk sorghum, buckwheat, millet, potato starch, xanthan gum, and sea salt in a bowl and set aside.
3. Combine milk and water in a glass measuring cup. Heat to between 110°F and 120°F. Add 2 teaspoons of agave nectar and yeast and stir to combine. Cover and set aside for a few minutes.
4. Combine the egg, olive oil, remaining agave, and vinegar in another mixing bowl. Add yeast and milk mixture. Pour wet ingredients into the bottom of bread pan.
5. Add all the dry ingredients to the bread pan in the order listed above.
6. Place the pan in the bread machine and close the lid.
7. Turn on the bread maker. Select the Gluten-Free setting, then the loaf size, and finally the crust color. Start the cycle.
8. After second kneading cycle, sprinkle with poppy seeds.
9. When the cycle is finished and the bread is baked, carefully remove the pan from the machine. Use a potholder as the handle will be very hot. Let rest for a few minutes.
10. Remove the bread from the pan and allow to cool on a wire rack for at least 10 minutes before slicing.

Gluten-free Oat & Honey Bread

Ingredients:
- 8 slices (1 pound)
- 1 1/4 cups warm water
- 3 tablespoons honey
- 2 eggs

- 3 tablespoons butter, melted
- 1 1/4 cups gluten-free oats
- 1 1/4 cups brown rice flour
- 1/2 cup potato starch
- 2 teaspoons xanthan gum
- 1 1/2 teaspoons sugar
- 3/4 teaspoon salt
- 1 1/2 tablespoons active dry yeast
- 12 slices (1 ½ pounds)
- 1 7/8 cups warm water
- 4 1/2 tablespoons honey
- 3 eggs
- 4 1/2 tablespoons butter, melted
- 1 7/8 cups gluten-free oats
- 1 7/8 cups brown rice flour
- 3/4 cup potato starch
- 3 teaspoons xanthan gum
- 2 1/4 teaspoons sugar
- 1 1/8 teaspoons salt
- 2 1/4 tablespoons active dry yeast
- 16 slices (2 pounds)
- 2 1/2 cups warm water
- 6 tablespoons honey
- 4 eggs
- 6 tablespoons butter, melted
- 2 1/2 cups gluten-free oats
- 2 1/2 cups brown rice flour
- 1 cup potato starch
- 4 teaspoons xanthan gum
- 3 teaspoons sugar
- 1 1/2 teaspoons salt
- 3 tablespoons active dry yeast

Directions:

1. Choose the size of loaf you would like to make and measure your ingredients.

2. Add the ingredients to the bread pan in the order listed above (except yeast).

3. Place the pan in the bread machine and close the lid.

4. Turn on the bread maker. Select the Gluten-Free setting, then the loaf size, and finally the crust color. Start the cycle.

5. When the cycle is finished and the bread is baked, carefully remove the pan from the machine. Use a potholder as the handle will be very hot. Let rest for a few minutes.

6. Remove the bread from the pan and allow to cool on a wire rack for at least 10 minutes before slicing.

Grain-free Chia Bread

Ingredients:

- 8 slices (1 pound)
- 1 cup warm water
- 3 large organic eggs, room temperature
- 1/4 cup olive oil
- 1 tablespoon apple cider vinegar
- 1 cup gluten-free chia seeds, ground to flour
- 1 cup almond meal flour
- 1/2 cup potato starch
- 1/4 cup coconut flour
- 3/4 cup millet flour
- 1 tablespoon xanthan gum
- 1 1/2 teaspoons salt
- 2 tablespoons sugar
- 3 tablespoons nonfat dry milk
- 6 teaspoons instant yeas
- 12 slices (1 ½ pounds)
- 1 1/2 cups warm water
- 4 1/2 large organic eggs, room temperature
- 3/8 cup olive oil
- 1 1/2 tablespoons apple cider vinegar
- 1 1/2 cups gluten-free chia seeds, ground to flour
- 1 1/2 cups almond meal flour
- 3/4 cup potato starch
- 3/8 cup coconut flour
- 1 1/8 cups millet flour
- 1 1/2 tablespoons xanthan gum
- 2 1/4 teaspoons salt
- 3 tablespoons sugar
- 4 1/2 tablespoons nonfat dry milk
- 9 teaspoons instant yeas
- 16 slices (2 pounds)
- 2 cups warm water
- 6 large organic eggs, room temperature
- 1/2 cup olive oil
- 2 tablespoons apple cider vinegar
- 2 cups gluten-free chia seeds, ground to flour

- 2 cups almond meal flour
- 1 cup potato starch
- 1/2 cup coconut flour
- 1 1/2 cups millet flour
- 2 tablespoons xanthan gum
- 3 teaspoons salt
- 4 tablespoons sugar
- 6 tablespoons nonfat dry milk
- 12 teaspoons instant yeas

Directions:

1. Choose the size of loaf you would like to make and measure your ingredients.

2. Whisk wet ingredients together and add to the bread pan.

3. Whisk dry ingredients, except yeast, together and add on top of wet ingredients.

4. Make a well in the dry ingredients and add yeast.

5. Place the pan in the bread machine and close the lid.

6. Turn on the bread maker. Select the Whole Wheat setting, then the loaf size, and finally the crust color. Start the cycle.

7. When the cycle is finished and the bread is baked, carefully remove the pan from the machine. Use a potholder as the handle will be very hot. Let rest for a few minutes.

8. Remove the bread from the pan and allow to cool on a wire rack for at least 10 minutes before slicing.

Gluten-free Crusty Boule Bread

Ingredients:
- 8 slices (1 pound)
- 2 1/6 cups gluten-free flour mix
- 2/3 tablespoon active dry yeast
- 1 teaspoon kosher salt
- 2/3 tablespoon guar gum
- 8/9 cup warm water
- 1 1/3 large eggs, room temperature
- 1 1/3 tablespoons, plus 2 teaspoons olive oil
- 2/3 tablespoon honey
- 12 slices (1 ½ pounds)
- 3 1/4 cups gluten-free flour mix
- 1 tablespoon active dry yeast
- 1 1/2 teaspoons kosher salt

- 1 tablespoon guar gum
- 1 1/3 cups warm water
- 2 large eggs, room temperature
- 2 tablespoons, plus 2 teaspoons olive oil
- 1 tablespoon honey
- 16 slices (2 pounds)
- 4 1/3 cups gluten-free flour mix
- 1 1/3 tablespoons active dry yeast
- 2 teaspoons kosher salt
- 1 1/3 tablespoons guar gum
- 1 7/9 cups warm water
- 2 2/3 large eggs, room temperature
- 2 2/3 tablespoons, plus 2 teaspoons olive oil
- 1 1/3 tablespoons honey

Directions:

1. Choose the size of loaf you would like to make and measure your ingredients.

2. Combine all of the dry ingredients, except the yeast, in a large mixing bowl and set aside.

3. Whisk together the water, eggs, oil, and honey in a separate mixing bowl.

4. Pour the wet ingredients into the bread pan.

5. Add the dry ingredients on top of the wet ingredients.

6. Make a well in the center of the dry ingredients and add the yeast.

7. Place the pan in the bread machine and close the lid.

8. Turn on the bread maker. Select the Gluten-Free setting, then the loaf size, and finally the crust color. Start the cycle.

9. When the cycle is finished and the bread is baked, carefully remove the pan from the machine. Use a potholder as the handle will be very hot. Let rest for a few minutes.

10. Remove the bread from the pan and allow to cool on a wire rack for at least 10 minutes before slicing.

11. Hollow out and fill with soup or dip to use as a boule, or slice for serving.

Gluten-free Pumpkin Pie Bread

Ingredients:
- 8 slices (1 pound)
- 1/4 cup olive oil

- 2 large eggs, beaten
- 1 tablespoon bourbon vanilla extract
- 1 cup canned pumpkin
- 4 tablespoons honey
- 1/4 teaspoon lemon juice
- 1/2 cup buckwheat flour
- 1/4 cup millet flour
- 1/4 cup sorghum flour
- 1/2 cup tapioca starch
- 1 cup light brown sugar
- 2 teaspoons baking powder
- 1 teaspoon baking soda
- 1/2 teaspoon sea salt
- 1 teaspoon xanthan gum
- 1 teaspoon ground cinnamon
- 1 teaspoon allspice
- 1-2 tablespoons peach juice
- 12 slices (1 ½ pounds)
- 3/8 cup olive oil
- 3 large eggs, beaten
- 1 1/2 tablespoons bourbon vanilla extract
- 1 1/2 cups canned pumpkin
- 6 tablespoons honey
- 3/8 teaspoon lemon juice
- 3/4 cup buckwheat flour
- 3/8 cup millet flour
- 3/8 cup sorghum flour
- 3/4 cup tapioca starch
- 1 1/2 cups light brown sugar
- 3 teaspoons baking powder
- 1 1/2 teaspoons baking soda
- 3/4 teaspoon sea salt
- 1 1/2 teaspoons xanthan gum
- 1 1/2 teaspoons ground cinnamon
- 1 1/2 teaspoons allspice
- 1 1/2-3 tablespoons peach juice
- 16 slices (2 pounds)
- 1/2 cup olive oil
- 4 large eggs, beaten
- 2 tablespoons bourbon vanilla extract
- 2 cups canned pumpkin
- 8 tablespoons honey
- 1/2 teaspoon lemon juice
- 1 cup buckwheat flour

- 1/2 cup millet flour
- 1/2 cup sorghum flour
- 1 cup tapioca starch
- 2 cups light brown sugar
- 4 teaspoons baking powder
- 2 teaspoons baking soda
- 1 teaspoon sea salt
- 2 teaspoons xanthan gum
- 2 teaspoons ground cinnamon
- 2 teaspoons allspice
- 2-4 tablespoons peach juice

Directions:

1. Choose the size of loaf you would like to make and measure your ingredients.
2. Mix dry ingredients together in a bowl and put aside.
3. Add wet ingredients to pan, except peach juice.
4. Add mixed dry ingredients to bread pan.
5. Place the pan in the bread machine and close the lid.
6. Turn on the bread maker. Select the Sweet bread setting, then the loaf size, and finally the crust color. Start the cycle.
7. As it begins to mix the ingredients, use a soft silicone spatula to scrape down the sides.
8. If the batter is stiff, add one tablespoon at a time of peach juice until the batter becomes slightly thinner than muffin batter.
9. When the cycle is finished and the bread is baked, carefully remove the pan from the machine. Use a potholder as the handle will be very hot. Let rest for a few minutes.
10. Remove the bread from the pan and allow to cool on a wire rack for at least 10 minutes before slicing.

Walnut Banana Bread

Ingredients:

- 8 slices (1 pound)
- 1/4 cup lukewarm water
- 1 1/2 tablespoons canola oil
- 1/2 teaspoon apple cider vinegar
- 1 egg, beaten
- 1 small banana, mashed
- 1/2 teaspoon table salt
- 3/8 cup brown rice flour

- 3/8 cup white rice flour
- 3/8 cup amaranth flour
- 1/4 cup corn starch
- 1/2 tablespoon xanthan gum
- 1/2 teaspoon cinnamon
- 1/4 teaspoon nutmeg
- 1 teaspoon bread machine yeast
- 1/2 cup walnuts, chopped
- 12 slices (1½ pounds)
- ⅓ cup lukewarm water
- 2 tablespoons canola oil
- ¾ teaspoon apple cider vinegar
- 2 eggs, beaten
- 1½ small bananas, mashed
- ¾ teaspoon table salt
- ½ cup brown rice flour
- ½ cup white rice flour
- ½ cup amaranth flour
- ⅓ cup corn starch
- ¾ tablespoon xanthan gum
- ¾ teaspoon cinnamon
- ⅓ teaspoon nutmeg
- 1½ teaspoons bread machine yeast
- ¾ cup walnuts, chopped
- 16 slices (2 pounds)
- ½ cup lukewarm water
- 3 tablespoons canola oil
- 1 teaspoon apple cider vinegar
- 2 eggs, beaten
- 2 small banana, mashed
- 1 teaspoon table salt
- ¾ cup brown rice flour
- ¾ cup white rice flour
- ¾ cup amaranth flour
- ½ cup corn starch
- 1 tablespoon xanthan gum
- 1 teaspoon cinnamon
- ½ teaspoon nutmeg
- 2 teaspoons bread machine yeast
- 1 cup walnuts, chopped

Directions:

1. Choose the size of loaf you would like to make and measure your ingredients.

2. Add the ingredients to the bread pan in the order listed above.

3. Place the pan in the bread machine and close the lid.

4. Turn on the bread maker. Select the Quick/Rapid setting, then the loaf size, and finally the crust color. Start the cycle.

5. When the cycle is finished and the bread is baked, carefully remove the pan from the machine. Use a potholder as the handle will be very hot. Let rest for a few minutes.

6. Remove the bread from the pan and allow to cool on a wire rack for at least 10 minutes before slicing.

Garlic Parsley Bread

Ingredients:

- 8 slices (1 pound)
- 3/4 cups almond or coconut milk
- 1/8 cup flax meal
- 6 tablespoons warm water
- 2 tablespoon butter
- 1 1/2 tablespoons maple syrup
- 1 1/2 teaspoon apple cider vinegar
- 1/8 cup parsley, loosely chopped
- 5–6 cloves garlic, minced
- 1/2 teaspoon table salt
- 1 5/8 cups brown rice flour
- 1/4 cup corn starch
- 1/8 cup potato starch
- 1 1/2 teaspoons xanthan gum
- 1 tablespoons garlic powder
- 1 tablespoons onion powder
- 1 teaspoons bread machine yeast
- 12 slices (1½ pounds)
- 1¼ cups almond or coconut milk
- 3 tablespoons flax meal
- ½ cup + 1 tablespoon warm water
- 3 tablespoons butter
- 2¼ tablespoons maple syrup
- 2¼ teaspoons apple cider vinegar
- 3 tablespoons parsley, loosely chopped
- 8–9 cloves garlic, minced
- ¾ teaspoon table salt
- 6 tablespoons + 2 teaspoons brown rice flour

- ⅓ cup corn starch
- 3 tablespoons potato starch
- 2 teaspoons xanthan gum
- 1½ tablespoons garlic powder
- 1½ tablespoons onion powder
- 1½ teaspoons bread machine yeast
- 16 slices (2 pounds)
- 1½ cups almond or coconut milk
- ¼ cup flax meal
- 12 tablespoons warm water
- 4 tablespoon butter
- 3 tablespoons maple syrup
- 3 teaspoon apple cider vinegar
- ¼ cup parsley, loosely chopped
- 10–12 cloves garlic, minced
- 1 teaspoon table salt
- 3¼ cups brown rice flour
- ½ cup corn starch
- ¼ cup potato starch
- 3 teaspoons xanthan gum
- 2 tablespoons garlic powder
- 2 tablespoons onion powder
- 2 teaspoons bread machine yeast

Directions:

1. Combine the water and flax meal in a bowl; set aside for 5–10 minutes to mix well.
2. Choose the size of loaf you would like to make and measure your ingredients.
3. Add the ingredients to the bread pan in the order listed above, including the flax meal.
4. Place the pan in the bread machine and close the lid.
5. Turn on the bread maker. Select the White/Basic or Gluten-Free (if your machine has this setting) setting, then the loaf size, and finally the crust color. Start the cycle.
6. When the cycle is finished and the bread is baked, carefully remove the pan from the machine. Use a potholder as the handle will be very hot. Let rest for a few minutes.
7. Remove the bread from the pan and allow to cool on a wire rack for at least 10 minutes before slicing.

Gluten-free Brown Bread

Ingredients:

- 8 slices (1 pound)
- 2 large eggs, lightly beaten
- 1 3/4 cups warm water
- 3 tablespoons canola oil
- 1 cup brown rice flour
- 3/4 cup oat flour
- 1/4 cup tapioca starch
- 1 1/4 cups potato starch
- 1 1/2 teaspoons salt
- 2 tablespoons brown sugar
- 2 tablespoons gluten-free flaxseed meal
- 1/2 cup nonfat dry milk powder
- 2 1/2 teaspoons xanthan gum
- 3 tablespoons psyllium, whole husks
- 2 1/2 teaspoons gluten-free yeast for bread machines
- 12 slices (1 ½ pounds)
- 3 large eggs, lightly beaten
- 2 5/8 cups warm water
- 4 1/2 tablespoons canola oil
- 1 1/2 cups brown rice flour
- 1 1/8 cups oat flour
- 3/8 cup tapioca starch
- 1 7/8 cups potato starch
- 2 1/4 teaspoons salt
- 3 tablespoons brown sugar
- 3 tablespoons gluten-free flaxseed meal
- 3/4 cup nonfat dry milk powder
- 3 3/4 teaspoons xanthan gum
- 4 1/2 tablespoons psyllium, whole husks
- 3 3/4 teaspoons gluten-free yeast for bread machines
- 16 slices (2 pounds)
- 4 large eggs, lightly beaten
- 3 1/2 cups warm water
- 6 tablespoons canola oil
- 2 cups brown rice flour
- 1 1/2 cups oat flour
- 1/2 cup tapioca starch
- 2 1/2 cups potato starch
- 3 teaspoons salt
- 4 tablespoons brown sugar
- 4 tablespoons gluten-free flaxseed meal

- 1 cup nonfat dry milk powder
- 5 teaspoons xanthan gum
- 6 tablespoons psyllium, whole husks
- 5 teaspoons gluten-free yeast for bread machines

Directions:

1. Choose the size of loaf you would like to make and measure your ingredients.

2. Add all the wet ingredients to the bread pan in the order listed above and stir until combined.

3. Whisk all of the dry ingredients except the yeast together in a large mixing bowl.

4. Add the dry ingredients on top of the wet ingredients.

5. Make a well in the center of the dry ingredients and add the yeast.

6. Place the pan in the bread machine and close the lid.

7. Turn on the bread maker. Select the Gluten-Free setting, then the loaf size, and finally the crust color. Start the cycle.

8. When the cycle is finished and the bread is baked, carefully remove the pan from the machine. Use a potholder as the handle will be very hot. Let rest for a few minutes.

9. Remove the bread from the pan and allow to cool on a wire rack for at least 10 minutes before slicing.

Cheese Potato Bread

Ingredients:

- 8 slices (1 pound)
- 5/8 cups lukewarm water
- 1 1/2 tablespoons vegetable oil
- 1 1/2 large eggs, beaten
- 1/4 cup dry skim milk powder
- 1/8 cup sugar
- 1/2 teaspoon apple cider vinegar
- 3/4 teaspoon table salt
- 1/4 cup cornstarch
- 3/8 cup cottage cheese
- 1/8 cup snipped chives
- 1/4 cup instant potato buds
- 1/4 cup potato starch
- 1/4 cup tapioca flour
- 1 cups white rice flour
- 1 1/8 teaspoon bread machine yeast
- 12 slices (1½ pounds)
- 1 cup lukewarm water
- 2¼ tablespoons vegetable oil
- 2 large eggs, beaten
- ⅓ cup dry skim milk powder
- 3 tablespoons sugar
- ¾ teaspoon apple cider vinegar
- 1⅛ teaspoons table salt
- ⅓ cup cornstarch
- ½ cup cottage cheese
- 3 tablespoons snipped chives
- ⅓ cup instant potato buds
- ⅓ cup potato starch
- ⅓ cup tapioca flour
- 1½ cups white rice flour
- 1½ teaspoons bread machine yeast
- 16 slices (2 pounds)
- 1¼ cups lukewarm water
- 3 tablespoons vegetable oil
- 3 large eggs, beaten
- ½ cup dry skim milk powder
- ¼ cup sugar
- 1 teaspoon apple cider vinegar
- 1½ teaspoons table salt
- ½ cup cornstarch
- ¾ cup cottage cheese
- ¼ cup snipped chives
- ½ cup instant potato buds
- ½ cup potato starch
- ½ cup tapioca flour
- 2 cups white rice flour
- 2¼ teaspoons bread machine yeast

Directions:

1. Choose the size of loaf you would like to make and measure your ingredients.

2. Add the ingredients to the bread pan in the order listed above.

3. Place the pan in the bread machine and close the lid.

4. Turn on the bread maker. Select the White/Basic or Gluten-Free (if your machine has this setting) setting, then the loaf size, and finally the crust color. Start the cycle.

5. When the cycle is finished and the bread is baked, carefully remove the pan from the machine. Use a potholder as the handle will be very hot. Let rest for a few minutes.

6. Remove the bread from the pan and allow to cool on a wire rack for at least 10 minutes before slicing.

Pecan Cranberry Bread

Ingredients:
- 8 slices (1 pound)
- 3/4 cups lukewarm water
- 1/8 cup canola oil
- 1/2 tablespoon orange zest
- 1/2 teaspoon apple cider vinegar
- 1 1/2 eggs, slightly beaten
- 1 1/2 tablespoons sugar
- 1/2 teaspoon table salt
- 1 cup white rice flour
- 1/3 cup nonfat dry milk powder
- 1/4 cup tapioca flour
- 1/4 cup potato starch
- 1/6 cup corn starch
- 1/2 tablespoon xanthan gum
- 1 teaspoon bread machine yeast
- 1/3 cup dried cranberries
- 1/3 cup pecan pieces
- 12 slices (1½ pounds)
- 1⅛ cups lukewarm water
- 3 tablespoons canola oil
- ¾ tablespoon orange zest
- ¾ teaspoon apple cider vinegar
- 2 eggs, slightly beaten
- 2¼ tablespoons sugar
- ¾ teaspoon table salt
- 1½ cups white rice flour
- ½ cup nonfat dry milk powder
- ⅓ cup tapioca flour
- ⅓ cup potato starch
- ¼ cup corn starch
- ¾ tablespoon xanthan gum
- 1½ teaspoons bread machine yeast
- ½ cup dried cranberries
- ½ cup pecan pieces

- 16 slices (2 pounds)
- 1½ cups lukewarm water
- ¼ cup canola oil
- 1 tablespoon orange zest
- 1 teaspoon apple cider vinegar
- 3 eggs, slightly beaten
- 3 tablespoons sugar
- 1 teaspoon table salt
- 2 cup white rice flour
- ⅔ cup nonfat dry milk powder
- ½ cup tapioca flour
- ½ cup potato starch
- ⅓ cup corn starch
- 1 tablespoon xanthan gum
- 2 teaspoons bread machine yeast
- ⅔ cup dried cranberries
- ⅔ cup pecan pieces

Directions:

1. Choose the size of loaf you would like to make and measure your ingredients.

2. Add all of the ingredients except for the pecans and cranberries to the bread pan in the order listed above.

3. Place the pan in the bread machine and close the lid.

4. Turn on the bread maker. Select the Gluten Free or Fruit/Nut (if your machine has this setting) setting, then the loaf size, and finally the crust color. Start the cycle. (If you don't have either of the above settings, use Basic/White.)

5. When the machine signals to add ingredients, add the pecans and cranberries. (Some machines have a fruit/nut hopper where you can add the pecans and cranberries when you start the machine. The machine will automatically add them to the dough during the baking process.)

6. When the cycle is finished and the bread is baked, carefully remove the pan from the machine. Use a potholder as the handle will be very hot. Let rest for a few minutes.

7. Remove the bread from the pan and allow to cool on a wire rack for at least 10 minutes before slicing.

Pecan Apple Spice Bread

Ingredients:

- 8 slices (1 pound)
- 1/4 cup lukewarm water
- 1 1/2 tablespoons canola oil
- 1/2 teaspoon apple cider vinegar
- 1 1/2 tablespoons light brown sugar, packed
- 1/2 cup Granny Smith apples, grated
- 3/2 eggs, room temperature, slightly beaten
- 3/8 cup brown rice flour
- 3/8 cup tapioca flour
- 3/8 cup millet flour
- 1/4 cup corn starch
- 1 tablespoon apple pie spice
- 1/2 tablespoon xanthan gum
- 1/2 teaspoon table salt
- 1 teaspoon bread machine yeast
- 1/4 cup pecans, chopped
- 12 slices (1½ pounds)
- ⅓ cup lukewarm water
- 2¼ tablespoons canola oil
- ¾ teaspoon apple cider vinegar
- 2¼ tablespoons light brown sugar, packed
- ¾ cup Granny Smith apples, grated
- 2 eggs, room temperature, slightly beaten
- ½ cup brown rice flour
- ½ cup tapioca flour
- ½ cup millet flour
- ⅓ cup corn starch
- 1½ tablespoons apple pie spice
- ¾ tablespoon xanthan gum
- ¾ teaspoon table salt
- 1¼ teaspoons bread machine yeast
- ⅓ cup pecans, chopped
- 16 slices (2 pounds)
- ½ cup lukewarm water
- 3 tablespoons canola oil
- 1 teaspoon apple cider vinegar
- 3 tablespoons light brown sugar, packed
- 1 cup Granny Smith apples, grated
- 3 eggs, room temperature, slightly beaten
- ¾ cup brown rice flour
- ¾ cup tapioca flour
- ¾ cup millet flour
- ½ cup corn starch
- 2 tablespoons apple pie spice
- 1 tablespoon xanthan gum
- 1 teaspoon table salt
- 2 teaspoons bread machine yeast
- ½ cup pecans, chopped

Directions:

1. Choose the size of loaf you would like to make and measure your ingredients.

2. Add all of the ingredients except for the pecans to the bread pan in the order listed above.

3. Place the pan in the bread machine and close the lid.

4. Turn on the bread maker. Select the White/Basic or Gluten-Free (if your machine has this setting) setting, then the loaf size, and finally the crust color. Start the cycle.

5. When the machine signals to add ingredients, add the chopped pecans.

6. When the cycle is finished and the bread is baked, carefully remove the pan from the machine. Use a potholder as the handle will be very hot. Let rest for a few minutes.

7. Remove the bread from the pan and allow to cool on a wire rack for at least 10 minutes before slicing.

Sorghum Bread Recipe

Ingredients:

- 8 slices (1 pound)
- 1 1/2 cups sorghum flour
- 1 cup tapioca starch
- 1/2 cup brown or white sweet rice flour
- 1 teaspoon xanthan gum
- 1 teaspoon guar gum
- 1/2 teaspoon salt
- 3 tablespoons sugar
- 2 1/4 teaspoons instant yeast
- 3 eggs (room temperature, lightly beaten)
- 1/4 cup oil
- 1 1/2 teaspoons vinegar
- 3/4-1 cup milk (105 - 115°F)
- 12 slices (1 ½ pounds)
- 2 1/4 cups sorghum flour

* 1 1/2 cups tapioca starch
* 3/4 cup brown or white sweet rice flour
* 1 1/2 teaspoons xanthan gum
* 1 1/2 teaspoons guar gum
* 3/4 teaspoon salt
* 4 1/2 tablespoons sugar
* 3 3/8 teaspoons instant yeast
* 4 1/2 eggs (room temperature, lightly beaten)
* 3/8 cup oil
* 2 1/4 teaspoons vinegar
* 1 1/8-1 1/2 cups milk (105 - 115°F)
* 16 slices (2 pounds)
* 3 cups sorghum flour
* 2 cups tapioca starch
* 1 cup brown or white sweet rice flour
* 2 teaspoons xanthan gum
* 2 teaspoons guar gum
* 1 teaspoon salt
* 6 tablespoons sugar
* 4 1/2 teaspoons instant yeast
* 6 eggs (room temperature, lightly beaten)
* 1/2 cup oil
* 3 teaspoons vinegar
* 1 1/2 - 2 cups milk (105 - 115°F)

Directions:

1. Choose the size of loaf you would like to make and measure your ingredients.
2. Combine the dry ingredients in a mixing bowl, except for yeast.
3. Add the wet ingredients to the bread pan, then add the dry ingredients on top.
4. Make a well in the center of the dry ingredients and add the yeast. Place the pan in the bread machine and close the lid.
5. Turn on the bread maker. Select the Basic setting, then the loaf size, and finally the crust color. Start the cycle.
6. When the cycle is finished and the bread is baked, carefully remove the pan from the machine. Use a potholder as the handle will be very hot. Let rest for a few minutes.
7. Remove the bread from the pan and allow to cool on a wire rack for at least 10 minutes before slicing.

Gluten-free Potato Bread

Ingredients:

* 8 slices (1 pound)
* 1/2 medium russet potato, baked, or mashed leftovers
* 1 packet gluten-free quick yeast
* 1 1/2 tablespoons honey
* 3/8 cup warm almond milk
* 1 egg, 1 egg white
* 1 5/6 cups almond flour
* 1 1/2 cups tapioca flour
* 1/2 teaspoon sea salt
* 1/2 teaspoon dried chives
* 1/2 tablespoon apple cider vinegar
* 1/8 cup olive oil
* 12 slices (1 ½ pounds)
* 3/4 medium russet potato, baked, or mashed leftovers
* 1 1/2 packets gluten-free quick yeast
* 2 1/4 tablespoons honey
* 9/16 cup warm almond milk
* 1 1/2 eggs, 1 1/2 eggs white
* 2 3/4 cups almond flour
* 2 1/4 cups tapioca flour
* 3/4 teaspoon sea salt
* 3/4 teaspoon dried chives
* 3/4 tablespoon apple cider vinegar
* 3/16 cup olive oil
* 16 slices (2 pounds)
* 1 medium russet potato, baked, or mashed leftovers
* 2 packets gluten-free quick yeast
* 3 tablespoons honey
* 3/4 cup warm almond milk
* 2 eggs, 1 egg white
* 3 2/3 cups almond flour
* 3/4 cup tapioca flour
* 1 teaspoon sea salt
* 1 teaspoon dried chives
* 1 tablespoon apple cider vinegar
* 1/4 cup olive oil

Directions:

1. Choose the size of loaf you would like to make and measure your ingredients.

2. Combine all of the dry ingredients, except the yeast, in a large mixing bowl and set aside.

3. Whisk together the milk, eggs, oil, apple cider, and honey in a separate mixing bowl.

4. Pour the wet ingredients into the bread pan.

5. Add the dry ingredients on top of the wet ingredients.

6. Create a well in the dry ingredients and add the yeast.

7. Place the pan in the bread machine and close the lid.

8. Turn on the bread maker. Select the Gluten-Free setting, then the loaf size, and finally the crust color. Start the cycle.

9. When the cycle is finished and the bread is baked, carefully remove the pan from the machine. Use a potholder as the handle will be very hot. Let rest for a few minutes.

10. Remove the bread from the pan and allow to cool on a wire rack for at least 10 minutes before slicing.

Basic Honey Bread

Ingredients:
- 8 slices (1 pound)
- 1 cup warm milk
- 1/6 cup unsalted butter, melted
- 1 egg, beaten
- 5/8 teaspoon apple cider vinegar
- 1/3 cup honey
- 5/8 teaspoon table salt
- 2 cups gluten-free flour(s) of your choice
- 1 teaspoon xanthan gum
- 1 teaspoon bread machine yeast
- 12 slices (1½ pounds)
- 1½ cups warm milk
- ¼ cup unsalted butter, melted
- 2 eggs, beaten
- 1 teaspoon apple cider vinegar
- ½ cup honey
- 1 teaspoon table salt
- 3 cups gluten-free flour(s) of your choice
- 1½ teaspoons xanthan gum
- 1¾ teaspoons bread machine yeast
- 16 slices (2 pounds)

- 2 cups warm milk
- ⅓ cup unsalted butter, melted
- 2 eggs, beaten
- 1¼ teaspoons apple cider vinegar
- ⅔ cup honey
- 1¼ teaspoons table salt
- 4 cups gluten-free flour(s) of your choice
- 2 teaspoons xanthan gum
- 2 teaspoons bread machine yeast

Directions:

1. Choose the size of loaf you would like to make and measure your ingredients.

2. Add the ingredients to the bread pan in the order listed above.

3. Place the pan in the bread machine and close the lid.

4. Turn on the bread maker. Select the White/Basic or Gluten-Free (if your machine has this setting) setting, then the loaf size, and finally the crust color. Start the cycle.

5. When the cycle is finished and the bread is baked, carefully remove the pan from the machine. Use a potholder as the handle will be very hot. Let rest for a few minutes.

6. Remove the bread from the pan and allow to cool on a wire rack for at least 10 minutes before slicing.

Mix Seed Bread

Ingredients:
- 8 slices (1 pound)
- 1 1/8 cups lukewarm milk
- 1/4cup + 1 /2tablespoon cooking oil
- 3/4 teaspoons vinegar
- 1 1/2eggs, slightly beaten
- 3/4 tablespoons sugar
- 3/4 teaspoons table salt
- 1 3/4 cups gluten-free flour(s) of your choice
- 1 1/2 tablespoons poppy seeds
- 1 1/2 tablespoons pumpkin seeds
- 1 1/2 tablespoons sunflower seeds
- 1 1/2 teaspoons bread machine yeast
- 12 slices (1½ pounds)
- 2 cups lukewarm milk
- 6 tablespoons cooking oil

- 1 teaspoon vinegar
- 2 eggs, slightly beaten
- 1 tablespoon sugar
- 1 teaspoon table salt
- 2⅔ cups gluten-free flour(s) of your choice
- 2 tablespoons poppy seeds
- 2 tablespoons pumpkin seeds
- 2 tablespoons sunflower seeds
- 2 teaspoons bread machine yeast
- 16 slices (2 pounds)
- 2¼ cups lukewarm milk
- ½ cup + 1 tablespoon cooking oil
- 1½ teaspoons vinegar
- 3 eggs, slightly beaten
- 1½ tablespoons sugar
- 1½ teaspoons table salt
- 3½ cups gluten-free flour(s) of your choice
- 3 tablespoons poppy seeds
- 3 tablespoons pumpkin seeds
- 3 tablespoons sunflower seeds
- 3 teaspoons bread machine yeast

Directions:

1. Choose the size of loaf you would like to make and measure your ingredients.

2. Add the ingredients to the bread pan in the order listed above.

3. Place the pan in the bread machine and close the lid.

4. Turn on the bread maker. Select the White/Basic or Gluten-Free (if your machine has this setting) setting, then the loaf size, and finally the crust color. Start the cycle.

5. When the cycle is finished and the bread is baked, carefully remove the pan from the machine. Use a potholder as the handle will be very hot. Let rest for a few minutes.

6. Remove the bread from the pan and allow to cool on a wire rack for at least 10 minutes before slicing.

Gluten-free Sourdough Bread

Ingredients:
- 8 slices (1 pound)
- 1 cup water
- 3 eggs

- 3/4 cup ricotta cheese
- 1/4 cup honey
- 1/4 cup vegetable oil
- 1 teaspoon cider vinegar
- 3/4 cup gluten-free sourdough starter
- 2 cups white rice flour
- 2/3 cup potato starch
- 1/3 cup tapioca flour
- 1/2 cup dry milk powder
- 3 1/2 teaspoons xanthan gum
- 1 1/2 teaspoons salt
- 12 slices (1 ½ pounds)
- 1 1/2 cups water
- 4 1/2 eggs
- 1 1/8 cups ricotta cheese
- 3/8 cup honey
- 3/8 cup vegetable oil
- 1 1/2 teaspoons cider vinegar
- 1 1/8 cups gluten-free sourdough starter
- 3 cups white rice flour
- 1 cup potato starch
- 1/2 cup tapioca flour
- 3/4 cup dry milk powder
- 5 1/4 teaspoons xanthan gum
- 2 1/4 teaspoons salt
- 16 slices (2 pounds)
- 2 cups water
- 6 eggs
- 1 1/2 cups ricotta cheese
- 1/2 cup honey
- 1/2 cup vegetable oil
- 2 teaspoons cider vinegar
- 1 1/2 cups gluten-free sourdough starter
- 4 cups white rice flour
- 1 1/3 cups potato starch
- 2/3 cup tapioca flour
- 1 cup dry milk powder
- 7 teaspoons xanthan gum
- 3 teaspoons salt

Directions:

1. Choose the size of loaf you would like to make and measure your ingredients.

2. Combine wet ingredients and pour into bread pan.

3. Mix together dry ingredients in a large mixing bowl, and add on top of the wet ingredients.

4. Place the pan in the bread machine and close the lid.

5. Turn on the bread maker. Select the Gluten-Free setting, then the loaf size, and finally the crust color. Start the cycle.

6. When the cycle is finished and the bread is baked, carefully remove the pan from the machine. Use a potholder as the handle will be very hot. Let rest for a few minutes.

7. Remove the bread from the pan and allow to cool on a wire rack for at least 10 minutes before slicing.

Classic White Bread

Ingredients:

- 8 slices (1 pound)
- 3/4 cup lukewarm water
- 1/8 cup canola oil
- ½ teaspoon apple cider vinegar
- 1 1/2 eggs, room temperature, slightly beaten
- 1 cup white rice flour
- 1/4 cup tapioca flour
- ⅓ cup nonfat dry milk powder
- 1/4 cup potato starch
- 1/6 cup cornstarch
- 1 1/2 tablespoons sugar
- ½ tablespoon xanthan gum
- ½ teaspoon table salt
- 1 teaspoon bread machine yeast
- 12 slices (1½ pounds)
- 1 1/8 cup lukewarm water
- 3 tablespoons canola oil
- ¾ teaspoon apple cider vinegar
- 2 eggs, room temperature, slightly beaten
- 1½ cups white rice flour
- ⅔ cup tapioca flour
- ½ cup nonfat dry milk powder
- ½ cup potato starch
- ⅓ cup cornstarch
- 2 tablespoons sugar
- ⅔ tablespoon xanthan gum
- ⅔ teaspoon table salt
- 1¼ teaspoons bread machine yeast

- 16 slices (2 pounds)
- 1½ cups lukewarm water
- ¼ cup canola oil
- 1 teaspoon apple cider vinegar
- 3 eggs, room temperature, slightly beaten
- 2 cups white rice flour
- ½ cup tapioca flour
- ⅔ cup nonfat dry milk powder
- ½ cup potato starch
- ⅓ cup cornstarch
- 3 tablespoons sugar
- 1 tablespoon xanthan gum
- 1 teaspoon table salt
- 2 teaspoons bread machine yeast

Directions:

1. Choose the size of loaf you would like to make and measure your ingredients.

2. Add the ingredients to the bread pan in the order listed above.

3. Place the pan in the bread machine and close the lid.

4. Turn on the bread maker. Select the White/Basic or Gluten-Free (if your machine has this setting) setting, then the loaf size, and finally the crust color. Start the cycle.

5. When the cycle is finished and the bread is baked, carefully remove the pan from the machine. Use a potholder as the handle will be very hot. Let rest for a few minutes.

6. Remove the bread from the pan and allow to cool on a wire rack for at least 10 minutes before slicing.

Gluten-free Pull-apart Rolls

Ingredients:

- 8 slices (1 pound)
- 1 cup warm water
- 2 tablespoons butter, unsalted
- 1 egg, room temperature
- 1 teaspoon apple cider vinegar
- 2 3/4 cups gluten-free almond-blend flour
- 1 1/2 teaspoons xanthan gum
- 1/4 cup sugar
- 1 teaspoon salt
- 2 teaspoons active dry yeast

- 12 slices (1 ½ pounds)
- 1 1/2 cups warm water
- 3 tablespoons butter, unsalted
- 1 1/2 eggs, room temperature
- 1 1/2 teaspoons apple cider vinegar
- 4 1/8 cups gluten-free almond-blend flour
- 2 1/4 teaspoons xanthan gum
- 3/8 cup sugar
- 1 1/2 teaspoons salt
- 3 teaspoons active dry yeast
- 16 slices (2 pounds)
- 2 cups warm water
- 4 tablespoons butter, unsalted
- 2 eggs, room temperature
- 2 teaspoons apple cider vinegar
- 5 1/2 cups gluten-free almond-blend flour
- 3 teaspoons xanthan gum
- 1/2 cup sugar
- 2 teaspoons salt
- 4 teaspoons active dry yeast

Directions:

1. Choose the size of loaf you would like to make and measure your ingredients.
2. Add wet ingredients to the bread pan.
3. Mix dry ingredients except for yeast, and put in the bread pan.
4. Make a well in the center of the dry ingredients and add the yeast.
5. Place the pan in the bread machine and close the lid.
6. Turn on the bread maker. Select the Dough setting, then the loaf size, and finally the crust color. Start the cycle.
7. Spray an 8-inch round cake pan with non-stick cooking spray.
8. When Dough cycle is complete, roll dough out into 9 balls, place in cake pan, and baste each with warm water.
9. Cover with a towel and let rise in a warm place for 1 hour.
10. Preheat oven to 400°F.
11. Bake for 26 to 28 minutes; until golden brown.
12. Brush with butter and serve.

Gluten-free Pizza Crust

Ingredients:

- 8 slices (1 pound)
- 2 large eggs, room temperature
- 1/3 cup olive oil
- 2/3 cup milk
- 1/3 cup water
- 1 1/3 cups rice flour
- 2/3 cup cornstarch, and extra for dusting
- 1/3 cup potato starch
- 1/3 cup sugar
- 1 1/3 tablespoons yeast
- 2 teaspoons xanthan gum
- 2/3 teaspoon salt
- 12 slices (1 ½ pounds)
- 3 large eggs, room temperature
- 1/2 cup olive oil
- 1 cup milk
- 1/2 cup water
- 2 cups rice flour
- 1 cup cornstarch, and extra for dusting
- 1/2 cup potato starch
- 1/2 cup sugar
- 2 tablespoons yeast
- 3 teaspoons xanthan gum
- 1 teaspoon salt
- 16 slices (2 pounds)
- 4 large eggs, room temperature
- 2/3 cup olive oil
- 1 1/3 cups milk
- 2/3 cup water
- 2 2/3 cups rice flour
- 1 1/3 cups cornstarch, and extra for dusting
- 2/3 cup potato starch
- 2/3 cup sugar
- 2 2/3 tablespoons yeast
- 4 teaspoons xanthan gum
- 1 1/3 teaspoons salt

Directions:

1. Choose the size of loaf you would like to make and measure your ingredients.
2. Combine the wet ingredients in a separate bowl and pour into the bread pan.

3.   Combine the dry ingredients (except yeast) and add to the bread pan.

4.   Make a well in the center of the dry ingredients and add the yeast.Place the pan in the bread machine and close the lid.

5.   Turn on the bread maker. Select the Dough setting, then the loaf size, and finally the crust color. Start the cycle.

6.   When the cycle is finished and the bread is baked, carefully remove the pan from the machine. Use a potholder as the handle will be very hot. Let rest for a few minutes.

7.   Press it out on a surface lightly sprinkled with corn starch and create a pizza shape.

8.   Remove the bread from the pan and allow to cool on a wire rack for at least 10 minutes before slicing.

Instant Cocoa Bread

Ingredients:
- 8 slices (1 pound)
- 3/4 cup lukewarm water
- 1 1/2 large eggs, beaten
- 1 1/2 tablespoons molasses
- 1 tablespoon canola oil
- 1/2 teaspoon apple cider vinegar
- 1 1/2 tablespoons light brown sugar
- 3/4 teaspoons table salt
- 1 cup white rice flour
- 1/3 cup potato starch
- 1/6 cup tapioca flour
- 1 1/4 teaspoons xanthan gum
- 1 teaspoon cocoa powder
- 1 teaspoon instant coffee granules
- 1 1/2 teaspoons bread machine yeast
- 12 slices (1½ pounds)
- 1⅛ cups lukewarm water
- 2 large eggs, beaten
- 2¼ tablespoons molasses
- 1½ tablespoons canola oil
- ¾ teaspoon apple cider vinegar
- 2¼ tablespoons light brown sugar
- 1⅛ teaspoons table salt
- 1½ cups white rice flour
- ½ cup potato starch
- ¼ cup tapioca flour
- 1½ teaspoons xanthan gum
- 1½ teaspoons cocoa powder
- 1½ teaspoons instant coffee granules
- 2 teaspoons bread machine yeast
- 16 slices (2 pounds)
- 1½ cups lukewarm water
- 3 large eggs, beaten
- 3 tablespoons molasses
- 2 tablespoons canola oil
- 1 teaspoon apple cider vinegar
- 3 tablespoons light brown sugar
- 1½ teaspoons table salt
- 2 cups white rice flour
- ⅔ cup potato starch
- ⅓ cup tapioca flour
- 2½ teaspoons xanthan gum
- 2 teaspoons cocoa powder
- 2 teaspoons instant coffee granules
- 3 teaspoons bread machine yeast

Directions:
1.   Choose the size of loaf you would like to make and measure your ingredients.

2.   Add the ingredients to the bread pan in the order listed above.

3.   Place the pan in the bread machine and close the lid.

4.   Turn on the bread maker. Select the White/Basic or Gluten-Free (if your machine has this setting) setting, then the loaf size, and finally the crust color. Start the cycle.

5.   When the cycle is finished and the bread is baked, carefully remove the pan from the machine. Use a potholder as the handle will be very hot. Let rest for a few minutes.

6.   Remove the bread from the pan and allow to cool on a wire rack for at least 10 minutes before slicing.

Onion Buttermilk Bread

Ingredients:
- 8 slices (1 pound)
- 5/8 cup lukewarm water
- 1/8 cup unsalted butter, melted

- 1/2 teaspoon apple cider vinegar
- 1/8 cup dry buttermilk powder
- 1 1/2 large eggs, beaten
- 1/8 cup sugar
- 3/4 teaspoon table salt
- 1/4 cup potato flour
- 1/4 cup tapioca flour
- 1 cup white rice flour
- 1/2 tablespoon dill, chopped
- 1/8 cup green onion, chopped
- 1 3/4 teaspoons xanthan gum
- 1 1/2 teaspoons bread machine yeast
- 12 slices (1½ pounds)
- 1 cup lukewarm water
- 3 tablespoons unsalted butter, melted
- ¾ teaspoon apple cider vinegar
- 3 tablespoons dry buttermilk powder
- 3 medium eggs, beaten
- 3 tablespoons sugar
- 1 teaspoon table salt
- ⅓ cup potato flour
- ⅓ cup tapioca flour
- 1½ cups white rice flour
- ¾ tablespoon dill, chopped
- 3 tablespoons green onion, chopped
- 2⅔ teaspoons xanthan gum
- 1½ teaspoons bread machine yeast
- 16 slices (2 pounds)
- 1¼ cups lukewarm water
- ¼ cup unsalted butter, melted
- 1 teaspoon apple cider vinegar
- ¼ cup dry buttermilk powder
- 3 large eggs, beaten
- ¼ cup sugar
- 1½ teaspoons table salt
- ½ cup potato flour
- ½ cup tapioca flour
- 2 cup white rice flour
- 1 tablespoon dill, chopped
- ¼ cup green onion, chopped
- 3½ teaspoons xanthan gum
- 2¼ teaspoons bread machine yeast

Directions:

1. Choose the size of loaf you would like to make and measure your ingredients.
2. Add the ingredients to the bread pan in the order listed above.
3. Place the pan in the bread machine and close the lid.
4. Turn on the bread maker. Select the White/Basic or Gluten-Free (if your machine has this setting) setting, then the loaf size, and finally the crust color. Start the cycle.
5. When the cycle is finished and the bread is baked, carefully remove the pan from the machine. Use a potholder as the handle will be very hot. Let rest for a few minutes.
6. Remove the bread from the pan and allow to cool on a wire rack for at least 10 minutes before slicing.

Easy Gluten-free, Dairy-free Bread

Ingredients:

- 8 slices (1 pound)
- 1 cup warm water
- 1 1/3 teaspoons active dry yeast
- 1 1/3 teaspoons sugar
- 1 1/3 eggs, room temperature
- 2/3 egg white, room temperature
- 1 tablespoon apple cider vinegar
- 3 tablespoons olive oil
- 2 2/9 cups multi-purpose gluten-free flour
- 12 slices (1 ½ pounds)
- 1 1/2 cups warm water
- 2 teaspoons active dry yeast
- 2 teaspoons sugar
- 2 eggs, room temperature
- 1 egg white, room temperature
- 1 1/2 tablespoons apple cider vinegar
- 4 1/2 tablespoons olive oil
- 3 1/3 cups multi-purpose gluten-free flour
- 16 slices (2 pounds)
- 2 cups warm water
- 2 2/3 teaspoons active dry yeast
- 2 2/3 teaspoons sugar
- 2 2/3 eggs, room temperature
- 1 1/3 egg whites, room temperature
- 2 tablespoons apple cider vinegar

- 6 tablespoons olive oil
- 4 4/9 cups multi-purpose gluten-free flour

Directions:

1. Choose the size of loaf you would like to make and measure your ingredients.

2. Add the yeast and sugar to the warm water and stir to mix in a large mixing bowl; set aside until foamy, about 8 to 10 minutes.

3. Whisk the 2 eggs and 1 egg white together in a separate mixing bowl and add to baking pan of bread maker.

4. Add apple cider vinegar and oil to bread pan.

5. Add foamy yeast/water mixture to bread pan.

6. Add the multi-purpose gluten-free flour on top.

7. Place the pan in the bread machine and close the lid.

8. Turn on the bread maker. Select the Gluten-Free setting, then the loaf size, and finally the crust color. Start the cycle.

9. When the cycle is finished and the bread is baked, carefully remove the pan from the machine. Use a potholder as the handle will be very hot. Let rest for a few minutes.

10. Remove the bread from the pan and allow to cool on a wire rack for at least 10 minutes before slicing.

Gluten-free Cinnamon Raisin Bread

Ingredients:
- 8 slices (1 pound)
- 3/4 cup almond milk
- 2 tablespoons flax meal
- 6 tablespoons warm water
- 1 1/2 teaspoons apple cider vinegar
- 2 tablespoons butter
- 1 1/2 tablespoons honey
- 1 2/3 cups brown rice flour
- 1/4 cup corn starch
- 2 tablespoons potato starch
- 1 1/2 teaspoons xanthan gum
- 1 tablespoon cinnamon
- 1/2 teaspoon salt
- 1 teaspoon active dry yeast
- 1/2 cup raisins
- 12 slices (1 ½ pounds)
- 1 1/8 cups almond milk
- 3 tablespoons flax meal
- 9 tablespoons warm water
- 2 1/4 teaspoons apple cider vinegar
- 3 tablespoons butter
- 2 1/4 tablespoons honey
- 2 1/2 cups brown rice flour
- 3/8 cup corn starch
- 3 tablespoons potato starch
- 2 1/4 teaspoons xanthan gum
- 1 1/2 tablespoons cinnamon
- 3/4 teaspoon salt
- 1 1/2 teaspoons active dry yeast
- 3/4 cup raisins
- 16 slices (2 pounds)
- 1 1/2 cups almond milk
- 4 tablespoons flax meal
- 12 tablespoons warm water
- 3 teaspoons apple cider vinegar
- 4 tablespoons butter
- 3 tablespoons honey
- 3 1/3 cups brown rice flour
- 1/2 cup corn starch
- 4 tablespoons potato starch
- 3 teaspoons xanthan gum
- 2 tablespoons cinnamon
- 1 teaspoon salt
- 2 teaspoons active dry yeast
- 1 cup raisins

Directions:

1. Choose the size of loaf you would like to make and measure your ingredients.

2. Mix together flax and water and let stand for 5 minutes.

3. Combine dry ingredients in a separate bowl, except for yeast.

4. Add wet ingredients to the bread pan.

5. Add the dry mixture on top and make a well in the middle of the dry mixture.

6. Add the yeast to the well.

7. Place the pan in the bread machine and close the lid.

8. Turn on the bread maker. Select the Gluten Free setting, then the loaf size, and finally the crust color. Start the cycle.

9. After first kneading and rise cycle, add raisins.

10. When the cycle is finished and the bread is baked, carefully remove the pan from the machine. Use a potholder as the handle will be very hot. Let rest for a few minutes.

11. Remove the bread from the pan and allow to cool on a wire rack for at least 10 minutes before slicing.

Gluten-free Simple Sandwich Bread

Ingredients:
- 8 slices (1 pound)
- 1 1/2 cups sorghum flour
- 1 cup tapioca starch or potato starch (not potato flour!)
- 1/2 cup gluten-free millet flour or gluten-free oat flour
- 2 teaspoons xanthan gum
- 1 1/4 teaspoons fine sea salt
- 2 1/2 teaspoons gluten-free yeast for bread machines
- 1 1/4 cups warm water
- 3 tablespoons extra virgin olive oil
- 1 tablespoon honey or raw agave nectar
- 1/2 teaspoon mild rice vinegar or lemon juice
- 2 organic free-range eggs, beaten
- 12 slices (1 ½ pounds)
- 2 1/4 cups sorghum flour
- 1 1/2 cups tapioca starch or potato starch (not potato flour!)
- 3/4 cup gluten-free millet flour or gluten-free oat flour
- 3 teaspoons xanthan gum
- 1 7/8 teaspoons fine sea salt
- 3 3/4 teaspoons gluten-free yeast for bread machines
- 1 7/8 cups warm water
- 4 1/2 tablespoons extra virgin olive oil
- 1 1/2 tablespoons honey or raw agave nectar
- 3/4 teaspoon mild rice vinegar or lemon juice
- 3 organic free-range eggs, beaten
- 16 slices (2 pounds)
- 3 cups sorghum flour

- 2 cups tapioca starch or potato starch (not potato flour!)
- 1 cup gluten-free millet flour or gluten-free oat flour
- 4 teaspoons xanthan gum
- 2 1/2 teaspoons fine sea salt
- 5 teaspoons gluten-free yeast for bread machines
- 2 1/2 cups warm water
- 6 tablespoons extra virgin olive oil
- 2 tablespoons honey or raw agave nectar
- 1 teaspoon mild rice vinegar or lemon juice
- 4 organic free-range eggs, beaten

Directions:
1. Choose the size of loaf you would like to make and measure your ingredients.

2. Whisk together the dry ingredients except the yeast and set aside.

3. Add the liquid ingredients to the bread pan first, then gently pour the mixed dry ingredients on top of the liquid.

4. Make a well in the center of the dry ingredients and add the yeast.

5. Place the pan in the bread machine and close the lid.

6. Turn on the bread maker. Select the Rapid setting, then the loaf size, and finally the crust color. Start the cycle.

7. When the cycle is finished and the bread is baked, carefully remove the pan from the machine. Use a potholder as the handle will be very hot. Let rest for a few minutes.

8. Remove the bread from the pan and allow to cool on a wire rack for at least 10 minutes before slicing.

Italian Herb Bread

Ingredients:
- 8 slices (1 pound)
- 1 2/3 cups lukewarm water
- 1 1/2 eggs, beaten
- 1/6 cup vegetable oil
- 1 teaspoons table salt
- 1/8 cup sugar
- 5/8 cups white bean flour
- 5/8 tablespoons mixed Italian herbs, dried
- 5/8 cups white rice flour

- 5/8 cups potato starch
- 1/3 cup tapioca flour
- 2/3 tablespoons xanthan gum
- 1 1/3–1 1/2 teaspoons bread machine yeast
- 12 slices (1½ pounds)
- 1½ cups lukewarm water
- 3 eggs, beaten
- ¼ cup vegetable oil
- 1½ teaspoons table salt
- 3 tablespoons sugar
- 1 cup white bean flour
- 1 tablespoon mixed Italian herbs, dried
- 1 cup white rice flour
- 1 cup potato starch
- ½ cup tapioca flour
- 1 tablespoon xanthan gum
- 2¼ teaspoons bread machine yeast
- 16 slices (2 pounds)
- 3⅓ cups lukewarm water
- 3 eggs, beaten
- ⅓ cup vegetable oil
- 2 teaspoons table salt
- ¼ cup sugar
- 1¼ cups white bean flour
- 1¼ tablespoons mixed Italian herbs, dried
- 1¼ cups white rice flour
- 1¼ cups potato starch
- ⅔ cup tapioca flour
- 1⅓ tablespoons xanthan gum
- 2⅔–3 teaspoons bread machine yeast

Directions:

1. Choose the size of loaf you would like to make and measure your ingredients.

2. Add the ingredients to the bread pan in the order listed above.

3. Place the pan in the bread machine and close the lid.

4. Turn on the bread maker. Select the White/Basic or Gluten-Free (if your machine has this setting) setting, then the loaf size, and finally the crust color. Start the cycle.

5. When the cycle is finished and the bread is baked, carefully remove the pan from the machine. Use a potholder as the handle will be very hot. Let rest for a few minutes.

6. Remove the bread from the pan and allow to cool on a wire rack for at least 10 minutes before slicing.

SPECIALITY FLOUR BREAD RECIPES

Gluten-free Buttermilk White Bread

Ingredients:
- 8 slices (1 pound)
- 2/3 cup buttermilk
- 1/3 cup water
- 2/3 teaspoon apple cider vinegar or rice vinegar
- 2 2/3 tablespoons butter or margarine, cut into pieces
- 2 2/3 large egg whites, beaten until foamy
- 2/3 cup white rice flour
- 2/3 cup brown rice flour
- 1/2 cup potato starch flour
- 1/6 cup tapioca flour
- 2 tablespoons light or dark brown sugar
- 2/3 tablespoon plus 1/3 teaspoon xanthan gum
- 1 teaspoon salt
- 2/3 tablespoon plus 2/3 teaspoon SAF yeast or 2/3 tablespoon plus 1/3 teaspoon machine yeast
- 12 slices (1 ½ pounds)
- 1 cup buttermilk
- 1/2 cup water
- 1 teaspoon apple cider vinegar or rice vinegar
- 4 tablespoons butter or margarine, cut into pieces
- 4 large egg whites, beaten until foamy
- 1 cup white rice flour
- 1 cup brown rice flour
- 3/4 cup potato starch flour
- 1/4 cup tapioca flour
- 3 tablespoons light or dark brown sugar
- 1 tablespoon plus 1/2 teaspoon xanthan gum
- 11/2 teaspoons salt
- 1 tablespoon plus 1 teaspoon SAF yeast or 1 tablespoon plus 1/2 teaspoon machine yeast
- 16 slices (2 pounds)
- 1 1/3 cups buttermilk
- 2/3 cup water
- 1 1/3 teaspoons apple cider vinegar or rice vinegar
- 5 1/3 tablespoons butter or margarine, cut into pieces
- 5 1/3 large egg whites, beaten until foamy
- 1 1/3 cups white rice flour
- 1 1/3 cups brown rice flour
- 1 cup potato starch flour
- 1/3 cup tapioca flour
- 4 tablespoons light or dark brown sugar
- 1 1/3 tablespoons plus 2/3 teaspoon xanthan gum
- 2 teaspoons salt
- 1 1/3 tablespoons plus 1 1/3 teaspoons SAF yeast or 1 1/3 tablespoons plus 2/3 teaspoon machine yeast

Directions:
1. Choose the size of loaf you would like to make and measure your ingredients.
2. Add the ingredients to the bread pan in the order listed above.
3. Place the pan in the bread machine and close the lid.
4. Turn on the bread maker. Select the Non-Gluten/Quick Yeast Bread setting, then the loaf size, and finally the crust color. Start the cycle.
5. When the cycle is finished and the bread is baked, carefully remove the pan from the machine. Use a potholder as the handle will be very hot. Let rest for a few minutes.
6. Remove the bread from the pan and allow to cool on a wire rack for at least 10 minutes before slicing.

Chickpea Flour Bread

Ingredients:
- 8 slices (1 pound)
- 3/4 cup evaporated milk or evaporated goat's milk
- 3/4 tablespoon olive oil
- 3/4 tablespoon honey
- 1 2/3 cups bread flour
- 1/3 cup chickpea flour
- 1 tablespoon gluten
- 1 teaspoon salt
- 1/6 teaspoon ground cinnamon
- 1/6 teaspoon crushed hot pepper flakes
- 1/2 tablespoon SAF yeast or 1/2 tablespoon plus 1/4 teaspoon bread machine yeast
- 12 slices (1½ pounds)
- 11/8 cups evaporated milk or evaporated goat's milk

- 1 tablespoon olive oil
- 1 tablespoon honey
- 21/2 cups bread flour
- 1/2 cup chickpea flour
- 1 tablespoon plus 2 teaspoons gluten
- 11/2 teaspoons salt
- 1/4 teaspoon ground cinnamon
- 1/4 teaspoon crushed hot pepper flakes
- 21/2 teaspoons SAF yeast or 1 tablespoon bread machine yeast
- 16 slices (2 pounds)
- 11/2 cups evaporated milk or evaporated goat's milk
- 11/2 tablespoons olive oil
- 11/2 tablespoons honey
- 31/3 cups bread flour
- 2/3 cup chickpea flour
- 2 tablespoons gluten
- 2 teaspoons salt
- 1/3 teaspoon ground cinnamon
- 1/3 teaspoon crushed hot pepper flakes
- 1 tablespoon SAF yeast or 1 tablespoon plus 1/2 teaspoon bread machine yeast

Directions:

1. Choose the size of loaf you would like to make and measure your ingredients.

2. Add the ingredients to the bread pan in the order listed above.

3. Place the pan in the bread machine and close the lid.

4. Turn on the bread maker. Select the Basic setting, then the loaf size, and finally the crust color. Start the cycle.

5. When the cycle is finished and the bread is baked, carefully remove the pan from the machine. Use a potholder as the handle will be very hot. Let rest for a few minutes.

6. Remove the bread from the pan and allow to cool on a wire rack for at least 10 minutes before slicing.

Brown Rice Flour Bread

Ingredients:
- 8 slices (1 pound)
- 5/6 cup water
- 1 1/2 tablespoons olive oil
- 1 1/2 tablespoons honey
- 7/8 cup whole wheat flour
- 5/8 cup bread flour
- 1/2 cup brown rice flour
- 1 tablespoon nonfat dry milk
- 1 tablespoon gluten
- 1 teaspoon salt
- 1/2 tablespoon plus 1/2 teaspoon SAF yeast or 1/2 tablespoon plus 3/4 teaspoon bread machine yeast
- 12 slices (1½ pounds)
- 11/4 cups water
- 2 tablespoons olive oil
- 2 tablespoons honey
- 11/4 cups whole wheat flour
- 1 cup bread flour
- 3/4 cup brown rice flour
- 11/2 tablespoons nonfat dry milk
- 11/2 tablespoons gluten
- 11/2 teaspoons salt
- 1 tablespoon SAF yeast or 1 tablespoon plus 1/2 teaspoon bread machine yeast
- 16 slices (2 pounds)
- 12/3 cups water
- 3 tablespoons olive oil
- 3 tablespoons honey
- 13/4 cups whole wheat flour
- 11/4 cups bread flour
- 1 cup brown rice flour
- 2 tablespoons nonfat dry milk
- 2 tablespoons gluten
- 2 teaspoons salt
- 1 tablespoon plus 1 teaspoon SAF yeast or 1 tablespoon plus 11/2 teaspoons bread machine yeast

Directions:

1. Choose the size of loaf you would like to make and measure your ingredients.

2. Add the ingredients to the bread pan in the order listed above.

3. Place the pan in the bread machine and close the lid.

4. Turn on the bread maker. Select the Whole Wheat setting, then the loaf size, and finally the crust color. Start the cycle.

5.   When the cycle is finished and the bread is baked, carefully remove the pan from the machine. Use a potholder as the handle will be very hot. Let rest for a few minutes.

6.   Remove the bread from the pan and allow to cool on a wire rack for at least 10 minutes before slicing.

Gluten-free Ricotta Potato Bread

Ingredients:
*   8 slices (1 pound)
*   11/3 cups water
*   3/4 cup ricotta cheese
*   1 teaspoon apple cider vinegar or rice vinegar
*   3 tablespoons vegetable or canola oil
*   3 large eggs, broken into a measuring cup to equal 3/4 cup (add water if needed)
*   21/4 cups white rice flour
*   1/2 cup instant potato flakes
*   1/3 cup potato starch flour
*   1/3 cup tapioca flour
*   1/2 cup dry buttermilk powder or nonfat dry milk
*   3 tablespoons sugar or powdered fructose
*   2 teaspoons xanthan gum
*   11/2 teaspoons salt
*   3/4 teaspoon baking soda
*   21/4 teaspoons SAF yeast or 23/4 teaspoons bread machine yeast
*   12 slices (1 ½ pounds)
*   2 cups water
*   1 1/8 cups ricotta cheese
*   1 1/2 teaspoons apple cider vinegar or rice vinegar
*   4 1/2 tablespoons vegetable or canola oil
*   4 1/2 large eggs, broken into a measuring cup to equal 3/4 cup (add water if needed)
*   3 3/8 cups white rice flour
*   3/4 cup instant potato flakes
*   1/2 cup potato starch flour
*   1/2 cup tapioca flour
*   3/4 cup dry buttermilk powder or nonfat dry milk
*   4 1/2 tablespoons sugar or powdered fructose
*   3 teaspoons xanthan gum
*   2 1/4 teaspoons salt
*   1 1/8 teaspoons baking soda
*   3 3/8 teaspoons SAF yeast or 4 teaspoons bread machine yeast
*   16 slices (2 pounds)
*   2 2/3 cups water
*   1 1/2 cups ricotta cheese
*   2 teaspoons apple cider vinegar or rice vinegar
*   6 tablespoons vegetable or canola oil
*   6 large eggs, broken into a measuring cup to equal 1 1/2 cups (add water if needed)
*   4 1/2 cups white rice flour
*   1 cup instant potato flakes
*   2/3 cup potato starch flour
*   2/3 cup tapioca flour
*   1 cup dry buttermilk powder or nonfat dry milk
*   6 tablespoons sugar or powdered fructose
*   4 teaspoons xanthan gum
*   3 teaspoons salt
*   1 1/2 teaspoons baking soda
*   4 1/2 teaspoons SAF yeast or 5 1/2 teaspoons bread machine yeast

Directions:
1.   Choose the size of loaf you would like to make and measure your ingredients.

2.   Add the ingredients to the bread pan in the order listed above.

3.   Place the pan in the bread machine and close the lid.

4.   Turn on the bread maker. Select the Non-Gluten/Quick Yeast Bread setting, then the loaf size, and finally the crust color. Start the cycle.

5.   When the cycle is finished and the bread is baked, carefully remove the pan from the machine. Use a potholder as the handle will be very hot. Let rest for a few minutes.

6.   Remove the bread from the pan and allow to cool on a wire rack for at least 10 minutes before slicing.

Buckwheat-millet Bread

Ingredients:
*   8 slices (1 pound)
*   3/4 cup water
*   1 tablespoon unsalted butter, cut into pieces
*   1 1/2 tablespoons dark honey
*   1 3/4 cups bread flour

- 1/4 cup light buckwheat flour
- 1/4 cup whole millet
- 2/3 tablespoon gluten
- 1 teaspoon salt
- 1 1/4 teaspoons SAF yeast or 1/2 tablespoon bread machine yeast
- 12 slices (1½ pounds)
- 11/8 cups water
- 1 tablespoon unsalted butter, cut into pieces
- 2 tablespoons dark honey
- 22/3 cups bread flour
- 1/3 cup light buckwheat flour
- 1/3 cup whole millet
- 1 tablespoon gluten
- 11/2 teaspoons salt
- 2 teaspoons SAF yeast or 21/2 teaspoons bread machine yeast
- 16 slices (2 pounds)
- 11/2 cups water
- 2 tablespoons unsalted butter, cut into pieces
- 3 tablespoons dark honey
- 31/2 cups bread flour
- 1/2 cup light buckwheat flour
- 1/2 cup whole millet
- 1 tablespoon plus 1 teaspoon gluten
- 2 teaspoons salt
- 21/2 teaspoons SAF yeast or 1 tablespoon bread machine yeast

Directions:

1. Choose the size of loaf you would like to make and measure your ingredients.

2. Add the ingredients to the bread pan in the order listed above.

3. Place the pan in the bread machine and close the lid.

4. Turn on the bread maker. Select the Basic setting, then the loaf size, and finally the crust color. Start the cycle.

5. When the cycle is finished and the bread is baked, carefully remove the pan from the machine. Use a potholder as the handle will be very hot. Let rest for a few minutes.

6. Remove the bread from the pan and allow to cool on a wire rack for at least 10 minutes before slicing.

Cornmeal And Hominy Bread

Ingredients:

- 8 slices (1 pound)
- 1/3 cup milk
- 1/3 cup water
- 1 1/2 tablespoons olive oil
- 2 cups bread flour
- 1/3 cup yellow cornmeal
- 1 1/2 tablespoons sugar
- 1 tablespoon gluten
- 1 teaspoon salt
- 1 1/4 teaspoons SAF yeast or 1/2 tablespoon bread machine yeast
- 3/4 cup canned hominy, rinsed
- 12 slices (1½ pounds)
- 1/2 cup milk
- 1/2 cup water
- 2 tablespoons olive oil
- 3 cups bread flour
- 1/2 cup yellow cornmeal
- 2 tablespoons sugar
- 11/2 tablespoons gluten
- 11/2 teaspoons salt
- 2 teaspoons SAF yeast or 21/2 teaspoons bread machine yeast
- 1 cup canned hominy, rinsed
- 16 slices (2 pounds)
- 2/3 cup milk
- 2/3 cup water
- 3 tablespoons olive oil
- 4 cups bread flour
- 2/3 cup yellow cornmeal
- 3 tablespoons sugar
- 2 tablespoons gluten
- 2 teaspoons salt
- 21/2 teaspoons SAF yeast or 1 tablespoon bread machine yeast
- 11/2 cups canned hominy, rinsed

Directions:

1. Choose the size of loaf you would like to make and measure your ingredients.

2. Add the ingredients to the bread pan in the order listed above (except the hominy).

3. Place the pan in the bread machine and close the lid.

4. Turn on the bread maker. Select the Basic/Fruit and Nut setting, then the loaf size, and finally the crust color. Start the cycle.

5. When the machine beeps, or between Knead 1 and Knead 2, add the hominy.

6. When the cycle is finished and the bread is baked, carefully remove the pan from the machine. Use a potholder as the handle will be very hot. Let rest for a few minutes.

7. Remove the bread from the pan and allow to cool on a wire rack for at least 10 minutes before slicing.

Chestnut Flour Bread

Ingredients:
- 8 slices (1 pound)
- 9/16 cup fat-free milk
- 1/2 large egg
- 2 tablespoons butter or margarine, cut into pieces
- 1 5/8 cups bread flour
- 3/8 cup chestnut flour
- 1 1/2 tablespoons dark brown sugar
- 1 1/2 tablespoons minced pecans
- 2/3 tablespoon gluten
- 1 teaspoon salt
- 1 1/4 teaspoons SAF yeast or 1/2 tablespoon bread machine yeast
- 12 slices (1½ pounds)
- 7/8 cup fat-free milk
- 1 large egg
- 3 tablespoons butter or margarine, cut into pieces
- 21/2 cups bread flour
- 1/2 cup chestnut flour
- 2 tablespoons dark brown sugar
- 2 tablespoons minced pecans
- 1 tablespoon gluten
- 11/2 teaspoons salt
- 2 teaspoons SAF yeast or 21/2 teaspoons bread machine yeast
- 16 slices (2 pounds)
- 11/8 cups fat-free milk
- 1 large egg
- 4 tablespoons butter or margarine, cut into pieces

- 31/4 cups bread flour
- 3/4 cup chestnut flour
- 3 tablespoons dark brown sugar
- 3 tablespoons minced pecans
- 1 tablespoon plus 1 teaspoon gluten
- 2 teaspoons salt
- 21/2 teaspoons SAF yeast or 1 tablespoon bread machine yeast

Directions:
1. Choose the size of loaf you would like to make and measure your ingredients.

2. Add the ingredients to the bread pan in the order listed above.

3. Place the pan in the bread machine and close the lid.

4. Turn on the bread maker. Select the Basic setting, then the loaf size, and finally the crust color. Start the cycle.

5. When the cycle is finished and the bread is baked, carefully remove the pan from the machine. Use a potholder as the handle will be very hot. Let rest for a few minutes.

6. Remove the bread from the pan and allow to cool on a wire rack for at least 10 minutes before slicing.

Quinoa Bread

Ingredients:
- 8 slices (1 pound)
- 1/3 cup water
- 1/3 cup buttermilk
- 3/8 cup firm-packed cooked quinoa (see cooking information here)
- 1 1/2 tablespoons sesame oil
- 1 1/2 tablespoons honey
- 2 cups bread flour
- 2/3 tablespoon gluten
- 1 teaspoon salt
- 1 1/4 teaspoons SAF yeast or 1/2 tablespoon bread machine yeast
- 12 slices (1½ pounds)
- 1/2 cup water
- 1/2 cup buttermilk
- 1/2 cup firm-packed cooked quinoa (see cooking information here)

- 2 tablespoons sesame oil
- 2 tablespoons honey
- 3 cups bread flour
- 1 tablespoon gluten
- 11/2 teaspoons salt
- 2 teaspoons SAF yeast or 21/2 teaspoons bread machine yeast
- 16 slices (2 pounds)
- 2/3 cup water
- 2/3 cup buttermilk
- 3/4 cup firm-packed cooked quinoa (see cooking information here)
- 3 tablespoons sesame oil
- 3 tablespoons honey
- 4 cups bread flour
- 1 tablespoon plus 1 teaspoon gluten
- 2 teaspoons salt
- 21/2 teaspoons SAF yeast or 1 tablespoon bread machine yeast

Directions:

1. Choose the size of loaf you would like to make and measure your ingredients.
2. Add the ingredients to the bread pan in the order listed above.
3. Place the pan in the bread machine and close the lid.
4. Turn on the bread maker. Select the Basic setting, then the loaf size, and finally the crust color. Start the cycle.
5. When the cycle is finished and the bread is baked, carefully remove the pan from the machine. Use a potholder as the handle will be very hot. Let rest for a few minutes.
6. Remove the bread from the pan and allow to cool on a wire rack for at least 10 minutes before slicing.

Gluten-free Mock Light Rye

Ingredients:
- 8 slices (1 pound)
- 5/6 cups water
- 2 tablespoons dark molasses
- 2/3 teaspoon apple cider or rice vinegar
- 1/6 cup vegetable or canola oil
- 2 large eggs, broken into a measuring cup to equal 1 1/8 cup (add water if needed)
- 1 1/2 cups white rice flour
- 2/3 cup brown rice flour
- 1/3 cup nonfat dry milk
- 1/6 cup dark brown sugar
- 2/3 tablespoon xanthan gum
- 2/3 tablespoon plus 2/3 teaspoon caraway seeds
- Grated zest of 2/3 large orange or 1 1/3 teaspoons dried orange peel
- 2 1/4 teaspoons salt
- 1 1/2 teaspoons SAF yeast or 1 5/6 teaspoons bread machine yeast
- 12 slices (1 ½ pounds)
- 11/4 cups water
- 3 tablespoons dark molasses
- 1 teaspoon apple cider or rice vinegar
- 1/4 cup vegetable or canola oil
- 3 large eggs, broken into a measuring cup to equal 3/4 cup (add water if needed)
- 21/4 cups white rice flour
- 7/8 cup brown rice flour
- 1/2 cup nonfat dry milk
- 1/4 cup dark brown sugar
- 1 tablespoon xanthan gum
- 1 tablespoon plus 1 teaspoon caraway seeds
- Grated zest of 1 large orange or 2 teaspoons dried orange peel
- 11/2 teaspoons salt
- 21/4 teaspoons SAF yeast or 23/4 teaspoons bread machine yeast
- 16 slices (2 pounds)
- 1 2/3 cups water
- 4 tablespoons dark molasses
- 1 1/3 teaspoons apple cider or rice vinegar
- 1/3 cup vegetable or canola oil
- 4 large eggs, broken into a measuring cup to equal 2 1/4 cup (add water if needed)
- 3 cups white rice flour
- 1 1/3 cups brown rice flour
- 2/3 cup nonfat dry milk
- 1/3 cup dark brown sugar
- 1 1/3 tablespoons xanthan gum
- 1 1/3 tablespoons plus 1 1/3 teaspoons caraway seeds

- Grated zest of 1 1/3 large oranges or 2 2/3 teaspoons dried orange peel
- 4 1/2 teaspoons salt
- 3 teaspoons SAF yeast or 3 2/3 teaspoons bread machine yeast

Directions:

1. Choose the size of loaf you would like to make and measure your ingredients.
2. Add the ingredients to the bread pan in the order listed above.
3. Place the pan in the bread machine and close the lid.
4. Turn on the bread maker. Select the Non-Gluten/Quick Yeast Bread setting, then the loaf size, and finally the crust color. Start the cycle.
5. When the cycle is finished and the bread is baked, carefully remove the pan from the machine. Use a potholder as the handle will be very hot. Let rest for a few minutes.
6. Remove the bread from the pan and allow to cool on a wire rack for at least 10 minutes before slicing.

Teff Honey Bread

Ingredients:

- 8 slices (1 pound)
- 3/4 cup water
- 1 1/2 tablespoons vegetable oil
- 1 1/2 tablespoons honey
- 1 5/8 cups bread flour
- 3/8 cup ivory or dark teff flour
- 2/3 tablespoon gluten
- 1 teaspoon salt
- 1/2 tablespoon SAF yeast or 1/2 tablespoon plus 1/4 teaspoon bread machine yeast
- 12 slices (1½ pounds)
- 11/8 cups water
- 2 tablespoons vegetable oil
- 2 tablespoons honey
- 21/4 cups bread flour
- 3/4 cup ivory or dark teff flour
- 1 tablespoon plus 1 teaspoon gluten
- 11/2 teaspoons salt
- 21/2 teaspoons SAF yeast or 1 tablespoon bread machine yeast

- 16 slices (2 pounds)
- 11/2 cups water
- 3 tablespoons vegetable oil
- 3 tablespoons honey
- 31/4 cups bread flour
- 3/4 cup ivory or dark teff flour
- 1 tablespoon plus 2 teaspoons gluten
- 2 teaspoons salt
- 1 tablespoon SAF yeast or 1 tablespoon plus 1/2 teaspoon bread machine yeast

Directions:

1. Choose the size of loaf you would like to make and measure your ingredients.
2. Add the ingredients to the bread pan in the order listed above.
3. Place the pan in the bread machine and close the lid.
4. Turn on the bread maker. Select the Basic setting, then the loaf size, and finally the crust color. Start the cycle.
5. When the cycle is finished and the bread is baked, carefully remove the pan from the machine. Use a potholder as the handle will be very hot. Let rest for a few minutes.
6. Remove the bread from the pan and allow to cool on a wire rack for at least 10 minutes before slicing.

Polenta-sunflower-millet Bread

Ingredients:

- 8 slices (1 pound)
- 3/4 cup water
- 1/8 cup honey
- 1 1/2 tablespoons sunflower seed oil
- 1 5/8 cups bread flour
- 3/8 cup whole wheat flour
- 1/6 cup polenta
- 1/8 cup whole raw millet
- 1/8 cup raw sunflower seeds
- 1 tablespoon gluten
- 1 teaspoon salt
- 1 1/4 teaspoons SAF yeast or 1/2 tablespoon bread machine yeast
- 12 slices (1½ pounds)
- 11/8 cups water

- 3 tablespoons honey
- 2 tablespoons sunflower seed oil
- 21/2 cups bread flour
- 1/2 cup whole wheat flour
- 1/4 cup polenta
- 3 tablespoons whole raw millet
- 3 tablespoons raw sunflower seeds
- 11/2 tablespoons gluten
- 11/2 teaspoons salt
- 13/4 teaspoons SAF yeast or 21/4 teaspoons bread machine yeast
- 16 slices (2 pounds)
- 11/2 cups water
- 1/4 cup honey
- 3 tablespoons sunflower seed oil
- 31/4 cups bread flour
- 3/4 cup whole wheat flour
- 1/3 cup polenta
- 1/4 cup whole raw millet
- 1/4 cup raw sunflower seeds
- 2 tablespoons gluten
- 2 teaspoons salt
- 21/2 teaspoons SAF yeast or 1 tablespoon bread machine yeast

Directions:

1. Choose the size of loaf you would like to make and measure your ingredients.

2. Add the ingredients to the bread pan in the order listed above.

3. Place the pan in the bread machine and close the lid.

4. Turn on the bread maker. Select the Basic/Whole Wheat setting, then the loaf size, and finally the crust color. Start the cycle.

5. When the cycle is finished and the bread is baked, carefully remove the pan from the machine. Use a potholder as the handle will be very hot. Let rest for a few minutes.

6. Remove the bread from the pan and allow to cool on a wire rack for at least 10 minutes before slicing.

Polenta-chestnut Bread

Ingredients:

- 8 slices (1 pound)
- 2/3 cup buttermilk
- 1/8 cup dark honey
- 1/8 cup olive oil
- 1 1/2 cups bread flour
- 3/8 cup chestnut flour
- 1/4 cup polenta
- 1 tablespoon gluten
- 1 teaspoon salt
- 1 3/8 teaspoons SAF yeast or 1/2 tablespoon plus 1/8 teaspoon bread machine yeast
- 12 slices (1½ pounds)
- 1 cup plus 1 tablespoon buttermilk
- 3 tablespoons dark honey
- 3 tablespoons olive oil
- 21/3 cups bread flour
- 1/2 cup chestnut flour
- 1/3 cup polenta
- 11/2 tablespoons gluten
- 11/2 teaspoons salt
- 21/4 teaspoons SAF yeast or 23/4 teaspoons bread machine yeast
- 16 slices (2 pounds)
- 11/3 cups buttermilk
- 1/4 cup dark honey
- 1/4 cup olive oil
- 3 cups bread flour
- 3/4 cup chestnut flour
- 1/2 cup polenta
- 2 tablespoons gluten
- 2 teaspoons salt
- 23/4 teaspoons SAF yeast or 1 tablespoon plus 1/4 teaspoon bread machine yeast

Directions:

1. Choose the size of loaf you would like to make and measure your ingredients.

2. Add the ingredients to the bread pan in the order listed above.

3. Place the pan in the bread machine and close the lid.

4. Turn on the bread maker. Select the Basic setting, then the loaf size, and finally the crust color. Start the cycle.

5. When the cycle is finished and the bread is baked, carefully remove the pan from the machine. Use a

potholder as the handle will be very hot. Let rest for a few minutes.

6. Remove the bread from the pan and allow to cool on a wire rack for at least 10 minutes before slicing.

Cornmeal Honey Bread

Ingredients:
- 8 slices (1 pound)
- 3/4 cup water
- 1 tablespoon unsalted butter cut into pieces
- 1/8 cup honey
- 1 3/4 cups bread flour
- 1/4 cup yellow cornmeal
- 1/4 cup dry buttermilk powder
- 1/2 tablespoon plus 1 teaspoons gluten
- 3/4 teaspoon salt
- 1 1/4 teaspoons SAF yeast or 1/2 tablespoon bread machine yeast
- 12 slices (1½ pounds)
- 11/8 cups water
- 11/2 tablespoons unsalted butter, cut into pieces
- 3 tablespoons honey
- 22/3 cups bread flour
- 1/3 cup yellow cornmeal
- 1/3 cup dry buttermilk powder
- 1 tablespoon plus 1 teaspoon gluten
- 1 teaspoon salt
- 13/4 teaspoons SAF yeast or 21/4 teaspoons bread machine yeast
- 16 slices (2 pounds)
- 11/2 cups water
- 2 tablespoons unsalted butter cut into pieces
- 1/4 cup honey
- 31/2 cups bread flour
- 1/2 cup yellow cornmeal
- 1/2 cup dry buttermilk powder
- 1 tablespoon plus 2 teaspoons gluten
- 11/2 teaspoons salt
- 21/2 teaspoons SAF yeast or 1 tablespoon bread machine yeast

Directions:
1. Choose the size of loaf you would like to make and measure your ingredients.

2. Add the ingredients to the bread pan in the order listed above.

3. Place the pan in the bread machine and close the lid.

4. Turn on the bread maker. Select the Basic setting, then the loaf size, and finally the crust color. Start the cycle.

5. When the cycle is finished and the bread is baked, carefully remove the pan from the machine. Use a potholder as the handle will be very hot. Let rest for a few minutes.

6. Remove the bread from the pan and allow to cool on a wire rack for at least 10 minutes before slicing.

Gluten-free Almond And Dried Fruit Holiday Bread

Ingredients:
- 8 slices (1 pound)
- For the dough:
- 11/2 cups water
- 2 teaspoons almond extract
- 1 teaspoon apple cider vinegar or rice vinegar
- 3 large eggs, broken into a measuring cup to equal 3/4 cup (add water if needed)
- 2 cups white rice flour
- 1/2 cup potato starch flour
- 1/2 cup tapioca flour or arrowroot
- 1/2 cup dry buttermilk powder or nonfat dry milk
- 1/3 cup sugar or 3 tablespoons powdered fructose
- 1 tablespoon xanthan gum
- 11/2 teaspoons ground cardamom
- 1/2 teaspoon ground mace or nutmeg
- Grated zest of 1 lemon or 1 teaspoon dried lemon peel
- 11/2 teaspoons salt
- 21/2 teaspoons SAF yeast or 1 tablespoon bread machine yeast
- 1/2 cup mixed dried fruit bits
- 2 tablespoons currants
- 1/3 cup toasted slivered almonds
- For the lemon glaze:
- 1 cup sifted confectioners' sugar
- 1 tablespoon melted butter or margarine
- 2 to 3 tablespoons fresh lemon juice, heated

- 12 slices (1 ½ pounds)
- For the dough:
- 2 1/4 cups water
- 3 teaspoons almond extract
- 1 1/2 teaspoons apple cider vinegar or rice vinegar
- 4 1/2 large eggs, broken into a measuring cup to equal 3/4 cup (add water if needed)
- 3 cups white rice flour
- 3/4 cup potato starch flour
- 3/4 cup tapioca flour or arrowroot
- 3/4 cup dry buttermilk powder or nonfat dry milk
- 1/2 cup sugar or 4 1/2 tablespoons powdered fructose
- 1 1/2 tablespoons xanthan gum
- 2 1/4 teaspoons ground cardamom
- 3/4 teaspoon ground mace or nutmeg
- Grated zest of 1 1/2 lemons or 1 1/2 teaspoons dried lemon peel
- 2 1/4 teaspoons salt
- 3 3/4 teaspoons SAF yeast or 1 1/2 tablespoons bread machine yeast
- 3/4 cup mixed dried fruit bits
- 3 tablespoons currants
- 1/2 cup toasted slivered almonds
- For the lemon glaze:
- 1 cup sifted confectioners' sugar
- 1 tablespoon melted butter or margarine
- 2 to 3 tablespoons fresh lemon juice, heated
- 16 slices (2 pounds)
- For the dough:
- 3 cups water
- 4 teaspoons almond extract
- 2 teaspoons apple cider vinegar or rice vinegar
- 6 large eggs, broken into a measuring cup to equal 3/4 cup (add water if needed)
- 4 cups white rice flour
- 1 cup potato starch flour
- 1 cup tapioca flour or arrowroot
- 1 cup dry buttermilk powder or nonfat dry milk
- 2/3 cup sugar or 6 tablespoons powdered fructose
- 2 tablespoons xanthan gum
- 3 teaspoons ground cardamom
- 1 teaspoon ground mace or nutmeg
- Grated zest of 2 lemons or 2 teaspoons dried lemon peel
- 3 teaspoons salt
- 5 teaspoons SAF yeast or 2 tablespoons bread machine yeast
- 1 cup mixed dried fruit bits
- 4 tablespoons currants
- 2/3 cup toasted slivered almonds
- For the lemon glaze:
- 1 cup sifted confectioners' sugar
- 1 tablespoon melted butter or margarine
- 2 to 3 tablespoons fresh lemon juice, heated

Directions:

1. Choose the size of loaf you would like to make and measure your ingredients.

2. Add the ingredients to the bread pan in the order listed above (except the raisins).

3. Place the pan in the bread machine and close the lid.

4. Turn on the bread maker. Select the Non-Gluten/Quick Yeast Bread setting, then the loaf size, and finally the crust color. Start the cycle.

5. Set a kitchen timer for 5 minutes. When the timer rings, open the lid and add the dried fruit and almonds.

6. When the cycle is finished and the bread is baked, carefully remove the pan from the machine. Use a potholder as the handle will be very hot. Let rest for a few minutes.

7. Remove the bread from the pan and allow to cool on a wire rack for at least 10 minutes before slicing.

8. To make the lemon glaze, combine the confectioners' sugar, butter, and lemon juice in a small bowl. Immediately pour over the top of the loaf, letting it dribble down the sides. Let cool to room temperature before slicing.

Wild Rice Bread

Ingredients:
- 8 slices (1 pound)
- 3/4 cup water
- 1/4 cup raw wild rice
- 1 1/2 tablespoons walnut oil
- 1/2 tablespoon light brown sugar
- 1 3/4 cups bread flour

- 1/4 cup pumpernickel rye flour
- 2/3 tablespoon gluten
- 1 teaspoon salt
- 1 1/8 teaspoons SAF yeast or 1 3/8 teaspoons bread machine yeast
- 12 slices (1½ pounds)
- 11/8 cups water
- 1/3 cup raw wild rice
- 21/2 tablespoons walnut oil
- 2 teaspoons light brown sugar
- 23/4 cups bread flour
- 1/3 cup pumpernickel rye flour
- 1 tablespoon plus 1 teaspoon gluten
- 11/2 teaspoons salt
- 2 teaspoons SAF yeast or 21/2 teaspoons bread machine yeast
- 16 slices (2 pounds)
- 11/2 cups water
- 1/2 cup raw wild rice
- 3 tablespoons walnut oil
- 1 tablespoon light brown sugar
- 31/2 cups bread flour
- 1/2 cup pumpernickel rye flour
- 1 tablespoon plus 2 teaspoons gluten
- 2 teaspoons salt
- 21/4 teaspoons SAF yeast or 23/4 teaspoons bread machine yeast

Directions:

1. Choose the size of loaf you would like to make and measure your ingredients.

2. Heat the water to a boil in a medium saucepan. Add the rice. Cover and simmer over low heat for 30 to 45 minutes, until the rice is tender. Strain the remaining cooking liquid into a 2-cup measure and add enough extra water to equal the original amount in the pan (11/8 cups for the 11/2-pound loaf or 11/2 cups for the 2-pound loaf). Set the liquid and rice aside separately to cool.

3. Add the ingredients to the bread pan in the order listed above (except the rice).

4. Place the pan in the bread machine and close the lid.

5. Turn on the bread maker. Select the Basic/Fruit and Nut setting, then the loaf size, and finally the crust color.

Start the cycle. (This recipe is not suitable for use with the Delay Timer.)

6. When the machine beeps, or between Knead 1 and Knead 2, add the rice.

7. When the cycle is finished and the bread is baked, carefully remove the pan from the machine. Use a potholder as the handle will be very hot. Let rest for a few minutes.

8. Remove the bread from the pan and allow to cool on a wire rack for at least 10 minutes before slicing.

Low-gluten White Spelt Bread

Ingredients:

- 8 slices (1 pound)
- 2/3 cup water
- 1/6 cup apple juice concentrate, thawed
- 1 tablespoon canola oil or soft butter
- 4 1/2 cups white spelt flour
- 1/6 cup oat bran or cornmeal
- 2/3 tablespoon full-fat soy flour
- 5/6 teaspoon salt
- 1 2/3 teaspoons SAF yeast or 2/3 tablespoon bread machine yeast
- 12 slices (1 ½ pounds)
- 1 cup water
- 1/4 cup apple juice concentrate, thawed
- 11/2 tablespoons canola oil or soft butter
- 3 cups white spelt flour
- 1/4 cup oat bran or cornmeal
- 1 tablespoon full-fat soy flour
- 11/4 teaspoons salt
- 21/2 teaspoons SAF yeast or 1 tablespoon bread machine yeast
- 16 slices (2 pounds)
- 1 1/3 cups water
- 1/3 cup apple juice concentrate, thawed
- 2 tablespoons canola oil or soft butter
- 9 cups white spelt flour
- 1/3 cup oat bran or cornmeal
- 1 1/3 tablespoons full-fat soy flour
- 1 2/3 teaspoons salt
- 1 1 /9 teaspoons SAF yeast or 1 1/3 tablespoons bread machine yeast

Directions:

1. Choose the size of loaf you would like to make and measure your ingredients.

2. Add the ingredients to the bread pan in the order listed above.

3. Place the pan in the bread machine and close the lid.

4. Turn on the bread maker. Select the Basic setting, then the loaf size, and finally the crust color. Start the cycle.

5. Test the dough ball, and add 1 to 2 teaspoons spelt flour or water as needed, but leave the dough moist and slightly tacky.

6. When the cycle is finished and the bread is baked, carefully remove the pan from the machine. Use a potholder as the handle will be very hot. Let rest for a few minutes.

7. Remove the bread from the pan and allow to cool on a wire rack for at least 10 minutes before slicing.

Barley Bread

Ingredients:

- 8 slices (1 pound)
- 3/4 cup water
- 1 1/2 tablespoons light brown sugar
- 1 1/2 tablespoons vegetable oil
- 1 1/2 cups bread flour
- 1/3 cup barley flour
- 1/6 cup whole wheat flour
- 1/8 cup dry buttermilk powder
- 1 tablespoon gluten
- 3/4 teaspoon ground cinnamon
- 1 teaspoon salt
- 1 1/4 teaspoons SAF yeast or 1/2 tablespoon bread machine yeast
- 12 slices (1½ pounds)
- 1 cup plus 3 tablespoons water
- 2 tablespoons light brown sugar
- 2 tablespoons vegetable oil
- 21/4 cups bread flour
- 1/2 cup barley flour
- 1/4 cup whole wheat flour
- 3 tablespoons dry buttermilk powder
- 1 tablespoon plus 2 teaspoons gluten
- 1 teaspoon ground cinnamon
- 11/2 teaspoons salt
- 21/4 teaspoons SAF yeast or 23/4 teaspoons bread machine yeast
- 16 slices (2 pounds)
- 11/2 cups water
- 3 tablespoons light brown sugar
- 3 tablespoons vegetable oil
- 3 cups bread flour
- 2/3 cup barley flour
- 1/3 cup whole wheat flour
- 1/4 cup dry buttermilk powder
- 2 tablespoons gluten
- 11/2 teaspoons ground cinnamon
- 2 teaspoons salt
- 21/2 teaspoons SAF yeast or 1 tablespoon bread machine yeast

Directions:

1. Choose the size of loaf you would like to make and measure your ingredients.

2. Add the ingredients to the bread pan in the order listed above.

3. Place the pan in the bread machine and close the lid.

4. Turn on the bread maker. Select the Basic/Whole Wheat setting, then the loaf size, and finally the crust color. Start the cycle.

5. When the cycle is finished and the bread is baked, carefully remove the pan from the machine. Use a potholder as the handle will be very hot. Let rest for a few minutes.

6. Remove the bread from the pan and allow to cool on a wire rack for at least 10 minutes before slicing.

Cornell Bread

Ingredients:

- 8 slices (1 pound)
- 3/4 cup water
- 1 1/2 tablespoons canola oil
- 1 1/2 tablespoons honey
- 1 1/2 tablespoons dark brown sugar
- 1/2 large egg
- 1 cup whole wheat flour
- 3/4 cup bread flour

- 1/4 cup full-fat soy flour
- 1 tablespoon wheat germ
- 1/6 cup nonfat dry milk
- 1 tablespoon gluten
- 1 teaspoon salt
- 1/2 tablespoon SAF yeast or 1/2 tablespoon plus 1/4 teaspoon bread machine yeast
- 12 slices (1½ pounds)
- 11/8 cups water
- 2 tablespoons canola oil
- 2 tablespoons honey
- 2 tablespoons dark brown sugar
- 1 large egg
- 11/2 cups whole wheat flour
- 1 cup plus 2 tablespoons bread flour
- 1/3 cup full-fat soy flour
- 11/2 tablespoons wheat germ
- 1/4 cup nonfat dry milk
- 11/2 tablespoons gluten
- 11/2 teaspoons salt
- 21/2 teaspoons SAF yeast or 1 tablespoon bread machine yeast
- 16 slices (2 pounds)
- 11/2 cups water
- 3 tablespoons canola oil
- 3 tablespoons honey
- 3 tablespoons dark brown sugar
- 1 large egg
- 2 cups whole wheat flour
- 11/2 cups bread flour
- 1/2 cup full-fat soy flour
- 2 tablespoons wheat germ
- 1/3 cup nonfat dry milk
- 2 tablespoons gluten
- 2 teaspoons salt
- 1 tablespoon SAF yeast or 1 tablespoon plus 1/2 teaspoon bread machine yeast

Directions:

1. Choose the size of loaf you would like to make and measure your ingredients.
2. Add the ingredients to the bread pan in the order listed above.
3. Place the pan in the bread machine and close the lid.
4. Turn on the bread maker. Select the Whole Wheat setting, then the loaf size, and finally the crust color. Start the cycle.
5. When the cycle is finished and the bread is baked, carefully remove the pan from the machine. Use a potholder as the handle will be very hot. Let rest for a few minutes.
6. Remove the bread from the pan and allow to cool on a wire rack for at least 10 minutes before slicing.

Orange-buckwheat Bread

Ingredients:
- 8 slices (1 pound)
- 2/3 cup buttermilk
- 1/2 large egg
- 1 1/2 tablespoons unsalted butter, cut into pieces
- 1 1/2 cups bread flour
- 1/2 cup whole wheat flour
- 1/4 cup light buckwheat flour
- 1 1/2 tablespoons dark brown sugar
- Grated zest of 1/2 large orange
- 2/3 tablespoon gluten
- 1 teaspoon salt
- 1 1/4 teaspoons SAF yeast or 1/2 tablespoon bread machine yeast
- 12 slices (1½ pounds)
- 1 cup buttermilk
- 1 large egg
- 2 tablespoons unsalted butter, cut into pieces
- 2 cups bread flour
- 3/4 cup whole wheat flour
- 1/3 cup light buckwheat flour
- 2 tablespoons dark brown sugar
- Grated zest of 1 large orange
- 1 tablespoon gluten
- 11/2 teaspoons salt
- 21/4 teaspoons SAF yeast or 23/4 teaspoons bread machine yeast
- 16 slices (2 pounds)
- 11/3 cups buttermilk
- 1 large egg
- 3 tablespoons unsalted butter, cut into pieces
- 3 cups bread flour

- 1 cup whole wheat flour
- 1/2 cup light buckwheat flour
- 3 tablespoons dark brown sugar
- Grated zest of 1 large orange
- 1 tablespoon plus 1 teaspoon gluten
- 2 teaspoons salt
- 21/2 teaspoons SAF yeast or 1 tablespoon bread machine yeast

Directions:

1. Choose the size of loaf you would like to make and measure your ingredients.

2. Add the ingredients to the bread pan in the order listed above.

3. Place the pan in the bread machine and close the lid.

4. Turn on the bread maker. Select the Basic setting, then the loaf size, and finally the crust color. Start the cycle.

5. When the cycle is finished and the bread is baked, carefully remove the pan from the machine. Use a potholder as the handle will be very hot. Let rest for a few minutes.

6. Remove the bread from the pan and allow to cool on a wire rack for at least 10 minutes before slicing.

Gluten-free Chickpea-, Rice-, And Tapioca-flour Bread

Ingredients:

- 8 slices (1 pound)
- 5/6 cups water
- 2/3 teaspoon apple cider vinegar or rice vinegar
- 2 tablespoons maple syrup
- 2 tablespoons olive oil
- 2 large eggs, broken into a measuring cup to equal 1/2 cup (add water if needed)
- 2/3 cup chickpea flour
- 2/3 cup brown rice flour
- 1/3 cup cornstarch
- 1/3 cup tapioca flour
- 1/3 cup nonfat dry milk
- 1 1/3 tablespoons light brown sugar
- 2/3 tablespoon plus 2/3 teaspoon xanthan gum

- 1 teaspoon salt
- 1 1/2 teaspoons SAF yeast or 1 5/6 teaspoons bread machine yeast
- 12 slices (1 ½ pounds)
- 11/4 cups water
- 1 teaspoon apple cider vinegar or rice vinegar
- 3 tablespoons maple syrup
- 3 tablespoons olive oil
- 3 large eggs, broken into a measuring cup to equal 3/4 cup (add water if needed)
- 1 cup chickpea flour
- 1 cup brown rice flour
- 1/2 cup cornstarch
- 1/2 cup tapioca flour
- 1/2 cup nonfat dry milk
- 2 tablespoons light brown sugar
- 1 tablespoon plus 1 teaspoon xanthan gum
- 11/2 teaspoons salt
- 21/4 teaspoons SAF yeast or 23/4 teaspoons bread machine yeast
- 16 slices (2 pounds)
- 11/4 cups water
- 1 teaspoon apple cider vinegar or rice vinegar
- 3 tablespoons maple syrup
- 3 tablespoons olive oil
- 3 large eggs, broken into a measuring cup to equal 3/4 cup (add water if needed)
- 1 cup chickpea flour
- 1 cup brown rice flour
- 1/2 cup cornstarch
- 1/2 cup tapioca flour
- 1/2 cup nonfat dry milk
- 2 tablespoons light brown sugar
- 1 tablespoon plus 1 teaspoon xanthan gum
- 11/2 teaspoons salt
- 21/4 teaspoons SAF yeast or 23/4 teaspoons bread machine yeast

Directions:

1. Choose the size of loaf you would like to make and measure your ingredients.

2. Add the ingredients to the bread pan in the order listed above.

3. Place the pan in the bread machine and close the lid.

4. Turn on the bread maker. Select the Non-Gluten/Quick Yeast Bread setting, then the loaf size, and finally the crust color. Start the cycle.

5. When the cycle is finished and the bread is baked, carefully remove the pan from the machine. Use a potholder as the handle will be very hot. Let rest for a few minutes.

6. Remove the bread from the pan and allow to cool on a wire rack for at least 10 minutes before slicing.

EVERYDAY/WHITE/BASIC BREAD RECIPES

Tomato Basil Bread

Ingredients:

- 8 slices (1 pound)
- 3/4 cup warm water
- 1/4 cup fresh basil, minced
- 1/4 cup parmesan cheese, grated
- 3 tablespoons tomato paste
- 1 tablespoon sugar
- 1 tablespoon olive oil
- 1 teaspoon salt
- 1/4 teaspoon crushed red pepper flakes
- 2 1/2 cups bread flour
- 1 package active dry yeast
- Flour, for surface
- 12 slices (1 ½ pounds)
- 1 1/8 cups warm water
- 3/8 cup fresh basil, minced
- 3/8 cup parmesan cheese, grated
- 4 1/2 tablespoons tomato paste
- 1 1/2 tablespoons sugar
- 1 1/2 tablespoons olive oil
- 1 1/2 teaspoons salt
- 3/8 teaspoon crushed red pepper flakes
- 3 3/4 cups bread flour
- 1 1/2 packages active dry yeast
- Flour, for surface
- 16 slices (2 pounds)
- 1 1/2 cups warm water
- 1/2 cup fresh basil, minced
- 1/2 cup parmesan cheese, grated
- 6 tablespoons tomato paste
- 2 tablespoons sugar
- 2 tablespoons olive oil
- 2 teaspoons salt
- 1/2 teaspoon crushed red pepper flakes
- 5 cups bread flour
- 2 packages active dry yeast
- Flour, for surface

Directions:

1. Choose the size of loaf you would like to make and measure your ingredients.
2. Add the ingredients to the bread pan in the order listed above (except yeast).
3. Make a well in the flour and pour the yeast into it.
4. Place the pan in the bread machine and close the lid.
5. Turn on the bread maker. Select the Dough setting, then the loaf size, and finally the crust color. Start the cycle.
6. When the cycle is finished and the bread is baked, turn finished dough out onto a floured surface and knead until smooth and elastic, about 3 to 5 minutes.
7. Place in a greased bowl, turning once to grease top. Cover and let rise in a warm place until doubled, about 1 hour.
8. Punch dough down and knead for 1 minute.
9. Shape into a round loaf. Place on a greased baking sheet. Cover and let rise until doubled, about 1 hour.
10. With a sharp knife, cut a large "X" in top of loaf. Bake at 375°F for 35-40 minutes or until golden brown.
11. Remove the bread from the pan and allow to cool on a wire rack for at least 10 minutes before slicing.

Southern Cornbread

Ingredients:

- 8 slices (1 pound)
- 1 1/3 fresh eggs, at room temperature
- 2/3 cup milk
- 1/6 cup butter, unsalted, at room temperature
- 1/2 cup sugar
- 2/3 teaspoon salt
- 1 1/3 cups unbleached all-purpose flour
- 2/3 cup cornmeal
- 2/3 tablespoon baking powder
- 12 slices (1 ½ pounds)
- 2 fresh eggs, at room temperature
- 1 cup milk
- 1/4 cup butter, unsalted, at room temperature
- 3/4 cup sugar
- 1 teaspoon salt
- 2 cups unbleached all-purpose flour

- 1 cup cornmeal
- 1 tablespoon baking powder
- 16 slices (2 pounds)
- 2 2/3 fresh eggs, at room temperature
- 1 1/3 cups milk
- 1/3 cup butter, unsalted, at room temperature
- 1 cup sugar
- 1 1/3 teaspoons salt
- 2 2/3 cups unbleached all-purpose flour
- 1 1/3 cups cornmeal
- 1 1/3 tablespoons baking powder

Directions:

1. Choose the size of loaf you would like to make and measure your ingredients.
2. Add the ingredients to the bread pan in the order listed above.
3. Place the pan in the bread machine and close the lid.
4. Turn on the bread maker. Select the Quick Bread setting, then the loaf size, and finally the crust color. Start the cycle.
5. When the cycle is finished and the bread is baked, carefully remove the pan from the machine. Use a potholder as the handle will be very hot. Let rest for a few minutes.
6. Remove the bread from the pan and allow to cool on a wire rack for at least 10 minutes before slicing.

Wine And Cheese Bread

Ingredients:
- 8 slices (1 pound)
- 3/4 cup white wine
- 1/2 cup white cheddar or gruyere cheese, shredded
- 1 1/2 tablespoons butter
- 1/2 teaspoon salt
- 3/4 teaspoon sugar
- 2 1/4 cups bread flour
- 1 1/2 teaspoons active dry yeast
- 12 slices (1 ½ pounds)
- 1 1/8 cups white wine
- 3/4 cup white cheddar or gruyere cheese, shredded
- 2 1/4 tablespoons butter
- 3/4 teaspoon salt
- 1 1/8 teaspoons sugar

- 3 3/8 cups bread flour
- 2 1/4 teaspoons active dry yeast
- 16 slices (2 pounds)
- 1 1/2 cups white wine
- 1 cup white cheddar or gruyere cheese, shredded
- 3 tablespoons butter
- 1 teaspoon salt
- 1 1/2 teaspoon sugar
- 4 1/2 cups bread flour
- 3 teaspoons active dry yeast

Directions:

1. Choose the size of loaf you would like to make and measure your ingredients.
2. Add the ingredients to the bread pan in the order listed above (except yeast).
3. Make a well in the flour and pour the yeast into it.
4. Place the pan in the bread machine and close the lid.
5. Turn on the bread maker. Select the Basic setting, then the loaf size, and finally the crust color. Start the cycle.
6. When the cycle is finished and the bread is baked, carefully remove the pan from the machine. Use a potholder as the handle will be very hot. Let rest for a few minutes.
7. Remove the bread from the pan and allow to cool on a wire rack for at least 10 minutes before slicing.

Rosemary Focaccia Bread

Ingredients:
- 8 slices (1 pound)
- 2/3 cup, plus 2 tablespoons water
- 2/3 tablespoon extra-virgin olive oil
- 2/3 teaspoon salt
- 1 1/3 teaspoons fresh rosemary, chopped
- 2 cups bread flour
- 1 teaspoon instant yeast
- For the topping:
- 3 tablespoons olive oil
- Coarse salt
- Red pepper flakes
- 12 slices (1 ½ pounds)
- 1 cup, plus 3 tablespoons water
- 1 tablespoon extra-virgin olive oil

- 1 teaspoon salt
- 2 teaspoons fresh rosemary, chopped
- 3 cups bread flour
- 1 1/2 teaspoons instant yeast
- For the topping:
- 3 tablespoons olive oil
- Coarse salt
- Red pepper flakes
- 16 slices (2 pounds)
- 1 1/3 cups, plus 4 tablespoons water
- 1 1/3 tablespoons extra-virgin olive oil
- 1 1/3 teaspoons salt
- 2 2/3 teaspoons fresh rosemary, chopped
- 4 cups bread flour
- 2 teaspoons instant yeast
- For the topping:
- 3 tablespoons olive oil
- Coarse salt
- Red pepper flakes

Directions:

1. Choose the size of loaf you would like to make and measure your ingredients.

2. Add the ingredients to the bread pan in the order listed above (except yeast).

3. Make a well in the center of the dry ingredients and add the yeast.

4. Place the pan in the bread machine and close the lid.

5. Turn on the bread maker. Select the Dough setting, then the loaf size, and finally the crust color. Start the cycle.

6. When the cycle is finished and the bread is baked, carefully remove the pan from the machine. Use a potholder as the handle will be very hot. Let rest for a few minutes.

7. Remove the bread from the pan and allow to cool on a wire rack for at least 10 minutes.

8. Form dough into a smooth ball and roll into a 12-inch round.

9. Place on a 12-inch pizza pan that has been lightly greased with olive oil. Poke dough randomly with fingertips to form dimples. Brush top with olive oil and sprinkle with salt and red pepper flakes to taste.

10. Let rise uncovered in warm, draft-free space for about 30 minutes.

11. Bake at 425°F for 18 to 22 minutes or until done.

Pepperoni Bread

Ingredients:

- 8 slices (1 pound)
- 2/3 cup plus 1 1/3 tablespoons warm water
- 1/4 cup mozzarella cheese, shredded
- 1 1/3 tablespoons sugar
- 1 teaspoon garlic salt
- 1 teaspoon dried oregano
- 2 1/6 cups bread flour
- 1 teaspoon active dry yeast
- 1/3 cup sliced pepperoni
- 12 slices (1 ½ pounds)
- 1 cup plus 2 tablespoons warm water
- 1/3 cup mozzarella cheese, shredded
- 2 tablespoons sugar
- 1 1/2 teaspoons garlic salt
- 1 1/2 teaspoons dried oregano
- 3 1/4 cups bread flour
- 1 1/2 teaspoons active dry yeast
- 2/3 cup sliced pepperoni
- 16 slices (2 pounds)
- 1 1/3 cups plus 2 2/3 tablespoons warm water
- 1/2 cup mozzarella cheese, shredded
- 2 2/3 tablespoons sugar
- 2 teaspoons garlic salt
- 2 teaspoons dried oregano
- 4 1/3 cups bread flour
- 2 teaspoons active dry yeast
- 2/3 cup sliced pepperoni

Directions:

1. Choose the size of loaf you would like to make and measure your ingredients.

2. Add the first six ingredients to the bread pan in the order listed above (except yeast).

3. Make a well in the flour and pour the yeast into it.

4. Place the pan in the bread machine and close the lid.

5. Turn on the bread maker. Select the Basic setting, then the loaf size, and finally the crust color. Start the cycle.

6.   Check dough after 5 minutes of mixing and add 1 to 2 tablespoons of water or flour if needed. Just before the final kneading, add the pepperoni.

7.   When the cycle is finished and the bread is baked, carefully remove the pan from the machine. Use a potholder as the handle will be very hot. Let rest for a few minutes.

8.   Remove the bread from the pan and allow to cool on a wire rack for at least 10 minutes before slicing.

Hungarian White Bread With Fennel Seeds

Ingredients:

- 8 slices (1 pound)
- 2/3 cup water
- 1 tablespoon unsalted butter, melted
- 2 cups bread flour
- 1 tablespoon sugar
- 1/2 tablespoon plus 1/2 teaspoon gluten
- 1/2 tablespoon fennel seeds
- 1 teaspoon salt
- 5/8 teaspoon SAF yeast or 1/2 tablespoon bread machine yeast
- 12 slices (1 ½ pounds)
- 11/8 cups water
- 11/2 tablespoons unsalted butter, melted
- 3 cups bread flour
- 11/2 tablespoons sugar
- 1 tablespoon gluten
- 21/2 teaspoons fennel seeds
- 11/2 teaspoons salt
- 2 teaspoons SAF yeast or 21/2 teaspoons bread machine yeast
- 16 slices (2 pounds)
- 11/3 cups water
- 2 tablespoons unsalted butter, melted
- 4 cups bread flour
- 2 tablespoons sugar
- 1 tablespoon plus 1 teaspoon gluten
- 1 tablespoon fennel seeds
- 2 teaspoons salt
- 21/2 teaspoons SAF yeast or 1 tablespoon bread machine yeast

Directions:

1.   Choose the size of loaf you would like to make and measure your ingredients.

2.   Add the ingredients to the bread pan in the order listed above.

3.   Place the pan in the bread machine and close the lid.

4.   Turn on the bread maker. Select the Basic setting, then the loaf size, and finally the crust color. Start the cycle.

5.   When the cycle is finished and the bread is baked, carefully remove the pan from the machine. Use a potholder as the handle will be very hot. Let rest for a few minutes.

6.   Remove the bread from the pan and allow to cool on a wire rack for at least 10 minutes before slicing.

Sampler Oatmeal Loaf

Ingredients:

- 8 slices (1 pound)
- 3/4 cup buttermilk
- 1 tablespoon honey or maple syrup
- 2 teaspoons butter or margarine, softened
- 13/4 cups bread flour
- 1/2 cup rolled oats
- 2 teaspoons gluten
- 1 teaspoon salt
- 11/4 teaspoons SAF yeast or 11/2 teaspoons bread machine yeast
- 12 slices (1 ½ pounds)
- 1 1/8 cups buttermilk
- 1 1/2 tablespoons honey or maple syrup
- 3 teaspoons butter or margarine, softened
- 2 5/8 cups bread flour
- 3/4 cup rolled oats
- 3 teaspoons gluten
- 1 1/2 teaspoons salt
- 17/8 teaspoons SAF yeast or 2 1/4 teaspoons bread machine yeast
- 16 slices (2 pounds)
- 1 1/2 cups buttermilk
- 2 tablespoon honey or maple syrup
- 4 teaspoons butter or margarine, softened
- 3 1/2 cups bread flour

- 1 cup rolled oats
- 4 teaspoons gluten
- 2 teaspoon salt
- 2 1/2 teaspoons SAF yeast or 3 teaspoons bread machine yeast

Directions:

1. Choose the size of loaf you would like to make and measure your ingredients.
2. Add the ingredients to the bread pan in the order listed above (except the nuts).
3. Place the pan in the bread machine and close the lid.
4. Turn on the bread maker. Select the Basic/Sweet Bread setting, then the loaf size, and finally the crust color. Start the cycle. (This recipe is not suitable for use with the Delay Timer.)
5. When the machine beeps, or between Knead 1 and Knead 2, add the nuts.
6. When the cycle is finished and the bread is baked, carefully remove the pan from the machine. Use a potholder as the handle will be very hot. Let rest for a few minutes.
7. Remove the bread from the pan and allow to cool on a wire rack for at least 10 minutes before slicing.

Prosciutto Parmesan Breadsticks

Ingredients:
- 8 slices (1 pound)
- 2/3 cup warm water
- 1/2 tablespoon butter
- 3/4 tablespoon sugar
- 3/4 teaspoon salt
- 2 cups bread flour
- 1 teaspoon yeast
- For the topping:
- 1/2 pound prosciutto, sliced very thin
- 1/2 cup of grated parmesan cheese
- 1 egg yolk
- 1 tablespoon of water
- 12 slices (1 ½ pounds)
- 1 cup warm water
- 3/4 tablespoon butter
- 1 1/8 tablespoons sugar
- 1 1/8 teaspoons salt
- 3 cups bread flour
- 1 1/2 teaspoons yeast
- For the topping:
- 1/2 pound prosciutto, sliced very thin
- 1/2 cup of grated parmesan cheese
- 1 egg yolk
- 1 tablespoon of water
- 16 slices (2 pounds)
- 1 1/3 cups warm water
- 1 tablespoon butter
- 1 1/2 tablespoons sugar
- 1 1/2 teaspoons salt
- 4 cups bread flour
- 2 teaspoons yeast
- For the topping:
- 1/2 pound prosciutto, sliced very thin
- 1/2 cup of grated parmesan cheese
- 1 egg yolk
- 1 tablespoon of water

Directions:

1. Choose the size of loaf you would like to make and measure your ingredients.
2. Add the ingredients to the bread pan in the order listed above (except yeast).
3. Make a well in the center of the dry ingredients and add the yeast.
4. Place the pan in the bread machine and close the lid.
5. Turn on the bread maker. Select the Dough setting, then the loaf size, and finally the crust color. Start the cycle.
6. When the cycle is finished and the bread is baked, drop the dough onto a lightly-floured surface.
7. Roll the dough out flat to about 1/4-inch thick, or about half a centimeter. Cover with plastic wrap and let rise for 20 to 30 minutes.
8. Sprinkle dough evenly with parmesan and carefully lay the prosciutto slices on the surface of the dough to cover as much of it as possible.
9. Preheat an oven to 400°F.
10. Cut the dough into 12 long strips, about one inch wide. Twist each end in opposite directions, twisting the toppings into the bread stick.

11. Place the breadsticks onto a lightly greased baking sheet.

12. Whisk the egg yolk and water together in a small mixing bowl and lightly baste each breadstick.

13. Bake for 8 to 10 minutes or until golden brown.

14. Remove from oven and serve warm.

Parsley And Chive Pull-apart Rolls

Ingredients:

- 8 slices (1 pound)
- 2/3 cup buttermilk
- 4 tablespoons unsalted butter, cut into 6 pieces
- 2 1/3 cups all-purpose flour
- 1 1/2 teaspoons instant yeast
- 1/4 cup granulated sugar
- 2/3 teaspoon salt
- 2 large egg yolks
- 1/6 cup chives, chopped
- 1/6 cup parsley, chopped
- For the topping:
- 1/4 cup butter, melted
- 12 slices (1 ½ pounds)
- 1 cup buttermilk
- 6 tablespoons unsalted butter, cut into 6 pieces
- 3 2/3 cups all-purpose flour
- 2 1/4 teaspoons instant yeast
- 1/3 cup granulated sugar
- 1 teaspoon salt
- 3 large egg yolks
- 1/4 cup chives, chopped
- 1/4 cup parsley, chopped
- For the topping:
- 1/4 cup butter, melted
- 16 slices (2 pounds)
- 1 1/3 cups buttermilk
- 8 tablespoons unsalted butter, cut into 6 pieces
- 4 2/3 cups all-purpose flour
- 3 teaspoons instant yeast
- 1/2 cup granulated sugar
- 1 1/3 teaspoons salt
- 4 large egg yolks
- 1/3 cup chives, chopped
- 1/3 cup parsley, chopped

- For the topping:
- 1/4 cup butter, melted

Directions:

1. Choose the size of loaf you would like to make and measure your ingredients.

2. Combine the buttermilk and the 6 tablespoons butter in a small saucepan and warm until the butter melts, stirring continuously. Add the packet of instant yeast and allow to stand for five minutes.

3. Mix the egg yolks with a fork and add to the above mixture and blend.

4. Combine the flour, sugar, salt and herbs.

5. Add the ingredients to the bread pan in the order listed above.

6. Place the pan in the bread machine and close the lid.

7. Turn on the bread maker. Select the Dough setting, then the loaf size, and finally the crust color. Start the cycle.

8. Lightly grease a 9-by-13-inch glass baking dish.

9. When the cycle is finished and the bread is baked, turn the dough out onto a clean work surface and press down gently. If the dough is too sticky add a little flour to the work surface. Using a bench scraper or a chef's knife, divide the dough into 16 equal pieces

10. Work one piece of dough at a time into a ball; keep the others covered with plastic wrap until ready to bake.

11. Cover the entire baking dish with plastic wrap and let the balls rise in a warm space, about 40 to 60 minutes.

12. Preheat an oven to 375°F and bake 20 to 25 minutes, or until lightly golden brown.

Classic White Bread Ii

Ingredients:

- 8 slices (1 pound)
- 3/4 cup water, lukewarm between 80 and 90°F
- 1 1/2 tablespoons unsalted butter, melted
- 1/2 tablespoon sugar
- 1 1/2 tablespoons dry milk powder
- 5/8 teaspoon table salt
- 2 cup white bread flour
- 3/4 teaspoon bread machine yeast
- 12 slices (1 ½ pounds)
- 1 1/4 cups water, lukewarm between 80 and 90°F

- 2 tablespoons unsalted butter, melted
- 2 teaspoons sugar
- 2 tablespoons dry milk powder
- 1 teaspoons table salt
- 3 1/4 cup white bread flour
- 1 1/4 teaspoons bread machine yeast
- 16 slices (2 pounds)
- 1 1/2 cups water, lukewarm between 80 and 90°F
- 3 tablespoons unsalted butter, melted
- 1 tablespoon sugar
- 3 tablespoons dry milk powder
- 1 1/4 teaspoons table salt
- 4 cups white bread flour
- 1 1/2 teaspoons bread machine yeast

Directions:

1. Choose the size of loaf you would like to make and measure your ingredients.

2. Add the ingredients to the bread pan in the order listed above.

3. Place the pan in the bread machine and close the lid.

4. Turn on the bread maker. Select the White/Basic setting, then the loaf size, and finally the crust color. Start the cycle.

5. When the cycle is finished and the bread is baked, carefully remove the pan from the machine. Use a potholder as the handle will be very hot. Let rest for a few minutes.

6. Remove the bread from the pan and allow to cool on a wire rack for at least 10 minutes before slicing.

Sour Cream Bread

Ingredients:
- 8 slices (1 pound)
- 3/8 cup plus 1/2 tablespoon water
- 5/8 cup sour cream
- 2 1/6 cups bread flour
- 3/4 tablespoon light brown sugar
- 1/2 tablespoon gluten
- 3/4 teaspoon salt
- 1/2 tablespoon SAF yeast or 1/2 tablespoon plus 1/4 teaspoon bread machine yeast
- 12 slices (1 ½ pounds)
- 1/2 cup plus 1 tablespoon water

- 1 cup sour cream
- 31/2 cups bread flour
- 1 tablespoon light brown sugar
- 2 teaspoons gluten
- 11/4 teaspoons salt
- 2 teaspoons SAF yeast or 21/2 teaspoons bread machine yeast
- 16 slices (2 pounds)
- 3/4 cup plus 1 tablespoon water
- 1 1/4 cups sour cream
- 4 1/3 cups bread flour
- 11/2 tablespoons light brown sugar
- 1 tablespoon gluten
- 11/2 teaspoons salt
- 1 tablespoon SAF yeast or 1 tablespoon plus 1/2 teaspoon bread machine yeast

Directions:

1. Choose the size of loaf you would like to make and measure your ingredients.

2. Add the ingredients to the bread pan in the order listed above, with the water and sour cream put in first, and adding the dry ingredients in on top.

3. Place the pan in the bread machine and close the lid.

4. Turn on the bread maker. Select the Basic setting, then the loaf size, and finally the crust color. Start the cycle.

5. When the cycle is finished and the bread is baked, carefully remove the pan from the machine. Use a potholder as the handle will be very hot. Let rest for a few minutes.

6. Remove the bread from the pan and allow to cool on a wire rack for at least 10 minutes before slicing.

Sampler Hawaiian Sweet Loaf

Ingredients:
- 8 slices (1 pound)
- 1/3 cup evaporated milk
- One 8-ounce can crushed pineapple in its own juice
- 1/4 cup pineapple juice reserved from draining the canned pineapple
- 1 tablespoon vegetable or nut oil
- 2 cups bread flour
- 1/3 cup flaked coconut

- 11/2 tablespoons light brown sugar
- 2 teaspoons gluten
- 1 teaspoon salt
- 1/2 teaspoon ground ginger
- 11/2 teaspoons SAF yeast or 2 teaspoons bread machine yeast
- 1/4 cup coarsely chopped macadamia nuts, rinsed and dried on a paper towel if salted
- 12 slices (1 ½ pounds)
- 1/2 cup evaporated milk
- One 12-ounce can crushed pineapple in its own juice
- 3/8 cup pineapple juice reserved from draining the canned pineapple
- 1 1/2 tablespoons vegetable or nut oil
- 3 cups bread flour
- 1/2 cup flaked coconut
- 2 1/4 tablespoons light brown sugar
- 3 teaspoons gluten
- 1 1/2 teaspoons salt
- 3/4 teaspoon ground ginger
- 3/4 teaspoons SAF yeast or 3 teaspoons bread machine yeast
- 3/8 cup coarsely chopped macadamia nuts, rinsed and dried on a paper towel if salted
- 16 slices (2 pounds)
- 2/3 cup evaporated milk
- One 16-ounce can crushed pineapple in its own juice
- 1/2 cup pineapple juice reserved from draining the canned pineapple
- 2 tablespoons vegetable or nut oil
- 4 cups bread flour
- 2/3 cup flaked coconut
- 3 tablespoons light brown sugar
- 4 teaspoons gluten
- 2 teaspoons salt
- 2 teaspoons ground ginger
- 3 teaspoons SAF yeast or 4 teaspoons bread machine yeast
- 1/2 cup coarsely chopped macadamia nuts, rinsed and dried on a paper towel if salted

Directions:

1. Choose the size of loaf you would like to make and measure your ingredients.

2. Add the ingredients to the bread pan in the order listed above.

3. Place the pan in the bread machine and close the lid.

4. Turn on the bread maker. Select the Whole Wheat setting, then the loaf size, and finally the crust color. Start the cycle.

5. When the cycle is finished and the bread is baked, carefully remove the pan from the machine. Use a potholder as the handle will be very hot. Let rest for a few minutes.

6. Remove the bread from the pan and allow to cool on a wire rack for at least 10 minutes before slicing.

Onion Loaf

Ingredients:

- 8 slices (1 pound)
- 2/3 tablespoon butter
- 1 1/3 medium onions, sliced
- 2/3 cup water
- 2/3 tablespoon olive or vegetable oil
- 2 cups bread flour
- 1 1/3 tablespoons sugar
- 2/3 teaspoon salt
- 5/6 teaspoon bread machine or quick active dry yeast
- 12 slices (1 ½ pounds)
- 1 tablespoon butter
- 2 medium onions, sliced
- 1 cup water
- 1 tablespoon olive or vegetable oil
- 3 cups bread flour
- 2 tablespoons sugar
- 1 teaspoon salt
- 1 1/4 teaspoons bread machine or quick active dry yeast
- 16 slices (2 pounds)
- 1 1/3 tablespoons butter
- 2 2/3 medium onions, sliced
- 1 1/3 cups water
- 1 1/3 tablespoons olive or vegetable oil
- 4 cups bread flour
- 2 2/3 tablespoons sugar
- 1 1/3 teaspoons salt

- 1 2/3 teaspoons bread machine or quick active dry yeast

Directions:
1. Choose the size of loaf you would like to make and measure your ingredients.
2. Preheat a large skillet to medium-low heat and add butter to melt. Add onions and cook for 10 to 15 minutes, stirring often, until onions are brown and caramelized; remove from heat.
3. Add the ingredients to the bread pan in the order listed above (except onions).
4. Place the pan in the bread machine and close the lid.
5. Turn on the bread maker. Select the Basic setting, then the loaf size, and finally the crust color. Start the cycle.
6. Add 1/2 cup of the onions 5 to 10 minutes before the last kneading cycle ends.
7. When the cycle is finished and the bread is baked, carefully remove the pan from the machine. Use a potholder as the handle will be very hot. Let rest for a few minutes.
8. Remove the bread from the pan and allow to cool on a wire rack for at least 10 minutes before slicing.

Brioche

Ingredients:
- 8 slices (1 pound)
- 1/4 cup milk
- 2 eggs
- 4 tablespoons butter
- 1 1/2 tablespoons vanilla sugar
- 1/4 teaspoon salt
- 2 cups flour
- 1 1/2 teaspoon yeast
- 1 egg white, for finishing
- 12 slices (1 ½ pounds)
- 3/8 cup milk
- 3 eggs
- 6 tablespoons butter
- 2 1/4 tablespoons vanilla sugar
- 3/8 teaspoon salt
- 3 cups flour
- 2 1/4 teaspoons yeast
- 1 1/2 egg whites, for finishing
- 16 slices (2 pounds)
- 1/2 cup milk
- 4 eggs
- 8 tablespoons butter
- 3 tablespoons vanilla sugar
- 1/2 teaspoon salt
- 4 cups flour
- 3 teaspoons yeast
- 2 egg whites, for finishing

Directions:
1. Choose the size of loaf you would like to make and measure your ingredients.
2. Add the ingredients to the bread pan in the order listed above (except yeast, egg white for finishing).
3. Make a well inside the flour and then add the yeast into the well.
4. Place the pan in the bread machine and close the lid.
5. Turn on the bread maker. Select the Dough setting, then the loaf size, and finally the crust color. Start the cycle.
6. When the cycle is finished and the bread is baked, remove dough, place dough on floured surface and divide into 12 equal size rolls.
7. Pinch walnut-sized ball of dough off each roll, making a smaller ball; make indent on top of roll and wet with milk; attach small ball to top making the traditional brioche shape.
8. Let rise for 30 minutes until almost double in size.
9. Preheat oven to 375°F.
10. Beat egg white, brush tops of brioche rolls, and bake at 375°F for 10 to 12 minutes, or until golden on top. Cool on rach before serving.

French Sandwich Pain Au Lait

Ingredients:
- 8 slices (1 pound)
- 5/6 cup water
- 3 tablespoons unsalted butter, cut into pieces
- 1 7/8 cups bread flour
- 1/8 cup barley flour
- 1/4 cup nonfat dry milk
- 1/2 tablespoon plus 1/2 teaspoon gluten

- 3/4 teaspoon sugar
- 1 teaspoon salt
- 1 1/8 teaspoons SAF yeast or 1 3/8 teaspoons bread machine yeast
- 12 slices (1 ½ pounds)
- 11/4 cups water
- 5 tablespoons unsalted butter, cut into pieces
- 27/8 cups bread flour
- 1/8 cup barley flour
- 1/3 cup nonfat dry milk
- 1 tablespoon gluten
- 1 teaspoon sugar
- 11/2 teaspoons salt
- 2 teaspoons SAF yeast or 21/2 teaspoons bread machine yeast
- 16 slices (2 pounds)
- 12/3 cups water
- 6 tablespoons unsalted butter, cut into pieces
- 33/4 cups bread flour
- 1/4 cup barley flour
- 1/2 cup nonfat dry milk
- 1 tablespoon plus 1 teaspoon gluten
- 11/2 teaspoons sugar
- 2 teaspoons salt
- 21/4 teaspoons SAF yeast or 23/4 teaspoons bread machine yeast

Directions:

1. Choose the size of loaf you would like to make and measure your ingredients.

2. Add the ingredients to the bread pan in the order listed above.

3. Place the pan in the bread machine and close the lid.

4. Turn on the bread maker. Select the Basic setting, then the loaf size, and finally the crust color. Start the cycle.

5. When the cycle is finished and the bread is baked, carefully remove the pan from the machine. Use a potholder as the handle will be very hot. Let rest for a few minutes.

6. Remove the bread from the pan and allow to cool on a wire rack for at least 10 minutes before slicing.

100% Whole Wheat Bread

Ingredients:

- 8 slices (1 pound)
- 2/3 cup warm water
- 1 1/3 tablespoons butter
- 2/3 teaspoon salt
- 2 cups 100% whole wheat flour
- 1 1/3 tablespoons dry milk
- 2/3 tablespoon sugar
- 1 1/3 teaspoons active dry yeast
- 12 slices (1 ½ pounds)
- 1 cup warm water
- 2 tablespoons butter
- 1 teaspoon salt
- 3 cups 100% whole wheat flour
- 2 tablespoons dry milk
- 1 tablespoon sugar
- 2 teaspoons active dry yeast
- 16 slices (2 pounds)
- 1 1/3 cups warm water
- 2 2/3 tablespoons butter
- 1 1/3 teaspoonS salt
- 4 cups 100% whole wheat flour
- 2 2/3 tablespoons dry milk
- 1 1/3 tablespoonS sugar
- 2 2/3 teaspoons active dry yeast

Directions:

1. Choose the size of loaf you would like to make and measure your ingredients.

2. Add the ingredients to the bread pan in the order listed above (except the yeast).

3. Make a well in the center of the bread flour and add the yeast.

4. Place the pan in the bread machine and close the lid.

5. Turn on the bread maker. Select the Wheat Bread setting, then the loaf size, and finally the crust color. Start the cycle.

6. When the cycle is finished and the bread is baked, carefully remove the pan from the machine. Use a potholder as the handle will be very hot. Let rest for a few minutes.

7. Remove the bread from the pan and allow to cool on a wire rack for at least 10 minutes before slicing.

Country White Bread

Ingredients:

- 8 slices (1 pound)
- 5/6 cup water
- 3/4 tablespoon vegetable or light olive oil
- 3/4 tablespoon sugar
- 2 cups bread flour
- 1 tablespoon instant potato flakes
- 1/8 cup nonfat dry milk
- 1/2 tablespoon plus 1/2 teaspoon gluten
- 1 teaspoon salt
- 1 1/4 teaspoons SAF yeast or 1/2 tablespoon bread machine yeast
- 12 slices (1 ½ pounds)
- 11/3 cups water
- 1 tablespoon vegetable or light olive oil
- 1 tablespoon sugar
- 3 cups bread flour
- 11/2 tablespoons instant potato flakes
- 3 tablespoons nonfat dry milk
- 1 tablespoon gluten
- 11/2 teaspoons salt
- 2 teaspoons SAF yeast or 21/2 teaspoons bread machine yeast
- 16 slices (2 pounds)
- 1 2/3 cups water
- 1 1/2 tablespoons vegetable or light olive oil
- 1 1/2 tablespoons sugar
- 4 cups bread flour
- 2 tablespoons instant potato flakes
- 1/4 cup nonfat dry milk
- 1 tablespoon plus 1 teaspoon gluten
- 2 teaspoons salt
- 2 1/2 teaspoons SAF yeast or 1 tablespoon bread machine yeast

Directions:

1. Choose the size of loaf you would like to make and measure your ingredients.
2. Add the ingredients to the bread pan in the order listed above.
3. Place the pan in the bread machine and close the lid.
4. Turn on the bread maker. Select the Basic setting, then the loaf size, and finally the crust color. Start the cycle.
5. When the cycle is finished and the bread is baked, carefully remove the pan from the machine. Use a potholder as the handle will be very hot. Let rest for a few minutes.
6. Remove the bread from the pan and allow to cool on a wire rack for at least 10 minutes before slicing.

Blue Cheese Bread

Ingredients:

- 8 slices (1 pound)
- 1/2 cup warm water
- 2/3 large egg
- 2/3 teaspoon salt
- 2 cups bread flour
- 2/3 cup blue cheese, crumbled
- 1 1/3 tablespoons nonfat dry milk
- 1 1/3 tablespoons sugar
- 2/3 teaspoon bread machine yeast
- 12 slices (1 ½ pounds)
- 3/4 cup warm water
- 1 large egg
- 1 teaspoon salt
- 3 cups bread flour
- 1 cup blue cheese, crumbled
- 2 tablespoons nonfat dry milk
- 2 tablespoons sugar
- 1 teaspoon bread machine yeast
- 16 slices (2 pounds)
- 1 cup warm water
- 1 1/3 large eggs
- 1 1/3 teaspoons salt
- 4 cups bread flour
- 1 1/3 cups blue cheese, crumbled
- 2 2/3 tablespoons nonfat dry milk
- 2 2/3 tablespoons sugar
- 1 1/3 teaspoons bread machine yeast

Directions:

1. Choose the size of loaf you would like to make and measure your ingredients.

2.   Add the ingredients to the bread pan in the order listed above (except yeast). Be sure to add the cheese with the flour.

3.   Make a well in the flour and pour the yeast into it.

4.   Place the pan in the bread machine and close the lid.

5.   Turn on the bread maker. Select the Basic setting, then the loaf size, and finally the crust color. Start the cycle.

6.   When the cycle is finished and the bread is baked, carefully remove the pan from the machine. Use a potholder as the handle will be very hot. Let rest for a few minutes.

7.   Remove the bread from the pan and allow to cool on a wire rack for at least 10 minutes before slicing.

French Bread

Ingredients:
*   8 slices (1 pound)
*   1 large egg whites
*   5/8 cup water
*   2 cups bread flour
*   1/2 tablespoon plus 1 teaspoons gluten
*   1/2 tablespoon sugar
*   5/8 teaspoon salt
*   1 1/8 teaspoons SAF yeast or 1 3/8 teaspoons bread machine yeast
*   12 slices (1 ½ pounds)
*   2 large egg whites
*   1 cup water
*   3 cups bread flour
*   1 tablespoon gluten
*   2 teaspoons sugar
*   13/4 teaspoons salt
*   2 teaspoons SAF yeast or 21/2 teaspoons bread machine yeast
*   16 slices (2 pounds)
*   2 large egg whites
*   11/4 cups water
*   4 cups bread flour
*   1 tablespoon plus 2 teaspoons gluten
*   1 tablespoon sugar
*   21/2 teaspoons salt

*   21/4 teaspoons SAF yeast or 23/4 teaspoons bread machine yeast

Directions:
1.   Choose the size of loaf you would like to make and measure your ingredients.

2.   Using an electric mixer, beat the egg whites until almost stiff and soft peaks are formed.

3.   Add the ingredients to the bread pan in the order listed above. Adding the egg whites in with the water.

4.   Place the pan in the bread machine and close the lid.

5.   Turn on the bread maker. Select the Basic/French setting, then the loaf size, and finally the crust color. Start the cycle. (This recipe is not suitable for use with the Delay Timer if using fresh eggs.)

6.   When the cycle is finished and the bread is baked, carefully remove the pan from the machine. Use a potholder as the handle will be very hot. Let rest for a few minutes.

7.   Remove the bread from the pan and allow to cool on a wire rack for at least 10 minutes before slicing.

Peasant Bread

Ingredients:
*   8 slices (1 pound)
*   2 tablespoons full rounded yeast
*   2 cups white bread flour
*   1 1/2 tablespoons sugar
*   1 tablespoon salt
*   7/8 cup water
*   For the topping:
*   Olive oil
*   Poppy seeds
*   12 slices (1 ½ pounds)
*   3 tablespoons full rounded yeast
*   3 cups white bread flour
*   2 1/4 tablespoons sugar
*   1 1/2 tablespoons salt
*   1 1/4 cups water
*   For the topping:
*   Olive oil
*   Poppy seeds
*   16 slices (2 pounds)
*   4 tablespoons full rounded yeast

- 4 cups white bread flour
- 3 tablespoons sugar
- 2 tablespoons salt
- 1 3/4 cups water
- For the topping:
- Olive oil
- Poppy seeds

Directions:

1. Choose the size of loaf you would like to make and measure your ingredients.

2. Add water first, then add the dry ingredients to the bread machine, reserving yeast.

3. Make a well in the center of the dry ingredients and add the yeast.

4. Place the pan in the bread machine and close the lid.

5. Turn on the bread maker. Select the French setting, then the loaf size, and finally the crust color. Start the cycle.

6. When bread is finished, coat the top of loaf with a little olive oil and lightly sprinkle with poppy seeds.

7. When the cycle is finished and the bread is baked, carefully remove the pan from the machine. Use a potholder as the handle will be very hot. Let rest for a few minutes.

8. Remove the bread from the pan and allow to cool on a wire rack for at least 10 minutes before slicing.

9. Add water first, then add the dry ingredients to the bread machine, reserving yeast.

10. Make a well in the center of the dry ingredients and add the yeast.

11. Choose French cycle, light crust color, and push Start.

Slider Buns

Ingredients:

- 8 slices (1 pound)
- 5/6 cup milk
- 2/3 egg
- 1 1/3 tablespoons butter
- 1/2 teaspoon salt
- 1/6 cup white sugar
- 2 1/2 cups all-purpose flour
- 2/3 package active dry yeast
- Flour, for surface
- 12 slices (1 ½ pounds)
- 1 1/4 cups milk
- 1 egg
- 2 tablespoons butter
- 3/4 teaspoon salt
- 1/4 cup white sugar
- 3 3/4 cups all-purpose flour
- 1 package active dry yeast
- Flour, for surface
- 16 slices (2 pounds)
- 1 2/3 cups milk
- 1 1/3 eggs
- 2 2/3 tablespoons butter
- 1 teaspoon salt
- 1/3 cup white sugar
- 5 cups all-purpose flour
- 1 1/3 packages active dry yeast
- Flour, for surface

Directions:

1. Choose the size of loaf you would like to make and measure your ingredients.

2. Add the ingredients to the bread pan in the order listed above.

3. Place the pan in the bread machine and close the lid.

4. Turn on the bread maker. Select the Dough setting, then the loaf size, and finally the crust color. Start the cycle.

5. When the cycle is finished and the bread is baked, c roll dough out on a floured surface to about a 1-inch thickness.

6. Cut out 18 buns with a biscuit cutter or small glass and place them on a greased baking sheet.

7. Let buns rise about one hour or until they have doubled in size.

8. Bake at 350°F for 10 minutes.

9. Brush the tops of baked buns with melted butter and serve.

Multigrain Bread

Ingredients:

- 8 slices (1 pound)
- 1 1/2 cups whole wheat flour
- 1/2 cup ground oatmeal
- 1 1/3 tablespoons wheat bran
- 1 1/3 tablespoons flaxseed meal
- 1 1/3 tablespoons vital wheat gluten
- 2/3 tablespoon dough enhancer
- 2/3 teaspoon salt
- 2 teaspoons active dry yeast
- 1 1/3 tablespoons olive oil
- 2/3 tablespoon agave nectar
- 2/3 tablespoon brown sugar
- 2/3 cup warm water (slightly warmer than room temperature)
- 12 slices (1 ½ pounds)
- 2 1/4 cups whole wheat flour
- 3/4 cup ground oatmeal
- 2 tablespoons wheat bran
- 2 tablespoons flaxseed meal
- 2 tablespoons vital wheat gluten
- 1 tablespoon dough enhancer
- 1 teaspoon salt
- 2 2/3 teaspoons active dry yeast
- 2 tablespoons olive oil
- 1 tablespoon agave nectar
- 1 tablespoon brown sugar
- 1 cup warm water (slightly warmer than room temperature)
- 16 slices (2 pounds)
- 3 cups whole wheat flour
- 1 cup ground oatmeal
- 2 2/3 tablespoons wheat bran
- 2 2/3 tablespoons flaxseed meal
- 2 2/3 tablespoons vital wheat gluten
- 1 1/3 tablespoons dough enhancer
- 1 1/3 teaspoons salt
- 4 teaspoons active dry yeast
- 2 2/3 tablespoons olive oil
- 1 1/3 tablespoons agave nectar
- 1 1/3 tablespoons brown sugar
- 1 1/3 cups warm water (slightly warmer than room temperature)

Directions:

1. Choose the size of loaf you would like to make and measure your ingredients.
2. Set the yeast aside and combine the remaining dry ingredients in a mixing bowl.
3. Add the liquids to the bread pan first, followed by the dry ingredients.
4. Make a small well in the flour and add the yeast.
5. Add the ingredients to the bread pan in the order listed above.
6. Place the pan in the bread machine and close the lid.
7. Turn on the bread maker. Select the Whole Wheat setting, then the loaf size, and finally the crust color. Start the cycle.
8. When the cycle is finished and the bread is baked, carefully remove the pan from the machine. Use a potholder as the handle will be very hot. Let rest for a few minutes.
9. Remove the bread from the pan and allow to cool on a wire rack for at least 10 minutes before slicing.

Homemade Hot Dog And Hamburger Buns

Ingredients:

- 8 slices (1 pound)
- 5/6 cup milk, slightly warmed
- 1 1/2 eggs, beaten
- 3 tablespoons butter, unsalted
- 1/6 cup white sugar
- 1/2 teaspoon salt
- 2 1/2 cups bread flour
- 5/6 teaspoon active dry yeast
- Flour, for surface
- 12 slices (1 ½ pounds)
- 1 1/4 cups milk, slightly warmed
- 1 egg, beaten
- 2 tablespoons butter, unsalted
- 1/4 cup white sugar
- 3/4 teaspoon salt
- 3 3/4 cups bread flour
- 1 1/4 teaspoons active dry yeast

- Flour, for surface
- 16 slices (2 pounds)
- 1 2/3 cups milk, slightly warmed
- 3 eggs, beaten
- 6 tablespoons butter, unsalted
- 1/3 cup white sugar
- 1 teaspoon salt
- 5 cups bread flour
- 1 2/3 teaspoons active dry yeast
- Flour, for surface

Directions:

1. Choose the size of loaf you would like to make and measure your ingredients.

2. Add the ingredients to the bread pan in the order listed above (except yeast, milk, egg, butter, sugar, salt, flour).

3. Make a well in the center of the dry ingredients and add the yeast.

4. Place the pan in the bread machine and close the lid.

5. Turn on the bread maker. Select the Dough setting, then the loaf size, and finally the crust color. Start the cycle.

6. Cut dough in half and roll each half out to a 1" thick circle.

7. Cut each half into 6 (3 1/2") rounds with inverted glass as a cutter. (For hot dog buns, cut lengthwise into 1-inch-thick rolls, and cut a slit along the length of the bun for easier separation later.)

8. Place on a greased baking sheet far apart and brush with melted butter.

9. Cover and let rise until doubled, about one hour; preheat an oven to 350°F.

10. Bake for 9 minutes.

Coconut Milk White Bread

Ingredients:
- 8 slices (1 pound)
- 3/4 cup canned coconut milk
- 2 cups bread flour
- 1/2 tablespoon plus 1/2 teaspoon gluten
- 1 teaspoon salt
- 5/8 teaspoon SAF yeast or 1/2 tablespoon bread machine yeast

- 12 slices (1 ½ pounds)
- 11/8 cups canned coconut milk
- 3 cups bread flour
- 1 tablespoon gluten
- 11/2 teaspoons salt
- 13/4 teaspoons SAF yeast or 21/4 teaspoons bread machine yeast
- 16 slices (2 pounds)
- 11/2 cups canned coconut milk
- 4 cups bread flour
- 1 tablespoon plus 1 teaspoon gluten
- 2 teaspoons salt
- 21/2 teaspoons SAF yeast or 1 tablespoon bread machine yeast

Directions:

1. Choose the size of loaf you would like to make and measure your ingredients.

2. Add the ingredients to the bread pan in the order listed above.

3. Place the pan in the bread machine and close the lid.

4. Turn on the bread maker. Select the Basic setting, then the loaf size, and finally the crust color. Start the cycle.

5. When the cycle is finished and the bread is baked, carefully remove the pan from the machine. Use a potholder as the handle will be very hot. Let rest for a few minutes.

6. Remove the bread from the pan and allow to cool on a wire rack for at least 10 minutes before slicing.

Sampler Buttermilk White Loaf

Ingredients:
- 8 slices (1 pound)
- 3/4 cup plus 1 tablespoon buttermilk
- 1 tablespoon dark honey
- 1 tablespoon butter or margarine, softened
- 2 cups bread flour
- 2 teaspoons gluten
- 1 teaspoon salt
- 11/4 teaspoons SAF yeast or 11/2 teaspoons bread machine yeast
- 12 slices (1 ½ pounds)
- 1 1/8 cup plus 1 tablespoon buttermilk

- 1 1/2 tablespoon dark honey
- 1 1/2 tablespoon butter or margarine, softened
- 3 cups bread flour
- 3 teaspoons gluten
- 1 1/2 teaspoon salt
- 1 7/8 teaspoons SAF yeast or 2 1/4 teaspoons bread machine yeast
- 16 slices (2 pounds)
- 1 1/2 cup plus 2 tablespoon buttermilk
- 2 tablespoon dark honey
- 2 tablespoon butter or margarine, softened
- 4 cups bread flour
- 4 teaspoons gluten
- 2 teaspoon salt
- 2 1/2 teaspoons SAF yeast or 3 teaspoons bread machine yeast

Directions:

1. Choose the size of loaf you would like to make and measure your ingredients.

2. Add the ingredients to the bread pan in the order listed above.

3. Place the pan in the bread machine and close the lid.

4. Turn on the bread maker. Select the Basic setting, then the loaf size, and finally the crust color. Start the cycle.

5. When the cycle is finished and the bread is baked, carefully remove the pan from the machine. Use a potholder as the handle will be very hot. Let rest for a few minutes.

6. Remove the bread from the pan and allow to cool on a wire rack for at least 10 minutes before slicing.

MULTIGRAIN BREAD RECIPES

Bohemian Black Bread

Ingredients:
- 8 slices (1 pound)
- 3/4 cup water
- 2 tablespoons butter, melted
- 1 tablespoon molasses
- 1 1/6 cups bread flour
- 2/3 cup medium or dark rye flour
- 1/6 cup wheat bran
- 1 1/2 tablespoons unsweetened Dutch-process cocoa powder
- 1/2 tablespoon plus 1/2 teaspoon gluten
- 1 teaspoon instant espresso powder
- 1 teaspoon caraway seeds
- 3/8 teaspoon fennel seeds
- 1 teaspoon salt
- 1 1/4 teaspoons SAF yeast or 1/2 tablespoon bread machine yeast
- 12 slices (1 ½ pounds)
- 11/8 cups water
- 3 tablespoons butter, melted
- 11/2 tablespoons molasses
- 13/4 cups bread flour
- 1 cup medium or dark rye flour
- 1/4 cup wheat bran
- 2 tablespoons unsweetened Dutch-process cocoa powder
- 1 tablespoon gluten
- 11/2 teaspoons instant espresso powder
- 11/2 teaspoons caraway seeds
- 1/2 teaspoon fennel seeds
- 11/2 teaspoons salt
- 2 teaspoons SAF yeast or 21/2 teaspoons bread machine yeast
- 16 slices (2 pounds)
- 11/2 cups water
- 4 tablespoons butter, melted
- 2 tablespoons molasses
- 21/3 cups bread flour
- 11/3 cup medium or dark rye flour
- 1/3 cup wheat bran
- 3 tablespoons unsweetened Dutch-process cocoa powder
- 1 tablespoon plus 1 teaspoon gluten
- 2 teaspoons instant espresso powder
- 2 teaspoons caraway seeds
- 3/4 teaspoon fennel seeds
- 2 teaspoons salt
- 21/2 teaspoons SAF yeast or 1 tablespoon bread machine yeast

Directions:
1. Choose the size of loaf you would like to make and measure your ingredients.
2. Add the ingredients to the bread pan in the order listed above.
3. Place the pan in the bread machine and close the lid.
4. Turn on the bread maker. Select the Basic/Whole Wheat setting, then the loaf size, and finally the crust color. Start the cycle.
5. When the cycle is finished and the bread is baked, carefully remove the pan from the machine. Use a potholder as the handle will be very hot. Let rest for a few minutes.
6. Remove the bread from the pan and allow to cool on a wire rack for at least 10 minutes before slicing

Old-fashioned Sesame-wheat Bread

Ingredients:
- 8 slices (1 pound)
- 3/8 cup water
- 3/8 cup milk
- 1 1/2 tablespoons butter, cut into pieces
- 1 1/2 cups bread flour
- 1/2 cup whole wheat flour
- 1 1/2 tablespoons light or dark brown sugar
- 1/2 tablespoon plus 1 teaspoon sesame seeds
- 1/2 tablespoon plus 1 teaspoon gluten
- 1 teaspoon salt
- 1 1/8 teaspoons SAF yeast or 1 3/8 teaspoons bread machine yeast
- 12 slices (1 ½ pounds)

- 3/4 cup water
- 3/8 cup milk
- 2 tablespoons butter, cut into pieces
- 21/4 cups bread flour
- 3/4 cup whole wheat flour
- 2 tablespoons light or dark brown sugar
- 1 tablespoon sesame seeds
- 1 tablespoon plus 1 teaspoon gluten
- 11/2 teaspoons salt
- 2 teaspoons SAF yeast or 21/2 teaspoons bread machine yeast
- 16 slices (2 pounds)
- 3/4 cup water
- 3/4 cup milk
- 3 tablespoons butter, cut into pieces
- 3 cups bread flour
- 1 cup whole wheat flour
- 3 tablespoons light or dark brown sugar
- 1 tablespoon plus 2 teaspoons sesame seeds
- 1 tablespoon plus 2 teaspoons gluten
- 2 teaspoons salt
- 21/4 teaspoons SAF yeast or 23/4 teaspoons bread machine yeast

Directions:

1. Choose the size of loaf you would like to make and measure your ingredients.

2. Add the ingredients to the bread pan in the order listed above.

3. Place the pan in the bread machine and close the lid.

4. Turn on the bread maker. Select the White/Basic setting, then the loaf size, and finally the crust color. Start the cycle.

5. When the cycle is finished and the bread is baked, carefully remove the pan from the machine. Use a potholder as the handle will be very hot. Let rest for a few minutes.

6. Remove the bread from the pan and allow to cool on a wire rack for at least 10 minutes before slicing.

Oat Bran Nutmeg Bread

Ingredients:

- 8 slices (1 pound)
- 1/2 cup lukewarm water
- 1 1/2 tablespoons unsalted butter, melted
- 1/8 cup blackstrap molasses
- 1/4 teaspoon table salt
- 1 1/2 cups whole-wheat bread flour
- 1/8 teaspoon ground nutmeg
- 1/2 cup oat bran
- 1 1/8 teaspoons bread machine yeast
- 12 slices (1 ½ pounds)
- ¾ cup lukewarm water
- 2¼ tablespoons unsalted butter, melted
- 3 tablespoons blackstrap molasses
- ⅓ teaspoon table salt
- 2¼ cups whole-wheat bread flour
- ¼ teaspoon ground nutmeg
- ¾ cup oat bran
- 1⅔ teaspoons bread machine yeast
- 16 slices (2 pounds)
- 1 cup lukewarm water
- 3 tablespoons unsalted butter, melted
- ¼ cup blackstrap molasses
- ½ teaspoon table salt
- 3 cups whole-wheat bread flour
- ¼ teaspoon ground nutmeg
- 1 cup oat bran
- 2¼ teaspoons bread machine yeast

Directions:

1. Choose the size of loaf you would like to make and measure your ingredients.

2. Add the ingredients to the bread pan in the order listed above.

3. Place the pan in the bread machine and close the lid.

4. Turn on the bread maker. Select the Whole Wheat/Wholegrain setting, then the loaf size, and finally the crust color. Start the cycle.

5. When the cycle is finished and the bread is baked, carefully remove the pan from the machine. Use a potholder as the handle will be very hot. Let rest for a few minutes.

6. Remove the bread from the pan and allow to cool on a wire rack for at least 10 minutes before slicing.

Oat Quinoa Bread

Ingredients:

- 8 slices (1 pound)
- 2/3 cup lukewarm milk
- 3/8 cup cooked quinoa, cooled
- 2 1/2 tablespoons unsalted butter, melted
- 2 teaspoons sugar
- 2/3 teaspoon table salt
- 1 cup white bread flour
- 2 1/2 tablespoons quick oats
- 1/2 cup whole-wheat flour
- 1 teaspoon bread machine yeast
- 12 slices (1 ½ pounds)
- 1 cup lukewarm milk
- ⅔ cup cooked quinoa, cooled
- ¼ cup unsalted butter, melted
- 1 tablespoon sugar
- 1 teaspoon table salt
- 1½ cups white bread flour
- ¼ cup quick oats
- ¾ cup whole-wheat flour
- 1½ teaspoons bread machine yeast
- 16 slices (2 pounds)
- 1⅓ cups lukewarm milk
- ¾ cup cooked quinoa, cooled
- 5 tablespoons unsalted butter, melted
- 4 teaspoons sugar
- 1⅓ teaspoons table salt
- 2 cups white bread flour
- 5 tablespoons quick oats
- 1 cup whole-wheat flour
- 2 teaspoons bread machine yeast

Directions:

1. Choose the size of loaf you would like to make and measure your ingredients.
2. Add the ingredients to the bread pan in the order listed above.
3. Place the pan in the bread machine and close the lid.
4. Turn on the bread maker. Select the White/Basic setting, then the loaf size, and finally the crust color. Start the cycle.
5. When the cycle is finished and the bread is baked, carefully remove the pan from the machine. Use a potholder as the handle will be very hot. Let rest for a few minutes.
6. Remove the bread from the pan and allow to cool on a wire rack for at least 10 minutes before slicing.

Sour Cream Rye

Ingredients:

- 8 slices (1 pound)
- 3/8 cup water
- 1 1/4 tablespoons balsamic vinegar
- 7/16 cup sour cream
- 1 1/2 tablespoons dark honey or molasses
- 1 1/2 tablespoons vegetable oil
- 1 1/4 cups bread flour
- 3/4 cup dark rye flour
- 3/4 tablespoon instant potato flakes
- 1/2 tablespoon plus 1 teaspoon gluten
- 1/2 tablespoon plus 1/2 teaspoon caraway seeds
- 3/4 teaspoon ground coriander seeds
- 1 teaspoon salt
- 1 1/4 teaspoons SAF yeast or 1/2 tablespoon bread machine yeast
- 12 slices (1 ½ pounds)
- 2/3 cup water
- 2 tablespoons balsamic vinegar
- 2/3 cup sour cream
- 2 tablespoons dark honey or molasses
- 2 tablespoons vegetable oil
- 13/4 cups bread flour
- 11/4 cups dark rye flour
- 1 tablespoon instant potato flakes
- 1 tablespoon plus 1 teaspoon gluten
- 1 tablespoon caraway seeds
- 1 teaspoon ground coriander seeds
- 11/2 teaspoons salt
- 21/4 teaspoons SAF yeast or 23/4 teaspoons bread machine yeast
- 16 slices (2 pounds)
- 3/4 cup water
- 21/2 tablespoons balsamic vinegar
- 7/8 cup sour cream
- 3 tablespoons dark honey or molasses
- 3 tablespoons vegetable oil

- 21/2 cups bread flour
- 11/2 cups dark rye flour
- 11/2 tablespoons instant potato flakes
- 1 tablespoon plus 2 teaspoons gluten
- 1 tablespoon plus 1 teaspoon caraway seeds
- 11/2 teaspoons ground coriander seeds
- 2 teaspoons salt
- 21/2 teaspoons SAF yeast or 1 tablespoon bread machine yeast

Directions:

1. Choose the size of loaf you would like to make and measure your ingredients.
2. Add the ingredients to the bread pan in the order listed above.
3. Place the pan in the bread machine and close the lid.
4. Turn on the bread maker. Select the Basic/Whole Wheat setting, then the loaf size, and finally the crust color. Start the cycle.
5. When the cycle is finished and the bread is baked, carefully remove the pan from the machine. Use a potholder as the handle will be very hot. Let rest for a few minutes.
6. Remove the bread from the pan and allow to cool on a wire rack for at least 10 minutes before slicing

Hearty Oatmeal Loaf

Ingredients:

- 8 slices (1 pound)
- ¾ cup water at 80 degrees F
- 2 tablespoons melted butter, cooled
- 2 tablespoons sugar
- 1 teaspoon salt
- ¾ cup quick oats
- 1½ cups white bread flour
- 1 teaspoon instant yeast
- 12 slices (1 ½ pounds)
- 1 1/8 cups water at 80 degrees F
- 3 tablespoons melted butter, cooled
- 3 tablespoons sugar
- 1 1/2 teaspoons salt
- 1 1/8 cups quick oats
- 2 1/4 cups white bread flour
- 1 1/2 teaspoons instant yeast

- 16 slices (2 pounds)
- 1 1/2 cups water at 80 degrees F
- 4 tablespoons melted butter, cooled
- 4 tablespoons sugar
- 2 teaspoons salt
- 1 1/2 cups quick oats
- 3 cups white bread flour
- 2 teaspoons instant yeast

Directions:

1. Choose the size of loaf you would like to make and measure your ingredients.
2. Add the ingredients to the bread pan in the order listed above.
3. Place the pan in the bread machine and close the lid.
4. Turn on the bread maker. Select the White/Basic setting, then the loaf size, and finally the crust color. Start the cycle.
5. When the cycle is finished and the bread is baked, carefully remove the pan from the machine. Use a potholder as the handle will be very hot. Let rest for a few minutes.
6. Remove the bread from the pan and allow to cool on a wire rack for at least 10 minutes before slicing.

Delicious Rice Bread

Ingredients:

- 8 slices (1 pound)
- 2 1/4 cups wheat flour
- 1/2 cup rice, cooked
- 1/2 whole egg, beaten
- 1 tablespoon milk powder
- 1 teaspoon active dry yeast
- 1 tablespoon butter
- 1/2 tablespoon sugar
- 1 teaspoon salt
- 5/8 cup water
- 12 slices (1 ½ pounds)
- 3 3/8 cups wheat flour
- 3/4 cup rice, cooked
- 3/4 whole egg, beaten
- 1 1/2 tablespoons milk powder
- 1 1/2 teaspoons active dry yeast
- 1 1/2tablespoons butter

- 3/4 tablespoon sugar
- 1 1/2 teaspoons salt
- 7/8 cup water
- 16 slices (2 pounds)
- 4½ cups wheat flour
- 1 cup rice, cooked
- 1 whole egg, beaten
- 2 tablespoons milk powder
- 2 teaspoons active dry yeast
- 2 tablespoons butter
- 1 tablespoon sugar
- 2 teaspoons salt
- 1 ¼ cups water

Directions:

1. Choose the size of loaf you would like to make and measure your ingredients.

2. Add the ingredients to the bread pan in the order listed above.

3. Place the pan in the bread machine and close the lid.

4. Turn on the bread maker. Select the White/Basic setting, then the loaf size, and finally the crust color. Start the cycle.

5. When the cycle is finished and the bread is baked, carefully remove the pan from the machine. Use a potholder as the handle will be very hot. Let rest for a few minutes.

6. Remove the bread from the pan and allow to cool on a wire rack for at least 10 minutes before slicing.

Swedish Rye Bread

Ingredients:

- 8 slices (1 pound)
- 13/16 cup water
- 1/8 cup honey
- 1 1/2 tablespoons vegetable oil
- 1 3/8 cups bread flour
- 7/8 cup medium rye flour
- 1/2 tablespoon plus 1 teaspoon gluten
- 1/2 tablespoon fennel seeds
- 1 teaspoon grated orange zest or dried orange peel
- 3/4 teaspoon salt
- 1 1/4 teaspoons SAF yeast or 1/2 tablespoon bread machine yeast

- 12 slices (1 ½ pounds)
- 11/4 cups water
- 3 tablespoons honey
- 2 tablespoons vegetable oil
- 2 cups bread flour
- 11/4 cups medium rye flour
- 1 tablespoon plus 1 teaspoon gluten
- 2 teaspoons fennel seeds
- 11/2 teaspoons grated orange zest or dried orange peel
- 11/4 teaspoons salt
- 2 teaspoons SAF yeast or 21/2 teaspoons bread machine yeast
- 16 slices (2 pounds)
- 15/8 cups water
- 1/4 cup honey
- 3 tablespoons vegetable oil
- 23/4 cups bread flour
- 13/4 cups medium rye flour
- 1 tablespoon plus 2 teaspoons gluten
- 1 tablespoon fennel seeds
- 2 teaspoons grated orange zest or dried orange peel
- 11/2 teaspoons salt
- 21/2 teaspoons SAF yeast or 1 tablespoon bread machine yeast

Directions:

1. Choose the size of loaf you would like to make and measure your ingredients.

2. Add the ingredients to the bread pan in the order listed above.

3. Place the pan in the bread machine and close the lid.

4. Turn on the bread maker. Select the Basic setting, then the loaf size, and finally the crust color. Start the cycle.

5. When the cycle is finished and the bread is baked, carefully remove the pan from the machine. Use a potholder as the handle will be very hot. Let rest for a few minutes.

6. Remove the bread from the pan and allow to cool on a wire rack for at least 10 minutes before slicing

Honey Wheat Berry Bread

Ingredients:

- 8 slices (1 pound)
- 3/8 cup wheat berries
- 1 1/2 tablespoons light or dark brown sugar
- 2/3 cup water
- 5/8 cup water
- 1/2 cup of the cooked and cooled wheat berries
- 1 1/2 tablespoons butter or margarine, cut into pieces
- 1/8 cup honey
- 1 cup bread flour
- 1 cup whole wheat flour
- 1 tablespoon gluten
- 1 teaspoon salt
- 1/2 tablespoon SAF yeast or 1/2 tablespoon plus 1/4 teaspoon bread machine yeast
- 12 slices (1½ pounds)
- 3/4 cup wheat berries
- 3 tablespoons light or dark brown sugar
- 11/3 cups water
- 1 cup water
- 2/3 cup of the cooked and cooled wheat berries
- 2 tablespoons butter or margarine, cut into pieces
- 3 tablespoons honey
- 11/2 cups bread flour
- 11/2 cups whole wheat flour
- 11/2 tablespoons gluten
- 11/2 teaspoons salt
- 21/2 teaspoons SAF yeast or 1 tablespoon bread machine yeast
- 16 slices (2 pounds)
- 3/4 cup wheat berries
- 3 tablespoons light or dark brown sugar
- 11/3 cups water
- 11/4 cups water
- 1 cup of the cooked and cooled wheat berries
- 3 tablespoons butter or margarine, cut into pieces
- 1/4 cup honey
- 2 cups bread flour
- 2 cups whole wheat flour
- 2 tablespoons gluten
- 2 teaspoons salt
- 1 tablespoon SAF yeast or 1 tablespoon plus 1/2 teaspoon bread machine yeast

Directions:

1. Choose the size of loaf you would like to make and measure your ingredients.
2. Combine the wheat berries, sugar, and 11/3 cups water in a saucepan. Bring to a boil. Reduce the heat to a simmer and partially cover. Simmer for 1 hour, until firm-chewy and slightly tender. Remove the mixture from the heat and let stand until room temperature, about 4 hours. You will have about 11/3 cups cooked wheat berries
3. Add the ingredients to the bread pan in the order listed above. (Store any extra cooked wheat berries in a covered container in the refrigerator up to 3 days or freeze them.)
4. Place the pan in the bread machine and close the lid.
5. Turn on the bread maker. Select the Basic setting, then the loaf size, and finally the crust color. Start the cycle.
6. When the cycle is finished and the bread is baked, carefully remove the pan from the machine. Use a potholder as the handle will be very hot. Let rest for a few minutes.
7. Remove the bread from the pan and allow to cool on a wire rack for at least 10 minutes before slicing.

Seven Grain Bread

Ingredients:

- 8 slices (1 pound)
- 1 1/3 cups warm water
- 1 tablespoon active dry yeast
- 3 tablespoons dry milk powder
- 2 tablespoons honey
- 2 teaspoons salt
- 1 whole egg
- 1 cup whole wheat flour
- 2½ cups bread flour
- ¾ cups 7-grain cereal
- 12 slices (1 ½ pounds)
- 2 cups warm water
- 1 1/2 tablespoons active dry yeast
- 4 1/2 tablespoons dry milk powder

- 3 tablespoons honey
- 3 teaspoons salt
- 1 1/2 whole eggs
- 1 1/2 cups whole wheat flour
- 3 3/4 cups bread flour
- 1 1/8 cups 7-grain cereal
- 16 slices (2 pounds)
- 2 2/3 cups warm water
- 2 tablespoons active dry yeast
- 6 tablespoons dry milk powder
- 4 tablespoons honey
- 4 teaspoons salt
- 2 whole eggs
- 2 cups whole wheat flour
- 5 cups bread flour
- 1 1/2 cups 7-grain cereal

Directions:

1. Choose the size of loaf you would like to make and measure your ingredients.

2. Add the ingredients to the bread pan in the order listed above.

3. Place the pan in the bread machine and close the lid.

4. Turn on the bread maker. Select the White/Basic setting, then the loaf size, and finally the crust color. Start the cycle.

5. When the cycle is finished and the bread is baked, carefully remove the pan from the machine. Use a potholder as the handle will be very hot. Let rest for a few minutes.

6. Remove the bread from the pan and allow to cool on a wire rack for at least 10 minutes before slicing.

Nine-grain Honey Bread

Ingredients:
- 8 slices (1 pound)
- 7/8 cup boiling water
- 1/3 cup 9-grain cereal
- 1/8 cup honey
- 2 tablespoons unsalted butter, cut into pieces
- 1 cup bread flour
- 2/3 cup whole wheat flour
- 1/3 cup dry buttermilk powder
- 1 tablespoon gluten
- 3/4 teaspoon salt
- 1/2 tablespoon SAF yeast or 1/2 tablespoon plus 1/4 teaspoon bread machine yeast
- 12 slices (1½ pounds)
- 11/4 cups boiling water
- 1/2 cup 9-grain cereal
- 3 tablespoons honey
- 3 tablespoons unsalted butter, cut into pieces
- 12/3 cups bread flour
- 1 cup whole wheat flour
- 1/3 cup dry buttermilk powder
- 11/2 tablespoons gluten
- 11/4 teaspoons salt
- 21/2 teaspoons SAF yeast or 1 tablespoon bread machine yeast
- 16 slices (2 pounds)
- 13/4 cups boiling water
- 2/3 cup 9-grain cereal
- 1/4 cup honey
- 4 tablespoons unsalted butter, cut into pieces
- 2 cups bread flour
- 11/3 cups whole wheat flour
- 2/3 cup dry buttermilk powder
- 2 tablespoons gluten
- 11/2 teaspoons salt
- 1 tablespoon SAF yeast or 1 tablespoon plus 1/2 teaspoon bread machine yeast

Directions:

1. Choose the size of loaf you would like to make and measure your ingredients.

2. Pour the boiling water over the cracked grain cereal in a bowl. Add the honey and butter. Let stand for 1 hour to soften the grains.

3. Add the ingredients to the bread pan in the order listed above. Adding the cereal and its soaking liquid as the liquid ingredients.

4. Place the pan in the bread machine and close the lid.

5. Turn on the bread maker. Select the Basic/Whole Wheat setting, then the loaf size, and finally the crust color. Start the cycle.

6. When the cycle is finished and the bread is baked, carefully remove the pan from the machine. Use a

potholder as the handle will be very hot. Let rest for a few minutes.

7. Remove the bread from the pan and allow to cool on a wire rack for at least 10 minutes before slicing.

Sennebec Hill Bread

Ingredients:
- 8 slices (1 pound)
- 5/6 cup water
- 1/8 cup canola oil
- 1 1/2 tablespoons molasses
- 1 1/2 large egg yolks
- 1 1/8 cups bread flour
- 1/2 cup whole wheat flour
- 1/6 cup medium or dark rye flour
- 1 3/4 tablespoons rolled oats
- 1 3/4 tablespoons yellow cornmeal
- 1 3/4 tablespoons toasted wheat germ
- 1/6 cup nonfat dry milk
- 1 tablespoon gluten
- 1 teaspoon salt
- 12 slices (1½ pounds)
- 11/4 cups water
- 3 tablespoons canola oil
- 2 tablespoons molasses
- 2 large egg yolks
- 11/2 cups bread flour
- 3/4 cup whole wheat flour
- 1/2 cup medium or dark rye flour
- 3 tablespoons rolled oats
- 3 tablespoons yellow cornmeal
- 3 tablespoons toasted wheat germ
- 1/2 cup nonfat dry milk
- 11/2 tablespoons gluten
- 11/2 teaspoons salt
- 21/2 teaspoons SAF yeast or 1 tablespoon bread machine yeast
- 16 slices (2 pounds)
- 12/3 cups water
- 1/4 cup canola oil
- 3 tablespoons molasses
- 3 large egg yolks
- 21/4 cups bread flour

- 1 cup whole wheat flour
- 1/3 cup medium or dark rye flour
- 31/2 tablespoons rolled oats
- 31/2 tablespoons yellow cornmeal
- 31/2 tablespoons toasted wheat germ
- 1/3 cup nonfat dry milk
- 2 tablespoons gluten
- 2 teaspoons salt
- 1 tablespoon SAF yeast or 1 tablespoon plus 1/2 teaspoon bread machine yeast

Directions:
1. Choose the size of loaf you would like to make and measure your ingredients.
2. Add the ingredients to the bread pan in the order listed above.
3. Place the pan in the bread machine and close the lid.
4. Turn on the bread maker. Select the Whole Wheat setting, then the loaf size, and finally the crust color. Start the cycle.
5. When the cycle is finished and the bread is baked, carefully remove the pan from the machine. Use a potholder as the handle will be very hot. Let rest for a few minutes.
6. Remove the bread from the pan and allow to cool on a wire rack for at least 10 minutes before slicing.

Scandinavian Light Rye

Ingredients:
- 8 slices (1 pound)
- 3/4 cup water
- 1 tablespoon canola oil
- 1 1/4 cups bread flour
- 3/4 cup medium rye flour
- 1 1/2 tablespoons brown sugar
- 1/2 tablespoon plus 1 teaspoon gluten
- 1 tablespoon caraway seeds
- 1 teaspoon salt
- 1/2 tablespoon SAF yeast or 1/2 tablespoon plus 1/4 teaspoon bread machine yeast
- 12 slices (1 ½ pounds)
- 11/8 cups water
- 11/2 tablespoons canola oil
- 17/8 cups bread flour

- 11/8 cups medium rye flour
- 2 tablespoons brown sugar
- 1 tablespoon plus 1 teaspoon gluten
- 11/2 tablespoons caraway seeds
- 11/2 teaspoons salt
- 21/2 teaspoons SAF yeast or 1 tablespoon bread machine yeast
- 16 slices (2 pounds)
- 11/2 cups water
- 2 tablespoons canola oil
- 21/2 cups bread flour
- 11/2 cups medium rye flour
- 3 tablespoons brown sugar
- 1 tablespoon plus 2 teaspoons gluten
- 2 tablespoons caraway seeds
- 2 teaspoons salt
- 1 tablespoon SAF yeast or 1 tablespoon plus 1/2 teaspoon bread machine yeast

Directions:

1. Choose the size of loaf you would like to make and measure your ingredients.
2. Add the ingredients to the bread pan in the order listed above.
3. Place the pan in the bread machine and close the lid.
4. Turn on the bread maker. Select the Basic setting, then the loaf size, and finally the crust color. Start the cycle.
5. When the cycle is finished and the bread is baked, carefully remove the pan from the machine. Use a potholder as the handle will be very hot. Let rest for a few minutes.
6. Remove the bread from the pan and allow to cool on a wire rack for at least 10 minutes before slicing.

Super-grain Bread

Ingredients:
- 8 slices (1 pound)
- 3/4 heaping tablespoon raw amaranth seeds
- 3/8 cup water
- 3/8 cup buttermilk
- 1/2 large egg
- 1 1/4 tablespoons butter, cut into pieces
- 1 1/4 tablespoons honey

- 1 1/6 cups bread flour
- 3/8 cup whole wheat or spelt flour
- 1 1/2 tablespoons quinoa flour
- 1 1/2 tablespoons barley flour
- 1 1/2 tablespoons brown rice flour
- 1 1/2 tablespoons instant potato flakes
- 1 1/2 tablespoons cornmeal
- 1 1/2 tablespoons rolled oats
- 1 tablespoon gluten
- 1 teaspoon salt
- 1/2 tablespoon plus 1/4 teaspoon SAF yeast or 1/2 tablespoon plus 1/2 teaspoon bread machine yeast
- 12 slices (1½ pounds)
- 1 heaping tablespoon raw amaranth seeds
- 1/2 cup water
- 2/3 cup buttermilk
- 1 large egg
- 2 tablespoons butter, cut into pieces
- 2 tablespoons honey
- 13/4 cups bread flour
- 1/2 cup whole wheat or spelt flour
- 2 tablespoons quinoa flour
- 2 tablespoons barley flour
- 2 tablespoons brown rice flour
- 2 tablespoons instant potato flakes
- 2 tablespoons cornmeal
- 2 tablespoons rolled oats
- 11/2 tablespoons gluten
- 11/2 teaspoons salt
- 1 tablespoon SAF yeast or 1 tablespoon plus 1/2 teaspoon bread machine yeast
- 16 slices (2 pounds)
- 11/2 heaping tablespoons raw amaranth seeds
- 3/4 cup water
- 3/4 cup buttermilk
- 1 large egg
- 21/2 tablespoons butter, cut into pieces
- 21/2 tablespoons honey
- 21/3 cups bread flour
- 3/4 cup whole wheat or spelt flour
- 3 tablespoons quinoa flour
- 3 tablespoons barley flour
- 3 tablespoons brown rice flour
- 3 tablespoons instant potato flakes

- 3 tablespoons cornmeal
- 3 tablespoons rolled oats
- 2 tablespoons gluten
- 2 teaspoons salt
- 1 tablespoon plus 1/2 teaspoon SAF yeast or 1 tablespoon plus 1 teaspoon bread machine yeast

Directions:

1. Choose the size of loaf you would like to make and measure your ingredients.
2. Heat a deep, heavy saucepan over medium heat. Place the amaranth in the pan. Stir immediately with a natural-bristle pastry brush. Stir constantly. The amaranth will pop like popcorn. Immediately remove to a bowl to cool.
3. Add the ingredients to the bread pan in the order listed above (including the popped amaranth).
4. Place the pan in the bread machine and close the lid.
5. Turn on the bread maker. Select the Whole Wheat setting, then the loaf size, and finally the crust color. Start the cycle.
6. When the cycle is finished and the bread is baked, carefully remove the pan from the machine. Use a potholder as the handle will be very hot. Let rest for a few minutes.
7. Remove the bread from the pan and allow to cool on a wire rack for at least 10 minutes before slicing.

Wheat Bran Bread

Ingredients:
- 8 slices (1 pound)
- 3/4 cup lukewarm milk
- 1 1/2 tablespoons unsalted butter, melted
- 1/8 cup sugar
- 1 teaspoon table salt
- 1/4 cup wheat bran
- 1 3/4 cups white bread flour
- 1 teaspoon bread machine yeast
- 12 slices (1 ½ pounds)
- 1⅛ cups lukewarm milk
- 2¼ tablespoons unsalted butter, melted
- 3 tablespoons sugar
- 1½ teaspoons table salt
- ⅓ cup wheat bran

- 2⅔ cups white bread flour
- 1½ teaspoons bread machine yeast
- 16 slices (2 pounds)
- 1½ cups lukewarm milk
- 3 tablespoons unsalted butter, melted
- ¼ cup sugar
- 2 teaspoons table salt
- ½ cup wheat bran
- 3½ cups white bread flour
- 2 teaspoons bread machine yeast

Directions:

1. Choose the size of loaf you would like to make and measure your ingredients.
2. Add the ingredients to the bread pan in the order listed above.
3. Place the pan in the bread machine and close the lid.
4. Turn on the bread maker. Select the White/Basic setting, then the loaf size, and finally the crust color. Start the cycle.
5. When the cycle is finished and the bread is baked, carefully remove the pan from the machine. Use a potholder as the handle will be very hot. Let rest for a few minutes.
6. Remove the bread from the pan and allow to cool on a wire rack for at least 10 minutes before slicing.

Classic Dark Bread

Ingredients:
- 8 slices (1 pound)
- 5/8 cup lukewarm water
- 1 tablespoon unsalted butter, melted
- 1/4 cup molasses
- 1/4 teaspoon table salt
- 1/2 cup rye flour
- 1 1/4 cups white bread flour
- 1 tablespoon unsweetened cocoa powder
- Pinch ground nutmeg
- 1 1/8 teaspoons bread machine yeast
- 12 slices (1 ½ pounds)
- 1 cup lukewarm water
- 1½ tablespoons unsalted butter, melted
- ⅓ cup molasses
- ⅓ teaspoon table salt

- ¾ cup rye flour
- 2 cups white bread flour
- 1½ tablespoons unsweetened cocoa powder
- Pinch ground nutmeg
- 1⅔ teaspoons bread machine yeast
- 16 slices (2 pounds)
- 1¼ cups lukewarm water
- 2 tablespoons unsalted butter, melted
- ½ cup molasses
- ½ teaspoon table salt
- 1 cup rye flour
- 2½ cups white bread flour
- 2 tablespoons unsweetened cocoa powder
- Pinch ground nutmeg
- 2¼ teaspoons bread machine yeast

Directions:

1. Choose the size of loaf you would like to make and measure your ingredients.

2. Add the ingredients to the bread pan in the order listed above.

3. Place the pan in the bread machine and close the lid.

4. Turn on the bread maker. Select the White/Basic setting, then the loaf size, and finally the crust color. Start the cycle.

5. When the cycle is finished and the bread is baked, carefully remove the pan from the machine. Use a potholder as the handle will be very hot. Let rest for a few minutes.

6. Remove the bread from the pan and allow to cool on a wire rack for at least 10 minutes before slicing.

Whole-grain Daily Bread

Ingredients:
- 8 slices (1 pound)
- 2/3 cup buttermilk
- 1/2 cup cooked whole grain of choice, firmly packed
- 1 1/2 tablespoons canola oil
- 1 1/2 tablespoons honey
- 1 2/3 cups bread flour
- 1/3 cup whole wheat flour
- 1/6 cup rolled oats
- 1/2 tablespoon plus 1/2 teaspoon gluten
- 1 teaspoon salt
- 1 1/4 teaspoons SAF yeast or 1/2 tablespoon bread machine yeast
- 12 slices (1½ pounds)
- 1 cup buttermilk
- 3/4 cup cooked whole grain of choice, firmly packed
- 2 tablespoons canola oil
- 2 tablespoons honey
- 21/2 cups bread flour
- 1/2 cup whole wheat flour
- 1/4 cup rolled oats
- 1 tablespoon gluten
- 11/2 teaspoons salt
- 2 teaspoons SAF yeast or 21/2 teaspoons bread machine yeast
- 16 slices (2 pounds)
- 11/3 cups buttermilk
- 1 cup cooked whole grain of choice, firmly packed
- 3 tablespoons canola oil
- 3 tablespoons honey
- 31/3 cups bread flour
- 2/3 cup whole wheat flour
- 1/3 cup rolled oats
- 1 tablespoon plus 1 teaspoon gluten
- 2 teaspoons salt
- 21/2 teaspoons SAF yeast or 1 tablespoon bread machine yeast

Directions:

1. Choose the size of loaf you would like to make and measure your ingredients.

2. Add the ingredients to the bread pan in the order listed above.

3. Place the pan in the bread machine and close the lid.

4. Turn on the bread maker. Select the Basic setting, then the loaf size, and finally the crust color. Start the cycle.

5. Reach in and touch the dough with your fingers, being careful to avoid the rotating blade. The dough ball will be quite soft. Add another tablespoon of flour if it is too sticky around the blade.

6. When the cycle is finished and the bread is baked, carefully remove the pan from the machine. Use a potholder as the handle will be very hot. Let rest for a few minutes.

7. Remove the bread from the pan and allow to cool on a wire rack for at least 10 minutes before slicing.

Zo's 14-grain Bread

Ingredients:

- 8 slices (1 pound)
- 1 cup water
- 1 1/2 tablespoons canola oil
- 1 1/2 tablespoons honey or sugar
- 7/8 cup whole wheat flour
- 1/2 cup kamut flour
- 1/2 cup spelt flour
- 1/3 cup raw 9-grain cereal
- 1 1/2 tablespoons raw sunflower seeds
- 3/4 tablespoon whole millet
- 3/4 tablespoon flax seed
- 3/4 tablespoon sesame seeds
- 3/4 tablespoon raw amaranth seeds
- 3/4 tablespoon lecithin granules (see here)
- 1/8 cup gluten
- 11 /2 tablespoons tofu powder or nonfat dry milk
- 1/2 tablespoon dough enhancer (see here)
- 1 teaspoon salt
- 1/2 tablespoon plus 1/4 teaspoon SAF yeast or 1/2 tablespoon plus 1/2 teaspoon bread machine yeast
- 12 slices (1½ pounds)
- 12/3 cups water
- 2 tablespoons canola oil
- 2 tablespoons honey or sugar
- 11/2 cups whole wheat flour
- 2/3 cup kamut flour
- 2/3 cup spelt flour
- 1/2 cup raw 9-grain cereal
- 2 tablespoons raw sunflower seeds
- 1 tablespoon whole millet
- 1 tablespoon flax seed
- 1 tablespoon sesame seeds
- 1 tablespoon raw amaranth seeds
- 1 tablespoon lecithin granules (see here)
- 3 tablespoons gluten
- 2 tablespoons tofu powder or nonfat dry milk
- 2 teaspoons dough enhancer (see here)
- 11/2 teaspoons salt
- 1 tablespoon SAF yeast or 1 tablespoon plus 1/2 teaspoon bread machine yeast
- 16 slices (2 pounds)
- 2 cups water
- 3 tablespoons canola oil
- 3 tablespoons honey or sugar
- 13/4 cups whole wheat flour
- 1 cup kamut flour
- 1 cup spelt flour
- 2/3 cup raw 9-grain cereal
- 3 tablespoons raw sunflower seeds
- 11/2 tablespoons whole millet
- 11/2 tablespoons flax seed
- 11/2 tablespoons sesame seeds
- 11/2 tablespoons raw amaranth seeds
- 11/2 tablespoons lecithin granules (see here)
- 1/4 cup gluten
- 3 tablespoons tofu powder or nonfat dry milk
- 1 tablespoon dough enhancer (see here)
- 2 teaspoons salt
- 1 tablespoon plus 1/2 teaspoon SAF yeast or 1 tablespoon plus 1 teaspoon bread machine yeast

Directions:

1. Choose the size of loaf you would like to make and measure your ingredients.

2. Add the ingredients to the bread pan in the order listed above.

3. Place the pan in the bread machine and close the lid.

4. Turn on the bread maker. Select the Whole Wheat setting, then the loaf size, and finally the crust color. Start the cycle.

5. When the cycle is finished and the bread is baked, carefully remove the pan from the machine. Use a potholder as the handle will be very hot. Let rest for a few minutes.

6. Remove the bread from the pan and allow to cool on a wire rack for at least 10 minutes before slicing.

Limpa

Ingredients:

- 8 slices (1 pound)
- 1/2 cup water
- 1/4 cup milk
- 1 tablespoon molasses
- 1 tablespoon brown sugar
- 1 1/2 tablespoons butter, cut into pieces

- 1 1/4 cups bread flour
- 1 1/4 cups medium rye flour
- 1/2 tablespoon plus 1/2 teaspoon gluten
- 3/8 teaspoon fennel seeds, crushed
- 3/8 teaspoon aniseed, crushed
- 1 teaspoon grated orange zest
- 7/8 teaspoon salt
- 1 1/8 teaspoons SAF yeast or 1 3/8 teaspoons bread machine yeast
- 12 slices (1 ½ pounds)
- 3/4 cup water
- 1/3 cup milk
- 1 tablespoon molasses
- 11/2 tablespoons brown sugar
- 2 tablespoons butter, cut into pieces
- 13/4 cups bread flour
- 11/4 cups medium rye flour
- 1 tablespoon gluten
- 1/2 teaspoon fennel seeds, crushed
- 1/2 teaspoon aniseed, crushed
- 11/2 teaspoons grated orange zest
- 11/2 teaspoons salt
- 2 teaspoons SAF yeast or 21/2 teaspoons bread machine yeast
- 16 slices (2 pounds)
- 1 cup water
- 1/2 cup milk
- 2 tablespoons molasses
- 2 tablespoons brown sugar
- 3 tablespoons butter, cut into pieces
- 21/2 cups bread flour
- 11/2 cups medium rye flour
- 1 tablespoon plus 1 teaspoon gluten
- 3/4 teaspoon fennel seeds, crushed
- 3/4 teaspoon aniseed, crushed
- 2 teaspoons grated orange zest
- 13/4 teaspoons salt
- 21/4 teaspoons SAF yeast or 23/4 teaspoons bread machine yeast

Directions:

1. Choose the size of loaf you would like to make and measure your ingredients.

2. Add the ingredients to the bread pan in the order listed above.

3. Place the pan in the bread machine and close the lid.

4. Turn on the bread maker. Select the Basic setting, then the loaf size, and finally the crust color. Start the cycle.

5. When the cycle is finished and the bread is baked, carefully remove the pan from the machine. Use a potholder as the handle will be very hot. Let rest for a few minutes.

6. Remove the bread from the pan and allow to cool on a wire rack for at least 10 minutes before slicing

Toasted Sesame–whole Wheat Bread

Ingredients:

- 8 slices (1 pound)
- 1 1/4 tablespoon sesame seeds
- 5/6 cup water
- 1 1/2 tablespoons honey
- 1/8 cup sesame oil
- 2 1/4 cups whole wheat flour
- 1 1/2 tablespoons gluten
- 1 1/8 teaspoons sea salt
- 1/2 tablespoon SAF yeast or 1/2 tablespoon plus 1/4 teaspoon bread machine yeast
- 12 slices (1 ½ pounds)
- 2 tablespoons sesame seeds
- 11/3 cups water
- 2 tablespoons honey
- 3 tablespoons sesame oil
- 31/2 cups whole wheat flour
- 2 tablespoons gluten
- 13/4 teaspoons sea salt
- 21/2 teaspoons SAF yeast or 1 tablespoon bread machine yeast
- 16 slices (2 pounds)
- 21/2 tablespoons sesame seeds
- 12/3 cups water
- 3 tablespoons honey
- 1/4 cup sesame oil
- 41/2 cups whole wheat flour
- 3 tablespoons gluten
- 21/4 teaspoons sea salt

- 1 tablespoon SAF yeast or 1 tablespoon plus 1/2 teaspoon bread machine yeast

Directions:

1. Choose the size of loaf you would like to make and measure your ingredients.

2. Place the sesame seeds in a dry skillet. Cook over medium heat, shaking constantly, until the seeds are lightly toasted, about 2 minutes. Set aside to cool.

3. Add the ingredients to the bread pan in the order listed above.

4. Place the pan in the bread machine and close the lid.

5. Turn on the bread maker. Select the Whole Wheat setting, then the loaf size, and finally the crust color. Start the cycle.

6. When the cycle is finished and the bread is baked, carefully remove the pan from the machine. Use a potholder as the handle will be very hot. Let rest for a few minutes.

7. Remove the bread from the pan and allow to cool on a wire rack for at least 10 minutes before slicing.

Three-seed Whole Wheat Bread

Ingredients:

- 8 slices (1 pound)
- 5/6 cup water
- 1 1/2 tablespoons sunflower seed oil
- 1 cup bread flour
- 1 cup whole wheat flour
- 1/8 cup nonfat dry milk
- 1 1/2 tablespoons brown sugar
- 1/2 tablespoon plus 1/2 teaspoon gluten
- 3/4 teaspoon salt
- 1 1/4 teaspoon SAF yeast or 1/2 tablespoon bread machine yeast
- 1/4 cup raw sunflower seeds
- 1 1/4 tablespoon sesame seeds
- 1 1/4 teaspoon poppy seeds
- 12 slices (1 ½ pounds)
- 11/4 cups water
- 2 tablespoons sunflower seed oil
- 11/2 cups bread flour
- 11/2 cups whole wheat flour
- 3 tablespoons nonfat dry milk
- 2 tablespoons brown sugar
- 1 tablespoon gluten
- 1 teaspoon salt
- 2 teaspoons SAF yeast or 21/2 teaspoons bread machine yeast
- 1/3 cup raw sunflower seeds
- 2 tablespoons sesame seeds
- 2 teaspoons poppy seeds
- 16 slices (2 pounds)
- 12/3 cups water
- 3 tablespoons sunflower seed oil
- 2 cups bread flour
- 2 cups whole wheat flour
- 1/4 cup nonfat dry milk
- 3 tablespoons brown sugar
- 1 tablespoon plus 1 teaspoon gluten
- 11/2 teaspoons salt
- 21/2 teaspoons SAF yeast or 1 tablespoon bread machine yeast
- 1/2 cup raw sunflower seeds
- 21/2 tablespoons sesame seeds
- 21/2 teaspoons poppy seeds

Directions:

1. Choose the size of loaf you would like to make and measure your ingredients.

2. Add the ingredients to the bread pan in the order listed above (except the seeds).

3. Place the pan in the bread machine and close the lid.

4. Turn on the bread maker. Select the Basic/Whole Wheat setting, then the loaf size, and finally the crust color. Start the cycle. (This recipe is not suitable for use with the Delay Timer.)

5. When the machine beeps, or between Knead 1 and Knead 2, add all the seeds.

6. When the cycle is finished and the bread is baked, carefully remove the pan from the machine. Use a potholder as the handle will be very hot. Let rest for a few minutes.

7. Remove the bread from the pan and allow to cool on a wire rack for at least 10 minutes before slicing.

Buttermilk Whole Wheat Bread

Ingredients:

- 8 slices (1 pound)
- 3/4 cup buttermilk
- 1 1/2 tablespoons canola oil
- 1 1/4 tablespoons maple syrup
- 1 cup whole wheat flour
- 1 cups bread flour
- 1/2 tablespoon plus 1 teaspoon gluten
- 1 teaspoon salt
- 1 1/8 teaspoons SAF yeast or 1 3/8 teaspoons bread machine yeast
- 12 slices (1 ½ pounds)
- 11/8 cups buttermilk
- 2 tablespoons canola oil
- 2 tablespoons maple syrup
- 11/2 cups whole wheat flour
- 11/2 cups bread flour
- 1 tablespoon plus 1 teaspoon gluten
- 11/2 teaspoons salt
- 2 teaspoons SAF yeast or 21/2 teaspoons bread machine yeast
- 16 slices (2 pounds)
- 11/2 cups buttermilk
- 3 tablespoons canola oil
- 21/2 tablespoons maple syrup
- 2 cups whole wheat flour
- 2 cups bread flour
- 1 tablespoon plus 2 teaspoons gluten
- 2 teaspoons salt
- 21/4 teaspoons SAF yeast or 23/4 teaspoons bread machine yeast

Directions:

1. Choose the size of loaf you would like to make and measure your ingredients.
2. Add the ingredients to the bread pan in the order listed above.
3. Place the pan in the bread machine and close the lid.
4. Turn on the bread maker. Select the Basic/Whole Wheat setting, then the loaf size, and finally the crust color. Start the cycle.
5. When the cycle is finished and the bread is baked, carefully remove the pan from the machine. Use a potholder as the handle will be very hot. Let rest for a few minutes.
6. Remove the bread from the pan and allow to cool on a wire rack for at least 10 minutes before slicing.

Flax Seed Whole Wheat Bread

Ingredients:

- 8 slices (1 pound)
- 3/4 cup water
- 1 1/2 tablespoons canola oil
- 1/8 cup honey
- 1 1/3 cups bread flour
- 2/3 cup whole wheat flour
- 1/6 cup nonfat dry milk
- 1 1/4 tablespoons flax seed
- 5/8 tablespoon gluten
- 3/4 teaspoon salt
- 1 1/8 teaspoons SAF yeast or 1 3/8 teaspoons bread machine yeast
- 12 slices (1 ½ pounds)
- 11/8 cups water
- 2 tablespoons canola oil
- 3 tablespoons honey
- 2 cups bread flour
- 1 cup whole wheat flour
- 1/4 cup nonfat dry milk
- 2 tablespoons flax seed
- 1 tablespoon gluten
- 1 teaspoon salt
- 2 teaspoons SAF yeast or 21/2 teaspoons bread machine yeast
- 16 slices (2 pounds)
- 11/2 cups water
- 3 tablespoons canola oil
- 1/4 cup honey
- 22/3 cups bread flour
- 11/3 cups whole wheat flour
- 1/3 cup nonfat dry milk
- 21/2 tablespoons flax seed
- 11/4 tablespoons gluten
- 11/2 teaspoons salt
- 21/4 teaspoons SAF yeast or 23/4 teaspoons bread machine yeast

Directions:

1. Choose the size of loaf you would like to make and measure your ingredients.

2. Add the ingredients to the bread pan in the order listed above.

3. Place the pan in the bread machine and close the lid.

4. Turn on the bread maker. Select the Basic/Whole Wheat setting, then the loaf size, and finally the crust color. Start the cycle.

5. When the cycle is finished and the bread is baked, carefully remove the pan from the machine. Use a potholder as the handle will be very hot. Let rest for a few minutes.

6. Remove the bread from the pan and allow to cool on a wire rack for at least 10 minutes before slicing.

Lou's Daily Bread

Ingredients:

- 8 slices (1 pound)
- Zest of 1 orange, cut into very thin strips
- 5/6 cup fat-free milk
- 1 1/2 tablespoons olive or walnut oil
- 1 1/2 tablespoons honey
- 1 1/8 cups whole wheat flour
- 1 cup bread flour
- 1/2 tablespoon plus 1/2 teaspoon gluten
- 3/4 teaspoon salt
- 1 1/8 teaspoons SAF yeast or 1 3/8 teaspoons bread machine yeast
- 12 slices (1 ½ pounds)
- Zest of 2 oranges, cut into very thin strips
- 11/4 cups fat-free milk
- 2 tablespoons olive or walnut oil
- 2 tablespoons honey
- 1 5/8 cups whole wheat flour
- 1 1/2 cups bread flour
- 1 tablespoon gluten
- 11/4 teaspoons salt
- 13/4 teaspoons SAF yeast or 21/4 teaspoons bread machine yeast
- 16 slices (2 pounds)
- Zest of 2 oranges, cut into very thin strips
- 12/3 cups fat-free milk

- 3 tablespoons olive or walnut oil
- 3 tablespoons honey
- 21/4 cups whole wheat flour
- 2 cups bread flour
- 1 tablespoon plus 1 teaspoon gluten
- 11/2 teaspoons salt
- 21/4 teaspoons SAF yeast or 23/4 teaspoons bread machine yeast

Directions:

1. In a food processor, chop the orange peel fine, or chop it fine by hand.

2. Place all the ingredients in the pan according to the order in the manufacturer's instructions. Set crust on medium and program for the Whole Wheat cycle; press Start. (This recipe is not suitable for use with the Delay Timer.)

3. When the baking cycle ends, immediately remove the bread from the pan and place it on a rack. Let cool to room temperature before slicing.

White Whole Wheat Bread

Ingredients:

- 8 slices (1 pound)
- 13/16 cup water
- 1 1/2 tablespoons nut oil or olive oil
- 1/6 cup maple syrup
- 2 1/6 cups white whole wheat flour
- 3/4 tablespoon gluten
- 1 teaspoon salt
- 1 1/4 teaspoons SAF yeast or 1/2 tablespoon bread machine yeast
- 12 slices (1 ½ pounds)
- 11/4 cups water
- 2 tablespoons nut oil or olive oil
- 1/4 cup maple syrup
- 31/4 cups white whole wheat flour
- 1 tablespoon gluten
- 11/2 teaspoons salt
- 2 teaspoons SAF yeast or 21/2 teaspoons bread machine yeast
- 16 slices (2 pounds)
- 15/8 cups water
- 3 tablespoons nut oil or olive oil

- 1/3 cup maple syrup
- 41/3 cups white whole wheat flour
- 11/2 tablespoons gluten
- 2 teaspoons salt
- 21/2 teaspoons SAF yeast or 1 tablespoon bread machine yeast

Directions:

1. Choose the size of loaf you would like to make and measure your ingredients.

2. Add the ingredients to the bread pan in the order listed above.

3. Place the pan in the bread machine and close the lid.

4. Turn on the bread maker. Select the Whole Wheat setting, then the loaf size, and finally the crust color. Start the cycle.

5. When the cycle is finished and the bread is baked, carefully remove the pan from the machine. Use a potholder as the handle will be very hot. Let rest for a few minutes.

6. Remove the bread from the pan and allow to cool on a wire rack for at least 10 minutes before slicing.

Pain De Paris

Ingredients:

- 8 slices (1 pound)
- For the pâte fermentée:
- 1/4 cup water
- 5/8 cup bread flour
- 1/8 teaspoon sea salt
- 1/4 teaspoon SAF or 1/2 teaspoon bread machine yeast
- For the dough:
- 2/3 cup water
- 1 1/2 cups bread flour
- 11/4 teaspoons gluten with vitamin C
- 5/8 teaspoon SAF yeast or 7/8 teaspoon bread machine yeast
- 3/8 cup pâte fermentée
- 3/4 teaspoon sea salt
- 12 slices (1 ½ pounds)
- For the pâte fermentée:
- 1/2 cup water
- 11/4 cups bread flour
- Pinch of sea salt
- 1/2 teaspoon SAF or 1 teaspoon bread machine yeast
- For the dough:
- 1 cup minus 1 tablespoon water
- 2 cups bread flour
- 11/2 teaspoons gluten with vitamin C
- 3/4 teaspoon SAF yeast or 11/4 teaspoons bread machine yeast
- 1/2 cup pâte fermentée
- 1 teaspoon sea salt
- 16 slices (2 pounds)
- For the pâte fermentée:
- 1/2 cup water
- 11/4 cups bread flour
- 1/4 teaspoon sea salt
- 1/2 teaspoon SAF or 1 teaspoon bread machine yeast
- For the dough:

- 11/3 cups water
- 3 cups bread flour
- 21/2 teaspoons gluten with vitamin C
- 11/4 teaspoons SAF yeast or 13/4 teaspoons bread machine yeast
- 3/4 cup pâte fermentée
- 11/2 teaspoons sea salt

Directions:

1. Choose the size of loaf you would like to make and measure your ingredients.

2. To make the pâte fermentée starter, place the starter ingredients in the bread pan. Program for the Dough cycle; press Start. Set a kitchen timer for 10 minutes. When the timer rings, press Pause and set the timer again for 10 minutes. Let the starter rest for 10 minutes (the autolyse). When the timer rings, press Start to continue and finish the Dough cycle. When the machine beeps at the end of the cycle, press Stop and unplug the machine. Gently deflate the spongy starter, and let it sit in the bread machine for 3 to 12 hours, deflating it about every 4 hours. (If you are making the starter ahead of time, remove it from the machine at this point and refrigerate it for up to 48 hours. Bring to room temperature before making the dough.)

3. Rinse out a plastic dry measure with cold water. With the measuring cup still wet, measure out the starter (the pâte fermentée) according to the chosen loaf size. If you have not already stored the pâte fermentée earlier, you can store the rest of the starter (enough for 2 to 3 batches of Pain de Paris) in the refrigerator for up to 48 hours.

4. Add the ingredients to the bread pan in the order listed above. (You don't have to wash out the bread pan from the starter.)

5. Place the pan in the bread machine and close the lid.

6. Turn on the bread maker. Select the French Bread setting, then the loaf size, and finally the crust color. Start the cycle.

7. After Knead 1, press Pause. Add the reserved pâte fermentée and the salt. Press Start to continue. The dough will be moist and smooth.

8. When the cycle is finished and the bread is baked, carefully remove the pan from the machine. Use a potholder as the handle will be very hot. Let rest for a few minutes.

9. Remove the bread from the pan and allow to cool on a wire rack for at least 10 minutes before slicing.

Pane Italiano

Ingredients:
- 8 slices (1 pound)
- 5/6 cup water
- 1 5/8 cups bread flour
- 7/16 cup semolina flour
- 3/4 tablespoon instant potato flakes
- 3/4 tablespoon sugar
- 1/2 tablespoon gluten
- 1 teaspoon salt
- 11/8 teaspoons SAF yeast or 1 3/8 teaspoons bread machine yeast
- 12 slices (1 ½ pounds)
- 11/3 cups water
- 21/2 cups bread flour
- 2/3 cup semolina flour
- 1 tablespoon instant potato flakes
- 1 tablespoon sugar
- 2 teaspoons gluten
- 11/2 teaspoons salt
- 2 teaspoons SAF yeast or 21/2 teaspoons bread machine yeast
- 16 slices (2 pounds)
- 12/3 cups water
- 31/4 cups bread flour
- 7/8 cup semolina flour
- 11/2 tablespoons instant potato flakes
- 11/2 tablespoons sugar
- 1 tablespoon gluten
- 2 teaspoons salt
- 21/4 teaspoons SAF yeast or 23/4 teaspoons bread machine yeast

Directions:
1. Choose the size of loaf you would like to make and measure your ingredients.

2. Add the ingredients to the bread pan in the order listed above.

3. Place the pan in the bread machine and close the lid.

4. Turn on the bread maker. Select the Basic/French Bread setting, then the loaf size, and finally the crust color. Start the cycle.

5. If using the Basic cycle, after Knead 2, press Stop, reset the machine, and start the cycle again, allowing the dough to be kneaded an extra time.

6. When the cycle is finished and the bread is baked, carefully remove the pan from the machine. Use a potholder as the handle will be very hot. Let rest for a few minutes.

7. Remove the bread from the pan and allow to cool on a wire rack for at least 10 minutes before slicing.

Pain De Maison Sur Poolish\

Ingredients:
- 8 slices (1 pound)
- For the poolish:
- 2/3cup water
- 5/6 cup organic bread flour
- 1/6 teaspoon SAF or bread machine yeast
- For the dough:
- 1/4 cup water
- 3/4 teaspoon SAF yeast or 1 teaspoon bread machine yeast
- 11/3 cups organic bread flour
- 3/4 tablespoon sugar
- 2/3 tablespoon gluten
- 1 teaspoon salt
- 12 slices (1 ½ pounds)
- For the poolish:
- 1 cup water
- 11/4 cups organic bread flour
- 1/4 teaspoon SAF or bread machine yeast
- For the dough:
- 1/3 cup water
- 11/2 teaspoons SAF yeast or 2 teaspoons bread machine yeast
- 2 cups organic bread flour
- 1 tablespoon sugar
- 1 tablespoon gluten

- 11/2 teaspoons salt
- 16 slices (2 pounds)
- For the poolish:
- 11/3 cups water
- 12/3 cups organic bread flour
- 1/3 teaspoon SAF or bread machine yeast
- For the dough:
- 1/2 cup water
- 11/2 teaspoons SAF yeast or 2 teaspoons bread machine yeast
- 22/3 cups organic bread flour
- 11/2 tablespoons sugar
- 1 tablespoon plus 1 teaspoon gluten
- 2 teaspoons salt

Directions:

1. Choose the size of loaf you would like to make and measure your ingredients.

2. To make the poolish starter, place the water, flour, and yeast in the bread pan. Program for the Dough cycle, and set a kitchen timer for 10 minutes. When the timer rings, press Stop and unplug the machine. Let the starter sit in the machine for about 6 hours.

3. Add all the ingredients to the bread pan in the order listed above (including the poolish).

4. Place the pan in the bread machine and close the lid.

5. Turn on the bread maker. Select the French Bread setting, then the loaf size, and finally the crust color. Start the cycle. (This recipe is not suitable for use with the Delay Timer.)

6. When the cycle is finished, check the bread. If the crust is still pale and loaf is not done, reset for Bake Only for 12 minutes longer.

7. When the bread is baked, carefully remove the pan from the machine. Use a potholder as the handle will be very hot. Let rest for a few minutes.

8. Remove the bread from the pan and allow to cool on a wire rack for at least 10 minutes before slicing.

Chuck Williams's Country French

Ingredients:
- 8 slices (1 pound)
- 5/6 cup water
- 11/2 cups bread flour

- 1/2 cup whole wheat flour
- 1/2 tablespoon gluten
- 1 teaspoon salt
- 11/8 teaspoons SAF yeast or13/8 teaspoons bread machine yeast
- 12 slices (1 ½ pounds)
- 11/4 cups water
- 21/4 cups bread flour
- 3/4 cup whole wheat flour
- 2 teaspoons gluten
- 11/2 teaspoons salt
- 13/4 teaspoons SAF yeast or 21/4 teaspoons bread machine yeast
- 16 slices (2 pounds)
- 12/3 cups water
- 3 cups bread flour
- 1 cup whole wheat flour
- 1 tablespoon gluten
- 2 teaspoons salt
- 21/4 teaspoons SAF yeast or 23/4 teaspoons bread machine yeast

Directions:

1. Choose the size of loaf you would like to make and measure your ingredients.

2. Add the ingredients to the bread pan in the order listed above.

3. Place the pan in the bread machine and close the lid.

4. Turn on the bread maker. Select the Basic/French Bread setting, then the loaf size, and finally the crust color. Start the cycle.

5. When the cycle is finished and the bread is baked, carefully remove the pan from the machine. Use a potholder as the handle will be very hot. Let rest for a few minutes.

6. Remove the bread from the pan and allow to cool on a wire rack for at least 10 minutes before slicing.

Pain Ordinaire Au Beurre

Ingredients:
- 8 slices (1 pound)
- 5/6 cup water
- 3/4 tablespoon unsalted butter, cut into pieces
- 2 cups unbleached all-purpose flour

- 1/2 tablespoon gluten
- 1 teaspoon fine sea salt
- 11/8 teaspoons SAF yeast or 1 3/8 teaspoons bread machine yeast
- 12 slices (1 ½ pounds)
- 11/4 cups water
- 1 tablespoon unsalted butter, cut into pieces
- 3 cups unbleached all-purpose flour
- 2 teaspoons gluten
- 11/2 teaspoons fine sea salt
- 2 teaspoons SAF yeast or 21/2 teaspoons bread machine yeast
- 16 slices (2 pounds)
- 12/3 cups water
- 11/2 tablespoons unsalted butter, cut into pieces
- 4 cups unbleached all-purpose flour
- 1 tablespoon gluten
- 2 teaspoons fine sea salt
- 21/4 teaspoons SAF yeast or 23/4 teaspoons bread machine yeast

Directions:

1. Choose the size of loaf you would like to make and measure your ingredients.

2. Add the ingredients to the bread pan in the order listed above.

3. Place the pan in the bread machine and close the lid.

4. Turn on the bread maker. Select the Basic/French Bread setting, then the loaf size, and finally the crust color. Start the cycle.

5. When the cycle is finished and the bread is baked, carefully remove the pan from the machine. Use a potholder as the handle will be very hot. Let rest for a few minutes.

6. Remove the bread from the pan and allow to cool on a wire rack for at least 10 minutes before slicing.

Semolina Country Bread

Ingredients:

- 8 slices (1 pound)
- 7/8 cup water
- 1 1/2 tablespoons olive oil
- 1 1/8 cups bread flour
- 7/8 cup semolina flour
- 1 tablespoon sesame seeds
- 1/2 tablespoon plus 1/2 teaspoon gluten
- 1 teaspoon salt
- 11/8 teaspoons SAF yeast or 13/8 teaspoons bread machine yeast
- 12 slices (1 ½ pounds)
- 11/3 cups water
- 2 tablespoons olive oil
- 13/4 cups bread flour
- 11/4 cups semolina flour
- 1 tablespoon plus 1 teaspoon sesame seeds
- 1 tablespoon gluten
- 11/2 teaspoons salt
- 2 teaspoons SAF yeast or 21/2 teaspoons bread machine yeast
- 16 slices (2 pounds)
- 13/4 cups water
- 3 tablespoons olive oil
- 21/4 cups bread flour
- 13/4 cups semolina flour
- 2 tablespoons sesame seeds
- 1 tablespoon plus 1 teaspoon gluten
- 2 teaspoons salt
- 21/4 teaspoons SAF yeast or 23/4 teaspoons bread machine yeast

Directions:

1. Choose the size of loaf you would like to make and measure your ingredients.

2. Add the ingredients to the bread pan in the order listed above.

3. Place the pan in the bread machine and close the lid.

4. Turn on the bread maker. Select the Basic/French Bread setting, then the loaf size, and finally the crust color. Start the cycle.

5. When the cycle is finished and the bread is baked, carefully remove the pan from the machine. Use a potholder as the handle will be very hot. Let rest for a few minutes.

6. Remove the bread from the pan and allow to cool on a wire rack for at least 10 minutes before slicing.

Pane Toscana

Ingredients:

- 8 slices (1 pound)
- 7/8 cup water
- 1 3/4 cups bread flour
- 1/4 cup whole wheat flour
- 1/2 tablespoon plus 1/2 teaspoon gluten
- 11/8 teaspoons SAF yeast or 1 3/8 teaspoons bread machine yeast
- Pinch of sugar
- Pinch of salt
- 12 slices (1 ½ pounds)
- 11/3 cups water
- 22/3 cups bread flour
- 1/3 cup whole wheat flour
- 1 tablespoon gluten
- 13/4 teaspoons SAF yeast or 21/4 teaspoons bread machine yeast
- Pinch of sugar
- Pinch of salt
- 16 slices (2 pounds)
- 13/4 cups water
- 31/2 cups bread flour
- 1/2 cup whole wheat flour
- 1 tablespoon plus 1 teaspoon gluten
- 21/4 teaspoons SAF yeast or 23/4 teaspoons bread machine yeast
- Pinch of sugar
- Pinch of salt

Directions:

1. Choose the size of loaf you would like to make and measure your ingredients.

2. To make the sponge, place the water, 1 cup of the bread flour, the whole wheat flour, the gluten, and the yeast in the pan according to the order in the manufacturer's instructions. Program for the Dough cycle, and set a kitchen timer for 10 minutes. When the timer rings, press Stop and unplug the machine. Let the sponge rest in the machine for 1 hour.

3. To make the dough, add the remaining 12/3 cups bread flour (for the 11/2-pound loaf) or 21/2 cups (for the 2-pound loaf), the sugar, and salt to the sponge in the bread pan.

4. Place the pan in the bread machine and close the lid.

5. Turn on the bread maker. Select the French Bread setting, then the loaf size, and finally the crust color. Start the cycle.

6. When the cycle is finished and the bread is baked, carefully remove the pan from the machine. Use a potholder as the handle will be very hot. Let rest for a few minutes.

7. Remove the bread from the pan and allow to cool on a wire rack for at least 10 minutes before slicing.

Olive Oil Bread

Ingredients:

- 8 slices (1 pound)
- For the biga starter:
- 1/2 cup water
- 1 cup bread flour
- 1/4 teaspoon SAF yeast or bread machine yeast
- For the dough:
- 1/4 cup water
- 1/8 cup olive oil
- 1 cup bread flour
- 1/2 tablespoon sugar
- 1 teaspoon gluten
- 1 teaspoon salt
- 3/4 teaspoon SAF yeast or 1 teaspoon bread machine yeast
- 12 slices (1 ½ pounds)
- For the biga starter:
- 3/4 cup water
- 11/2 cups bread flour
- 1/2 teaspoon SAF yeast or bread machine yeast
- For the dough:
- 1/4 cup water
- 3 tablespoons olive oil
- 11/2 cups bread flour
- 2 teaspoons sugar
- 1 teaspoon gluten
- 11/2 teaspoons salt
- 11/4 teaspoons SAF yeast or 13/4 teaspoons bread machine yeast
- 16 slices (2 pounds)
- For the biga starter:

- 1 cup water
- 2 cups bread flour
- 1/2 teaspoon SAF yeast or bread machine yeast
- For the dough:
- 1/2 cup water
- 1/4 cup olive oil
- 2 cups bread flour
- 1 tablespoon sugar
- 2 teaspoons gluten
- 2 teaspoons salt
- 11/2 teaspoons SAF yeast or 2 teaspoons bread machine yeast

Directions:

1. Choose the size of loaf you would like to make and measure your ingredients.

2. To make the biga starter, place starter ingredients in the bread pan. Program for the Dough cycle and set a timer for 10 minutes. When the timer rings, press Stop and unplug the machine. Let the starter sit in the machine for 12 to 18 hours.

3. To make the dough, with a rubber spatula, break up the starter into 6 or 8 pieces and leave in the machine.

4. Add all the dough ingredients to the bread pan in the order listed above.

5. Place the pan in the bread machine and close the lid.

6. Turn on the bread maker. Select the French Bread setting, then the loaf size, and finally the crust color. Start the cycle.

7. When the cycle is finished and the bread is baked, carefully remove the pan from the machine. Use a potholder as the handle will be very hot. Let rest for a few minutes.

8. Remove the bread from the pan and allow to cool on a wire rack for at least 10 minutes before slicing.

INTERNATIONAL BREAD RECIPES

British Hot Cross Buns

Ingredients:

- 8 slices (1 pound)
- 1/2 cup warm milk
- 2 tablespoons butter, unsalted
- 1/6 cup white sugar
- 1/3 teaspoon salt
- 2/3 egg
- 2/3 egg white
- 2 cups all-purpose flour
- 2/3 tablespoon active dry yeast
- 1/2 cup dried raisins
- 2/3 teaspoon ground cinnamon
- For Brushing:
- 1 egg yolk
- 2 tablespoons water
- For the Crosses:
- 2 tablespoons flour
- Cold water
- 1/2 tablespoon sugar
- 12 slices (1 ½ pounds)
- 3/4 cup warm milk
- 3 tablespoons butter, unsalted
- 1/4 cup white sugar
- 1/2 teaspoon salt
- 1 egg
- 1 egg white
- 3 cups all-purpose flour
- 1 tablespoon active dry yeast
- 3/4 cup dried raisins
- 1 teaspoon ground cinnamon
- For Brushing:
- 1 egg yolk
- 2 tablespoons water
- For the Crosses:
- 2 tablespoons flour
- Cold water
- 1/2 tablespoon sugar
- 16 slices (2 pounds)
- 1 cup warm milk
- 4 tablespoons butter, unsalted
- 1/3 cup white sugar
- 2/3 teaspoon salt

- 1 1/3 eggs
- 1 1/3 egg whites
- 4 cups all-purpose flour
- 1 1/3 tablespoons active dry yeast
- 1 cup dried raisins
- 1 1/3 teaspoons ground cinnamon
- For Brushing:
- 1 egg yolk
- 2 tablespoons water
- For the Crosses:
- 2 tablespoons flour
- Cold water
- 1/2 tablespoon sugar

Directions:

1. Choose the size of loaf you would like to make and measure your ingredients.
2. Add the first eight ingredients to the bread pan in the order listed above.
3. Place the pan in the bread machine and close the lid.
4. Turn on the bread maker. Select the Dough setting, then the loaf size, and finally the crust color. Start the cycle.
5. Add raisins and cinnamon 5 minutes before kneading cycle ends.
6. When the cycle is finished and the bread is baked, allow to rest in machine until doubled, about 30 minutes.
7. Punch down on a floured surface, cover, and let rest 10 minutes.
8. Shape into 12 balls and place in a greased 9-by-12-inch pan.
9. Cover and let rise in a warm place until doubled, about 35-40 minutes.
10. Mix egg yolk and 2 tablespoons water and baste each bun.
11. Mix the cross ingredients to form pastry.
12. Roll out pastry and cut into thin strips. Place across the buns to form crosses.
13. Bake at 375°F for 20 minutes.
14. Remove the bread from the pan and allow to cool on a wire rack for at least 10 minutes before slicing.

Italian Panettone

Ingredients:

- 8 slices (1 pound)
- 1/2 cup warm water
- 2 2/3 large egg yolks
- 1 1/3 teaspoons vanilla extract
- 1/3 cup sugar
- 2/3 teaspoon lemon zest
- 2/3 teaspoon orange zest
- 1/3 teaspoon salt
- 1/3 cup unsalted butter, softened and cut into pieces
- 2 1/6 cups unbleached flour
- 2/3 package bread machine yeast
- 1/3 cup golden raisins
- 1/3 cup raisins
- 1 egg white, slightly beaten
- 2 2/3 sugar cubes, crushed
- 12 slices (1 ½ pounds)
- 3/4 cup warm water
- 4 large egg yolks
- 2 teaspoons vanilla extract
- 1/2 cup sugar
- 1 teaspoon lemon zest
- 1 teaspoon orange zest
- 1/2 teaspoon salt
- 1/2 cup unsalted butter, softened and cut into pieces
- 3 1/4 cups unbleached flour
- 1 package bread machine yeast
- 1/2 cup golden raisins
- 1/2 cup raisins
- 1 egg white, slightly beaten
- 4 sugar cubes, crushed
- 16 slices (2 pounds)
- 1 cup warm water
- 5 1/3 large egg yolks
- 2 2/3 teaspoons vanilla extract
- 2/3 cup sugar
- 1 1/3 teaspoons lemon zest
- 1 1/3 teaspoons orange zest
- 2/3 teaspoon salt
- 2/3 cup unsalted butter, softened and cut into pieces
- 4 1/3 cups unbleached flour
- 1 1/3 packages bread machine yeast
- 2/3 cup golden raisins
- 2/3 cup raisins
- 2 egg whites, slightly beaten
- 5 1/3 sugar cubes, crushed

Directions:

1. Choose the size of loaf you would like to make and measure your ingredients.
2. Add the ingredients to the bread pan in the order listed above.
3. Lay pieces of butter around the outside of the pan on top of the flour.
4. Press a well into the flour and add the yeast.
5. Place the pan in the bread machine and close the lid.
6. Turn on the bread maker. Select the Dough setting, then the loaf size, and finally the crust color. Start the cycle.
7. At the second kneading cycle add golden raisins.
8. Let dough rise until doubled.
9. Prepare the pan/baking case: cut a circle of parchment paper to line the bottom of the 6-inch cake pan and spray with non-stick cooking spray.
10. Cut another piece of parchment to line the inside of the brown paper bag after you have cut the bottom out of the bag.
11. Fold the top edge down to form a cuff then spray the inside of the parchment with cooking spray. Place the paper case in the pan.
12. Punch the dough down and knead into a ball.
13. Add it to the paper-lined pan case and allow to rise until almost doubled.
14. Preheat the oven to 350°F.
15. Baste the top of the panettone dough with the beaten egg white and sprinkle with the crushed sugar cubes.
16. Bake for 30 minutes, then reduce heat to 325°F and bake another 30 minutes.
17. Remove from oven and allow to cool in pan for about 15 minutes, then cool on a rack until ready to serve.

Greek Easter Bread

Ingredients:

- 8 slices (1 pound)
- 1/3 cup fresh butter

- 1/2 cup milk
- 1/2 cup sugar
- 1/2 teaspoon mastic
- 1/4 teaspoon salt
- 1/2 package active dry yeast
- 1 1/2 eggs
- 2 1/2 cups strong yellow flour
- 1/2 egg, for brushing blended with 1 teaspoon water
- 12 slices (1 ½ pounds)
- 1/2 cup fresh butter
- 3/4 cup milk
- 3/4 cup sugar
- 3/4 teaspoon mastic
- 3/8 teaspoon salt
- 3/4 package active dry yeast
- 2 1/4 eggs
- 3 3/4 cups strong yellow flour
- 3/4 egg, for brushing blended with 1 1/2 teaspoons water
- 16 slices (2 pounds)
- 2/3 cup fresh butter
- 1 cup milk
- 1 cup sugar
- 1 teaspoon mastic
- 1/2 teaspoon salt
- 1 package active dry yeast
- 3 eggs
- 5 cups strong yellow flour
- 1 egg, for brushing blended with 2 teaspoons water

Directions:

1. Choose the size of loaf you would like to make and measure your ingredients.

2. Heat milk and butter until melted in a saucepan (do not boil). Add to the bread pan.

3. Add sugar and mastic to a food processor and blend. Add to the bread pan.

4. Add remaining ingredients to the bread pan.

5. Place the pan in the bread machine and close the lid.

6. Turn on the bread maker. Select the Dough setting, then the loaf size, and finally the crust color. Start the cycle.

7. When the cycle is finished and the bread is baked, leave the dough to rise for one hour.

8. Shape into 2 loaves, cover, and leave to rise for 50 more minutes.

9. Baste with egg wash.

10. Bake at 320°F for 30 to 40 minutes or until golden brown.

11. Remove the bread from the pan and allow to cool on a wire rack for at least 10 minutes before slicing.

Russian Rye Bread

Ingredients:

- 8 slices (1 pound)
- 1 1/4 cups warm water
- 1 3/4 cups rye flour
- 1 3/4 cups whole wheat flour
- 2 tablespoons malt (or beer kit mixture)
- 1 tablespoon molasses
- 2 tablespoons white vinegar
- 1 teaspoon salt
- 1/2 tablespoon coriander seeds
- 1/2 tablespoon caraway seeds
- 2 teaspoons active dry yeast
- 12 slices (1 ½ pounds)
- 1 7/8 cups warm water
- 2 5/8 cups rye flour
- 2 5/8 cups whole wheat flour
- 3 tablespoons malt (or beer kit mixture)
- 1 1/2 tablespoons molasses
- 3 tablespoons white vinegar
- 1 1/2 teaspoons salt
- 3/4 tablespoon coriander seeds
- 3/4 tablespoon caraway seeds
- 3 teaspoons active dry yeast
- 16 slices (2 pounds)
- 2 1/2 cups warm water
- 3 1/2 cups rye flour
- 3 1/2 cups whole wheat flour
- 4 tablespoons malt (or beer kit mixture)
- 2 tablespoons molasses
- 4 tablespoons white vinegar
- 2 teaspoons salt
- 1 tablespoon coriander seeds
- 1 tablespoon caraway seeds
- 2 teaspoons active dry yeast

Directions:

1. Choose the size of loaf you would like to make and measure your ingredients.

2. Mix dry ingredients together in a bowl, except for yeast.

3. Add wet ingredients to bread pan first; top with dry ingredients.

4. Make a well in the center of the dry ingredients and add the yeast.

5. Place the pan in the bread machine and close the lid.

6. Turn on the bread maker. Select the Basic setting, then the loaf size, and finally the crust color. Start the cycle.

7. When the cycle is finished and the bread is baked, carefully remove the pan from the machine. Use a potholder as the handle will be very hot. Let rest for a few minutes.

8. Remove the bread from the pan and allow to cool on a wire rack for at least 10 minutes before slicing.

Russian Black Bread

Ingredients:

- 8 slices (1 pound)
- 5/6 cup dark rye flour
- 1 2/3 cups unbleached flour
- 2/3 teaspoon instant coffee
- 1 1/3 tablespoons unsweetened cocoa powder
- 2/3 tablespoon whole caraway seeds
- 1/3 teaspoon dried minced onion
- 1/3 teaspoon fennel seeds
- 2/3 teaspoon sea salt
- 1 1/3 teaspoons active dry yeast
- 1 cup water, at room temperature
- 2/3 teaspoon sugar
- 1 tablespoon dark molasses
- 1 tablespoon apple cider vinegar
- 2 tablespoons vegetable oil
- 12 slices (1 ½ pounds)
- 1 1/4 cups dark rye flour
- 2 1/2 cups unbleached flour
- 1 teaspoon instant coffee
- 2 tablespoons unsweetened cocoa powder
- 1 tablespoon whole caraway seeds
- 1/2 teaspoon dried minced onion
- 1/2 teaspoon fennel seeds
- 1 teaspoon sea salt
- 2 teaspoons active dry yeast
- 1 1/3 cups water, at room temperature
- 1 teaspoon sugar
- 1 1/2 tablespoons dark molasses
- 1 1/2 tablespoons apple cider vinegar
- 3 tablespoons vegetable oil
- 16 slices (2 pounds)
- 1 2/3 cups dark rye flour
- 3 1/3 cups unbleached flour
- 1 1/3 teaspoons instant coffee
- 2 2/3 tablespoons unsweetened cocoa powder
- 1 1/3 tablespoons whole caraway seeds
- 2/3 teaspoon dried minced onion
- 2/3 teaspoon fennel seeds
- 1 1/3 teaspoons sea salt
- 2 2/3 teaspoons active dry yeast
- 2 cups water, at room temperature
- 1 1/3 teaspoons sugar
- 2 tablespoons dark molasses
- 2 tablespoons apple cider vinegar
- 4 tablespoons vegetable oil

Directions:

1. Choose the size of loaf you would like to make and measure your ingredients.

2. Mix dry ingredients together in a bowl, except for yeast.

3. Add wet ingredients to bread pan first; top with dry ingredients.

4. Make a well in the center of the dry ingredients and add the yeast.

5. Place the pan in the bread machine and close the lid.

6. Turn on the bread maker. Select the Basic setting, then the loaf size, and finally the crust color. Start the cycle.

7. When the cycle is finished and the bread is baked, carefully remove the pan from the machine. Use a potholder as the handle will be very hot. Let rest for a few minutes.

8. Remove the bread from the pan and allow to cool on a wire rack for at least 10 minutes before slicing.

Fiji Sweet Potato Bread

Ingredients:

- 8 slices (1 pound)
- 5/6 cup sweet potato, mashed
- 6 2/3 tablespoons canned coconut milk
- 2/3 teaspoon ginger, fresh grated
- 2/3 tablespoon lemon zest
- 1 1/3tablespoons honey
- 1 1/3 tablespoons olive oil
- 2 cups bread flour
- 2/3 teaspoon salt
- 1 1/2 teaspoons rapid rise yeast
- 12 slices (1 ½ pounds)
- 1 1/4 cups sweet potato, mashed
- 10 tablespoons canned coconut milk
- 1 teaspoon ginger, fresh grated
- 1 tablespoon lemon zest
- 2 tablespoons honey
- 2 tablespoons olive oil
- 3 cups bread flour
- 1 teaspoon salt
- 2 1/4 teaspoons rapid rise yeast
- 16 slices (2 pounds)
- 1 2/3 cups sweet potato, mashed
- 13 1/3 tablespoons canned coconut milk
- 1 1/3 teaspoons ginger, fresh grated
- 1 1/3 tablespoons lemon zest
- 2 2/3tablespoons honey
- 2 2/3 tablespoons olive oil
- 4 cups bread flour
- 1 1/3 teaspoons salt
- 3 teaspoons rapid rise yeast

Directions:

1. Choose the size of loaf you would like to make and measure your ingredients.

2. Add the ingredients to the bread pan in the order listed above (except yeast).

3. Make a well in the center of the dry ingredients and add the yeast.

4. Place the pan in the bread machine and close the lid.

5. Turn on the bread maker. Select the Basic setting, then the loaf size, and finally the crust color. Start the cycle.

6. When the cycle is finished and the bread is baked, carefully remove the pan from the machine. Use a potholder as the handle will be very hot. Let rest for a few minutes.

7. Remove the bread from the pan and allow to cool on a wire rack for at least 10 minutes before slicing.

Za'atar Bread

Ingredients:

- 8 slices (1 pound)
- 1/4 cup za'atar seasoning
- 1 1/3 tablespoons onion powder
- 2/3 cup warm water
- 1 1/3 tablespoons agave nectar
- 1/6 cup applesauce
- 2 cups bread flour
- 2/3 teaspoon salt
- 1 1/2 teaspoons rapid rise yeast
- 12 slices (1 ½ pounds)
- 1/3 cup za'atar seasoning
- 2 tablespoons onion powder
- 1 cup warm water
- 2 tablespoons agave nectar
- 1/4 cup applesauce
- 3 cups bread flour
- 1 teaspoon salt
- 2 1/4 teaspoons rapid rise yeast
- 16 slices (2 pounds)
- 1/2 cup za'atar seasoning
- 2 2/3 tablespoons onion powder
- 1 1/3 cups warm water
- 2 2/3 tablespoons agave nectar
- 1/3 cup applesauce
- 4 cups bread flour
- 1 1/3 teaspoons salt
- 3 teaspoons rapid rise yeast

Directions:

1. Choose the size of loaf you would like to make and measure your ingredients.

2. Add the ingredients to the bread pan in the order listed above (except yeast).

3. Make a well in the center of the dry ingredients and add the yeast.

4. Place the pan in the bread machine and close the lid.

5. Turn on the bread maker. Select the Basic setting, then the loaf size, and finally the crust color. Start the cycle.

6. When the cycle is finished and the bread is baked, carefully remove the pan from the machine. Use a potholder as the handle will be very hot. Let rest for a few minutes.

7. Remove the bread from the pan and allow to cool on a wire rack for at least 10 minutes before slicing.

Portuguese Corn Bread

Ingredients:
- 8 slices (1 pound)
- 1 cup yellow cornmeal
- 1 1/4 cups cold water, divided
- 1 1/2 teaspoons active dry yeast
- 1 1/2 cups bread flour
- 2 teaspoons sugar
- 3/4 teaspoon salt
- 1 tablespoon olive oil
- 12 slices (1 ½ pounds)
- 1 1/2 cup yellow cornmeal
- 1 7/8 cups cold water, divided
- 2 1/4 teaspoons active dry yeast
- 2 1/4 cups bread flour
- 3 teaspoons sugar
- 1 1/8 teaspoons salt
- 1 1/2 tablespoons olive oil
- 16 slices (2 pounds)
- 2 cups yellow cornmeal
- 2 1/2 cups cold water, divided
- 3 teaspoons active dry yeast
- 3 cups bread flour
- 4 teaspoons sugar
- 1 1/2 teaspoons salt
- 2 tablespoons olive oil

Directions:

1. Choose the size of loaf you would like to make and measure your ingredients.

2. Stir cornmeal into 3/4 cup of the cold water until lumps disappear.

3. Add cornmeal mixture and the remaining ingredients to the bread pan in the order listed above (except yeast).

4. Make a well in the center of the dry ingredients and add the yeast.

5. Place the pan in the bread machine and close the lid.

6. Turn on the bread maker. Select the Sweet Bread setting, then the loaf size, and finally the crust color. Start the cycle.

7. When the cycle is finished and the bread is baked, carefully remove the pan from the machine. Use a potholder as the handle will be very hot. Let rest for a few minutes.

8. Remove the bread from the pan and allow to cool on a wire rack for at least 10 minutes before slicing.

Hawaiian Bread

Ingredients:
- 8 slices (1 pound)
- 1/2 cup pineapple juice
- 2/3 egg
- 1 1/3 tablespoons olive oil
- 1 1/3 tablespoons whole milk
- 3 3/4 tablespoons sugar
- 1/2 teaspoon salt
- 2 cups bread flour
- 1 teaspoon active dry yeast
- 12 slices (1 ½ pounds)
- 3/4 cup pineapple juice
- 1 egg
- 2 tablespoons olive oil
- 2 tablespoons whole milk
- 2 1/2 tablespoons sugar
- 3/4 teaspoon salt
- 3 cups bread flour
- 1 1/2 teaspoons active dry yeast
- 16 slices (2 pounds)
- 1 cup pineapple juice
- 1 1/3 eggs
- 2 2/3 tablespoons olive oil
- 2 2/3 tablespoons whole milk
- 7 1/2 tablespoons sugar
- 1 tcaspoon salt

- 4 cups bread flour
- 2 teaspoons active dry yeast

Directions:

1. Choose the size of loaf you would like to make and measure your ingredients.
2. Add the ingredients to the bread pan in the order listed above (except yeast).
3. Make a well in the center of the dry ingredients and add the yeast.
4. Place the pan in the bread machine and close the lid.
5. Turn on the bread maker. Select the Basic setting, then the loaf size, and finally the crust color. Start the cycle.
6. When the cycle is finished and the bread is baked, carefully remove the pan from the machine. Use a potholder as the handle will be very hot. Let rest for a few minutes.
7. Remove the bread from the pan and allow to cool on a wire rack for at least 10 minutes before slicing.

Mexican Sweet Bread

Ingredients:

- 8 slices (1 pound)
- 2/3 cup whole milk
- 1/6 cup butter
- 2/3 egg
- 1/6 cup sugar
- 2/3 teaspoon salt
- 2 cups bread flour
- 1 teaspoon yeast
- 12 slices (1 ½ pounds)
- 1 cup whole milk
- 1/4 cup butter
- 1 egg
- 1/4 cup sugar
- 1 teaspoon salt
- 3 cups bread flour
- 1 1/2 teaspoons yeast
- 16 slices (2 pounds)
- 1 1/3 cups whole milk
- 1/3 cup butter
- 1 1/3 eggs
- 1/3 cup sugar

- 1 1/3 teaspoons salt
- 4 cups bread flour
- 2 teaspoons yeast

Directions:

1. Choose the size of loaf you would like to make and measure your ingredients.
2. Add the ingredients to the bread pan in the order listed above (except yeast).
3. Make a well in the center of the dry ingredients and add the yeast.
4. Place the pan in the bread machine and close the lid.
5. Turn on the bread maker. Select the Sweet Bread setting, then the loaf size, and finally the crust color. Start the cycle.
6. When the cycle is finished and the bread is baked, carefully remove the pan from the machine. Use a potholder as the handle will be very hot. Let rest for a few minutes.
7. Remove the bread from the pan and allow to cool on a wire rack for at least 10 minutes before slicing.

Amish Wheat Bread

Ingredients:

- 8 slices (1 pound)
- 1 1/8 cups warm water
- 1 package active dry yeast
- 2 3/4 cups wheat flour
- 1/2 teaspoon salt
- 1/3 cup sugar
- 1/4 cup canola oil
- 1 large egg
- 12 slices (1 ½ pounds)
- 1 3/4 cups warm water
- 1 1/2 packages active dry yeast
- 4 cups wheat flour
- 3/4 teaspoon salt
- 1/2 cup sugar
- 3/8 cup canola oil
- 1 1/2 large eggs
- 16 slices (2 pounds)
- 2 1/4 cups warm water
- 2 packages active dry yeast
- 5 1/2 cups wheat flour

- 1 teaspoon salt
- 2/3 cup sugar
- 1/2 cup canola oil
- 2 large eggs

Directions:

1. Choose the size of loaf you would like to make and measure your ingredients.

2. Add warm water, sugar and yeast to bread maker pan; let sit for 8 minutes or until it foams.

3. Add the remaining ingredients to the bread pan in the order listed above.

4. Place the pan in the bread machine and close the lid.

5. Turn on the bread maker. Select the Basic setting, then the loaf size, and finally the crust color. Start the cycle.

6. When the cycle is finished and the bread is baked, carefully remove the pan from the machine. Use a potholder as the handle will be very hot. Let rest for a few minutes.

7. Remove the bread from the pan and allow to cool on a wire rack for at least 10 minutes before slicing.

Challah

Ingredients:
- 8 slices (1 pound)
- 1/2 cup warm water
- 1 package active dry yeast
- 1 tablespoon sugar
- 3 tablespoons butter, softened
- 1/2 teaspoon kosher salt
- 2 to 2 1/2 cups kosher all-purpose flour
- 2 eggs
- 1 egg yolk
- 1 teaspoon water
- 12 slices (1 ½ pounds)
- 3/4 cup warm water
- 1 1/2 packages active dry yeast
- 1 1/2 tablespoons sugar
- 4 1/2 tablespoons butter, softened
- 3/4 teaspoon kosher salt
- 3 to 3 3/4 cups kosher all-purpose flour
- 3 eggs
- 1 1/2 egg yolks

- 1 1/2 teaspoons water
- 16 slices (2 pounds)
- 1 cup warm water
- 2 packages active dry yeast
- 2 tablespoons sugar
- 6 tablespoons butter, softened
- 1 teaspoon kosher salt
- 4 to 5 cups kosher all-purpose flour
- 4 eggs
- 2 egg yolks
- 2 teaspoons water

Directions:

1. Choose the size of loaf you would like to make and measure your ingredients.

2. Add the first six ingredients to the bread pan in the order listed above.

3. Place the pan in the bread machine and close the lid.

4. Turn on the bread maker. Select the Dough setting, then the loaf size, and finally the crust color. Start the cycle.

5. When the cycle is finished and the bread is baked, transfer dough to a large mixing bowl sprayed with non-stick cooking spray. Spray dough with non-stick cooking spray and cover. Let rise in a warm place until doubled in size; about 45 minutes.

6. Punch dough down. Remove dough to lightly floured surface; pat dough and shape into a 10-by-6-inch rectangle.

7. Divide into 3 equal strips with a pizza cutter. Braid strips and place into a 9-by-5-inch loaf pan sprayed with non-stick cooking spray. Cover and let rise in warm place for about 30 to 45 minutes.

8. Beat egg yolk with 1 teaspoon water and baste loaf.

9. Bake at 375°F for 25 to 30 minutes, or until golden.

10. Remove the bread from the pan and allow to cool on a wire rack for at least 10 minutes before slicing.

Bread Of The Dead (pan De Muertos)

Ingredients:
- 8 slices (1 pound)
- 1/3 cup water
- 4 1/2 tablespoons butter
- 4 1/2 eggs

- 3/8 cup sugar
- 3/4 teaspoon salt
- 1/3 teaspoon orange zest
- 1/8 teaspoon star anise
- 2 1/3 cups bread flour
- 1 1/2 teaspoons bread machine yeast
- 12 slices (1 ½ pounds)
- 1/2 cup water
- 6 3/4 tablespoons butter
- 6 3/4 eggs
- 1/2 cup sugar
- 1 1/8 teaspoons salt
- 1/2 teaspoon orange zest
- 1/5 teaspoon star anise
- 3 1/2 cups bread flour
- 2 1/4 teaspoons bread machine yeast
- 16 slices (2 pounds)
- 2/3 cup water
- 9 tablespoons butter
- 9 eggs
- 3/4 cup sugar
- 1 1/2 teaspoons salt
- 2/3 teaspoon orange zest
- 1/4 teaspoon star anise
- 4 2/3 cups bread flour
- 3 teaspoons bread machine yeast

Directions:

1. Choose the size of loaf you would like to make and measure your ingredients.

2. Whisk together the dry ingredients and set aside.

3. Add the liquid ingredients to the bread pan first, then gently pour the mixed dry ingredients on top of the liquid.

4. Place the pan in the bread machine and close the lid.

5. Turn on the bread maker. Select the Sweet setting, then the loaf size, and finally the crust color. Start the cycle.

6. When the cycle is finished and the bread is baked, carefully remove the pan from the machine. Use a potholder as the handle will be very hot. Let rest for a few minutes.

7. Remove the bread from the pan and allow to cool on a wire rack for at least 10 minutes before slicing.

Italian Bread

Ingredients:
- 8 slices (1 pound)
- 2 cups unbleached flour
- 1/2 tablespoon light brown sugar
- 2/3 cups warm water
- 3/4 teaspoons salt
- 3/4 teaspoons olive oil
- 1/2 package active dry yeast
- 1/2 egg
- 1/2 tablespoon water
- 1 tablespoon cornmeal
- 12 slices (1 ½ pounds)
- 3 cups unbleached flour
- 3/4 tablespoon light brown sugar
- 1 cup warm water
- 1 1/8 teaspoons salt
- 1 1/8 teaspoons olive oil
- 3/4 package active dry yeast
- 3/4 egg
- 3/4 tablespoon water
- 1 1/2 tablespoons cornmeal
- 16 slices (2 pounds)
- 4 cups unbleached flour
- 1 tablespoon light brown sugar
- 1 1/3 cups warm water
- 1 1/2 teaspoons salt
- 1 1/2 teaspoons olive oil
- 1 package active dry yeast
- 1 egg
- 1 tablespoon water
- 2 tablespoons cornmeal

Directions:

1. Choose the size of loaf you would like to make and measure your ingredients.

2. Add the ingredients to the bread pan in the order listed above.

3. Place the pan in the bread machine and close the lid.

4. Turn on the bread maker. Select the Dough setting, then the loaf size, and finally the crust color. Start the cycle.

5. When the cycle is finished and the bread is baked, punch down the dough and turn it out onto a lightly floured surface.

6. Form into two loaves and place them seam-side down on a cutting board.

7. Generously sprinkle with cornmeal and cover the loaves with a damp cloth.

8. Let rise until doubled in volume, about 40 minutes.

9. Beat egg and 1 tablespoon of water in a small mixing bowl.

10. Baste loaves with egg wash.

11. Cut down the center of loaves with a sharp knife.

12. Bake in 475°F preheated oven for 30 to 35 minutes, or until loaves sound hollow when tapped on the bottom.

13. Remove the bread from the pan and allow to cool on a wire rack for at least 10 minutes before slicing.

RECIPE INDEX

S

Sampler Buttermilk White Loaf 180
Sampler Hawaiian Sweet Loaf 172
Sampler Oatmeal Loaf 169
Sauerkraut Rye Bread 86
Scandinavian Light Rye 189
Semolina Country Bread 202
Sennebec Hill Bread 189
Sesame Seeds & Onion Bread 54
Seven Grain Bread 187
Shortcut Vanilla Pound Cake 93
Slider Buns 178
Sorghum Bread Recipe 140
Sour Cream Bread 172
Sour Cream Rye 184
Sourdough Banana Nut Bread 125
Sourdough Bread With Fresh Pears And Walnuts 124
Sourdough Buckwheat Bread 130
Sourdough Carrot Poppy Seed Bread 122
Sourdough Cornmeal Bread 128
Sourdough Cottage Cheese Bread With Fresh Herbs 127
Sourdough Pesto Bread 126
Sourdough Raisin Bread 123
Sourdough Sunflower Seed Honey Bread 129
Sourdough Tomato Bread With Feta 128
Sourdough Whole Wheat Bread 130
Southern Cornbread 166
Spice Peach Bread 28
Spice Pumpkin Bread 69
Spicy Hot Red Pepper Bread 73
St. Patrick's Rum Bread 105
Strawberry Oat Bread 38
Succulent Cranberry Cinnamon Bread 34
Sunflower Oatmeal Bread 47
Sunflower Seeds & Oatmeal Bread 48
Super Spice Bread 34
Super-grain Bread 190
Swedish Rye Bread 186

Sweet Almond Anise Bread 98
Sweet Applesauce Bread 100
Sweet Challah 101
Sweet Potato Bread 81
Sweet Vanilla Bread 88

T

Teff Honey Bread 157
Three-seed Whole Wheat Bread 195
Toasted Coconut Bread 31
Toasted Sesame–whole Wheat Bread 194
Toasted Walnut Bread 42
Tomato Basil Bread 166
Tomato Bread 29
Turmeric Raisin Saffron Loaf 60

V

Veggie Bread 79

W

Walnut Banana Bread 135
Wheat Bran Bread 191
White And Dark Chocolate Tea Cake 89
White Chocolate Bread 93
White Chocolate Cranberry Party Loaf 116
White Sourdough Bread 127
White Whole Wheat Bread 197
Whole Wheat Basil Bread 57
Whole-grain Daily Bread 192
Wild Rice Bread 160
Wild Rice Cranberry Delight 30
Wine And Cheese Bread 167

Z

Za'atar Bread 209
Zo's 14-grain Bread 193
Zucchini Bread 77
Zucchini Herbed Bread 73
Zucchini Lemon Bread 81
Zucchini Spice Bread 76
Zuni Indian Bread 40